Caribbean Crime and Criminal Justice

Despite high crime rates among men in the Caribbean, rising rates of violence against women in the region, and a significant number of Caribbean nationals incarcerated abroad due to drug smuggling, existing research has yet to offer explanations that are tailored to the unique Caribbean societies and the individuals in them.

This edited volume adds to the existing body of scientific, empirical and theoretical work on crime (victimisation), and criminal justice in the Caribbean, with a specific focus on impacts of post-colonialism and gender. To investigate these impacts on a developing Caribbean criminology, the contributions in this volume focus on how impacts of post-colonialism, associated racial stereotypes, and/or gender throughout the Caribbean impact on (a) types of offending, (b) victimisation, and (c) criminal justice system responses and policies.

Bringing together a broad range of experts, this book sheds light on key criminological topics in the Caribbean, including victimisation, risk factors for offending, subcultures of violence and particularly gendered violence, and the role of motherhood within matrifocal societies. It is essential reading for those engaged with Caribbean – or decolonial – Criminology and those engaged with comparative and international studies in crime and justice more generally.

Katharina J. Joosen is a Postdoctoral Research Fellow at the NSCR, the Netherlands. She has coordinated the project Caribbean Women & Crime on pathways to offending among Dutch Caribbean women for which data has been collected in the Netherlands, Curacao and Aruba.

Corin Bailey is a Senior Research Fellow at the Sir Arthur Lewis Institute of Social and Economic Studies on the UWI, Cave Hill Campus, Barbados. He has been working on issues related to crime and violence in the Caribbean for approximately 13 years.

Routledge Studies in Crime and Society

For a full list of titles in this series, please visit www.routledge.com/criminology/series/RSCS

26 Cybercrime Through an Interdisciplinary Lens
Edited by Thomas J. Holt

27 Domestic Violence in International Context
Edited by Diana Scharff Peterson and Julie A. Schroeder

28 Child Trafficking in the EU
Policing and Protecting Europe's Most Vulnerable
Pete Fussey and Paddy Rawlinson

29 Resettlement of Sex Offenders after Custody
Circles of Support and Accountability
David Thompson and Terry Thomas with Susanne Karstedt

30 Cybercrime and its Victims
Edited by Elena Martellozzo and Emma A. Jane

31 Gender, Technology and Violence
Edited by Marie Segrave and Laura Vitis

32 Money and the Governance of Punishment
A Genealogy of the Penal Fine
Patricia Faraldo Cabana

33 Violence, Sex Offenders, and Corrections
Rose Ricciardelli and Dale C. Spencer

34 Caribbean Crime and Criminal Justice
Impacts of Post-Colonialism and Gender
Edited by Katharina J. Joosen and Corin Bailey

35 Skinhead History, Identity, and Culture
Robin Maria Valeri and Kevin Borgeson

Caribbean Crime and Criminal Justice

Impacts of Post-colonialism and Gender

Edited by Katharina J. Joosen and Corin Bailey

Routledge
Taylor & Francis Group
LONDON AND NEW YORK

First published 2018
by Routledge
2 Park Square, Milton Park, Abingdon, Oxon OX14 4RN

and by Routledge
711 Third Avenue, New York, NY 10017

Routledge is an imprint of the Taylor & Francis Group, an informa business

British Library Cataloguing-in-Publication Data
A catalogue record for this book is available from the British Library

Library of Congress Cataloging-in-Publication Data
A catalog record for this book has been requested

ISBN: 978-1-138-22377-6 (hbk)
ISBN: 978-1-315-40378-6 (ebk)

Typeset in Times New Roman
by Apex CoVantage, LLC

Contents

List of figures viii
List of tables ix
List of contributors xi
Abbreviations xvii

Introduction 1
CORIN BAILEY

SECTION A
Historical perspectives 7

1 Reframing criminalised resistance strategies of female slaves in the Dutch Caribbean and Suriname during the era of colonialism 9
ASPHA BIJNAAR, KARIN LURVINK AND KATHARINA J. JOOSEN

2 Honour, gender and violence in the Dutch Caribbean and Suriname 33
JANINE JANSSEN

SECTION B
Crime and victimisation 51

3 Prevalence of public fraud and corruption in the Dutch Caribbean: impacts of (post)colonialism explored 53
P.C.M. (NELLY) SCHOTBORGH - VAN DE VEN

4 Ethnicity and crime victimisation in Trinidad and Tobago 73
RANDY SEEPERSAD AND SCOT WORTLEY

5 **Child domestic slavery in Haiti** 105
BENEDETTA FAEDI DURAMY

6 **The language of partner violence in the Caribbean: a decolonial feminist analysis** 123
HALIMAH A. F. DESHONG

7 **Participatory action research: identifying and addressing sexual violence in St. Lucia** 139
REBECCA HAYES, CHRISTINA DEJONG, SOUYENNE DATHORNE AND VELIKA LAWRENCE

SECTION C
Causes and risk factors for offending 161

8 **The influence of gender on social capital resources and youth problem behaviour outcomes in Trinidad and Tobago** 163
ALVINELLE MATTHEW

9 **Trouble in paradise? Pathways to prison among Caribbean women incarcerated in the Netherlands** 189
KATHARINA J. JOOSEN

10 **Constructing crime in Antigua: perceptions of structural explanations of crime in post-colonial era** 208
JANEILLE Z. MATTHEWS

11 **Psychosis and crime among Caribbean migrants: a social defeat perspective** 232
DAVID J. VINKERS

12 **Crime, identity and community: a post-colonial analysis on Kingston, Jamaica** 247
NICOLA D. SATCHELL

SECTION D
Criminal justice systems and policies 265

13 **Perceptions of familial responsibility as a practical constraint in judicial decision-making: focal concerns and gender bias in sentencing on the island of Barbados** 267
CORIN BAILEY

14 Intellectual disability among male prisoners in Bonaire: translating and validating psychological and intellectual diagnostic tools in the local Creole language 285
MICHA VAN DE VORST

15 Crime control and punishment in Dominica: perspectives of community leaders and offenders 300
KYRA PAUL

16 Migrant sex work or sex trafficking? Reflections on "trafficking in women": a Caribbean post-colonial perspective 318
JOAN PHILLIPS

Discussion 325
KATHARINA J. JOOSEN

Index 335

Figures

1.1	Map of Paramaribo with the corner of Keizerstraat and Zwarthovenbrugstraat where Hendrika Reims de Vries' house was located	15
1.2	Area map including Coro in Venezuela, and the Dutch colonies Aruba, Curacao, St. Eustatius, St. Maarten, and Suriname	19
1.3	Map with marronage communities Aluku, Kwinti, and Ndjuka	20
4.1	Ethnicity of murder victims (2001–2013)	78
4.2	Murder rates, by ethnicity of the victim (2001–2013)	79
4.3	Ethnicity of wounding and shooting victims (2010–2014)	80
4.4	Wounding and shooting rates, by ethnicity of the victim (2010–2014)	80
4.5	Ethnicity of robbery victims (2010–2014)	81
4.6	Robbery rates, by ethnicity of the victim (2010–2014)	82
4.7	Ethnicity of sexual offence victims (2010–2014)	83
4.8	Sexual offence rates, by ethnicity of the victim (2010–2014)	84
4.9	Ethnicity of burglary and break-in victims (2010–2014)	85
4.10	Burglary and break-in rates, by ethnicity of the victim (2010–2014)	86
4.11	Ethnicity of larceny and larceny of motor vehicle victims (2010–2014)	88
4.12	Larceny and larceny of motor vehicle rates, by ethnicity of the victim (2010–2014)	89
4.13	Ethnicity of domestic violence victims (2012–2014)	90
4.14	Domestic violence rates, by ethnicity of the victim (2012–2014)	91

Tables

1.1 Number of runaway slaves in Suriname divided by gender in the period 1779–1792 18
3.1 Differentiation of appeal cases of (alleged) public fraud and corruption per judicial area 59
3.2 Categorisation as to petty, grand, and political fraud as well as corruption 60
4.1 Cross tabulation of gender and ethnicity of murder victims (2001–2013) 78
4.2 Per cent of victims of specified sexual offences, by ethnicity (2010–2014) 84
4.3 Average annual rates for specified sexual offences, burglary and break-in offences, and larceny and larceny of motor vehicle offences by ethnicity of the victim (2010–2014) 87
4.4 Average annual rates for specified domestic violence offences, by ethnicity of the victim (2012–2014) 92
4.5 Per cent of victims, and victimisation rates by ethnic background of victims 93
4.6 Per cent of persons victimised within the last 10 years and within the last year in Trinidad and Tobago 95
4.7 Per cent of households victimised in 2009 97
4.8 Per cent of respondents who have been a victim of crime within the past five years and past year, by ethnicity. 98
7.1 Proportion of extent of lifetime sexual victimisation, by gender and class (self-reported, $N = 158$) 149
7.2 Average rating for "Belief in rape myths", by gender ($N = 158$) 150
7.3 Awareness of sexual assault laws and resources in St Lucia, among self-reported victims of sexual assault 151
8.1 Descriptive statistics on study's variables 172
8.2 Spearman's correlations between crime covariates, peer deviance and social capital variables for males 173
8.3 Spearman's correlations between crime covariates, peer deviance and social capital variables for females 174

8.4 Negative binomial regression models for family, school and community social capital on delinquency 175
8.5 Negative binomial regression models for family, school and community social capital on violent behaviour 176
9.1 Prevalence of potential risk and protective factors for offending and incarceration among Caribbean and Dutch incarcerated women in the Netherlands 198
9.2 Variables related to periods of incarceration across the life span for Caribbean and Dutch female inmates 199
9.3 Variables related to periods of incarceration across the life span for Caribbean and Dutch female inmates: the impact of single motherhood 200
14.1 Number of suspects and origin in the Netherlands 286
14.2 Information on school dropout percentages in Curacao, Census 2011 of Curacao 295

Contributors

Corin Bailey has been working on issues related to crime and violence in the Caribbean for approximately 13 years. This began with work on the effects of social exclusion on levels of crime in Kingston, Jamaica in fulfilment of his PhD at the University of the West Indies (UWI) in 2004. Since then, he has continued his work on crime with specific focus on children in violent circumstances and research on gender and crime. Corin is currently a Senior Research Fellow at the Sir Arthur Lewis Institute of Social and Economic Studies on the UWI, Cave Hill Campus. His current teaching includes Qualitative research methods and Deviance.

Aspha Bijnaar studied Sociology. She accomplished her PhD at the University of Amsterdam on "*Kasmoni*: Traditional Saving in Suriname and in The Netherlands". She is (co)author of many Dutch publications like "Op zoek naar de stilte. Sporen van het slavernijverleden in Nederland", "Jacquelina. Slavin van plantage Driesveld", "Kind aan de ketting. Opgroeien in slavernij, toen en nu", and "Meer dan vijftig tinten zwart. Slavernijverleden in de kunst". She initiated and coordinated several exhibitions, educational (digital) projects (www.slavernijenjij) and theatre plays. She initiated the research about rebellious enslaved women in Suriname and the Dutch Antilles, and developed the basic idea for the theatre play "Rebelse Vrouwen. Theatervoorstelling over verzet van vrouwen in slavernij". Aspha Bijnaar is an independent researcher and director of foundation "Educatie Studio" in Amsterdam. Educatie Studio explores and represents colonial history and its legacy in order to create critical minds and contemporary citizenship.

Souyenne Dathorne co-founder of PROSAF, grew up on the Caribbean island of St. Lucia. She developed a keen interest in the area of sexual violence whilst pursuing her undergraduate degree in Forensic Psychology. Upon returning from her studies she put forth the idea of starting a campaign to address the issues of sexual violence on her native island. The campaign, the brain child of Souyenne and a childhood friend, grew into PROSAF.

Christina DeJong is an Associate Professor in the School of Criminal Justice at Michigan State University (US). She received her PhD in Criminology and Criminal Justice from the University of Maryland, College Park (US). Her research is focused on areas of gender and justice, corrections, and genocide.

Halimah A. F. DeShong is a lecturer at the Institute for Gender & Development Studies: Nita Barrow Unit at the University of the West Indies, Cave Hill Campus. Her research interests and peer-reviewed publications include a focus on feminist studies of crime and violence, feminist epistemologies and methodologies, and anti-colonial/decolonial feminisms. Her essays can be found in *Journal of Gender Studies, Global Public Health, Caribbean Review of Gender Studies, Social and Economic Studies, Journal of Eastern Caribbean Studies, Love and Power: Caribbean Discourses on Gender*, and *Doing Gender, Doing Love: Interdisciplinary Voices*. She is the co-editor of two special issues on feminist methodologies and men and masculinities for the *Caribbean Review of Gender Studies*. A passionate advocate for gender justice, she has advised Caribbean governments and civil society organisations on domestic violence law and policies, and policies to combat gender-based violence. Recently, she completed a national gender-based violence action plan for the Government of St. Vincent and the Grenadines. A devoted educator for all of her adult life, her scholarship and advocacy comes to life as she teaches courses in feminist theories, feminist epistemologies and methodologies, men and masculinities in the Caribbean, crimes by and against women, and theoretical concepts and sources of knowledge in women's studies.

Benedetta Faedi Duramy is a Professor of Law and Associate Dean for Faculty Scholarship at Golden Gate University School of Law where she teaches Family Law, International Human Rights, Gender and Children's issues in International Law, and Property, among others. The author of several of book chapters and articles, Professor Faedi Duramy completed her doctoral program at Stanford Law School where she has been the recipient of numerous awards for her extensive research and scholarship on gender-based violence, with a special focus on Haiti. Her book "Gender and Violence in Haiti: Women's Path from Victims to Agents" was published in 2014 by Rutgers University Press, and her edited volume "International Perspectives and Empirical Findings on Child Participation" was published in 2015 by Oxford University Press. She received an LLM from the London School of Economics and Political Sciences, an MA in Political Science from the University of Florence, and an LLB from the University of Rome "La Sapienza" (summa cum laude).

Rebecca Hayes is an Associate Professor in the Department of Sociology, Anthropology and Social Work at Central Michigan University (US). She received her PhD in Criminology from the University of Florida (US). Her research is focused on social justice, violence against women, and media impacts on the justice system.

Janine Janssen is head of research of the National Centre of Expertise on Honour-based Violence (Landelijk Expertise Centrum Eer Gerelateerd Geweld – LEC EGG) of the Dutch National Police Force. She is also professor of Violence in Dependency Relations at the Avans University for Applied Sciences in the Netherlands.

Katharina J. Joosen graduated in Clinical and Health Psychology from Utrecht University (2005). She completed her Master's thesis (on homesickness) and clinical internship (on psychosis) in the UK. Her PhD, at the Centre for Child and Family Studies of Leiden University, focused on early maternal behavioural and physiological indicators of harsh discipline among lower educated mothers (2012). As a Postdoctoral Research Fellow at the NSCR, Katharina studied female pathways into prison in the Netherlands from 2012 till 2015. For this project she interviewed 400 incarcerated women on their life histories prior to incarceration and co-founded the international Spinhuis Centre for Research on Incarcerated Females. In 2014 she received a grant from the Caribbean Research Program together with Anne-Marie Slotboom (VU) and Catrien Bijleveld (NSCR). Since 2015, she coordinated this international project, which focuses specifically on pathways to offending among Dutch Caribbean women, and for which data of 330 women has been collected in the Netherlands, Curacao, and Aruba. Over the years her research interests have broadened from clinical psychology, child development, attachment, parenting, and physiological underpinnings of behaviour, to forensic psychology, criminology, injustice, and the impact of racism.

Velika Lawrence is the co-founder of PROSAF and The Power of One, and is from St. Lucia.

Karin Lurvink obtained her PhD from the VU University Amsterdam in 2016. The title of her dissertation is "Beyond racism and poverty: The truck system on Louisiana plantations and Dutch peateries, 1865–1920". She is currently a postdoc researcher at the VU University Amsterdam, where she works on the project "Slaves, commodities, and logistics" on the long-term impact of slavery on the Dutch economy in the eighteenth and nineteenth centuries. Her research on resistance acts of female slaves resulted as well in the theatre play "Rebelse Vrouwen".

Alvinelle Matthew recently completed her PhD studies in Public Policy with the Sir Arthur Lewis Graduate School of Economic Studies, St. Augustine. Her thesis explored the interconnections between HRD and social capital in reducing youth problem behaviour. Her main research areas are crime prevention, social capital, social networks, and youth development perspectives. She has worked as a research assistant in the University of Alberta, Canada and with the Department of Geography, University of the West Indies, St. Augustine campus.

Janeille Z. Matthews is a criminal law scholar who teaches criminal law and criminology at the University of the West Indies, Mona Campus. Dr Matthews holds a Juris Doctor and Masters in Public Administration from Harvard University and a PhD in Social Policy from the London School of Economics and Political Science. Her substantive area of research is criminal justice policy in the Caribbean with a particular focus on crime and crime policy in Antigua and Barbuda. Her doctoral dissertation was entitled "Competing constructions: A mixed methods investigation of the popular and media framing of the Antigua crime story". She is called to the New York State Bar as well as the Bar of

Antigua and Barbuda and has enjoyed a diverse career that includes consulting for UNDP on issues relating to Caribbean crime and security and time spent in Arusha, Tanzania working on the International Criminal Tribunal for Rwanda.

Kyra Paul is currently the Social Development Planner in the Ministry of Planning, Economic Development and Investment after being promoted from the position of Director of the Bureau of Gender Affairs in the Ministry of Social Services, Family and Gender affairs. Her responsibilities include providing advice on the formulation of human and social development, and gender-sensitive policies. Kyra holds a Bachelor's of Science in Management (first class honours) and her PhD in Social Policy was obtained from the University of the West Indies in 2016. She also holds certificates in Gender and Development and Climate Change. Both Kyra's work and research focuses on poverty reduction, social protection, gender, crime prevention, and community building.

Joan Phillips is a Senior Lecturer and Coordinator of Sociology in the Department of Government, Sociology and Social Work at the University of the West Indies, Cave Hill. She is a graduate of the University of the West Indies, Cave Hill, and completed her PhD at the University of Bedfordshire. She is also a recipient of a Leverhulme Postdoctoral fellowship from the University of London, Royal Holloway. She has extensive research and teaching experience both in the region and internationally. Her previous employment includes Lecturer at the University of Brighton, University of London and University of Reading. She was a Research Fellow at the Policy Studies Institute in the United Kingdom and is a reviewer for a number of academic journals. She has written extensively on sex tourism, return migration, and the relationship between race, sexuality, and post-coloniality. Recently her research interests have focused on issues relating to sex work and trafficking and development.

Nicola D. Satchell is a lecturer in the Department of Government, University of the West Indies (UWI) where she teaches in the areas of criminal justice and political sociology. She is currently engaged in graduate work in the Department of Sociology. Her research uses community psychology to explain the relationship between social identity processes and attitudes to crime and violence. She is passionate about community and youth development. She has worked with the Kingston Restoration Company as a researcher where she focused on the problems affecting effective community development in Kingston. She was engaged with the Institute of Criminal Justice and Security, UWI as Project Manager/Researcher. Here she was involved in several initiatives and projects geared towards enhancing research, teaching and learning in crime and security concerns across the Caribbean. She has also worked on several technical reports including the Office of the Contractor General's Youth Corruption Survey, 2016 and Jamaica's UN Habitat III report. Ms. Satchell is currently developing a monograph on youth values and attitudes in Jamaica. She is a member of the Violence Prevention Alliance, Jamaica and a Senior Research Fellow in the Centre for Leadership and Governance, UWI.

P.C.M. (Nelly) Schotborgh-van de Ven studied Cultural Anthropology and Criminology at Utrecht University in the Netherlands. She started her career as scientific officer at the central intelligence service of the Dutch police. In 1999 she moved to Curacao. In the first 10 years of her stay in the Dutch Caribbean she worked for the financial forensic department of Ernst & Young and for Forensic Services Caribbean. In 2010 she started her own research and training bureau SRA-Caribbean. With almost 17 years of work experience Schotborgh has thorough knowledge of corruption, fraud, and integrity issues in the Dutch Caribbean. In 2012 she was hired by Transparency International to conduct the National Integrity Assessment in Curacao. Schotborgh has been lecturing Criminology since 2005 and in 2017 she also teaches Corporate Governance at the University of Curacao. In addition to the foregoing, Schotborgh is writing a PhD thesis about the causes of fraud and corruption in the Dutch Caribbean at the VU University Amsterdam (VU).

Randy Seepersad is a Criminologist and Head of the Criminology Department at the University of the West Indies, Trinidad and Tobago. Dr. Seepersad holds a PhD from the University of Toronto and an M.Phil. degree from the University of Cambridge. He specialises in research methodology and statistics and has a research interest in economic deprivation and crime, gang violence, youth crime and justice, and penology. Recent books which were published by Dr. Seepersad include “Gangs in the Caribbean” (2013), “Making deterrence work: Problems and possibilities” (2014) and “Crime and security in Trinidad and Tobago” (2016). He has also published in a number of peer refereed journals including the *Caribbean Journal of Criminology*, *Justice Report*, and the *Journal of Gang Research.*

Micha van de Vorst, being half Dutch, half French, has been part of different cultures since childhood. After finishing an internship at the psychiatric department of the Curacao prison, and receiving a master’s degree at Tilburg University in the Netherlands, Micha moved to Curacao with his wife. Micha started working at Psychiatric Corporation Antilles and embraced the unique Papiamento language. He works as a psychologist in three different prisons on the islands of Curacao and Bonaire and works as a court reporter for different Dutch Caribbean islands. He is specialised in treating trauma (EMDR) and personality disorders (schema therapy). He took on the challenge to translate and validate assessment tools for the Papiamento language, which is a mainly spoken language, and has published on this matter. He is an advocate for the use of low-cost open-source technology to increase the quality of treatment and psychological assessment. He has been experimenting with the use of text-to-speech in psychological assessment, among other things. He organises international conferences and initiated the first international Criminal Law & Forensic Psychiatry conference on the island of Curacao.

David J. Vinkers studied medicine and philosophy at Leiden University. He worked two years as an intern on Curacao more than fifteen years ago, where he met his wife. After that he has focused his research and work as a psychiatrist on Afro-Caribbean patients. He speaks the native language Papiamento fluently. On a regularly basis, he provides consultations regarding mental health issues in Afro-Caribbean nationals for the Municipality, the Public Prosecutor, the Mayor of Rotterdam, and Dutch Ministries. He is recognised in the Netherlands as an independent researcher outside of traditional academia. He has instigated a study among more than 20,000 pre-trial reported defendants in the Netherlands and described for the first time a high prevalence of psychosis in immigrant defendants. He set up several studies among Afro-Caribbean nationals, including studies on CYP and MAOA, COMT and 5-HTTPLR genotypes in Afro-Caribbean nationals in the Netherlands and Curacao and on social defeat in Afro-Caribbean immigrants in Rotterdam.

Scot Wortley has been a Professor at the Centre of Criminology, University of Toronto since 1996. In 2001 he was appointed the Justice and Law Domain Leader at the Centre of Excellence for Research on Immigration and Settlement (CERIS). He has also recently conducted research on youth violence as the Research Director for both the Toronto District School Board and the Ontario Government. From 2009 to 2012 he was the lead evaluator for Prevention Intervention Toronto (PIT) – a major gang prevention program. He also helped design and implement the 2006, 2009, 2013, and 2016 Jamaican National Crime Victimization Surveys. Additionally, he wrote reports for the Government of Jamaica based on these surveys. Professor Wortley teaches both undergraduate and graduate courses on criminology, justice systems, interpersonal violence, and youth culture, and crime. He is currently involved in several research projects concerning street gangs in Toronto, migration, minority perceptions of the Canadian justice system, and youth radicalisation and offending.

Abbreviations

ACASI	Audio Computer Assisted Self-Interview
ANOVA	Analysis of Variance
BES	Bonaire, St. Eustatius, Saba
CAPA	Crime and Problem Analysis
CAPI	Computer Assisted Personal Interview
CARICOM	Caribbean Community and Common Market
CBS	Central Bureau of Statistics
CDB	Caribbean Development Bank
CDPF	Commonwealth of Dominica Police Force
CERCO	Ethics Committee for Legal and Criminological Research, VU University Amsterdam
COHADDE	Coalition Haïtienne pour la Defence des Droits de l'Enfant
CSJP	Citizen Security and Justice program
EU	European Union
HBV	Honour-based Violence
HRD	Human Research Development
IBESR	Institut du bien-être social et de la recherche
ILO	International Labour Organization
IMF	International Monetary Fund
IPEC	International Program on the Elimination of Child Labour
IPSOFA	Institut Psycho-Social de la Famille
IPV	– Intimate Partner Violence
IQ	Intelligence Quotient
LEC	Landelijk Expertise Centrum Eergerelateerd Geweld
LHC	Life History Calendar
MMPI	Minnesota Multiphasic Personality Inventory
NGO	Non-Governmental Organisation
OAS	Organization of American States
OCT	Overseas Countries and Territories
OHCHR	The Office of the United Nations High Commissioner for Human Rights
OLS	Ordinary Least Squares
PMI	Peace Management Initiative

PROSAF	Positive Reactions Over Secrets and Fear
PSA	Public Service Announcement
SES	Sexual Experiences Survey
SHSA	Special Hospitals Service Authority
SIDS	Sudden Infant Death Syndrome
TTPS	Trinidad and Tobago Police Service
TTS	Text-to-Speech
UN	United Nations
UNA	University of Netherlands Antilles
UNDP	United Nations Development Program
UNICEF	United Nations Children's Fund
UNODC	United Nations Office on Drugs and Crime
USD	United States Dollars
USSC	United States Sentencing Commission
VRI	Violence Related Injuries
WTO	World Trade Organization

Introduction

Corin Bailey

The changing nature of Caribbean crime

For some time, the Caribbean has been experiencing increases in levels of crime leading to considerable concern among citizens and policy makers. This has been accompanied too, by changes in the nature of crime experienced across the region. Rapid urbanisation in the nineteenth and early twentieth centuries led to an increase in rates of property crime. Diversification in the form of a switch from agriculture to the service industry and light manufacturing during the 1960s led to a considerable increase in rates of property crime (McElroy & Albuquerque, 1982). Levels of this form of crime however remained low when compared to other developing countries around the world.

Today however, the main feature of crime in the Caribbean is the high level of violent offences with one study suggesting that the Caribbean as a region, has the highest per capita murder rate in the world (UNODC, 2011). Indeed, while for much of the world, violent crimes have been on a downward trend (Harrendorf, Heiskanen, & Malby, 2010), for most of the Caribbean, with Barbados as a notable exception, the opposite is true (UNDP, 2012). Youth figure prominently in Caribbean statistics for crime and violence both as victims and perpetrators. Particularly troubling is the fact that in many countries, the proportion of violent crimes being committed by youth and juveniles appears to be increasing steadily (UNODC, 2002). Evidence suggests that the Latin America and Caribbean region has the highest rate of homicide among men aged 15–29 in the world. A rate of 68.6 per 100,000 for the region is alarming when compared to those of countries such as Canada (2.5 per 100,000) and Chile (5.2 per 100,000) (UNODC/World Bank, 2007). A troubling manifestation of this increase in violence is the corresponding increase in violence towards young women. As with general violent crime, the Caribbean also suffers from disproportionately high rates of violence against girls. Although young women are less likely to be victims of homicides than men, their lives are severely affected by their increased vulnerability to violent attacks. Violence within intimate partner relationships and within families is common within the Caribbean context and women and young girls are particularly affected by this trend (Pan American Health Organisation, 2004).

Another disturbing area of criminal activity across the Caribbean is organised crime, which takes several forms with drug trafficking predominating. The location of the Caribbean has made it one of the world's major drug transhipment points as it is situated between South America – the world's largest producer of cocaine, and its main markets in the United States and Europe. Geographical location is only one of the factors explaining the importance of this type of activity. The inability of Caribbean governments to secure the long stretches of coastline and surrounding territorial waters and the inadequacies of the criminal justice system are also explanatory variables (Harriott, 2003). Although drug trafficking is the predominant form of organized crime, and is associated with sharp increases in violent crime, other forms of organised crime too affect the region. These include money laundering and the corruption of local officials, and increasingly human trafficking (UNODC/World Bank, 2007).

Crime and gender

The nature of crime in the Caribbean, therefore, has helped to shape the research agenda of Caribbean criminology such that it has thus far been characterised primarily by research examining the trends, or motivations for the perpetration of violent crimes. As such, one feature of Caribbean criminology is that relatively little attention has been paid to other forms of offending. A second feature, particularly relevant to this collection, is that despite ground-breaking scholarship in Caribbean gender studies (Barriteau, 2001; Leo-Rhynie, 2002; Reddock, 1998), its application to the field of criminology has been somewhat inequitable. Crime in the Caribbean, has been investigated almost exclusively from the perspective of male perpetration or victimisation, with women's involvement given little attention. This neglect of women and the justice system in the Caribbean can undoubtedly be attributed to the low numbers of women that come into contact with the system when compared to their male counterparts (Clarke & Henry-Lee, 2005). Thus when gender has been considered, it has been examined primarily against the background of male offending. Beckles (2004) for example, traced the aggression of Caribbean males back to the period of slavery where the masculinity of enslaved blacks interacted with the dominant masculinity of white slave owners. This interaction was characterised by an often violent struggle in which a differentiated, marginalised, subordinated, and stigmatised black masculinity attempted to achieve an *autonomous positional identity*. Plummer and Simpson (2007) too, observed physicality to be an important part of contemporary Caribbean life as men continue to struggle for ways to differentiate themselves from the opposite sex. Central to gender identity formation, the consequence of this for relationships is that men are more likely to use physicality to solve disputes. Walking away from violence risks his status as a man. While there have been recent attempts at addressing this imbalance through a focus on the offending and victimisation of women (Bailey, 2013; DeShong, 2011), research on gender and crime in the Caribbean continues to be limited in its scope.

Crime and post-colonialism

Simply put, as a discipline, the field of post-colonial studies refers to an examination of the consequences of imperial or colonial rule. Unpacking the concept further however, is a somewhat challenging undertaking. Loomba (1998) offered an explanation for this complexity, suggesting that the primary hurdle to overcome was the diversity that existed within and among the cultures encompassed by the term. This complexity has spawned a number of debates surrounding the use, as well as the application of the term to contemporary scholarship. The failures of traditional discourses to effectively address the issues that have arisen as a result of the histories of formerly colonised societies have however highlighted the relevance of a specific analysis aimed at doing so. The publication of "Post-colonial Studies" precipitated the interrogation of a variety of issues using a post-colonial lens, including among others, economics, sociology, the environment, literature, and religion (Ashcroft, Griffiths, & Tiffin, 2007).

It is important to conceptualise the post-colonial as an ongoing process rather than a historical event – that the imperial past significantly informs the present. The *critical aftermath* of colonialism has had considerable and ongoing cultural effects both on the colonisers, as well as the formerly colonised. Cunneen (2011) highlighted for example, the manner in which post-colonial theory has been used by legal scholars to critique the relevance of Western laws, to the contemporary cultures of colonial people. Despite the existence of such debates however, the application of a similar analysis to the field of criminology has been lacking, with relatively few scholars addressing this need (Agozino, 2003; Cunneen, 2011; Oriola, 2006). Indeed, Agozino (2003, p. 1) saw his work as a timely and "transdisciplinary theoretico-methodological intervention aimed at decolonizing theories and methods of imperialistic reason in criminology". He believed that within criminology, there was a deeply entrenched bias towards dominant societal groups that has manifested for example, in the preoccupation of contemporary criminology with lower-class crime, in the face of rampant offending by the more privileged.

Caribbean society and culture has been, and continues to be significantly influenced by its colonial past. Economic exploitation, migration, political fragmentation, racial stereotypes, continued colonial control, and in some cases the forced use of European language as opposed to local dialects, are some of the more significant features of these societies struggling to cope with the long-term consequences of imperialism. While there are limited examples of scholarship focused on the role of post-colonialism at the regional level (Girvan, 2012; Nettleford, 1998; Wagg, 2005), there is a need to extend these debates into the field of Caribbean criminology.

Aims of the book

The main aim of this collection therefore, is to address the current dearth of Caribbean criminological literature in these two critical areas – gender and post-colonialism. To this end, the book is organised into four sections. Section A provides historical discourse on gender violence from the perspective of the Dutch Caribbean. Section B looks at crime and victimisation occurring at various levels such as the State in the case of Schotborgh-van de Ven, as well as at the individual level, by way of submissions on child (Faedi Duramy), intimate partner (Deshong), and sexual violence (Hayes, DeJong, Dathorne, and Lawrence). In this section too, Seepersad and Wortley offer a timely discourse on ethnicity and victimisation, a feature of post-colonial criminology that has thus far been absent from Caribbean scholarship. Section C addresses risk factors for offending. While Matthew and Joosen discuss this issue from a gendered perspective, submissions from Matthews, Vinkers, and Satchell use post-colonial theory to explain crime perpetration in Antigua, the Netherlands (Caribbean migrants), and Jamaica, respectively. Finally, section D looks at the effects of criminal justice systems and policies within the Caribbean region. Here, the gendered nature of sentencing decisions by Bailey highlight the manner in which gender intersects with criminal justice systems. Furthermore, Van de Vorst shows in his study the importance of using measures in local creole – as opposed to the colonial Dutch – in validly diagnosing intellectual disability among male prisoners. In addition, Paul and Phillips place the issues of crime control and migrant sex work/trafficking within a post-colonial context. Together, these studies are suggesting Caribbean specific conceptualisations and solutions to contemporary crime problems.

The second aim of this collection is to address an existing imbalance in the study of crime in the Caribbean. It is an unfortunate paradox that despite growing public concern over rising levels of crime, research into crime and violence in the Caribbean – its causes, incidence and effects – remains in its infancy. That which has been done however, has focused primarily on larger, high crime islands such as Trinidad and Tobago, and Jamaica, with very little attention being paid to smaller islands, particularly those of the Eastern and Dutch Caribbean. This is likely a result of the numbers, with the majority of regional crime occurring in these larger islands. Important also is the fact that research into crime and other disciplines tends to be focused in those islands in which a University of the West Indies campus is located (Jamaica, Trinidad and Tobago, and Barbados). The lack of research in other territories has a deleterious effect, since policy decisions relating to crime reduction necessitate a continuous supply of empirical work that will provide decision makers with a full understanding of the regional crime problem, and the evidence needed to make rational choices regarding possible strategies. We thought it critical, therefore, that this collection includes the investigation of issues related to crime and violence in otherwise sparsely researched territories so as to assist in addressing this ongoing cycle of empirical neglect.

References

Agozino, B. (2003). *Counter-colonial criminology: A critique of imperialist reason*. London: Pluto Press.

Ashcroft, B., Griffiths, G., & Tiffin, H. (2007). *Post-colonial studies: The key concepts* (2nd ed.). London and New York: Routledge.

Bailey, C. (2013). Exploring female motivations for drug smuggling on the island of Barbados: Evidence from her Majesty's Prison. *Feminist Criminology*, *8*(2), 117–141.

Barriteau, E. (2001). *The political economy of gender in the twentieth century Caribbean*. Hampshire, UK: Palgrave.

Beckles, H. (2004). Black masculinity in Caribbean slavery. In R. Reddock (Ed.), *Interrogating Caribbean masculinities: Theoretical and empirical analyses* (pp. 225–243). Kingston: University of the West Indies Press.

Clarke, M., & Henry-Lee, A. (2005). *Women in prison: The impact of the incarceration of Jamaican women on themselves and their families*. Jamaica: Planning Institute of Jamaica.

Cunneen, C. (2011). Postcolonial perspectives for criminology. In M. Bosworth, & C. Hoyte (Eds.), *What is criminology* (pp. 1–15). Oxford, UK: Oxford University Press.

DeShong, H. (2011). Gender, sexuality and sexual violence: A feminist analysis of Vincentian women's experiences in violent heterosexual relationships. *Journal of Eastern Caribbean Studies*, *36*(2), 63–96.

Girvan, N. (2012). *Colonialism and neo colonialism in the Caribbean: An overview*. IV International Seminar Africa, the Caribbean, and Latin America. St. Vincent and the Grenadines.

Harrendorf, S., Heiskanen, M., & Malby, S. (2010). *International statistics on crime and justice: HEUNI Publication Series 64*. Helsinki: European Institute for Crime Prevention and Control. Vienna: UNODC.

Harriott, A. (2003). The Jamaican crime problem: New developments and new challenges for public policy. In A. Harriott (Ed.), *Understanding crime in Jamaica: New challenges for public policy* (pp. 1–12). Jamaica: University of the West Indies Press.

Leo-Rhynie, E. (2002). Women in development studies. In P. Mohammed (Ed.), *Gendered realities: Essays in Caribbean feminist thought* (pp. 147–163). Mona: University of the West Indies Press.

Loomba, A. (1998). *Colonialism/postcolonialism: The new critical idiom*. London: Routledge.

McElroy, J., & Albuquerque, K. (1982). *Crime and modernization: The US Virgin Islands experience*. Seventh Annual Conference of the Caribbean Studies Association, Kingston.

Nettleford, R. (1998). *Mirror mirror: Race and protest in Jamaica*. Kingston: Kingston Publishers Limited.

Oriola, T. (2006). Biko Agozino and the rise of post-colonial criminology. *African Journal of Criminology and Justice Studies*, *2*(1), 104–131.

Pan American Health Organisation. (2004). *Activa project: Cultural norms and attitudes towards violence in selected cities in Latin America and Spain*. Washington, DC: PAHO.

Plummer, D., & Simpson, J. (2007). *HIV and Caribbean masculinities*. St Augustine: University of the West Indies Press.

Reddock, R. (1998). Feminism and feminist thought: Consensus and controversy. In P. Mohammed, & C. Shepherd (Eds.), *Gender in Caribbean development* (pp. 53–73). Jamaica, Trinidad and Tobago, Barbados: University of the West Indies, Women and Development Studies Project.

UNDP. (2012). *Caribbean human development report: Human development and the shift to better citizen security*. New York: UNDP.

UNODC. (2002). *Crime trends in the Caribbean and responses*. Vienna: UNODC.

UNODC. (2011). *Global study on homicide: Trends, contexts, data*. Vienna: UNODC.

UNODC/World Bank. (2007). *Crime, violence and development: Trends, costs and policy options in the Caribbean*. Washington, DC: World Bank.

Wagg, S. (Ed.). (2005). *Cricket and national identity in the post-colonial age: Following on*. New York: Routledge.

Section A

Historical perspectives

1 Reframing criminalised resistance strategies of female slaves in the Dutch Caribbean and Suriname during the era of colonialism

Aspha Bijnaar, Karin Lurvink and Katharina J. Joosen

Introduction

Unshaken and with her head held high Flora faces the soldiers of the colonial army. "Oh my God, they have discovered their hiding-place!" This is bad news for Flora's friend Sery and her little baby girl Patienta. The soldiers have no mercy and brutally try to force Flora to answer questions about herself and all the other formerly enslaved refugees: "Who is your slave master? Where are the others hiding? With how many are they? How strong are they? Are they armed and what kind of weapons do they have?" Without fear she looks the soldiers straight in the eyes and lifts her hair above her head to symbolise a rope. In a true contempt for death she ignores each of the questions fired at her by the soldiers by pressing two fingers to her lips, pointing to the sky, and striking her hand along her neck. Savagely the rebellious Flora is beheaded even after she has already been shot dead. Sery is next. They pierce her body with an arrow and cut off her head (Wolbers, 1861). Nobody knows what the soldiers did with Sery's baby girl Patienta. We can only imagine Sery's thoughts concerning little Patienta and the intense fear she must have gone through during those horrifying last moments (De Kom, 1981).

This story is one of many accounts of courageous enslaved women who resisted enslavement in Suriname and, by doing so, played a remarkable role in the Dutch history of slavery. This contribution investigates acts of resistance of enslaved women living in the Dutch Caribbean and Suriname during the era of colonialism. So far, few scholars in the field have systematically studied acts of resistance by enslaved women. Literature that focuses on female slaves is mainly based on historical accounts from the Americas (e.g. Brent, 1861; White, 1999). To offer a more inclusive perspective on slave resistance, the current study will explore and describe the different types of acts of resistance employed by female slaves in Suriname and the Dutch Caribbean during the era of slavery. Furthermore, we will critically examine the way these acts have been classified and described as resisting – and therefore criminal – by the Dutch colonial ruler. Last, we discuss the potential impact criminalisation of such acts of resistance could have on current-day viewpoints concerning women and crime in the Caribbean.

Historical views on female slaves and their (lack of) resistance

Brent's (1861) autobiography of female victimisation and resistance during slavery is one of few written. This void in literature on the history of female slave resistance holds especially true as it relates to the former Dutch colonies. We know much more about acts of resistance by enslaved males such as escape attempts, riots, and marronage.[1] Well-known are the acts of resistance by Baron, Boni, and Joli Coeur (Hoogbergen, 1990), as well as by the Boston Band in Suriname (Dragtenstein, 2010). In the Dutch Caribbean we recollect the acts of resistance by Tula (Paula, 1974), Carpata (Paula, 1974), and Thico (Paula, 1974). Furthermore, research conducted in other parts of the Caribbean are predominantly male-oriented as well, such as the accounts of the Jamaican rebel Samuel Sharpe (Reid-Salmon, 2012).

Female slaves are rarely pictured as heroic, neither in unilateral written literature nor across visual presentations in art, culture, or history. In the television series "Roots" (Margulies et al., 1977), and in movies such as "Amistad" (Allen & Spielberg, 1997), "Django Unchained" (Hudlin, Savone, Sher, & Tarantino, 2012), "Lincoln" (Kennedy & Spielberg, 2012), "Tula" (Leinders, Nije, Van Stapele, 2013) and "Twelve Years a Slave" (Gardner et al., 2013), the starring roles are predominantly performed by powerful, heroic enslaved males. Contrarily, in such visual presentations, female slaves are characterised mainly as victims, damsels in distress, and/or concubines; such as the enslaved Patsy in "Twelve Years a Slave" (Gardner et al., 2013) or Cecil Gaines's mother Hattie Pearl in "The Butler" (Elwes, Patrick, Williams, Ziskin, & Daniels, 2013). According to authors such as Wood, "Popular stereotypes [. . .] have portrayed them as passive and downtrodden work-horses who did little to advance the struggle for freedom" (2003, p. 551).

However, some critics have painted an even more negative picture of enslaved women. For example, Wilson (1973) argued that enslaved women did not protest against slavery but in fact embraced the lifestyle of being enslaved by their white oppressors. As house slaves and especially as concubines of white planters these women lived relatively privileged lives, even though this "privilege" increased their risk of being sexually violated by their master. This fact seems to have been too easily overridden by scholars such as Wilson and his supporters. In her book "Incidents in the life of a slave girl" Brent (1861) wrote about the Jezebel stereotype[2] and how some enslaved women would at least attempt to escape the worst pains of enslavement by using their sexuality. She discussed how enslaved women were not only victimised by sexual abuse of slave owners, but how they managed to have some agency by employing their sexuality in order to "choose" partners opportunistically. In doing so they could attempt to escape from more severe oppression. However, such overtures bore many risks as well when white "lovers" would end up bored, happily married, or had jealous wives – all of which were situations that would ultimately lead such fallen women to be sold away (White, 1999).

Gendered types of resistance?

After colonizers realised the procreative potential of female slaves for a natural increase of the slave population, childbirth and childcare of this new generation of slaves became ingrained in the responsibilities of enslaved women on the plantations. Motivations to resist oppression – for example by running away – were likely similar across gender (i.e. (fear of) cruel treatment, (fear of) sale (of loved ones), or the desire to be free). However, the procreative role of female slaves and their attachments to and daily care of their children negatively impacted the patterns of female resistance. For example, in the antebellum South more than three-quarters of runaways were male slaves (White, 1999). Although the fear of children being sold off or victimised could be the main motivation to flee, at the same time, attempts to escape with children were highly unlikely to be successful. "Such desperate decisions inevitably induced emotional trauma and psychological torment" among female slaves (White, 1999, p. 74).

Instead of openly resisting, some scholars have suggested that women created an indigenous counterculture by committing hidden acts of resistance against colonial oppression during and after slavery. For example, during conflicts with slaveholders they would scream particularly loudly. Other attempts consisted of hiding out in the woods, looting estates, sabotaging family planning, refusing work, feigning illness, or achieving some autonomy as market vendors (Besson, 1995; Bush, 1990; Mair, 2007; White, 1999). This, according to Besson (1995), was the way women created a general spirit of resistance. In a broader sense, the development of a culture of resistance is mainly attributed to enslaved women; known as the process of creolisation (e.g. patrons of kinship, language, songs, dance, music, and local economic patrons). Furthermore, Cowling (2013) showed that enslaved women in Brazil and Cuba played a dominant role in achieving freedom for themselves and their children through court. In addition, a minority of female slaves resorted to more violent options by committing suicide, infanticide, murder, and (self)poisoning (Plet, 2002; Van Stipriaan, 1993).

Even though in essence enslaved women were seeking ways to take a stand against the cruelties of slavery, the general literature about slave resistance has classified women's protest as *hidden* and *discrete*, while the protest of enslaved men has been labelled as predominantly *open* and *striking*. This classification has been derived from Scott's famous anthropological resistance framework on peasant societies (Scott, 1985). Open protest actions against the oppression of slavery were visible and striking (e.g. riots, rebellion, or escape) and, moreover, were unambiguous in their aim. Hidden acts of resistance were less visible and striking (e.g. sabotage, abortion, and creolisation) with the aim of resistance more or less concealed. According to Plet, such hidden acts of resistance were aimed to determine "the limits of power in order to force change, for example to achieve more space to move and act" (2002, p. 112).

The distinction between open and hidden resistance has long been used to interpret the actions of the enslaved. However, from a gendered perspective the connection between gender and certain types of resistance (i.e. open versus hidden) seems to overly contrast the concept of the strong man against that of the vulnerable woman. Who is to say with absolute certainty that enslaved women did not physically resist their oppressors? Moreover, why do we assume that enslaved men did not commit hidden acts of resistance as well, such as suicide, feigning illness and so on? In addition, the examples coinciding with these categories seem to assume that risk and violence could only be labelled as characteristics of open resistance, while in fact certain violent acts of resistance, such as (the planning of) murder, in fact could be both violent and hidden. Furthermore, the division between open and hidden resistance gives little insight into the actual motivations for resistance among enslaved men and women.

Current study

Thus, it appears that the simple classification of resistance strategies into either open or hidden protest is somewhat lacking and insufficient to describe and categorise strategies of enslaved women. In the current study we will explore a new perspective on acts of resistance by enslaved women in the Dutch western colonies in order to develop a new framework for interpretation. We use the results of the research conducted by Plet (1994, 1998, 2000, 2002; Plet & Ten Hove, 2003). Following Plet's research we have identified additional acts of resistance by enslaved woman in Suriname and the Dutch Caribbean. All these examples were collected by Lurvink (2009) in light of her research "Slavinnen in verzet" *["Resistance of female slaves"]* for the National Dutch Institute on Slavery ([NiNsee]; Bijnaar, 2005), which will form the basis for this chapter. Our main research questions are formulated as follows:

(a) How did women who were forced into slavery – and thus forced to live a life characterized by servitude, physical and mental violence, captivity, and racism – behave and respond?
(b) How can we interpret their behaviour and responses to enslavement? Are their reactions expressions of deliberate resistance or signs of the mental impact of trauma, which was inherent to the experience of slavery? Did these enslaved women consciously or unconsciously use strategies in order to cope with such trauma?

We will present additional examples of acts of resistance and will combine these examples with supplementary information on these women. Even though this contribution does not cover much newly found source material, it does give an innovative interpretation of female acts of resistance from a psychological and criminological point of view. As our ultimate aim is to reinterpret the individual acts of resistance of enslaved women, we will explore an alternative classification on slave resistance that diverges from the existing open-versus-hidden classification. In this alternative classification we will differentiate between *violent* and *non-violent resistance*. The latter is subdivided into resisting by (a) using the rules, (b) breaking the rules, and (c) reclaiming autonomy and agency (outside of official colonial rules). In addition, we will investigate whether certain acts of resistance could potentially be interpreted from a psychological perspective, by using theoretical frameworks on traumatic stress and coping. Last, we will incorporate this innovative classification of female resistance into a broader discussion on how the labelling of female slave behaviour and responses by colonial rulers might still impact today's stereotyping of Afro-Caribbean women as violent and criminal.

Methods

In this research we have mainly used colonial sources created by slave owners or the colonial government such as criminal records from the Governing Council, accounts of white travellers, plantation notebooks, governmental reports, and newspapers. Existing literature on female slaves was used as a starting point, in which we searched for their stories, and (new) original documents. In doing so, we inventoried the known acts of female resistance, enriched these stories with more details from the original sources, and found new stories by searching the same type of archival sources in which examples had been found before.

However, the historical data sources we consulted have limitations. Although we found information in these sources on resisting women, their acts of protest, as well their first names and the plantations or household they lived on/in, these utilised sources did not contain elaborate information regarding the women's age, profession, character, and/or agency in the context of protest. In addition, we did not find sufficient information on the actual motives for their resisting behaviour, with the exemption of the police interrogation files which occasionally did reveal (in part) the perspective of these women. Unfortunately, no written records created by the enslaved themselves have remained. Last, we need to state that this classification is of course purely instrumental, as it is likely that enslaved people were continuously protesting against slavery in divergent ways.

Results

Violent resistance

In this paragraph, two types of violent resistance in which female slaves played an important role will be discussed, namely, (1) protests or uprisings, and (2) individual (attempted) murder.

Protests

In February of the year 1750, 11 men and one woman – enslaved on plantation Bethlehem in Suriname – laid down their involuntary work in protest. They plundered the plantation and killed the 60-year-old planter Amand Thomas. As a previous member of the Court of Police as well as an Elder of the *Nederduytsche* [Dutch] Reformed Church, he was a powerful man, which made this act of resistance extraordinarily risky and brave. According to historians Thoden van Velzen and Hoogbergen (2011), Thomas regularly (sexually) assaulted women on the plantation, and his "relationship" with the wife of Maroon leader *Basiya* Coridon was the final straw for the slaves on the plantation. Although initiators of slave uprisings were usually male, and women generally are thought not to have participated in slave uprisings or protests, one of the 12 slaves in the Bethlehem protest was in fact female (Raad van Politie, 1750). Unfortunately, the administrative sources do not reveal details about her personality, her life, or her actions. Women were often present during protests on the plantations: their involvement ranging from observing to presenting themselves militantly and loudly at the forefront. For example, during the famous strike led by male slave Tula in 1795 in Curacao, two female slaves were accused of hiding guns in their houses (Paula, 1974). Another enslaved woman was one of nine slaves who were part of the *conspiracy of rebellious* slaves owned by Johanna Lesire (Cain, 2009, p. 71).

Murder

The story of Serafina and her daughter Jansie is one of the examples described by Plet (2002) in which female slaves committed murder as an act of resistance. This enslaved mother and daughter could no longer tolerate the brutal and degrading ways in which their slave mistress Hendrika Reims de Vries – a 37-year-old widow – disciplined her house slaves. They decided together that murder would be the only way to put an end to the suffering imposed by De Vries. In their murderous plot Serafina paid a visit to Damon, a medicine man who dealt in poison. First, he gave her an unidentified substance (i.e. "something") to rub on her own body. Then, he ordered her to bring a curl of De Vries's hair and a piece from the sole of her shoe that had to be permeated with her sweat. He said these ingredients were necessary to prepare a lethal potion. Serafina was then instructed to add this potion daily to the dish she would prepare for De Vries' dinner, which was guaranteed to kill her.

Oddly enough, De Vries did not die at all. Desperate for the potion to take its toll, Serafina and her daughter decided to give fate a helping hand. It was early in the morning, June 16 of 1823, when Jansie called De Vries out of her house – located on the corner of Keizerstraat and Zwarthovenbrugstraat in Paramaribo (see Figure 1.1).[3] While Jansie invented an excuse to urge De Vries to come to the open water well on the yard, Serafina stayed on the veranda on the lookout. When De Vries bent over the pit, Jansie dove down and grabbed the ladies' ankles in an attempt to throw De Vries into the well and drown her. Unfortunately for Jansie and Serafina, the mistress responded quickly and started screaming as loud as she could. This immediately prompted her son and two slaves to come running, which saved De Vries. Jansie, fully aware of the consequences of her actions, started to run, but was caught soon. After her arrest, Jansie did not have much choice but to confess. First she proclaimed that the incident at the water well was

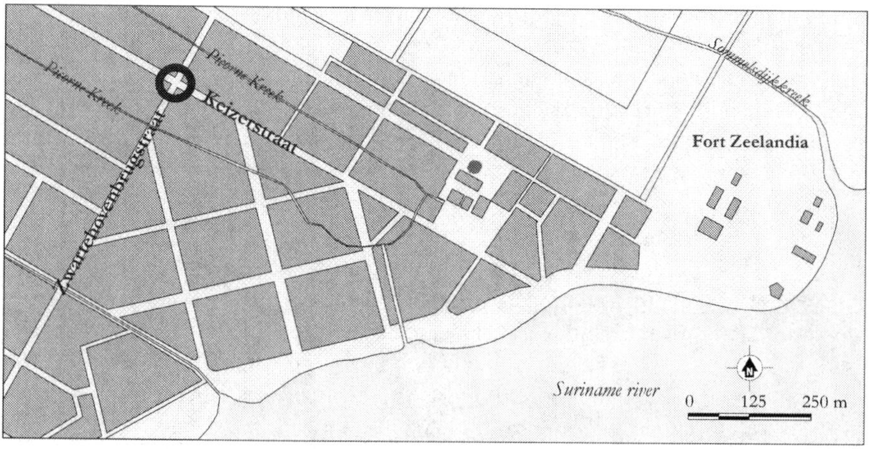

Figure 1.1 Map of Paramaribo with the corner of Keizerstraat and Zwarthovenbrugstraat where Hendrika Reims de Vries' house was located

meant as a joke; however, the authorities did not believe her and accused Jansie of the attempted murder of De Vries. Serafina was suspected immediately as well, despite her denial of involvement. In fact, she was labelled by the court as the mastermind behind the attempted murder. Allegedly Serafina had said to Jansie that nobody would find out if De Vries would be pushed into the well and that her slaves would be sold after she had died. Ultimately, both Serafina and Jansie were convicted for murder, although sources do not reveal whether this judgment was in fact executed. Ironically and coincidentally, De Vries died suddenly right before the adjudication. The cause of her death has never been brought to light.

Another dramatic story of murder as an act of resistance is that of the young girl Jacquelina from plantation Driesveld, Paramaribo in 1829 (Feenstra, 1842). Her master Van Halm did not want her to engage in a love affair with an unknown boy and punished her every time she disobeyed him. Finally, Jacquelina worked out a plan to kill Van Halm by adding rat poison to his chocolate drink; a plan that worked out successfully. Unfortunately, she was betrayed by the pharmacist and one of the house slaves, whom she had asked for the rat poison. After Van Halm died, Jacquelina was convicted of murder and executed on February 27 of 1830. Jacqueline's story is one of the few that is quite well documented and, therefore, has been published as a graphic novel (Bijnaar, Mok, & Stam, 2010). In addition, more examples are known of enslaved women who (attempted to) kill their oppressors. For example, the story of Diana, a female slave in Curacao who tried to kill her mistress by choking her. For her punishment the authorities chopped off Diana's hands and "strangled her to a pole until death" (Paula, 1974, p. 109), as a method of deterrence to others. After her death her body was dumped into the ocean.

By killing their masters, the enslaved were not just defending themselves, but were attacking the oppressor directly (Hira, 1984). Many slaveholders feared that their enslaved workers would poison them sooner or later and for some of them this fear became an obsession (Brenneker, 1976). The enslaved used animal and plant extracts to create poison. They could easily get these ingredients at pharmacies and via the indigenous people in surrounding areas. Sometimes poison was only used to threaten someone (Beeldsnijder, 1994). By the eighteenth century, a substantial number of slaves were using poison to kill their masters, to kill each other, and to kill other enemies. In December 1745, the use of poison was legally prohibited by law. Authorities would cut off the tongue and ears of the perpetrator who violated this ban, after which he or she would be branded on the forehead and chained to a pole for life. In addition, these enslaved convicts would be given a lifelong sentence of working and living in complete isolation. The colonial authorities sought refuge in such drastic discipline as they were convinced that slaves preferred death to punishment, for death would offer them redemption. As a result of these severe sentences, the use of poison declined during the 1860s, even though it never disappeared completely (Dragtenstein, 2004).

Non-violent resistance

By resisting non-violently, enslaved women tried to create personal freedom for themselves within the restricting and oppressing system of slavery. This type of resistance was less obvious than violent acts of resistance and ranged from escaping or marronage to refusing to convert to Christianity, from bureaucratic to non-bureaucratic. In the first part of this paragraph we will present how some enslaved women used the existing colonial rules to resist their lack of freedom. Furthermore, in this paragraph we will discuss examples of women who dared to break these rules in their resistance, and women who tried to claim their autonomy and agency with strategies not involving colonial rules.

Using the rules

Some women used the existing colonial rules and bureaucracy to protest against their lack of personal freedom. An example is Badina, a rebellious priestess within the Winti faith, which mainly had followers among the slaves on the wood plantations in the Para District of Suriname (Lenders, 1996). In 1863, 70 per cent of the slave population in Suriname had been or was about to be converted to Christianity (MacLeod, 1996). However, not all slaves were in favour of this Christianisation, and responded rebelliously and disobediently. To illustrate, during a religious and socially critical dance in 1782, a group of "heathen" slaves showed the Christianised slaves that they did not want to have anything to do with the new faith (Everaert, 1999). The general view in the literature has been that women were more likely to convert to Christianity than men (Lenders, 1996). However, not all women did convert out of their own free will and were consciously disobedient instead. Some enslaved women were priestesses of their own faith and actively hampered missionaries' efforts to eradicate the religious beliefs of the slaves (Lamur, 1985; Everaert, 1848).

Badina was one of these constantly disobedient enslaved priestesses. She managed to discourage many slaves from converting to Christianity (Lenders, 1996). Notwithstanding the many exhortations and threats from the Moravian missionaries, she continued to practice her faith publicly. One day in 1849, Badina and Thomas, one of the overseers and an assistant of the Moravians, got into an argument. The exact details of the clash are unknown, but it resulted in Badina biting Thomas on his arm, and him chasing her with a whip. For Badina, this incident gave reason to head to Paramaribo to complain to one of the influential white administrators that one of the missionaries had assaulted her because of her faith. One of the administrators took her complaint seriously and was about to punish the overseer, when this was prevented by the intermediary of the director. Later on, the administrator visited the plantation and told the slaves: "The Moravians have deprived you from all joy, I will return this [joy] to you" (Lenders, 1986, p. 188). He organised a party that lasted three nights. Thereafter, the administrator publicly insulted the director of the plantation and let the slaves openly spill their dismay as well. After this offence, the director had no choice but to leave the plantation. Though the administrator was more than willing to play this heroic role, Badina was the real hero: she violated the rules of the missionaries, defended her religion and identity, and resisted the imposition of Christianity – which actually served to control and discipline the slaves. Thus, Badina used the (limited) bureaucratic options she had to the fullest in order to maintain her personal religious freedom.

Breaking the rules

Some enslaved women were brave enough to protest against the colonial rules. A good example is the Aruban enslaved woman Virginia Dementricia. She disobeyed the colonial rules, was rebellious, and escaped many times. She has been called "the most punished enslaved woman of Aruba" (Alofs, 2009, p. 20). As one of the 20 slaves of Protestant colonist Jan van der Biest, Virginia repeatedly violated the colonial law. Between 1859 and 1863, five trials were held against her. She was accused of theft, running away, causing street noise, and resisting the police. It all started in March 1859, when she was 17 years old and stole some clothes from Van der Biest. She was punished, but repeated this offence in July. She was punished again, after which she escaped the plantation in November, and was punished once more. In July of the next year she was convicted of "running away and false accusation, accompanied by impiety" (Alofs, 2009, p. 20). After serving eight days in prison, she was arrested again for causing street noise and resisting the police. Despite the punishments she received for her disobedient and rebellious behaviour, Virginia kept resisting the colonial rules and the rules of Van der Biest until Van der Biest sold Virginia to slave owner Jesserun in Curacao (Alofs, 2009).

According to the Dutch colonial law, slaves who tried to escape slavery were guilty of "theft of their own body" (Archives of Curacao, Bonaire, and Aruba, 1821, inventory no. 1685). When escaped slaves were captured, they received

Table 1.1 Number of runaway slaves in Suriname divided by gender in the period 1779–1792

Year	*Men*	*Women*
1779	75	8
1780	97	5
1781	301	14
1782	147	14
1790	171	23
1791	325	26
1792	105	3
Total	1221	93

Note: (Hoogbergen & De Theye, 1986, p. 148).

the death penalty as a deterrent. Virginia was not the only enslaved woman who escaped or tried to escape. However, in Suriname enslaved women escaped less often than enslaved men during the period 1779–1792 (Hoogbergen & De Theye, 1986; see Table 1.1). On average, in 1770 the ratio of female and male slaves in Suriname was 1.04 (Van Stipriaan, 1993). Van Stipriaan argues that women rarely escaped alone, especially when they had children. However, according to Plet (2002), advertisements from the Suriname newspaper reveal that many enslaved women escaped with their children but without men. More research is needed to determine the exact number of enslaved women that escaped (without men). Examples of enslaved women who escaped together without men were Monkie, Sabina, and Wilhelmina who left plantation Vrouwenvlijt by boat (Brenneker, 1976; Van Stipriaan, 1993).

Where did the formerly enslaved women seek refuge after they had escaped slavery? Slaves from the islands Aruba and Curacao usually escaped by boat to the Spanish colonies on the mainland of South America. In the period 1729–1774, 585 slaves escaped from Curacao to Coro (see Figure 1.2) of which 89 (15 per cent) were female (Rupert, 2007). Slaves in Suriname escaped into the jungle and founded their own communities, also called marronage communities (see Figure 1.3). The vast majority of escaped slaves were male and between 1767 and 1802, 5,028 males escaped compared to 503 female slaves (Van der Putten, 2005). Although women were in the minority in the early periods of marronage, they did play important roles within the marron communities (Beeldsnijder, 1994), as those responsible for food and religion (De Groot, 2009). Famous marron leader Boni became part of the marron community Lowéman because his mother, Ma Awitya, escaped slavery by running away and resorting to marronage (Thoden van Velzen, & Hoogbergen, 2011).

Another famous and fierce female escapee was Ma Cato. She did not only protest against the rules when she escaped, but also used the colonial rules to negotiate peace for the marrons (De Groot, 2009). In the 1730s, Ma Cato broke away from the plantation and never returned to her masters. She escaped with two of her sisters, a brother-in-law, her uncle, and two nephews and aligned with a Maroon society in

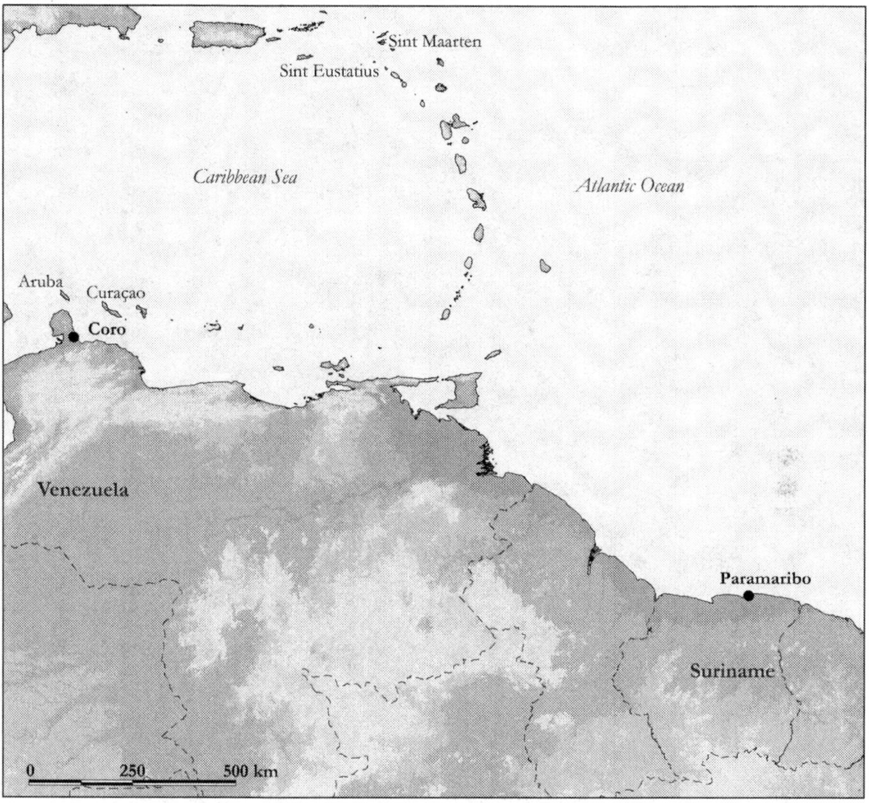

Figure 1.2 Area map including Coro in Venezuela, and the Dutch colonies Aruba, Curacao, St. Eustatius, St. Maarten, and Suriname

the Ndjuka area. Since she was an African priest and spiritual medium, she played an important role in creating and consolidating the culture and identity of the Marrons. She was indispensable when the Maroons started their negotiations about freedom with the colonial authorities in 1760 and was also responsible for introducing education to the Maroons. We may conclude that with the supervision of Ma Cato the Maroons were able to maintain their freedom and develop themselves.

Reclaiming autonomy and agency

Lydia was a young and good-looking woman, and the house slave of a free black woman named Johanna (Van Hoëvell, 1855). It was Lydia's job to employ activities outside the household and hand over a fixed amount of 32 cents to Johanna every day. Everything went fine until she met Frans, a young light-skinned and free man. As a concierge of several government buildings he earned quite a good salary.

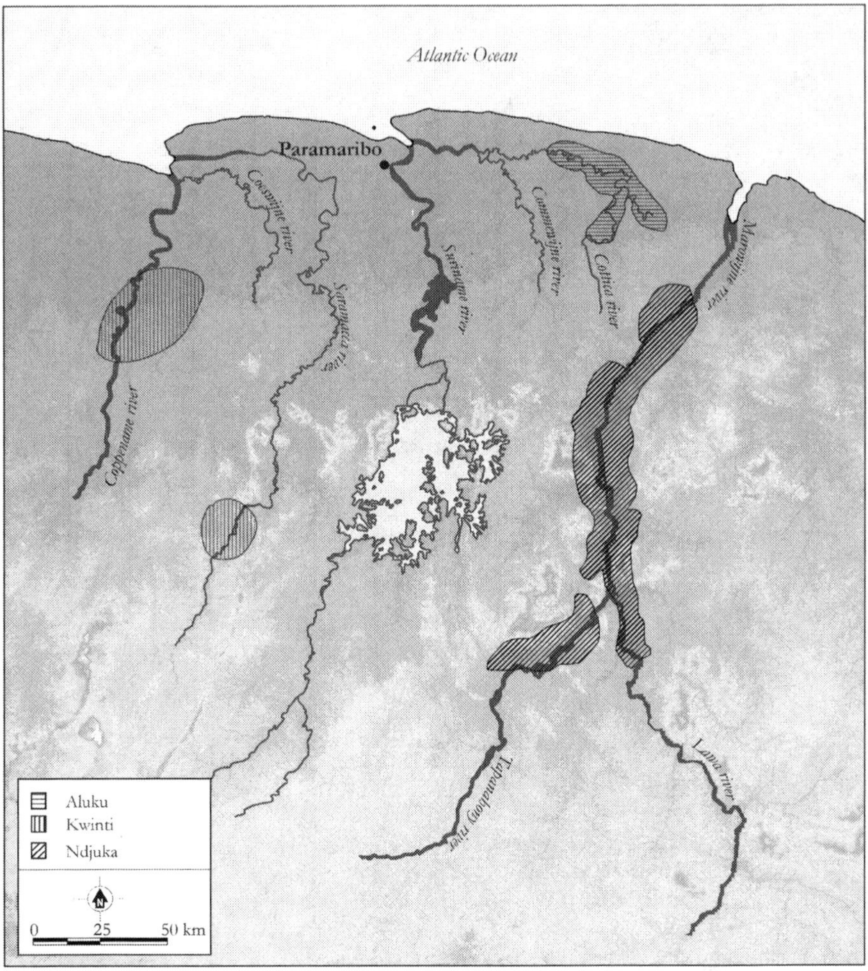

Figure 1.3 Map with marronage communities Aluku, Kwinti, and Ndjuka

Lydia and Frans fell in love with each other and spent many hours together in his house. Lydia cleaned and helped out with other things in his household. Naturally, Frans took responsibility of the 32 cents she had to hand Johanna daily. As months were going by, they were becoming really devoted to each other, displaying an outstanding love and loyalty. However, they both feared that Johanna would discover their relationship, which ultimately happened one day, after which Johanna responded furiously and insisted Lydia should look for another man. Lydia continued to disobey, and as a result was locked up in a sty in the yard for 24 hours without any food or water. However, this punishment had the opposite effect and only increased Lydia's longing for Frans. The day after her punishment she went back to Frans immediately. When Johanna found out she warned and threated Lydia several times, but Lydia played deaf and continued her visits to Frans. Ultimately Johanna called the police to complain, who sentenced Lydia to 15 whiplashes on her naked body. When the whiplash came down on her, she tried to cover up her body. But the executioner had no mercy: he chained her hands to a pole above her head so he could do his job efficiently. The historical data do not reveal whether this tragic turn led to the separation of Lydia and Frans.

Many enslaved women used these kinds of strategies against slavery without using any violence nor trespassing of the official rules. Though enslaved people were depersonalised as human beings, by resisting, many enslaved made it clear that the oppressor could break their bones, but not their spirit. They pursued their human dignity and integrity within the ambivalent boundaries of the slave society. For example, an enslaved woman who was brought to Amsterdam by her master had to take Dutch classes and convert herself to Christianity. After seven years she returned to Suriname where she explained that she was no longer a Christian but preferred the African religion of the enslaved instead (Herlein, 1718). As mentioned above, more women rejected their conversion to Christianity and continued practicing their African religion. Another example of an act of resistance not related to rules was the prevention of pregnancy. After the abolition of the slave trade in 1808, many enslaved women refused to obey the planter's wishes to "produce" as many slaves as possible, and therefore, consciously tried to prevent pregnancy (Campbell, Miers, & Miller, 2005). Van Stipriaan (1993) researched enslaved women on 14 Suriname plantations in the period 1820–1863. Despite a surplus of men, 23.5 per cent of the women did not have any children. Van Stipriaan argues with reasonable certainty that the low fertility of these women was the result of their own autonomous decisions.

Responding to experiences of trauma and loss

Life for the enslaved was inhumane, degrading, and potentially traumatizing for men, women, and children (DeGruy, 2005). The endured violence and associated overwhelming fear that accompanied the unpredictably cruel life circumstances of slavery clearly must have taxed many men and women to the limits of their physical and psychological coping mechanisms and strength. Furthermore, as the era of slavery transcended generations many enslaved were born and buried under its reign, experiencing to its full extent, slavery's cycle of violence. From a psychological perspective, certain life-threatening and frightening events, which lie outside of the "normal" human experience, can be described as potentially damaging and traumatizing (American Psychiatric Association, 2013). Prolonged exposure to (sexual) violence and abuse is known to cause symptoms of severe psychopathology such as post-traumatic stress, depression, anxiety, dissociation, psychosis, borderline- or antisocial personality disorders, suicide attempts, and/or self-harming behaviour (e.g. Senn, Carey, & Vanable, 2008; Widom, 2014). The negative impact of trauma and abuse on mental health has been found across cultures, both in general and within the context of war (Betancourt, Newnham,

McBain, & Brennan, 2013; Feldman, Vengrober, Eidelman-Rothman, & Zagoory-Sharon, 2013; Mels, Derluyn, Broekaert, & García-Pérez, 2015; Widom, 2014). Especially in the case of prolonged child sexual abuse and later sexual victimisation in adolescence and adulthood, coping responses to such behaviour may involve violent/aggressive behaviour, running away, sexual risk-taking behaviour (i.e. promiscuity), and/or survival sex (Daly, 1994; Siegel & Williams, 2003; Layne, et al., 2014; Littleton, Breitkopf, & Berenson, 2007; Senn et al., 2008, Wilson & Widom, 2010). Thus, some acts of enslaved women which have been interpreted as acts of resistance or consorting with the enemy could perhaps also be interpreted in light of (failing) coping efforts after prolonged (sexual) victimisation. Some critics such as Wilson (1973) have judged this behaviour to be sleeping with the enemy. Other researchers like Besson (1995), on the contrary, have interpreted these as acts of resistance.

For example, several instances of hypersexual behaviour or prostitution have been recorded regarding enslaved women in the Dutch colonies. Most of these instances involved concubines, who were enslaved women that entered into sexual relationships with their suppressors. However, records also show that these behaviours were not exclusively aimed at or related to sex with the suppressor. To illustrate, in 1861, a group of missionaries expressed their disapproval of the "whorish" behaviour of Hermine, a young slave, directed at the newly arrived overseer. Two months later a complaint was filed about the enslaved woman Europa for prostituting herself to two men: a slave of plantation Goudmijn and a white overseer (Oostindie, 2007). In addition, the enslaved woman Christina lived in 1768 in the Netherlands as the house slave of Adrianus van der Geugten and his wife. History records have shown that Christina continuously escaped the house to beg and prostitute herself (Schout en Schepenen, 1768; Dors, 2002).

Unfortunately, only their perceived acts of deviance have been recorded in time; therefore, we can only hypothesise about potential explanations. However, as (sexual) violence has been described as a common denominator in the lives of the enslaved, it could be possible that, for example, Christina's "excessive" sexual behaviour and prostitution stemmed from her own (sexual) victimisation. Also in recent studies a history of childhood sexual abuse is associated with sexualised behaviour problems (Putnam, 2003) and significantly higher arrest rates for sex crimes and prostitution (Widom & Ames, 1994). Furthermore, as a concubine, also called *sisi*, women had a greater chance to increase their quality of life in some ways as well as better chances to gain their freedom papers (Terborg, 2002). Research has shown, for example, that two-thirds of the manumitted slaves in Suriname were women, of whom many had been concubines (Plet & Ten Hove, 2003). The question remains if and to what degree the decision of enslaved women to become concubines was always a voluntary one. Furthermore, for enslaved women resisting the demand of a slave master to be his concubine meant putting yourself at risk for severe whipping (Wolbers, 1853). Thus, women whose behaviour potentially became sexualised as a result of severe enduring sexual victimisation were criminalised in some instances. At the same time refusal to cooperate with a slave master's desire to become his concubine would lead to severe punishment as well. In the context of slavery, the interpretation of such acts of deviance are problematic because (a) history was recorded by white colonial powers, and therefore, coloured by their racist frame of mind and stereotypes of the black hypersexual Jezebel, and (b) the context of slavery in which history was recorded dehumanised the enslaved and, therefore, dehumanised their human responses to this oppressive system and potentially traumatizing experiences.

This lack of consideration by the colonial powers for the psychological impact of trauma endured by the enslaved is also shown in several examples of responses to traumatic loss and bereavement. For example, Melanie was a young enslaved woman who was owned by a woman named Van het Kruis who had bought Melanie when she was still a child and had since tyrannised her. It was Melanie's task to maintain the upkeep of the household, to take care of the seven children of the woman, and to sell goods on the street. Whenever Van het Kruis was not content with the amount of money Melanie handed over, the woman gave her severe beatings. After some time, Melanie got pregnant and delivered a child, after which her problems only became worse. Van het Kruis did not want Melanie to breastfeed the baby, since this would impede her from doing her work properly. One day Melanie's baby got sick but still Van het Kruis did not give Melanie permission to stay at home with her infant. Regardless of Melanie's maternal worries, Van het Kruis instructed her to sell products on the street. When Melanie returned home late in the evening she found her baby dead. It was clear that the baby had been murdered. To prevent Melanie from screaming the mistress grabbed her tight and put a gag in her mouth.

The death of her child was a severe turning point in Melanie's life. After the burial she escaped from Van het Kruis. Walking along the Suriname River she met a few enslaved who were heading for the Para District, which was a plantation area further away. The enslaved allowed her to join them, but since they were afraid to bring her to their own living area she had to eventually leave the group. Melanie walked for days and nights, suffering extreme hunger when all of a sudden she heard some cocks crowing. She started to follow the sound and found several slave houses. She was so hungry that she decided she was going to ask for food, regardless of the risk to be captured. To her luck she had arrived at plantation Loefbeek, a plantation left by its owners since the plantation was not profitable anymore. The owner had been permitted by the colonial authorities to deport his slaves to another plantation. He had taken the strong and vital ones with him and had left the sick ones alone at plantation Loefbeek. Melanie moved in with this small community of no more than 10 inhabitants; all runaway slaves or slaves who hung around several plantations to sell their goods (i.e. *schuilders*). However, life at Loefbeek was not without stress as they were living in constant fear of being caught by military expeditions who were heading for these schuilders constantly. Nonetheless, Melanie fell in love with one of the slaves living at Loefbeek; a man called Mei who was suffering from a severe case of leprosy. Together they had two children and lived a relatively peaceful life for some time. Unfortunately, their luck was brutally ended when a patrol discovered their hiding place at Loefbeek and Melanie and her two children got caught. Unfortunately, the historical data do not reveal what happened to Melanie and her children (Hoogbergen & De Theye, 1986).

As described in the introduction, the daily care of children and the fear of loss and separation from their children often impeded and prevented enslaved women from running away as an act of resistance. However, losing this responsibility due to the loss of a child through death or murder would imply that these enslaved women could feel like they no longer had anything to lose. Furthermore, in psychology the loss of an attachment figure, especially the loss of a child, is seen as a psychologically taxing and potentially traumatic event (e.g. Bowlby, 1980). "Unexpected and untimely deaths, particularly when associated with violence and the witnessing of horrific events, have emerged from many studies as predictors of poor outcome following bereavement" (Parkes, 2001, p. 39). Responses to (traumatic types of) loss and bereavement are known to encompass, for example, severe anxiety, depression, suicidal ideation or suicide, anger, and even mortality (for a review see Stroebe, Schut, & Stroebe, 2007). Thus, when Melanie ran away after losing her child at the hands of her mistress, her decision to run away could have been an act of resistance (as she had nothing left to loose), but perhaps also as an indication of traumatic bereavement.

Furthermore, certain homicidal behaviours of female slaves could then also be explained by reactions and indications of potential traumatic loss experiences. Suicide attempts by enslaved women usually involved hanging themselves in a tree, jumping from a cliff, or drowning in a well or in the sea (Brenneker, 1976). For example, an enslaved woman drowned herself in Suriname (Beeldsnijder, 1994). Unfortunately, there are no records as to any potentially specific events leading up to these suicides. However, across general populations it has been found that both mothers and fathers are at increased risk for suicide after the death of a child, especially in the first month of bereavement and when the child was still young at the time of death (Qin & Mortensen, 2003). The difference with the context of slavery is that the behavioural reactions of the enslaved to loss were not recorded by colonial historians as such, due to the fact that behaviour of the enslaved in general was dehumanised. Instead, potential behavioural responses to trauma and loss were more likely interpreted as proof of the hypersexual nature of the enslaved (i.e. Jezebel stereotype), or as criminal acts of resistance in need of punishment.

Discussion

In this chapter we have placed the historically documented acts of female slave resistance in Suriname and the Dutch Caribbean in a new perspective. We have amended the standardly used distinction between open and hidden acts of resistance into the following categories: (1) violent acts of resistance, (2) non-violent acts of resistance, and (3) responses to trauma and loss. Furthermore, the category of non-violent acts of resistance was further subdivided into acts in which women (1) used the rules, (2) broke the rules, or (3) reclaimed their autonomy and agency. It has to be emphasised that the categorisation used is purely instrumental as the true motivations of each of these brave women will never be fully uncovered and we can only hypothesise based on the historical records at hand. Furthermore, we experienced difficulty in placing some of the acts recorded in history as resistance into this categorisation, for example, the act of aborting a pregnancy or infanticide committed by enslaved women. According to one example from 1857, an enslaved woman was accused of feeding her child with something that caused its death (Everaert, 1857). Unfortunately, too little historical information has been recorded to interpret these acts and the motivations of this particular enslaved woman.

Moreover, a critical note needs to be made regarding historical accounts of both feigning illness and infanticide. Due to the hard work under inhumane conditions, of course the likelihood of actually getting sick was extremely high (White, 1999). Furthermore, what we know of such instances of "feigned" illness was recorded in history mainly by those in power. Therefore, it remains hard to interpret whether women feigned illness as deliberate attempts to resist, or whether they were actually sick and were unjustly labelled by their slave master as dishonestly escaping their "workloads". Similarly, recent historical and medical research suggest that many instances of infanticide by suffocation were in fact more likely accidental infant deaths by Sudden Infant Death Syndrome (SIDS) or *crib death* (Johnson, 1981). Such interpretation of slave mothers as careless and/or murderous could also be seen as examples of how behaviour of female slaves was dehumanised and overly criminalised by colonial rulers.

Current viewpoints concerning Caribbean women and crime

Does the criminalizing of acts of resistance by enslaved women still impact current-day viewpoints concerning Caribbean women and crime, especially, concerning women from African descent in post-colonial societies? Is the behaviour of black women still misinterpreted and unjustly labelled as overly aggressive, dangerous, and/or criminal? Although one cannot empirically show that such a bias would be directly related to the era of slavery and the labelling of these acts as resisting (as opposed to human reactions to trauma), existing literature and statistics do show that black women are over-represented in the justice system as compared to native/white women across, for example, the United Sates (e.g. Steffensmeier, Ulmer, & Kramer, 1998), the United Kingdom (Coid et al., 2002), and the Netherlands (Central Bureau of Statistics [CBS], 2016). In the 1990s the incarceration odds for black women in the United States were higher than for white women for all included age groups. Additionally, African American women also received longer sentences than white women regardless of age (Steffensmeier et al., 1998). In 2003 during the enduring *war on drugs*, black women were incarcerated for drug offences at a rate almost 5 times as high compared to white women across the United States (Human Rights Watch, 2008 in Brennan, Chesney-Lind, Vandenberg, & Wulf-Ludden, 2015). Continuing this trend, in 2014 the imprisonment rate for African American women was more than twice as high compared to white women (Porter, 2016). Also in the Netherlands, Surinamese and (Dutch) Caribbean women together form the largest ethnic minority group among the female prison population (CBS, 2016).

This international over-representation of black women (of African descent) across criminal justice systems occurs at a time in which negative stereotyping of black women is also continuingly present (e.g. Brennan et al., 2015). In line with negative racial stereotypes of the black female slave, black women currently are still portrayed and typified as dominant, angry, dangerous/violent, and hypersexual (e.g. Brennan, 2006). In fact, in their study on media portrayals of female offenders Brennan et al. (2015) found that minority women who offend are more often characterised by the media as culpable for their actions and are more likely portrayed as "beyond reformation" compared to descriptions of white female offenders. Moreover, newspaper stories about minority offenders more often focused on the harm that had been inflicted onto victims by these particular female offenders. On the contrary, newspaper stories on white female offenders more likely included justifications for the offence and/or a focus on "forces beyond control" (i.e. mental health problems) in relation to the committed/alleged crime (Brennan & Vandenberg, 2009). As the media has a strong impact in our (social) media-driven societies, individuals' perceptions on minorities and blacks in particular could be negatively influenced by these different, seemingly racially motivated, nuances in newspaper articles on female offenders.

These specific negative stereotypes of black women have been suggested to unconsciously defeminise black women by labelling their behaviours as more masculine. "This masculinization perspective suggests that female offenders, especially violent girls, abandon their femininity and take on the masculine traits of their male counterparts" (Irwin & Chesney-Lind, 2008, p. 839). Furthermore, stereotyping violent girls as masculine has been suggested to warrant the harsher treatment of these girls by the criminal justice system as they are then more likely perceived as part of the social threat of the *super predator* violent juveniles (Brennan et al., 2015; Irwin & Chesney-Lind, 2008). Indeed, racially typifying violent delinquency as committed relatively more often by blacks was indirectly related to increased punitiveness (Metcalfe, Pickett, & Mancini, 2015). In summary, black women (of African descent) are over-represented in official crime statistics internationally, and at the same time, are being continuously stereotyped as more violent, more masculine, more culpable, and more deserving of harsher sentences than white women. Clearly, more research is needed on the potential impacts of institutionalised racism and racial stereotypes stemming from the era of transatlantic slavery on the over-representation of female black ethnic minorities in post-colonial criminal justice systems.

Conclusion

From a gendered perspective the categorisation of female acts of resistance to slavery as proposed in this chapter seems to fit better with the specific motivations and the opportunities for resistance in the daily lived experience of enslaved women in the era of transatlantic slavery. During slavery, the human nature of the enslaved was denied and constantly undermined, Thus, by taking into account the impact of potentially traumatic experiences of (sexual) victimisation and violent deaths of children and/or partners, we have managed to reframe acts that were criminalised by colonial rulers into potential efforts to cope with psychological torment and trauma. In doing so, known historical acts of enslaved women become more humanised as their potential experiences, reactions, and motivations are placed in a broader psychological perspective.

Notes

1 People who escaped slavery and created independent groups and communities in remote locations.
2 The Jezebel stereotype characterized black women as entirely driven by hyper-sexuality and an inflated libido.
3 All figures were prepared for this chapter by Jaap Fokkema from the Faculty of Humanities, VU University Amsterdam.

References

Allen, D., & Spielberg, S. (1997). *Amistad [Motion picture]*. USA: DreamWorks SKG in association with Home Box Office.

Alofs, L. (2009). Virginia dementricia. In E. Kloek, M. Hell, F. Maas, & V. Wetering (Eds.), *Digitaal vrouwenlexicon van Nederland [Digital women lexicon of The Netherlands]*. Retrieved from http://resources.huygens.knaw.nl/vrouwenlexicon/lemmata/data/Virginia.

American Psychiatric Association. (2013). *Diagnostic and statistical manual of mental disorders (DSM-5®)*. Arlington, VA: American Psychiatric Publishing.

Beeldsnijder, R.O. (1994). *"Om werk van jullie te hebben": Plantageslaven in Suriname, 1730–1750 [To get your work: Plantation slaves in Suriname 1730–1750]*. Utrecht: CLACS & IBS Utrecht.

Besson, J. (1995). Women's use of ROSCAS in the Caribbean: Reassessing the literature. In S. Ardener, & S. Burman (Eds.), *Money-go-rounds: The importance of rotating saving and credit associations for women* (pp. 236–288). Oxford: Berg.

Betancourt, T.S., Newnham, E.A., McBain, R., & Brennan, R.T. (2013). Post-traumatic stress symptoms among former child soldiers in Sierra Leone: Follow-up study. *The British Journal of Psychiatry*, *203*(3), 196–202.

Bijnaar, A. (2002). *Kasmoni–een spaartraditie in Suriname en Nederland [Kasmoni: A money saving tradition in Suriname and The Netherlands]*. Amsterdam: Bert Bakker.

Bijnaar, A. (2005). *Rebelse slavinnen: Een zoektocht naar vrouwelijke slaven die onverschrokken slavernij aan de kaak stelden [Rebellious female slaves: A search for female slaves who fearlessly challenged slavery]*. Amsterdam: Research proposal NiNsee.

Bijnaar, A., Mok, I., & Stam, D. (2010). *Jacquelina: Slavin van plantage Driesveld [Jacquelina: Slave of plantation Driesveld]*. Amsterdam: NiNsee, KIT Publishers.

Bowlby, J. (1980). *Attachment and loss. Vol. 3: Loss: Sadness and depression*. New York: Basic Books.

Brennan, P.K. (2006). Sentencing female misdemeanants: An examination of the direct and indirect effects of race/ethnicity. *Justice Quarterly*, *23*(1), 60–95.

Brennan, P.K., Chesney-Lind, M., Vandenberg, A.L., & Wulf-Ludden, T. (2015). The saved and the damned: Racial/ethnic differences in media construction of female drug offenders. *Radical Criminology*, *5*, 47–98.

Brennan, P.K., & Vandenberg, A.L. (2009). Depictions of female offenders in front-page newspaper stories: The importance of race/ethnicity. *International Journal of Social Inquiry*, *2*(2), 141–175.

Brenneker, P.H.F. (1976). *Sambumbu: Volkskunde van Curaçao, Aruba en Bonaire I [Sambumbu; Ethnology of Curacao, Aruba and Bonaire I]*. Willemstad: Scherpenheuvel N.V.

Brent, L. (1861). *Incidents in the life of a slave girl*. Boston: L. Maria Child.

Bush, B. (1990). *Slave women in Caribbean society 1650–1838*. Bloomington: Indiana University Press.

Cain, A. (2009). *Tula: De slavenopstand van 1795 op Curaçao [Tula: The slave revolt of 1795 on Curacao]*. Amsterdam: Amrit Consultancy.

Campbell, G., Miers, S., & Miller, J.C. (2005). Women in Western systems of slavery: Introduction. *Slavery and Abolition, 26*(2), 161–179.

Central Bureau of Statistics. (2016). *Verdachten: Delictgroep, geslacht, leeftijd en herkomstgroepering [Suspects: Offense type, sex, age, and country of birth]*. Retrieved from http://statline.cbs.nl/Statweb/publication/?DM=SLNL&PA=81947NED&D1=0&D2=2&D3=0&D4=0-1,6-7&D5=l&HDR=G4,G3,G1,G2&STB=T&VW=T.

Coid, J., Petruckevitch, A., Bebbington, P., Brugha, T., Bhugra, D., Jenkins, R., . . . Singleton, N. (2002). Ethnic differences in prisoners: Criminality and psychiatric morbidity. *The British Journal of Psychiatry, 181*(6), 473–480.

Cowling, C. (2013). *Conceiving freedom: Women of color, gender, and the abolition of slavery in Havana and Rio de Janeiro*. Chapel Hill: The University of North Carolina Press.

Daly, K. (1994). *Gender, crime, and punishment*. New Haven and London: Yale University Press.

De Groot, S.W. (2009). *Agents of their own emancipation: Topics in the history of Suriname Maroons*. Amsterdam: de Groot.

DeGruy, J. (2005). *Post-traumatic slave syndrome: America's legacy of enduring injury and healing*. Milwaukie, OR: Uptone Press.

De Kom, A. (1981). *Wij slaven van Suriname [Us slaves of Suriname]*. Bussum: Uitgeverij Contact.

Dors, H.G. (Ed.). (2002). *De kleine geschiedenis van de slavernij: Sporen in Amsterdam [The little history of slavery: Traces in Amsterdam]*. Amsterdam: KIT Publishers.

Dragtenstein, R.F. (2004). *'Trouw aan de blanken': Quassie van Nieuw Timotibo, twist en strijd in de 18e eeuw in Suriname [Loyalty to the whites: Quassie of New Timotibo, dispute and strife in 18th century Suriname]*. Amsterdam: KIT Publishers.

Dragtenstein, R.F. (2010). *"Alles voor de vrede", De brieven van Boston Band tussen 1757 en 1763 [All for peace: The Letters of Boston Band between 1757 and 1763]*. Amsterdam: Amrit Consultancy.

Elwes, C., Patrick, B., Williams, P.O., Ziskin, L., & Daniels, L. (2013). *The Butler [Motion picture]*. USA: Follow Through Productions.

Everaert, H., Specialien Schevening. (1848, October 26). Private collection.

Everaert, H., Specialien Fairfield. (1857, February). Private collection.

Everaert, H. (1999). *Een zoektocht naar de aard van man-vrouw relaties onder Surinaamse slaven: de suikerplantages Fairfield, Breukelerwaard, Cannewapibo en La Jalousie in de periode voorafgaande aan de emancipatie [In search of the nature of men-women relationships among Surinamese slaves: The sugar plantations Fairfield, Breukelerwaard, Cannewagibo and La Jalousie in the period prior to emancipation]*. Amsterdam: Atelier Rijksbouwmeester.

Feenstra, M.D. (1842). *De negerslaven in de kolonie Suriname en de uitbreiding van het Christendom onder de heidensche bevolking [The negro slaves in the colony of Suriname and the expansion of Christianity among the heathen population]*. Dordrecht: H. Lagerweij.

Feldman, R., Vengrober, A., Eidelman-Rothman, M., & Zagoory-Sharon, O. (2013). Stress reactivity in war-exposed young children with and without posttraumatic stress disorder: Relations to maternal stress hormones, parenting, and child emotionality and regulation. *Development and Psychopathology*, *25*(4pt1), 943–955.

Gardner, D., Katagas, A., Kleiner, J., Milchan, A., Pitt, B., Pohlad, B., & McQueen, S. (2013). *Twelve years a slave [Motion picture]*. USA/UK: Regency Enterprises.

Herlein, J.H. (1718). *Beschryvinge van de volk-plantinge Zuriname [Description of the population of plantation Suriname]*. Leeuwarden: Meindert Injema.

Hira, S. (1984). *Van Priary tot en met De Kom: De geschiedenis van het verzet in Suriname 1630–1940 [Van Priary till De Kom: The history of resistance in Suriname, 1630–1940]*. Den Haag: Blok & Flohr.

Hoogbergen, W.S.M. (1990). *The Boni maroon wars in Suriname*. Leiden, New York, Kopenhagen and Keulen: E.J. Brill.

Hoogbergen, W.S.M., & De Theye, M. (1986). Surinaamse vrouwen in de slavernij [Surinamese women in slavery]. *Jaarboek voor Vrouwengeschiedenis*, *7*, 126–151.

Hudlin, R., Savone, P., Sher, S., & Tarantino, Q. (2012). *Django unchained [Motion picture]*. USA: The Weinstein Company and Columbia Pictures.

Irwin, K., & Chesney-Lind, M. (2008). Girls' violence: Beyond dangerous masculinity. *Sociology Compass*, *2*(3), 837–855.

Johnson, M.P. (1981). Smothered slave infants: Were slave mothers at fault? *The Journal of Southern History*, *47*(4), 493–520.

Kennedy, K., & Spielberg, S. (2012). *Lincoln [Motion picture]*. USA: DreamWorks.

Lamur, H.E. (1985). *De kerstening van de slaven van de Surinaamse plantage Vossenburg: 1847–1878 [Christening of the slaves of Surinamese plantation Vossenburg: 1848–1878]*. Amsterdam: Universiteit van Amsterdam.

Layne, C.M., Greeson, J.K., Ostrowski, S.A., Kim, S., Reading, S., Vivrette, R.L. . . . Pynoos, R.S. (2014). Cumulative trauma exposure and high risk behaviour in adolescence: Findings from the National Child Traumatic Stress Network Core Data Set. *Psychological Trauma: Theory, Research, Practice, and Policy*, *6*(S1), S40–S49.

Leinders, J., Nije, R., & Van Stapele, D. (2013). *Tula: The revolt [Motion picture]*. Nederland: Fisheye Feature Films.

Lenders, M. (1986). Misi Hartmann. Een leven als zendelinge in de kolonie Suriname [Misi Hartmann: A life as a missionary in the colony Suriname]. *Jaarboek voor Vrouwengeschiedenis*, *7*, 172–191.

Lenders, M. (1996). *Strijders voor het lam: leven en werk van hernhutter broeders en zusters in Suriname, 1735–1900 [Fighters for the lam: Life and work of 'hernhutter' brothers and sisters in Suriname, 1735–1900]*. Leiden: KITLV.

Littleton, H., Breitkopf, C.R., & Berenson, A. (2007). Sexual and physical abuse history and adult sexual risk behaviours: Relationships among women and potential mediators. *Child Abuse & Neglect*, *31*(7), 757–768.

Lurvink, K. (2009). *Slavinnen in verzet. Een zoektocht naar 'rebelse' of 'markante' slavinnen in Suriname en de Nederlandse Antillen [Slave women in resistance: A search for rebel or distinctive female slaves in Suriname and the Dutch Antilles]*. Unpublished Research Report. NiNsee/Vrije Universiteit Amsterdam.

MacLeod, C. (1996). *Elisabeth Samson*. Schoorl: Conserve.

Mair, L. (2007). *The rebel women in the British West Indies during slavery*. Jamaica, Barbados, Trinidad and Tobago: University of the West Indies Press.

Margulies, S., Wolper, D.L., Chomsky, M.J., Erman, J., Greene, D., & Moses, G. (1977). *Roots [TV mini-series]*. USA: David L. Wolper Productions/Warner Bros.

Mels, C., Derluyn, I., Broekaert, E., & García- Pérez, C. (2015). Coping behaviours and post- traumatic stress in war- affected eastern Congolese adolescents. *Stress and Health, 31*(1), 83–88.

Metcalfe, C., Pickett, J.T., & Mancini, C. (2015). Using path analysis to explain racialized support for punitive delinquency policies. *Journal of Quantitative Criminology, 31*, 699–725.

Oostindie, G. (2007). Kerstening en familieleven: Hernhutters, slaven en vrijgemaakten in de Boven-Commewijne, 1852–1878 [Christening and family life: 'Hernhutters', slaves, and freed in the Boven-Commewijne, 1852–1878]. In P.J.J. Meel, H.K. Ramsoedh, & W.S.M. Hoogbergen (Eds.), *Ik ben een haan met een kroon op mijn hoofd Pacificatie en verzet in koloniaal en postkoloniaal Suriname: Opstellen voor Wim Hoogbergen* (pp. 109–132). Amsterdam: Bakker.

Parkes, C.M. (2001). A historical overview of the scientific study of bereavement. In M.S. Stroebe, R.O. Hansson, W. Stroebe, & H. Schut (Eds.), *Handbook of bereavement research* (pp. 25–46). Washington, DC: American Psychological Association.

Paula, A.F. (1974). *1795 de slavenopstand op Curaçao. Een bronnenstudie van de originele overheidsdocumenten [1795 the slave revolt on Curacao. A study of original governmental sources]*. Curaçao: Curaçao Centraal Historisch Archief 1974.

Plet, P. (1994). *Verborgen verzet: Verzets- en overlevingsstrategieën van slavinnen in Rio de Janeiro (1850–1871) [Concealed resistance: Resistance and survival strategies of female slaves in Rio de Janeiro]* (Unpublished Master's thesis). Universiteit Utrecht, Utrecht.

Plet, P. (1998). Overleven en overlevering: Historisch onderzoek naar Surinaamse slavinnen [Survival and surrendering: Historical research on Surinamese female slaves]. *Lover: Driemaandelijkse Literatuuroverzicht voor de Vrouwenbeweging, 25*(3), 20–22.

Plet, P. (2000). Johanna Christina Jonas (1799–1849), een zwarte Surinaamse onderwijzeres [Johanna Christina Jonas (1799–1849), a black Surinamese female teacher]. *OSO–Tijdschrift voor Surinamistiek, 19*(2), 144–146.

Plet, P. (2002). Rebelse vrouwen: Slavinnen in verzet in het negentiende-eeuwse Paramaribo [Rebellious women: Slaves in resistances in nineteenth century Paramaribo]. In R. Daalder, A. Kieskamp, & D.J. Tang (Eds.), *Slaven en schepen* (pp. 110–116). Leiden: Primavera Pers.

Plet, P., & Ten Hove, O. (2003). Magdalena Geurig, Elisa Christina Weefsel en Ketty Bekoorlijk: Gender aspecten in Creools-Surinaamse familienamen [Magdalena Geurig, Elisa Christina Weefsel en Ketty Bekoorlijk: Gender aspects of Creole-Surinamese family names]. *OSO–Tijdschrift voor Surinamistiek, 22*(2), 308–325.

Porter, N.D. (2016). *The state of sentencing 2015: Developments in policy and practice*. Washington, DC: The Sentencing Project.

Putnam, F.W. (2003). Ten-year research update review: Child sexual abuse. *Journal of the American Academy of Child & Adolescent Psychiatry, 42*(3), 269–278.

Qin, P., & Mortensen, P.B. (2003). The impact of parental status on the risk of completed suicide. *Archives of General Psychiatry, 60*(8), 797–802.

Raad van Politie. (1750, March 4–28; April 1–2; May 28–29; June 2,9,19,30; July 12). *Betreffende een slavencomplot tegen Amand Thomas, plantager van de plantage Bethlehem aan de Boven-Commewijne [Concerning a slave conspiracy against Amand Thomas, planter of plantation Bethlehem at the Boven-Commewijne]*. Oud Archief Suriname (Inv. nr.801; microfilm), (HvP/CP). Nationaal Archief: Den Haag.

Reid-Salmon, D. (2012). *Burning for freedom: A theology for the black Atlantic struggle for liberation*. Kingston: Ian Randle Publishers.

Rupert, L.M. (2007). Waters of faith, currents of freedom: Gender, religion, and ethnicity in inter-imperial trade between Curacao and Tierra Firme. In N. Jaffary (Ed.), *Race, religion, and gender in the colonization of the Americas* (pp. 151–164). Aldershot: Ashgate Publishing.

Schout en Schepenen. (1768). Betreffende de 'swartin' Christina uit Indië die veroordeeld werd tot opsluiting in het spinhuis *[Concerning the black woman Christina from Indië who was sentenced to imprisonment in "het spinhuis"]*. Archief van Schout en Schepenen (Inv.nr.1276). Amsterdam: Gemeente Archief Amsterdam.

Scott, J.C. (1985). *Weapons of the weak: Everyday forms of peasant resistance*. New Haven: Yale University Press.

Senn, T.E., Carey, M.P., & Vanable, P.A. (2008). Childhood and adolescent sexual abuse and subsequent sexual risk behaviour: Evidence from controlled studies, methodological critique, and suggestions for research. *Clinical Psychology Review*, *28*(5), 711–735.

Siegel, J.A., & Williams, L.M. (2003). The relationship between child sexual abuse and female delinquency and crime: A prospective study. *Journal of Research in Crime and Delinquency*, *40*(1), 71–94.

Steffensmeier, D., Ulmer, J., & Kramer, J. (1998). The interaction of race, gender, and age in criminal sentencing: The punishment cost of being young, black, and male. *Criminology*, *36*(4), 763–798.

Stroebe, M., Schut, H., & Stroebe, W. (2007). Health outcomes of bereavement. *The Lancet*, *370*(9603), 1960–1973.

Terborg, J. (2002). *Liefde en conflict. Seksualiteit en gender in de Afro-Surinaamse familie [Love and conflict. Seksuality and gender in the Afro-Surinamese family]*. Amsterdam: Universiteit van Amsterdam.

Thoden van Velzen, H.U.E., & Hoogbergen, W. (2011). *Een zwarte vrijstaat in Suriname: De Okaanse samenleving in de achttiende eeuw [A black free state in Surinam: The Okan society in the 18th century]*. Amsterdam: Amsterdam University Press.

Van der Putten, R. (2005). Surinaamse 'weglopers' van de jaren 1767–1802 [Surinamese runaways in the years 1767–1802]. *OSO–Tijdschrift voor Surinamistiek*, *24*(2), 276–288.

Van Hoëvell, W.R. (1855). *Slaven en vrijen onder de Nederlandsche wet [Slaves and freed under Dutch law]*. Zaltbommel: Noman en Zoon.

Van Stipriaan, A. (1993). *Surinaams contrast: Roofbouw en overleven in een Caraïbische plantage-economie, 1750–1863 [Surimese contrast: Overcropping and survival in a Caribbean plantation economy, 1750–1863]*. Amsterdam: Centrale Huisdrukkerij Vrije Universiteit.

White, D.G. (1999). *Ar'n't I a woman? Female slaves in the Plantation South*. New York and London: W.W. Norton & Company.

Widom, C.S. (2014). Longterm consequences of child maltreatment. In J.E. Korbin, & R.D. Krugman (Eds.), *Handbook of child maltreatment* (pp. 225–247). Dordrecht, Netherlands: Springer.

Widom, C.S., & Ames, M.A. (1994). Criminal consequences of childhood sexual victimization. *Child Abuse & Neglect*, *18*(4), 303–318.

Wilson, H.W., & Widom, C.S. (2010). The role of youth problem behaviours in the path from child abuse and neglect to prostitution: A prospective examination. *Journal of Research on Adolescence*, *20*(1), 210–236.

Wilson, P.J. (1973). *Crab antics: The social anthropology of English-speaking Negro societies of the Caribbean*. New Haven: Yale University Press.

Wolbers, J. (1853). *De slavernij in Suriname, of dezelfde gruwelen der slavernij, die in de 'negerhut' geschetst zijn, bestaan ook in onze West-Indische koloniën! [The slavery in Suriname, the same horrors of slavery sketched in the 'negerhut', also exist in our west Indian colonies!]*. Amsterdam: H. de Hoogh.

Wolbers, J. (1861). *Geschiedenis van Suriname [History of Suriname]*. Amsterdam: H. de Hoogh.

Wood, B. (2003). Some aspects of female resistance to chattel slavery in low country Georgia, 1763–1815. In G. Heuman, & J. Walvin (Eds.), *The slavery reader* (pp. 511–568). London: Routledge.

2 Honour, gender, and violence in the Dutch Caribbean and Suriname

Janine Janssen

Introduction

In 2013 an interesting book was published regarding interventions aimed at *multi-problem* families comparing Dutch native families with immigrated Curaçaoan families. Part of the research had also been conducted on this island in the Caribbean. The researcher had tried to make a comparison between the material that she collected in Europe and the data she collected in Curacao. But she came to the conclusion that this was a 'mission impossible'. One of the problems was that the adjective multi-problem referred to families that had contact with social workers and not to a specific type of family. Furthermore, Dutch policy makers did not see eye to eye when it came to a definition of this concept. Next to that, social workers in Curacao were not familiar with this concept and when asked, they had their own interpretation of what a multi-problem family was. They did not use this term and when confronted with it, they spoke about *deprived families, families lacking opportunities,* or *poor families* (Verhallen, 2013). An important lesson to be learned from this example is that (criminological) concepts might have different meanings on both sides of the Atlantic Ocean. From a critical post-colonial perspective, it would be condescending to ignore these differences, meaning that history and societal development in this part of the world is denied. Therefore, a comparative study might deepen our insight into potentially cultural-specific aspects of family life and violent phenomena in the Caribbean as well as among migrated Caribbean nationals and help prevention and treatment of violence among these populations.

In this chapter attention will be paid to honour-based violence (HBV). In contemporary Europe HBV is generally associated with views on family relationships and morals regarding sexual behaviour. Sexual relations outside of marriage, for example, are not accepted. In classical anthropological research the question had been posed as to the purpose of honour. A commonly heard answer is that honour is an important factor in societies in which people are unable to rely on a strong central authority and are consequently left to their own devices in the struggle for survival. By adhering to codes of honour, rivals competing for scarce resources are kept at a distance. Presenting themselves as honourable is a way for people to protect loved ones and possessions, because it gives one scope to defend one's position and possessions independently. An honour code, in other words, creates the legitimation for taking the law into one's own hands. In the Netherlands honour-based violence is often associated with honour codes from North Africa and the Middle East used by men in order to control and limit women (Janssen, 2008). It must be admitted, however, the honour of men and women is not necessarily identical, and there are gender-specific interpretations of the concept of honour. Some anthropologists have even stated that women cannot claim honour. The anthropologist Blok, for example, even asserts that in literature it is wrongly assumed that women have honour. He states that – in the Mediterranean context of farming communities that he has studied – women are viewed as possessions and that they at best can lay claim to virtue (Blok, 1980). All over the world examples can be found of a gender-specific interpretation of the concept of honour (Gilmore, 1990), also in the Caribbean and among migrants from these islands in the Netherlands. But even those that only have paid superficial attention to women with a Caribbean background and those that have to deal with concepts of honour from North Africa and the Middle East can immediately see huge differences, for example regarding ideas concerning femininity and decent behaviour.

Does honour as a motive for violent behaviour exist in the Caribbean? What problems arise when the concept of HBV as it is perceived nowadays in the Netherlands, is applied to the Caribbean? Reflections on that particular question should help in answering one final question: can a breath of fresh air from the Caribbean help us to see new (potentially gendered) aspects of honour or can we see already known and described features in a new light? In other words, does looking at the relationship between honour and violence in a different context bring new insights (Janssen & Van San, 2014)? This contribution is based on the study of literature with a special focus on studies about the (former) Dutch Caribbean islands. In the first paragraph of this chapter a brief overview will be given regarding the process of (de) colonisation in the (former) Dutch parts of the Caribbean. The second paragraph continues with a description of dominant features as described in the literature on family structures in the (Dutch) Caribbean. In the third paragraph attention will be paid to the prevalence of violence within the family and its causes as described in the existing literature. The fourth paragraph is entirely dedicated to the question to what extent honour pops up as a motive for explaining violence in Caribbean families. In the fifth paragraph some final remarks will be presented.

(De)colonisation in the Dutch Caribbean

Dutch Caribbean islands

In the Caribbean two groups of islands were colonised by the Dutch. These islands of the former Dutch Antilles are all part of the Lesser Antilles. Some islands form part of the Leeward Islands in the eastern part of the Caribbean: St Maarten, Saba and St Eustatius. Three other islands can be found in the so-called Leeward Antilles in the southern part of the Caribbean Sea: Aruba, Bonaire, and Curacao.

The Dutch started to colonise these islands in the seventeenth century. The islands became an import centre for the slave trade. In 1863, 11,800 slaves were set free on the Dutch islands in the Caribbean. The consequences of the abolition of slavery in the Caribbean were different from those in Suriname. On the islands, trade had always been an important pillar of the economy. Therefore, not all slaves worked in agriculture but also in other branches of the economy, such as salt production. Next to that, agriculture on the islands was more focused on the production of food for local consumption than on export. In comparison to Suriname, slaves formed a smaller part of the entire population. During the nineteenth century slaves on the islands received more privileges and liberties than Surinamese slaves. Before the official abolition, for example, some slaves on the islands were already paid but still enslaved.[1]

In 1954 the islands were united as a country named the Dutch Antilles. Together with Suriname and the Netherlands they became a composite kingdom. The former colonies had been granted autonomy, except for matters such as defence and foreign affairs. In 1986 Aruba was allowed to secede from the Dutch Antilles and in 2010 the Dutch Antilles were dissolved entirely (Oostindie & Klinkers, 2001). Curacao and Saint Maarten acceded to the same country status as Aruba within the kingdom of the Netherlands, while Bonaire, Saint Eustatius and Saba were granted a status similar to Dutch municipalities. They are now referred to as the "Caribbean Netherlands", but they are also known by this abbreviation: the BES islands. On the first of January 2015 the Netherlands had approximately 17,000,000 inhabitants. About 150,000 inhabitants had a Dutch Caribbean background meaning that these individuals or one of their parents were born on one of the islands of the former Dutch Antilles or Aruba.[2]

Suriname

Although Suriname is not an island or even directly bordered by the Caribbean Sea, this smallest country in South America is often considered to be one of the largest Caribbean territories. There are several reasons for this. First of all, Suriname shares the unique heritage of sugar cane plantations and the way this economic system – especially through the application of slavery – has influenced social and political structures. Next to that, it is considered to be rather deterministic to define the Caribbean region solely by its relationship with the sea. It is also stated that some continental areas might experience insularity due to remoteness and isolation. In the case of Suriname one might speak of *green insularity* in a sense that the country is not only surrounded by the sea, but also by large rivers and forests that cover most parts of the territory (Taglioni & Cruse, 2013).

In 1650 Francis Lord Willoughby, the British governor of Barbados, furnished out a vessel, and by treaty with the natives of that part of Guiana called Suriname began to settle a colony there. At his own cost he equipped a ship of 20 guns, and two smaller vessels with things necessary for the support of the plantation. But in 1667 the Dutch under Crijnsen captured the colony. At first governor Byam refused to surrender but finally had to give in. Approximately six months after the Dutch had obtained Suriname, the English appeared with a large fleet and reclaimed their possession. In accordance with the Treaty of Breda the Dutch amongst other things exchanged New Netherland – that includes present-day New York City – for Suriname.[3] An agricultural economy developed, based on slavery. Around 1860 half of the slaves in Suriname worked on sugar cane plantations. As stated before, when the Dutch abolished slavery in 1863, 34,8 thousand slaves received their liberty in Suriname. Former slaves between 15 and 60 years of age remained under the supervision of the state in order to work as indentured labourer on the plantations. After this obligation ended, a lot of them left the plantations in 1873. The former slaves were then replaced by indentured labourers from India, Indonesia, and China. In contract, the Dutch government did not expect a decline in the workforce after slavery was abolished on the Caribbean islands. Due to this expectation, former slaves on the islands were not placed under supervision by the state.[4] Internal self-governance was granted to Suriname in 1954 after which full independence followed in 1975 (Oostindie & Klinkers, 2001). The prospect of independence prompted mass migration to the Netherlands. In 2015, 350,000 inhabitants of the Netherlands had a Surinamese background, meaning that these individuals or one of their parents were born in Suriname.[5]

Summarizing this paragraph, the reader should keep in mind that the (Dutch) Caribbean as a geographical area with a homogeneous culture and history does not exist (Knight, 1978). This brief overview can never do justice to the cultural diversity among these different parts of the Caribbean (Bijl, Pommer, Turkenburgen, & Briene, 2015; Marcha &Verweel, 2003a). It is important to keep in mind that due to their rich history and related migratory tides the various communities that make up the Caribbean nowadays have formed complex and colourful patchworks.

Dominant features in Caribbean family structures

Young mothers and single parenthood

According to figures from the Dutch Bureau of Statistics (Centraal Bureau voor de Statistiek) women in the Caribbean Netherlands (BES) give birth to their first child at the average age of 25.2.[6] Women in the European part of the Netherlands give birth to their first child at the age of 29.4. Women with a Dutch Caribbean background who live in the Netherlands become a mother for the first time at the age of 25.9. In the BES islands, the mother is still a teenager in one out of 10 births, while on the other islands and Aruba that figure is 6.8 per cent. In the Netherlands in only 1.3 per cent of births is a teenage Caribbean mother involved. It seems that in the Netherlands the level of teenage pregnancies among Dutch Caribbean women has been slowly declining to the level of all women in the Netherlands. Women raising a child without the father is not exceptional (see also Roopnarine & Yildirim, 2016).

In 2012 about a third of children born that year in the BES islands had a single parent. That figure is the same for Dutch Caribbean women living in the Netherlands. But in 2012 in only 8 per cent of the births the child was born to a single mother.[7] In 2014 in Suriname approximately one out of five new born children had a teenage mother.[8] Among women with a Surinamese background living in the Netherlands, the percentage of single mothers is also relatively high: in 2013 almost one-third of Surinamese women in their forties were single mothers. For Dutch Caribbean women that figure was four out of 10. In the Netherlands Surinamese and Dutch Caribbean women were most likely to become a single parent.[9] In literature these families are often called *matrifocal*.

Matrifocality

The term *matrifocality* was first coined by Smith (1956) in his work on British Guyana. In communities all over the world matrifocality has been identified and studied, for example on Java (Geertz, 1961), the poor parts of Naples (Parsons, 1969), and in African American communities (Smith, 1973; Stack, 1974).[10] But what is matrifocality? It is important to understand that matrifocality is not a kinship system such as matriarchy – where the mother or the oldest female heads the family – or matriliny – where the descent is traced through the female line. Matrifocality can be found in different kinship systems, also in those where men have a dominant position. For example, in southern Spain, matrifocality coexists with male dominance and machismo within an honour-and-shame value system (Brogger & Gilmore, 1997). This has also been noticed in the Caribbean (see for example, Bull, 1998; Chevannes, 2003; Jones, Jemmott, Maharai, & Da Breo, 2014; Momsen, 2012). Matrifocality means as much as *mother-centeredness*. Tanner (1974) tried to come up with a definition. She argued that in family life the mother is structurally, culturally, and affectively the key person. Next to that the centrality of the mother is legitimate and society values especially the bond between mother and children, while the conjugal relationship is expected to be less an expression of solidarity and affection (Tanner, 1974). Although there has been some discussion regarding this definition, summarizing, one could state that some agreement emerges from the literature: in matrifocal households the mother is central structurally and effectively, and when compared to men, women have a stronger authority position. Men have a reduced or even absent role as husband or father (Girigori, 2015). Often men are not only emotionally absent, but also physically, due to, for example, migration. Matrifocality goes hand in hand with forms of (male) economic insecurity, such as seasonal unemployment (Brogger & Gilmore, 1997).

Although matrifocal families can be found in different socioeconomic contexts,[11] this association with economic trouble that forces them to solely take control over the well-being of their families is one of the factors influencing the bad reputation of matrifocality. These families are often seen as dysfunctional. In several studies regarding young men from Curacao, for example, the link has been made between being raised by a single parent and the establishment of a criminal career (Bos & Van Hulst, 1993; Leuw, 1997). Bovenkerk (1994) has argued that in the United States crime by African Americans is often explained by the fact that these young men were raised by single mothers. However, Bovenkerk reasoned that within the matrifocal context offspring can be socialised just as well as within the traditional Western family (see also UNA, 2010). What makes these families more vulnerable is their economic position: the absentee fathers do not always contribute economically to the household (Ayres, 1998; Bailey, 2013; Bailey, Branche, & Le Franc, 1998; Barrow, 2000; Evans & Davies, 1997; Krishnakumar, Narine, Roopnarine, & Logie, 2014; Richardson, Brakle, & St Vil, 2014; Roopnarine & Yildirim, 2016; Safa, 1998; Van San, 1998).

Two sets of explanations are usually offered for the presence of matrifocality in the Caribbean: there are historical and more functional-structural explanations (Marks, 1973). From a historical point of view several outlooks on the dominance of matrifocality are presented. Some state that the slaves that had been imported from Africa brought with them polygamous family structures that already knew some form of matrifocality (Herskovits & Herskovits, 1947). Others have issued that due to slavery it was almost impossible for the captive slaves to lead a family life as they or their ancestors once did in Africa (Frazier, 1939). In the system of slavery long-lasting intimate relations between men and wife were sabotaged, while on the other hand slaves were expected to provide slave owners with offspring (Römer, 1981). Moreover, (upper-class) slave owners often had extramarital relations with slaves or free black women. So it seemed desirable and attractive for lower-class men to copy the way of life of males in the upper class (Hoetink, 1958). Although these historical explanations shed an interesting light upon matrifocality, they cannot explain to the full extent the contemporary omnipresence of these female-headed households in the Caribbean. It has already been mentioned that in literature a link is seen between matrifocality, a troublesome economy, and absent fathers (Girigori, 2015). In general, one might state that history provides a reason for the birth of matrifocality, but the contemporary structure of society mainly explains the continued existence of matrifocality (Van San, 1998, see also UNA, 2010). But probably reality is more complex, because we are all products of our past. Historical patterns have ingrained the way in which attachments are valued by men and women and which roles they serve, and how this is transferred over generations by attitudes, expectations, and experiences with their own (absent) fathers.

Family and violence: prevalence and causes

Prevalence

In 2012 the Kingdom of the Netherlands signed the Council of Europe Convention on preventing and combating violence against women and domestic violence,[12] also known as the "Istanbul convention".[13] The purpose of this convention is amongst other things to protect women against all forms of violence, and prevent, prosecute, and eliminate violence against women and domestic violence. This convention also covers the BES islands. The Minister of Safety and Justice ordered a report that dealt with the question of what the implications of the implementation of this convention would be for the Caribbean parts of the Dutch Kingdom (De Bruijn, Kriek, & De Vaan, 2014). One of the important findings of this research project was that the registration of domestic violence on Bonaire, St Eustatius, and Saba remains troublesome. There is, for example, no central reporting service for domestic violence. Next to that, the registration by the police does not give a complete insight into the prevalence of this type of violence: domestic violence is still considered to be taboo – similar conclusions could be drawn regarding sexual offences (Zuring, 2015) – and as a result the readiness to report such crimes to the police is low. As had been mentioned before, it is difficult to obtain reliable crime statistics. Nevertheless, in (group) interviews all partners in law enforcement tend to agree that domestic violence is a common phenomenon. They are also under the impression that in these parts of the kingdom in comparison with the European part, more often severe forms of physical domestic violence can be found (Bruijn et al., 2014). The approach of domestic violence is fragmented and not very intensive. There is little or no (structural) information given in schools and on other sites. General public information is absent. Prevention activities, specifically aimed at risk groups, are very limited and the help for victims of domestic violence is minimal (De Bruijn et al., 2014). For the other parts of the Dutch Caribbean there are some rough indications: one out of three people (25 per cent of men, 38 per cent of women) in Curacao have experienced some form of domestic violence at some point in their adult lives (Van Wijk & De Bruijn, 2012). Linden (2007) estimated that each year 5 to 10 per cent of the population of this island suffers from domestic violence. In Suriname the police registered only 290 cases of domestic violence in 2013.[14]

While looking at the existing literature, it comes to mind that the phenomenon of domestic violence is often not defined. In the Dutch context, for example, the definition of domestic violence has changed over the years: nowadays also male victims and even victimised pets are included and a distinction is made between violence that takes place within the nuclear and the extended family (Janssen, 2016). The question of how violence within the family is perceived and defined within the Dutch Caribbean does not seem to receive enough attention. Besides, literature does not always offer insight into (different) patterns among the various regions of the Dutch Caribbean and among different ethnic groups (Bijl et al., 2015).

Causes

In a publication on domestic violence in Curacao, the most significant risk factors for domestic violence was summed up: female gender, a young age, low education, and experiencing domestic violence victimisation in childhood. Divorce, single parenthood, and unemployment increased the risk for women, but not for men (Van Wijk & De Bruijn, 2012). In this section, socioeconomic status and matrifocality will be addressed. However, it is important to note that these different causes do not exist in isolation. On the contrary, they influence each other, with some intersection taking place (Althoff, 2013).

Due to the small scale of Dutch Caribbean islands, the socioeconomic infrastructure is limited. Stable employment is problematic. In the event of unemployment people leave for other islands or go to the Netherlands. Dutch Caribbean youths leave for the Netherlands in order to get an education. If employment suddenly increases, for example, because of seasonal work, there is much immigration from Colombia, Peru, the Dominican Republic, and Venezuela to the Dutch Caribbean. All in all, this makes it difficult to maintain a good balance between the educational system and the demands of the labour market on these small islands. In additon, on the BES islands a considerable number of youth skip school or even drop out. For these young people there are not many job opportunities and a life on the street or in the subculture of drugs may look tempting under these circumstances. In addition, these subcultures are often tied up with gangs who provide the family feeling often lacking among these neglected youngsters (e.g. Smith & Green, 2007).

In general, the average income of the working population in the European part of the Netherlands is 2.6 times as high as the average income of the workforce in the BES islands. Furthermore, in the Dutch Caribbean the cost of living has skyrocketed, which puts households with a low income under permanent stress. It is challenging to survive on one income. Often mothers are (partially) dependent on financial support from (absent) fathers. If the father is not a part of the family, it is even more difficult to get him to contribute financially. Mothers who have to handle several jobs lack time to spend with their children. Children at times even have to take on jobs in order to keep the family income afloat. That situation can have a negative influence on the development of the school career. The financial dependency of women can be an important influence in making the decision to stay in a relationship or even relationships with several partners. It is not surprising that conflicts between lovers are often about money. This type of fight can turn sour and end in violence. What adds fuel to the conflict is the housing conditions: people live in small houses with very little privacy and limited social control. Another important factor influencing violence within the family is the use of alcohol and drugs (Bijl et al., 2015; De Bruijn et al., 2014). A typical feature of island communities is that it is difficult to escape the wandering eye of your neighbours. People do not have the luxury of anonymity. They are often scared that secrets, for example, regarding sexual abuse within the family, might get known within the community. It is seen as an aspect of a culture of poverty in which outing such secrets is experienced as underlining one's marginal position in society (De Bruijn et al., 2014, see also DeShong, 2011; Marcha & Verweel, 2003b; Pasura et al., 2013; Samms & Cholewa, 2014).

As has been mentioned before, in the Dutch Caribbean matrifocality is widely spread. Women become mothers at an early age and stay with their own mothers. These grandmothers play an important role in family life. The father remains part of the household of his own mother and often starts a relationship with another young woman. Due to this practice, men often have children with several women and women have children from different fathers. Men have a limited role in the upbringing of their offspring. Due to this fact it is rather difficult for mothers to force the fathers to provide financial support. These rather loose relations between men and women fuel disagreements that might lead to violence. Furthermore, physical violence is considered to be an appropriate tool in the upbringing of children (De Bruijn et al., 2014; Kloosterboer, 2013).

Another important factor influencing violence within the family is the use of alcohol and drugs (Bijl et al., 2015; De Bruijn et al., 2014). In literature one particular aspect of gender roles in the Caribbean is often mentioned: the existence of a so-called *macho-culture*. Machismo is, among other things, associated with alcohol and drug abuse and dominant male behaviour (Janssen, 2008). One could say that machismo is described as the flipside of matrifocal households. As a consequence, young girls are raised with less self-esteem. Some say that that makes them vulnerable in dealing with men. Males might abuse their position in order to receive sexual favours (De Bruijn et al., 2014). On the other hand, women who have become mothers make a very strong impression (De Bruijn et al., 2014; Van San, 1998). These active mothers who are engaged in fights with the fathers of their children over financial and other forms of support, are also vulnerable: these fights might lead to domestic violence (De Bruijn et al., 2014).

Honour as a motive for violence

What is honour-based violence?

Given the fact that honour is damaged and restored in a large variety of ways, defining this phenomenon is far from simple. Current Dutch policy with regard to HBV has focused on group pressure within the context of the family (Janssen & Sanberg, 2013). Dutch policy applies the following definition of HBV:

> any form of mental or physical violence on the basis of a collective mentality and in response to (the threat of) damage inflicted on the honour of a man or a woman, and the honour of his or her family as a consequence, of which the outside world is aware or is likely to become aware.
>
> (Ferwerda & Van Leiden, 2005, p. 25)

As a consequence, governmental institutions working on HBV focus on cases of family conflict and moral aspects regarding sexuality and parenthood. The Dutch national police force has a centre of expertise on HBV that deals with HBV cases and carries out research on the backgrounds of this type of violence and effective policing practices. The cases treated at this centre show that honour conflicts often revolve around resisting strict (gender) rules, partner choice, sexuality, and (illegitimate) pregnancies and parenthood (Janssen & Sanberg, 2010).

Dutch policy does not regard HBV as violence against women, but defines it in a gender-neutral way (Brenninkmeijer, Geerse, & Roggeband, 2009). At the Dutch centre of expertise on HBV, police files show that despite the fact that more women seem to suffer from HBV, there are cases involving female offenders and male victims (Janssen & Sanberg, 2013). In communities where honour is important for social interaction, different behaviour is expected from women and men. Honour conflicts often start when women misbehave according to gender rules in the community, such as having sex before marriage (Janssen & Sanberg, 2010). Male family members are expected to act upon this and restore the family honour. Nevertheless, men too can become victims of HBV. In cases where they are pressured to commit violence to restore the family honour, or when they have a relationship with a married woman, they can fall victim to violence from that women's husband or family. Men can also be victimised for being openly gay while their families consider homosexuality to be a violation of honour. These are examples from the police files at the Dutch Centre of Expertise on HBV (Janssen & Sanberg, 2013).

Most of the cases of HBV in the Dutch context can be related to a North African and Middle Eastern context (LEC EGG, 2015). Another, smaller ethnic group in the Netherlands in which HBV plays an important role is the Hindustani community. They originate from the Dutch former colony of Suriname. Their forbearers came to Suriname from India as indentured labourers in the nineteenth century and a large number of them migrated to the Netherlands in the second half of the twentieth century (see paragraph on Suriname). During the last few years, there has been an influx of honour cases in communities of refugees and their offspring from Middle Eastern countries such as Afghanistan, Syria, and Iraq as well as from countries in eastern Africa, such as Somalia, and Eritrea. These migratory movements are the result of changing political dependency relationships. A post-colonial perspective offers insight in the way ethnic background, gender, and the relation between the Western world and other less privileged parts of the globe influence the process of forming an identity (Cunneen & Stubbs, 2004). Spivak (1993), for example, has elaborated a post-colonial feminist perspective and illustrated how feminism in the Western world builds on two polarised images: the image of the emancipated, White, Western woman versus the victim of patriarchal oppression.

Rèspèt and honour

Ingredients of HBV that are often highlighted in literature regarding this violent phenomenon can also be found in the Caribbean, for example, different gender roles, fear of gossip, and the use of violence in conflicts. In the Netherlands not that many cases of HBV among people from the Caribbean can be found. Most of these cases involve (Surinamese) people with a Hindustani background. Of note also is the fact that the word 'honour' does not feature frequently in literature. Work in the Southern United States has been particularly instructive (Nisbett & Cohen, 1996). Greenberg (1996), for example, has done impressive work on the relationship between slavery and honour (see also Fletchman Smith, 2011). His work offers some insight in the way societies with slavery functioned. Among other things, he explains that slaves were deprived by their masters of all the elements necessary for the formal duels of gentlemen of honour. The word of a gentleman needed to be treated with honour, while the word of a slave could be treated with contempt. One could state that honour was considered to be the exclusive domain of white masters. Slaves underlined the honourable position of their masters by being obedient. Although masters were never pleased with disobedience, it was more or less accepted. It was considered to be a flaw in the slave's character and a symptom of dishonour. Greenberg formulated the thought that the exclusion of slaves from the language of honour was a factor of influence regarding the creation of a semiautonomous space on the plantation. Of course, although in the slave owner's view of the world the possession of honour seemed to be strictly limited to their privileged class and other whites, this did not mean that the slaves themselves had no notion of the honour concept. Iliffe (2005) was the first to publish an historical account on the role played by ideas of honour in African history from the fourteenth century to the present-day. He pointed out that before European conquest ideas regarding honour were cultivated. Some of these values conflicted and others blended with Islamic and Christian teachings, which were introduced in the colonial period.

Another author who mentions a culture of honour, is Van San. In her PhD thesis (1998) she described that for young males from Curacao it is important that a damaged sense of honour is restored with a violent reaction. This is especially the case with offensive behaviour or remarks by individuals in a more or less similar social position: it is not considered to be an honourable act to use violence in order to restore one's honour against women, children, or elderly persons. Within the Dutch Caribbean context, a word that features more frequently than honour, is *rèspèt* [Papiamento for "respect"]. In studies regarding the violent involvement of Antillean youngsters in the Caribbean as well as in the Netherlands, for example, it is mentioned that violence is used as a means to obtain respect (Van San, 1998; Van San, Boom, & Van Wijk, 2007). It seems that not all these authors make a distinction between respect and honour and the meaning of these concepts for men and women. Adding to this confusion is that in the literature, often concepts are used that overlap to a certain extent, including, respect, prestige, dignity, esteem, and honour (Broek, 2007; Sennet, 2003).

First and foremost, the word comes up in the context of violent behaviour by young men, for example:

> But what it boils down to is that respect in the sense used by gun toting youths, club wielding guards, crotch scratching, gold-chain-rattling, thru-their-gold-teeth-spitting, down-town terrorizing drug lords and criminologists who take a good look (. . .) is nothing but a plain old excuse for plain old macho behaviour.
>
> (Menckeberg, 1999, p. 196)

Van San (1998) noticed that youngsters from Curacao legitimise violent behaviour by referring to their economic deprived position in society, especially as it relates to defending instrumental forms of violence (i.e. goal-oriented violence). Committing expressive forms of violence (i.e. violence triggered by emotions and impulse), on the other hand, tends to be defended by referring to *rèspèt* (see also Gray, 2003).

Van Hulst and Bos (1993) have described how the term *rèspèt* played an important role in the political context and was related to the topic of (neo)colonialism. They referred especially to the 1969 uprising in Curacao, a series of riots that took place from May 30 to June 1. During this turmoil, protesters pleaded for "pan y rekonsimentu [bread and recognition]" and "nos lo sinjanan respetanos [we will teach them- that is the white people – to respect us]". As a consequence of the rise of the oil industry, a number of civil servants, mostly from the Netherlands, were brought in. In May 1969, there was a labour dispute that revolved around the issue that Antillean employees received lower wages than employees from the Netherlands. Another issue that came up was the relationship between the island and the Netherlands. Matters of foreign policy and national defence were decided by the Council of Ministers of the Netherlands. Although some stated that it would be very costly for the islands to manage foreign affairs and defence, others were not satisfied with this construction: they saw it as (post)colonial treatment. (Anderson & Dynes, 1975; Oostindie & Klinkers, 2001).

The word *rèspèt* does not seem to be used frequently when it comes down to family life. Van San, for example, used the word *status* in describing the position of women and mothers. Within the family a woman's position is based on her motherhood. Van San (1998) stated that for women from lower strata of society, motherhood is often the only channel through which she can obtain respectability and status. It does not matter that the offspring is born out of wedlock. Having children is important when social and economic conditions are severe. Having children offers a road to welfare and offers women prestige when they are not succeeding in getting that through marriage and/or a career. Women feel ashamed when they receive criticism regarding the upbringing of their children. By having children men from lower social and economic strata can prove their manliness and potency. The emotional connection between mother and son is special and intense. Although the single mothers do not expect much from the fathers of their children, they turn to their sons for (financial) help. To a certain extent one might say that women gain authority due to the fact that their spouses fail. They become "strong women". Van San (1998) also referred to honour regarding family life: young men can become very aggressive when their mother is insulted. Due to the fact that their fathers are often absent, young men feel that they have to protect their mothers and sisters. Van San noticed that although mothers often have children with different fathers, mothers and sons do not speak openly about these relationships.

Final remarks

We started out with the question to what extent honour as a motive for violent behaviour exists in the Caribbean? Although in the Netherlands, attention is paid towards HBV, this phenomenon nowadays tends to be associated mainly with groups from North Africa and the Middle East. In the statistics provided by the Dutch police not that many cases can be found that can be traced back to people that come from the Caribbean. An exception is the Hindustani community. The cases of HBV that are dealt with in the Netherlands focus on honour concepts related to family life. In the Netherlands policy makers have decided that their policies regarding violence in the name of honour are limited to issues in family life. While looking at literature about the Caribbean, it shows that not only the word honour is used, but also the term *rèspèt*. The key question is whether both terms can be used as synonyms. A glimpse at literature shows that *rèspèt* is also associated with violent behaviour by youngsters and in a political context. It is not without risk when policy makers and academics with a Dutch background address violent phenomena in the Caribbean without paying attention to the local context and attribution of meaning to words such as *rèspèt* and honour. Then we are at risk of missing that breath of fresh air and we will create the same confusion, which was described at the beginning of this chapter regarding the concept of the multi-problem family. Confusion about concepts entails much more than a purely semantic problem. If researchers want to contribute to the development of knowledge that can be used by policy makers and professionals to address violence, they should pay attention to the way victims, offenders, and bystanders of violence experience, perceive – and as a consequence define – what has happened to them. This also makes sense from a post-colonial perspective: people from the Caribbean want to analyse and describe phenomena in their societies in and on their own terms. It is all about honour.

Notes

1 De Jong (2013, July 1). Op 1 juli 1863 47 duizend slaven vrijgemaakt in Suriname en op de Antillen [On July 1 47 thousand slaves were freed in Suriname and the Antilles]. Retrieved from: https://www.cbs.nl/nl-nl/achtergrond/2013/27/op-1-juli-1863-47-duizend-slaven-vrijgemaakt-in-suriname-en-op-de-antillen.

2 Central Bureau of Statistics (2016, December 1). Bevolking per maand; leeftijd, geslacht, herkomst, generatie [Population per month; age, sex, origin, generation]. Retrieved from: http://statline.cbs.nl/Statweb/publication/?DM=SLNL&PA=71090ned&D1=0&D2=0&D3=0&D4=a&D5=0&D6=96-114&VW=T.

3 Sainsbury, W.N. (1880, April 15). Calendar of state papers colonial, America and West Indies: Volume 5, 1661–1668. Retrieved from: www.british-history.ac.uk/cal-state-papers/colonial/america-west-indies/vol5/vii-lxxxiii

4 www.cbs.nl/nl-NL/menu/themas/dossiers/historische-reeksen/publicaties/artikelen/archief/2013/2013-47-duizend-slaven-vrijgemaakt-pub.htm (accessed 20 February 2017).

5 http://statline.cbs.nl/Statweb/publication/?DM=SLNL&PA=71090ned&D1=0&D2=0&D3=0&D4=a&D5=0&D6=96-114&VW=T (accessed 20 February 2017).

6 Since the Caribbean Netherlands are also part of the Netherlands, the Dutch Bureau of Statistics also collects data regarding these specific islands. These data are not (always) available for all the other islands and Suriname.

7 Loozen, S. & Harmsen, C. (2015). Moeders in Caribisch Nederland [Mothers in Caribbean Netherlands]. *Demos, 31*(4), 8.

8 Van Maele, P. (2014, March 19). Schoolbanken onveilig voor Surinaamse tienermoeders [Schools unsafe for Surinamses teenage mothers]. De Groene Amsterdammer. Retrieved from: www.groene.nl/artikel/schoolbanken-onveilig-voor-surinaamse-tienermoeders

Nog veel Surinaamse tienermoeders [Still many Surinamese teenage mothers]. Retrieved from: http://sioweb.nl/nog-veel-surinaamse-tienermoeders-2.

9 Rijksoverheid (2014, January 24). Huishoudens, 2000-2013 [Households 2000-2013]. Retrieved from: www.compendiumvoordeleefomgeving.nl/indicatoren/nl2114-Huishoudens.html?i=35-172.

10 Hogarth, H-K. K. Matrifocality in Korean society: Hindrance or help towards gender equality? Retrieved from: http://sydney.edu.au/arts/korean/downloads/KSAA2009/Global_Korea_Proceedings_104-114_Hogarth.pdf

11 http://sydney.edu.au/arts/korean/downloads/KSAA2009/Global_Korea_Proceedings_104-114_Hogarth.pdf (accessed 20 February 2017).
12 Council of Europe Convention on preventing and combating violence against women and domestic violence, Istanbul, 11.V.2011. Retrieved from: https://rm.coe.int/168008482e.
13 www.coe.int/en/web/istanbul-convention/home(accessed 20 February 2017).
14 Meeste slachtoffers huiselijk geweld vrouwen [Most victims of domestic violence are female]. (2014, March 11). Retrieved from: http://www.nospang.com/index.php?option=com_content&view=article&id=38984:meeste-slachtoffers-huiselijk-geweld-vrouwen&catid=73:binnenland&Itemid=65.

References

Althoff, M. (2013). Multiple identities and crime: A study of Antillean women and girls in the Netherlands. *European Journal of Criminology*, *10*(4), 394–407.

Anderson, W.A., & Dynes, R.R. (1975). *Social movements, violence, and change: The may movement in Curacao*. Columbus: Ohio State University Press.

Ayres, R.L. (1998). *Crime and violence as development issues in Latin America and the Caribbean*. Washington, DC: World Bank Publications.

Bailey, C. (2013). Exploring female motivations for drug smuggling on the island of Barbados: Evidence from her Majesty's Prison, Barbados. *Feminist Criminology*, *8*(2), 117–141.

Bailey, W., Branche, C., & Le Franc, E. (1998). Parenting and socialisation in Caribbean family systems. *Caribbean Dialogue*, *4*(1), 21–28.

Barrow, C. (2000). *Family in the Caribbean: Themes and perspectives*. Kingston: Ian Randle Publishers.

Bijl, R., Pommer, E., Turkenburgen, M., & Briene, M. (2015). Gesprekken op de eilanden: Het verhaal achter de cijfers. In E. Pommer, & R. Bijl (Eds.), *Vijf jaar Caribisch Nederland. Gevolgen voor de bevolking [Five years Caribbean Netherlands. Consequences for the population]* (pp. 267–308). Den Haag: SCP.

Blok, A. (1980). Eer en de fysieke persoon [Honour and the physical person]. *Tijdschrift voor de Sociale Geschiedenis*, *6*, 211–230.

Bos, J., & Van Hulst, H. (1993). *Pan i rèspet. Criminaliteit van geïmmigreerde Curaçaose jongeren [Criminality of immigrated Curacaoan youth]*. Utrecht: OKU.

Bovenkerk, F. (1994). Over de oorzaken van de criminaliteit van allochtone jongeren [On causes of crime among ethnic minority youth]. In G.W. Montfrans-Hartman (Ed.), *Met de neus op de feiten* (pp. 51–63). Den Haag: Ministerie van Justitie.

Brenninkmeijer, N., Geerse, M., & Roggeband, C. (2009). *Eergerelateerd geweld in Nederland. Onderzoek naar de beleving en aanpak van eergerelateerd geweld [Honor-based violence in the Netherlands]*. Den Haag: Sdu Uitgevers.

Broek, A.G. (2007). *De terreur van de schaamte. Brandstof voor agressie [The terror of shame. Fuel for aggression]*. Haarlem: In de Knipscheer.

Brogger, J., & Gilmore, D. (1997). The matrifocal family in Iberia: Spain and Portugal compared. *Ethnology*, *36*(1), 13–30.

Bull, S.S. (1998). Machismo/marianismo attitudes, employment, education, and sexual behavior among women in Ecuador and the Dominican Republic. *Journal of Gender, Culture and Health*, *3*(1), 1–27.

Chevannes, B. (2003). The role of the street in the socialization of Caribbean males. In L. Lewis, The culture of gender and sexuality in the Caribbean (pp. 215–233). Gainesville: University Press of Florida.

Cunneen, C., & Stubbs, J. (2004). Cultural criminology and engagement with race, gender and postcolonial identities. In J. Ferrell, K. Hayward, W. Morrison, & M. Presdee (Eds.), *Cultural criminology unleashed* (pp. 97–108). London: Glasshouse Press.

De Bruijn, J. de, Kriek, F., & De Vaan, K. (2014). *De aanpak van huiselijk geweld op de BES-eilanden [Approach to domestic violence on BES-islands]*. Amsterdam: Regioplan.

DeShong, H. (2011). Gender, sexuality and sexual violence: A feminist analysis of Vincentian women's experiences in violent heterosexual relationships. *Journal of Eastern Caribbean Studies*, *36*(2), 63–97.

Evans, H., & Davies, R. (1997). Overview of issues in childhood socialization in the Caribbean. In J.L. Roopnarine, & J. Brown (Eds.), *Caribbean families: Diversity among ethnic groups*, 14 (pp. 1–24). London: JAI Press Ltd.

Ferwerda, H., & Van Leiden, I. (2005). *Eerwraak of eergerelateerd geweld? Naar een werkdefinitie [Honour vengenge or honour-related violence? Towards a working definition]*. Arnhem: Onderzoeksgroep Beke.

Fletchman Smith, B. (2011). *Transcending the legacies of slavery: A psychoanalytic view*. London: Karnac Books.

Frazier, F. (1939). *The Negro family in the United States*. Chicago: University of Chicago Press.

Geertz, H. (1961). *Javanese family: A study of kinship and socialization*. New York: The Free Press of Glencoe.

Gilmore, D.D. (1990). *Manhood in the making: Cultural concepts of masculinity*. New Haven: Yale University Press.

Girigori, O. (2015). *Father absence: The consequences for reproductive behavior and mating strategies among females* (Unpublished doctoral thesis). University of Groningen, Groningen.

Greenberg, K.S. (1996). *Honor & slavery*. Princeton: Princeton University Press.

Gray, O. (2003). Badness-honour. In A. Harriott (Ed.), *Understanding crime in Jamaica: New challenges for public policy* (pp. 13–48). Kingston: University of West Indies Press.

Herskovits, M.J., & Herskovits, F.S. (1947). *Trinidad village*. New York: Knopf.

Hoetink, H. (1958). *Het patroon van de oude Curaçaose samenleving. Een sociologische studie [The pattern of the old Curaçaoan society. A sociological study]*. Assen: Van Gorcum.

Iliffe, J. (2005). *Honour in African history*. Cambridge: The Cambridge University Press.

Janssen, J. (2008). Machismo. In R. Bos (Ed.), *Antillianen. Crimineel of gewoon anders? [Antilleans, criminal or just different?]* (pp. 50–57). Zutphen: Walburg Pers.

Janssen, J. (2016). Geweld in afhankelijkheidsrelaties [Violence in dependent relationships]. In M. Liem, & E. Muller (Eds.), *Geweld en geweldsbeheersing in Nederland* (pp. 393–411). Deventer: Wolters Kluwer.

Janssen, J., & Sanberg, R. (2010). *Mogelijke eerzaken nader bekeken. Een onderzoek naar casuïstiek uit 2006 [Possible honor cases further investigated. An examination of cases from 2006]*. Den Haag: Ministerie van Justitie, Ministerie van Binnenlandse Zaken, LEC EGG.

Janssen, J., & Sanberg, R. (2013). Als de nood aan de man komt: Slachtofferschap van mannen bij eergerelateerd geweld [Victimization of honor-related violence among men]. *Justitiële Verkenningen*, *39*(5), 61–80.

Janssen, J., & Van San, M. (2014). In de leer over eer bij Curaçaose jongens. Mogelijkheden voor verdieping van het begrip 'eergerelateerd geweld' [Learning about honor from Curacaoan boys]. *Proces*, *93*(6), 432–439.

Jones, A.D., Jemmott, E.T., Maharaj, P.E., & Da Breo, H. (2014). *An integrated systems model for preventing child sexual abuse*. Basingstoke, UK: Palgrave Macmillan.

Kloosterboer, K. (2013). *Kind op Bonaire, Sint Eustatius en Saba. Kinderrechten in Caribisch Nederland. Samenvatting [Children's rights in Caribbean Netherlands, Summary].* Voorburg: UNICEF.

Knight, F.W. (1978). *The Caribbean. The genesis of a fragmented nationalism.* New York: Oxford University Press.

Krishnakumar, A., Narine, L., Roopnarine, J.L., & Logie, C. (2014). Multilevel and cross-level effects of neighborhood and family influences on children's behavioral outcomes in Trinidad and Tobago: The intervening role of parental control. *Journal of Abnormal Child Psychology, 42*(6), 1057–1068.

LEC EGG. (2015). *Terugblik op 2014. Jaarverslag van het Landelijk Expertise Centrum EerGerelateerdGeweld.* Den Haag: LEC EGG.

Leuw, E. (1997). *Criminaliteit en etnische minderheden. Een criminologische analyse [Crime and ethnic minorities: An criminologic analysis].* Den Haag: WODC.

Linden, E. (2007). *Vooronderzoek relationeel geweld op Curaçao [Pilot study relational violence on Curacao].* Willemstad, NA: Geneeskundige-en Gezondheidsdienst.

Marcha, V., & Verweel, P. (2003a). *De waarheid van Curaçao [The truth of Curacao].* Amsterdam: Uitgeverij SWP.

Marcha, V., & Verweel, P. (2003b). *De cultuur van angst. Paradoxale ketenen van angst en zwijgen op Curaçao [Culture of fear. Paradocal chains of fear and silence on Curacao].* Amsterdam: Uitgeverij SWP.

Marks, A.F. (1973). *Man, vrouw en huishoudgroep. De Afro-Amerikaanse familie in de samenleving van Curaçao [Man, woman and household. The African-American family in the society of Curacao].* Leiden: Rijksuniversiteit Leiden.

Menckeberg, H. (1999). What's respect got to do with it? In A.B. Hoogenboom, & L.J.J. Rogier (Eds.), *Rèspèt. 61 essays over criminaliteit op Curaçao en St. Maarten.* Curaçao: Universiteit van de Nederlandse Antillen.

Momsen, J.H. (2012). Patriarchy in absentia: Women and development in the Caribbean. *Different Contexts, Different Facets, 71.* Retrieved from www.niew.gov.my/review/docs-224-66.pdf#page=72.

Nisbett, R.E., & Cohen, D. (1996). *Culture of honor. The psychology of violence in the South.* Boulder: Westview Press, Inc.

Oostindie, G., & Klinkers, I. (2001). *Het Koninkrijk in de Caraïben. Een korte geschiedenis van het Nederlandse dekolonisatiebeleid, 1940–2000 [The kingdom in the Caribbean. A short history of the Dutch de-colonisation policy, 1940–2000].* Amsterdam: Amsterdam University Press.

Parsons, A. (1969). *Belief, magic and anomie: Essays in psychosocial anthropology.* New York: Free P. US.

Pasura, D., Jones, A.D., Hafner, J.A., Maharaj, P.E., Nathaniel-DeCaires, K., & Johnson, E.J. (2013). Competing meanings of childhood and the social construction of child sexual abuse in the Caribbean. *Childhood, 20*(2), 200–214.

Richardson, J.B., Brakle, M., & St Vil, C. (2014). Taking boys out of the hood: Exile as a parenting strategy for African American male youth. *New Directions for Child and Adolescent Development, 2014*(143), 11–31.

Römer, R.A. (1981). *Samenleven op een Caraïbisch eiland. Een sociologische verkenning [Living together on a Caribbean island. A sociological exploration].* Curaçao: Van Dorp Eddine NV.

Roopnarine, J.L., & Yildirim, E.D. (2016). Family structure and socialization patterns in Caribbean and Caribbean immigrant families: Developmental outcomes. In U.P Gielen, &

J.L. Roopnarine (Eds.), *Childhood and adolescence: Cross-cultural perspectives and applications* (pp. 151–176). Santa Barbara, US: Praeger/ABC-CLIO, LLC.

Safa, H.I. (1998). Female-headed households in the Caribbean: Sign of pathology or alternative form of family organization. *The Brown Journal of World Affairs*, *5*(2), 203–214.

Samms, K.M., & Cholewa, B.E. (2014). Exploring the context of child sexual abuse in Jamaica: Addressing the deficits. *Journal of Child Sexual Abuse*, *23*(2), 115–127.

Sennet, R. (2003). *Respect in a world of inequality*. New York: W.W. Norton & Company, Inc.

Smith, D.E., & Green, K.E. (2007). Violence among youth in Jamaica: A growing public health risk and challenge. *Revista Panamericana de Salud Pública*, *22*(6), 417–424.

Smith, R.T. (1956). *The negro family in British Guiana*. London: Routledge and Kegan Paul.

Smith, R.T. (1973). The matrifocal family. In J. Goody (Ed.), *The character of kinship* (pp. 121–145). Cambridge: Cambridge University Press.

Spivak, G. (1993). Can the subaltern speak? In L. Chrisman, & P. Williams (Eds.), *Colonial discourse and post-colonial theory: A reader* (pp. 66–111). New York: Columbia University Press.

Stack, C.B. (1974). Sex roles and survival strategies in an urban black community. In M.Z. Rosaldo, & L. Lamphere (Eds.), *Woman, culture and society* (pp. 113–128). Stanford: Stanford University Press.

Taglioni, F., & Cruse, R. (2013). Is Suriname a Caribbean island like the others? In R. Cruse, & K. Rhiney (Eds.), *Caribbean atlas*. Retrieved from www.caribbean-atlas.com/en/themes/what-is-the-caribbean/is-suriname-a-caribbean-island-like-the-others.html.

Tanner, N. (1974). *Matrifocality in Indonesia and Africa and among Black Americans*. In M.Z. Rosaldo, & L. Lamphere (Eds.), *Woman, culture and society* (pp. 129–156). Stanford: Stanford University Press.

UNA. (2010). *Vrouwen van de Nederlandse Antillen en Aruba. Naar een betere toekomst. De positie van de Antilliaanse en Arubaanse vrouw in het heden, verleden en in de toekomst [Women from the Dutch Antilles and Aruba]*. Den Haag: Ministerie van Binnenlandse Zaken en Koninkrijksrelaties.

Van Hulst, H., & Bos, J. (1993). *Pan i rèspèt. Criminaliteit van gemigreerde Curaçaose jongeren [Criminality of migrated Curacaoan youth]*. Utrecht: OKU.

Van San, M. (1998). *Stelen en steken. Delinquent gedrag van Curaçaose jongens in Nederland [Stealing and stabbing. Delinquent behaviour of Curacaoan boys in the Netherlands]*. Amsterdam: Het Spinhuis.

Van San, M., De Boom, J., & Van Wijk, A. (2007). *Verslaafd aan een flitsende levensstijl [Addicted to a flashy lifestyle]*. Rotterdam: Risbo.

Van Wijk, N.P.L., & De Bruijn, J.G.M. (2012). Risk factors for domestic violence in Curacao. *Journal of Interpersonal Violence*, *27*(15), 3032–3053.

Verhallen, T. (2013). *Gezinsinterventies bij Nederlandse en Nederlands Curaçaose 'multiprobleem' gezinnen [Family interventions in Dutch and Dutch Curacaoan 'multiproblem' families]*. Den Haag: Boom Lemma Uitgevers.

Zuring, R. (2015). Ik handelde naar de omstandigheden [I acted under the circumstances]. *Blauw: Politievakblad*, *3*, 42–44.

Section B

Crime and victimisation

3 Prevalence of public fraud and corruption in the Dutch Caribbean

Impacts of (post)colonialism explored

P.C.M. (Nelly) Schotborgh-van de Ven

Introduction

The islands of the Dutch Caribbean – Aruba, Curacao, St Maarten, Bonaire, Saba, and St Eustatius, are known for their rich history, sunny beaches, and luxurious tourist resorts. However, they are simultaneously portrayed as the breeding ground for fraud and corruption, and indeed, many Caribbean islands have suffered from failing governments and corrupted public officials (Blickman, 1997; Collier, 2005; Goede, 2013; Ilegems & Sauviller, 1995; Weenink, Klein, Haarhuis, Bokhorst, & Smit, 2011). Scholars have suggested these failing Caribbean governments are the result of a colonial legacy of administrative cultures based on inequality. In fact, existing literature does show a greater prevalence of fraud and corruption across countries with a colonial past (Gurgur & Shah, 2005; Serra, 2006).

Nevertheless, hardly any empirical qualitative studies on the nature of public fraud and corruption in the Dutch Caribbean have as yet been published. The numerous reports on the lack of good governance and crime in the Dutch Caribbean have provided little insight into the nature and extent of public fraud and corruption across these islands (De Wit, 2015; Mesu, Stoffers, & Harrigan, 2011; Schotborgh-van de Ven & Van Velzen, 2013; Verhoeven, Bokhorst, Leeuw, Bogaerts, & Schotborgh-van de Ven, 2007; Weenink & Brug, 2009). Therefore, the current study aims to bring to the fore the prevalence of officially registered cases of public fraud and corruption in the Dutch Caribbean by investigating court cases in which public officials have been implicated. Furthermore, the results will be shortly viewed in the light of international literature, with a special focus on post-colonial characteristics.

Defining fraud and corruption

As public fraud and corruption form the central focus of this study, clear definitions are needed to interpret the results, and subsequently, guide the discussion on the discourse of public fraud and corruption throughout the Dutch Caribbean. The definition of the term public official in this study is broad based and includes all employees who are considered to work as civil servants under the National ordinance substantive civil servants law of the autonomous countries.[1] The definition of public official used in this article also covers ministers, lieutenant governors, chief-prosecutors, and the Ombudsman. In addition, employees of government-owned companies and entities, where government is a deciding factor in the manner in which business is conducted, are also considered public officials.

In the Penal Code, no description of fraud and corruption is provided. Generally, the activities of theft, embezzlement, deception, and bribery are considered criminal offences. In this article, the focus is on public officials who use their position to benefit themselves, their family, their political party, or other private interests at the expense of public funds. This specifically refers to public monies, goods, information, jobs, permits, and services which have been obtained from the government in an unlawful manner. In relevant literature, fraud is often referred to as a form of corruption (Hollinger & Davis, 2006; Huberts, 2003, 2005; Levi, 2006); however, a more specific criterion can be distinguished in that fraud can also refer to cases in which the perpetrator can profit personally without benefitting others. In this context, fraud pertains to public officials who act on their own accord and, for example, steal cash money or submit inflated expense reports. Corruption, however, always involves two parties: the corruptor and the corrupted. Reciprocity is central and inherent in the case of corruption: the corrupted receives money or other privileges or perks, while the corruptor stands to win something in return, such as a permit or a government job (Huberts, 2005).

Existing literature on fraud and corruption across the Dutch Caribbean

The first examples of fraud and corruption in the Dutch Caribbean that can be found in the literature go back to the seventeenth century. The trade of the West Indian Company between Europe and the Caribbean went conjointly with illegal trade of different kind. There were illegal transactions with their Spanish and French enemy, and goods such as stockfish, wood, lime, salt, alcohol, and weapons were illegally traded. The executive and judicial branch were not separated at the time. The absence of separation of powers made it possible for the governor to create a climate in which patronage, nepotism, and slavery were considered normal (Nederlof, 2008; Rupert, 2012).

In recent years, various cases have been brought before the Joint Court of Justice of Aruba, Curacao, St Maarten and Bonaire, St Eustatius and Saba where public officials such as ministers, commissioners, and public officers were suspected of serious fraud and corruption-related crimes. Although much has been written in the media about those cases, academic literature about contemporary fraud and corruption in the Dutch Caribbean does not exist. In a study on the perception of corruption in Curacao and Bonaire (Central Bureau of Statistics, 2005), the majority of respondents of both islands stated that especially political systems of the islands exhibit signs of corruption. Thus, corruption seems to have affected the values of the political climate. The perception of corruption in Curacao was more negative than in Bonaire. Furthermore, results of the study showed that the experience of an impact of corruption on personal life decreases with the level of income.

The World Bank[2] conducted another corruption perception study in a number of Caribbean countries. The Bahamas scored best on integrity, Aruba best on democracy and lawfulness, and Barbados best on effectiveness. The (former) Netherlands Antilles and Trinidad and Tobago were performing second best, and Belize, Jamaica, and Suriname followed, with Guyana and Haiti performing the worst. In addition to these perception studies there have been a few studies on criminality in the Dutch Caribbean. Although these reports cover various aspects of criminal activities, no evidence-based statistics could be found on fraud and corruption. Due to the lack of resources in supervisory bodies and inspection services, limited information is available. Therefore, these criminological reports concluded that several instances of fraud and corruption by public officials and suspicions of abuse of power of personal gain are suspected, but cannot be substantiated (De Wit, 2015; Mesu et al., 2011; Mooij, Tijssens, & Van der Mark, 2013; Schotborgh-van de Ven & Van Velzen, 2013).

Impacts of (post-)colonialism on fraud and corruption across the Dutch Caribbean

The geographical research area of this study is the Dutch Caribbean, which is part of the Kingdom of the Netherlands. The Dutch Caribbean was annexed as a colony by the Dutch in the seventeenth century, at which time the Dutch West India Company had a dominant role. In 1954, the constitutional status of the six islands of the Dutch Caribbean was established as a country within the Dutch Kingdom, known as the Netherlands Antilles. Aruba opted to leave this constellation in 1986, becoming a separate country within the Dutch Kingdom. On October 10, 2010, the remainder of the Netherlands Antilles was split up in two separate countries and three public entities.

The Dutch Kingdom is now comprised of four autonomous countries: the Netherlands, Aruba, Curacao, and St Maarten and three public entities: Bonaire, Saba and St Eustatius, which fall under the jurisdiction of the Netherlands and are known as the Caribbean Netherlands, also called BES.[3] Aruba, Curacao, and St Maarten each have a separate Constitution, Governor, and government. Their autonomous status entails a high degree of autonomy in internal government, while Dutch nationality, foreign relations, national defence, and the Supreme Court fall under the jurisdiction of the Kingdom as a whole. The total population of the six islands of the Dutch Caribbean is currently comprised of approximately 300,000 people. Even though the Dutch Caribbean is often qualified as a unity, the islands' (colonial) history, political situation, and social and cultural characteristics are very different. People in St Maarten, St Eustatius, and Saba speak English and the islands are orientated towards the British/American culture. Papiamentu is the native language of Aruba, Bonaire, and Curacao. These latter islands show great similarities with the neighbouring countries in South America.

International literature mentions different post-colonial impacts that are relevant to this study. In 1964 Riggs, for instance, posited his theory of the prismatic society that formed the connection between the modern and traditional society.

Riggs (1964) based this theory on his perception that the new modern society did not match the traditional society that already existed before colonisation. Other authors (Blockman, 1988; Campbell, 1989; De Zwart, 2010; Hoetjes, 1977; Huiskamp, 1991; Riggs, 1964; Rupert, 2012) have also mentioned this disconnection. According to them, the governmental orders to public officials stood diametrically opposed to the needs of the people of the colonised land. Therefore, the public officials stood in between the State and the will of their fellow citizens, including their family and friends. This position made them vulnerable to bribes, especially because bribing or paying to achieve the desired results was not considered to be bad or undesirable behaviour in the traditional society. Herewith, corruption of public officials formed the glue, the cement, between the wishes that were routed in the traditional society and the orders of the current government. Corrupt public officials were the middlemen between the government at the central level, and the citizens (Wagenaar, Van der Meij, & Van der Heijden, 2005). However, Rose-Ackerman (2010) does not agree with this perspective. In her view, deep historical factors do not have to be fundamental determinants of corruption. The massive transformations that have occurred in Latin America and Asia show that countries are able to change and to escape from their past, according to this researcher.

Nonetheless, in line with Riggs (1964) and Price (1975), researchers in the Dutch Caribbean also see a connection between the current society and its colonial history. Rupert (2012) writes about the importance of contraband trade and smuggling in Curacao, which formed the society. Other researchers discuss the tradition of patronage and the impact of generations that perpetuated patronage relationships based on inequality. These relations were focused on the exchange of gifts and services: "give a little, take a little" (Collier, 2005; Oostindie, 2010; Römer, 2003; Rupert, 2012). The poor islander was accustomed to turn to his/her wealthy island-mate for survival. In return they were loyal to each other, work was performed or services were rendered. According to Verton (2006), this loyalty continued after the colonial period in a part of the population and is indicated with *political patronage*. Political leaders started to fulfil the role of the former wealthy island-mates. Political followers could count on public housing, a scholarship, a government license, leasehold land, and so on (Verton, 2006).

Other researchers have emphasised the impact of the colonial past and its influence on the democratic political structures of the Dutch Caribbean (Nauta, 2011). Those structures were created by institutional architects from the Netherlands in the early 1950s, when the former colonies were granted self-government. According to those researchers, it is a mistake to consider the Dutch Caribbean as a "scaled down" version of the Netherlands (Oostindie & Sutton, 2006). They argue that those structures do not fit to small-scale societies, as the detailed legislation is ineffective and vulnerable for bad governance.

Other relevant cultural characteristics are identified in the literature with concepts as the *culture of fear*, *culture of silence,* and *culture of victimisation*. These characteristics are attributed to colonialism and slavery. The fear of reprisals in the slave-master relationship – "You were nothing, you may nothing, and this certainly not in formal situations" (Marcha & Verweel, 2009, p. 11) – would have evolved to fear of the religious leader, fear of the boss, fear of the journalist, fear of colleagues, and/or fear of the politicians. According to Marcha and Verweel (2009), fear is a broad social, institutional, relational, and personal phenomenon encountered at all levels. This fear is not only due to the centuries-long totalitarian system of colonialism and slavery, but also a result of social institutions such as education, religion, and politics. According to researchers in the Caribbean, the limited responsibility people feel for their own social and task-oriented behaviour and the lack of mutual trust, is a result of this culture of fear (Marcha & Verweel, 2009; Paula, 2003; Schrills, 2003). People do not dare to take responsibility as they fear to do something wrong. Related to this culture of fear is the emphasis on *law-abiding* and respect for authority, implying people will avoid contradicting the authority of elected or appointed leaders. From this perspective, questioning the authority of a leader is seen as a lack of respect towards him/her (Verton, 2006).

Current study

In sum, fraud and corruption form an ongoing problem throughout the Dutch Caribbean, while very little empirical attention has been focused on this issue. Therefore, the current study will investigate the following research question: What is the nature of the (alleged) public fraud and corruption cases that are known by law enforcement agencies and judiciary in the Dutch Caribbean, and do these cases show characteristics that are rooted in the colonial past? To answer this question several sub-questions have been formulated:

- Is fraud more prevalent than corruption in the Dutch Caribbean or vice versa?
- Which forms of fraud and corruption are most common?
- Which sectors of government are most prone to fraud and corruption and on which level of government do these crimes take place, i.e. what is the function and governmental status of the public official involved?
- Do the cases show impacts of post-colonial characteristics?

Methods

Data

The research methods used in this study included studying literature and reports, carrying out judicial research (e.g. the verdicts), conducting interviews, and exploring newspaper-based databanks. I researched and studied all known public fraud and corruption cases that were tried between 2000 and 2014 before the Court of Appeal of the Joint Court of Aruba, Curacao, St Maarten and Bonaire, St Eustatius and Saba, formerly the Joint Court of the Netherlands Antilles and Aruba. This yielded 46 studied cases in total, which were all covered by the definition provided above; all cases involved a public official who had misused the trust placed in him – as one who had accepted the duty of public office – to obtain personal gain.

Procedure

To facilitate the interpretation of the empirical information yielded by the 46 studied cases, a classification of various categories is provided. The researched cases were divided into those involving public fraud and others involving public corruption, based on the indictment handed down in the particular case. Fraud included (a) theft and embezzlement, and (b) forgery, fraud, and deception. Corruption included (c) favouritism and (d) bribery. Due to the fact that in certain cases public officials were indicted for numerous crimes, the division into distinct categorisation was not always clear cut. While some cases were clear examples of fraud or corruption, many cases contained elements of both. In those cases, various categories of fraud and corruption were combined, such as deceit and acceptance of bribes, as well as money laundering and forgery. In this context, where different forms of public fraud and corruption overlapped, (suspected) fraudulent and/or corrupt practices could be placed in various categories. In those instances, I chose to categorise the case under the most critical indictment handed down in the verdict.

To further the classification of the studied cases, an additional differentiation was added to the classification provided above. In terms of fraud and corruption, the levels *petty, grand,* and *political* were introduced. Global organisations such as Transparency International and the World Bank use these categorisations because it helps to understand the effects of fraud and corruption on an economic or political system.[4] The categorisation *petty, grand,* and *political* has a bearing on the level of government in which the public official is employed, the manner in which the case impacts society at large, as well as the financial implications of the crime (Blundo & Sardan, 2006; Killias, Mugellini, Isenring, & Villettaz, 2016; World Bank Group, 1997).[5] Petty corruption refers to everyday abuse of entrusted power by low- and mid-level public officials in their interactions with ordinary citizens, who are often trying to access basic goods or services in locations such as hospitals, schools, police departments, and/or other agencies. Grand corruption consists of acts committed at a high level of government that distort policies or the central functioning of the state, enabling leaders to benefit at the expense of the public good. Political corruption is the manipulation of policies, institutions, and rules of procedure in the allocation of resources and financing by political decision makers, who abuse their position to sustain their power, status, and wealth.

Limitations

In comparison to other crimes, fraud and corruption are known to harbour a relatively large area of uncertainty as to factual numbers. The main reason for this is comprised of the fact that many fraud and corruption cases are so-called victimless crimes: as both parties involved are implicated, neither the corrupted nor the corruptor stand to gain by filing a police report against the other. In addition, witnesses often do not file a report out of lack of confidence in legal authorities and/or fear of repercussions (Central Bureau of Statistics, 2008;

Raad voor Rechtshandhaving, 2012). Moreover, while the majority of those cases that do end up being investigated and tried lead to appeal cases, not all reach the Court of Appeal, in which case they would not be included in this study. The number of 46 cases cannot be taken as an indication of the range of public fraud and corruption in the Dutch Caribbean, owing to the fact that the study solely focuses on the cases which were tried by the Court of Appeal between 2000 and 2014.

It is also prudent to note that substantial differences exist between cases in both range and complexity. The 46 studied cases entail larger and smaller manifestations of fraud and corruption. A case can be contained in a certain area of government, but it can also consist of a much broader network of international divisions. Some cases are centred around one suspect, while others involve almost 20 public officials. In the same vein, some cases involve smaller amounts of money, while others entail millions of guilders. The complexity of a case often also determines the length of the investigative process. Investigative work can take months but it can also take years. In some cases, it can take up to a decade to reach a verdict by the Court of Appeal.

Results

The (alleged) fraud and corruption in the 46 studied cases took place within various judicial areas involving criminal law, civil law, as well as administrative law. Table 3.1 presents the number of cases per judicial area. The table demonstrates that the majority (70%) of the studied cases involved criminal law, followed by cases which were tried before a civil law judge. Not all appeal cases have resulted in a conviction of public officials: in three (7%) of the 46 cases the Court of Appeal decided to acquit the defendant. In one case the public prosecutor was declared inadmissible by the Court of Appeal.

Fraud

A categorisation along the lines of petty, grand, and political fraud is presented in Table 3.2.

Table 3.1 Differentiation of appeal cases of (alleged) public fraud and corruption per judicial area

Judicial area	*Total number of cases (%)*	*Per country*			
		Aruba	*Curaçao*	*Sint Maarten*	*BES*
Criminal law	33 (70)	5	17	10	1
Civil law	9 (19)	5	3	1	
Administrative law	5 (11)	1	3		1
Total	46 (100)	11	23	11	2

Table 3.2 Categorisation as to petty, grand, and political fraud as well as corruption

	Number of cases	*Petty*	*Grand*	*Political*
Fraud				
Theft and embezzlement	5	5		
Forgery, fraud, and deception	15	3	10	2
Subtotal (%)	20 (43)			
Corruption				
Favouritism	6			6
Bribery	20	8	7	5
Subtotal (%)	26 (57)			
Total (%)	46 (100)	16 (35)	17 (37)	13 (28)

Petty fraud

Eight (40 per cent) of the 20 fraud cases were categorised as petty fraud, of which five were based on theft and embezzlement and three on forgery, fraud, and deception. These petty fraud cases involved low-ranking public officials who abused entrusted power in their interactions with ordinary citizens for personal gain, in ways that were not aimed at derailing government or the specific organisations' policies. The theft and embezzlement cases, which were considered petty fraud, concerned cases where a treasurer or administrative officer used or trafficked funds and goods he had been entrusted with for personal enrichment. Even though these cases were classified as petty fraud, the monetary amounts overall were substantial – up to several tens of thousands Antillean or Aruban guilders. In this context, the impact for the organisations involved was consequential.

In St Maarten's Point Blanche prison, an employee embezzled more than 100,000 Antillean guilders (55,555 US dollars). The money belonged to a foundation which administered funds of prisoners in the detention centre and penitentiary of the Point Blanche prison.[6] Furthermore, three cases of forgery, fraud, and deception involved instances in which undocumented workers were aided to enter the country in an unlawful manner and government documents were forged. In one case the *Bureau Rijbewijzen* [Bureau of Drivers' Licensing] of the Aruban Police Force was involved. A drivers' license could be bought for approximately 600 Aruban guilders (333 US dollars). Duplicate licenses and added categories on the license – to legally operate additional types of vehicles – were for sale, often through third-party liaisons. This resulted in approximately 1,200 counterfeit drivers' licenses. Three bureau employees, some 22 third-party liaisons, and approximately 60 customers who bought counterfeit licenses were arrested.

Grand fraud

Ten (50 per cent) of the 20 fraud cases were categorised as grand fraud, all of which were based on forgery, fraud, and deception. These cases involved high-ranking public officials, who were often highly creative: documents were especially designed to carry out deviating policies, expenses were made in name of the government that had not been budgeted for nor approved, and/or payments were made to non-existing companies. These cases overall involved substantial amounts of money and had a major impact on the organisations. Most cases entailed the cooperation of several public officials/colleagues, and/or third parties. A police commissioner, formerly the head of Immigration in St Maarten, designed "re-entry" documents for undocumented immigrants. These "re-entry" documents allowed people to travel to their respective countries and legally return to St Maarten. A similar document had been used during an earlier Immigration Grace Period; however, this period had been revoked. The newly designed documents had no legal basis either in St Maarten's or in Netherlands Antillean's government policy. Moreover, due to the fact that no legal basis had been set, the so-called "re-entry" documents were administrated at random and/or linked to the highest bidder. The chief of police was also convicted in this case; by signing the "re-entry" permits he was found guilty of forgery.[7]

Political fraud

Two (10 per cent) of the 20 fraud cases were based on political fraud. These cases involved public officials working at the highest level of government, who creatively adjusted the policies of state-owned companies as well as undermined international regulations on economic trade agreements. These public officials often worked within or established a network of accomplices, often political affiliates and/or civil servants, to enable the execution of fraudulent practices. Both political fraud cases involved one and the same public official/politician. A European Union regulation stipulated sugar from Overseas Countries & Territories (OCT's) to be imported into the EU without import duties. If the sugar had been refined up to 24 per cent in the OCT, the zero import-duty regulation also held. The public official and six co-perpetrators counterfeited export permits, the bill of lading, the sales invoice, as well as the certificate of origin. In addition, a refinement from light brown to white sugar was feigned. In reality, there was no refinery of sugar in Curacao, meaning the EU-import regulations were abused. This case received a lot of (international) media attention.[8] A few years later, two directors of a government bank embezzled 400,000 Antillean guilders (222,222 US dollars) using a stock exchange transaction. They also managed to increase the amount of money that could be loaned at any one time and gave out mortgages lacking sufficient collateral to (political) relations, including the public official/politician involved in the EU-sugar regulation case and his political party members.[9]

An in-depth analysis of the 20 studied fraud cases, and a closer examination of petty, grand, and political fraud cases, demonstrated that forgery, fraud, and deception made up the largest category (15 out of 20). The majority of these cases were classified as grand fraud. This indicates that in those cases, the crimes were committed at a high level of government in a way that distorted governmental policies and/or the central functioning of the state, with the aim of personal benefit at the expense of the common good.

Corruption

A categorisation along the lines of petty, grand, and political corruption is presented in Table 3.2.

Petty corruption

Eight (31 per cent) of the total 26 corruption cases were categorised as petty corruption, all involving bribery. In those petty corruption cases, relatively small amounts of payments, ranging from several hundred to several thousand guilders, were made to facilitate (illegal) actions. Two of those cases involved bribery for undocumented immigrants to obtain a legal status, three other cases entailed the delivery of contraband – including drugs – into a prison. Three other cases had to do with evading import duties, while one case was based on deliberately turning a blind eye to drug trafficking. In another case, an immigration official employed at the Curacaoan airport helped Dominican women illegally enter the country to obtain employment in the sex work industry. The Dominican women were instructed to seek out the immigration official sporting a nose ring. The official in question would lead the women through a restricted area and out the door, circumventing immigration. Outside the women would be collected by a brothel owner, whose Dominican wife was instrumental in recruiting the women in the Dominican Republic and guiding them on the plane to Curacao.[10]

Grand corruption

A total of seven (27 per cent) cases were deemed grand corruption cases. Grand corruption involves either high-ranking public officials or instances in which the impact on society is so severe that the case has to be categorised as a high level, grand corruption case. Four of these cases were connected to comprehensive drug trafficking networks, one case involved a high-ranking public official who was looking to financially benefit from granting a construction permit, and one other case entailed a conflict of interest in hiring a third party for government work. A customs officer became part of a criminal organisation that exported drugs in large quantities from Curacao to the Netherlands. The cooperation between the drug ring and the public officer resulted in a situation where the insides of airplanes, namely the compartments where electricity cables were housed, were opened up to remove isolation materials and insert drugs packages instead. The official did not hold a high rank position within government, yet the impact of the case was such that many passengers' lives were endangered, categorizing it as a grand corruption case.[11]

Political corruption: favouritism and bribery

Out of the 26 studied corruption cases, 11 (42 per cent) were categorised as political corruption. Six involved favouritism, while five were based on bribery. In all these cases, manipulation of government policies, institutions, and rules of procedure were the directive in the allocation of resources and financing by political decision makers, who abused their public position to sustain their personal power, status, and wealth.

Favouritism

Concerning favouritism, all six cases involved appointments or job nominations by a minister or a public official in a place of authority. The political appointments were tied to job positions that were created by the accused minister and for which no public job application process had taken place. In fact, no application processes entailing job interviews or assessments were involved at all. Moreover, the perks and working conditions for the appointed civil servant tended to be disproportional in comparison to other civil servants in similar positions. A policy advisor in Aruba was hired on the basis of a contract that was very beneficial to the policy advisor and very disadvantageous for the state-owned company involved. The overall pay was relatively high, considering the nature of the work to be executed, and the arrangements made in light of redundancy were out of bounds considering regular government contracts. Up until the time the advisor reached retirement, the state-owned company had to pay the advisor a salary comparable to that of a parliamentarian, regardless of whether the advisor reported on the job or not. The total expense to tax payers' money came up to 2,219,200 Aruban guilders (1,232,888 US dollars).[12]

Bribery

In the political corruption category, the category involving bribery denoted cases in which ministers, chief commissioners, department heads, and private parties engaged in clandestine barter deals. This could manifest itself in various forms, namely (a) public officials providing confidential information to certain companies, giving them a heads-up in a tender process, (b) allowing only a small number of companies to submit a bid in a tender process, and (c) evading procedures for public tender processes. In such cases, the government was being swindled, forgery was committed, and accountability and budget regulations were circumvented. Accountability was usually only adhered to after contracts had already been signed. In such cases, civil servants were often bribed or intimidated.

Cases involving bribery in the category of political corruption were increasingly complex. In general, an enduring and thorough police investigation was necessary, often spanning several years. In some cases, criminals established a complex web of legal entities, making it difficult to determine the paper trail. Cases in this category also involved large amounts of money, often up to millions of guilders or US dollars.

Four (20 per cent) of the bribery cases involved the real estate/construction sector. In these cases, bribes had been paid to obtain building permits and/or tenders. The "Curinta-affair" is the largest public fraud and corruption case in Curacaoan history. New roads were built as part of a plan to upgrade the infrastructure surrounding the Curacaoan airport. The tender was awarded to a Curacaoan construction company for 7,2 million Antillean guilders (4 million US dollars). Two years prior, this company had paid bribes to Curacaoan politicians and political parties. A total of 17 public officials were involved in this case, including several politicians of different political parties. All politicians were linked to the case due to the fact that their positions were related to the planning of infrastructure. The "Curinta-affair" not only drew attention to the bribes paid by the construction company to win the bid for road construction at the airport, but also to the monies received by public officials for benefitting certain companies in a public tender. The importance and scope of this case was determined by the large number of public officials involved and the high level of these government officials, more so than the amounts of money involved.[13]

A closer look at the – in total – 26 studied corruption cases, and a closer examination of petty, grand, and political corruption cases, demonstrated that bribery amounted to the largest category, 20 out of 26 cases, of which the majority (11) was classified as political corruption. These political corruption cases were often during the entire police investigations featured in the media, resulting in much reputation damage for the Dutch Caribbean.

Table 3.2 demonstrates that 43 per cent of the cases were classified as fraud and 57 per cent as corruption. Out of a total of 46 cases, most cases (20) were based on bribery (43 per cent), where the corruptor paid a fee or offered a service in order to get preferential treatment from a public official. Sixteen (35 per cent) of the 46 selected cases were classified as petty, 17 (37 per cent) cases fell under grand and 13 (28 per cent) cases could be categorised as political fraud and corruption. The large number of high level cases signifies that the majority of fraud and corruption cases brought before the Court of Appeal either involved high-ranking government officials, entrusted with a high level of authority, or were of a large scale and/or impact on society.

Verdicts

The distinction between petty, grand, and political fraud and corruption was not reflected in the verdicts handed down by the Court of Appeal. Studying the verdicts in these 46 cases, it became apparent that the differences in punishment administered in petty, grand, or political fraud and corruption cases were negligible. Besides a more than 10-year prison sentence in a grand fraud case, the most far-reaching punishment was handed down in a petty fraud case, namely a four-year unconditional prison sentence in combination with an eight-year ban from holding public office. However, both cases involved the use of violence. As mentioned above, in four cases, all grand and political corruption cases, the Appeal Court decided to either acquit the defendant or not hold him liable in the case. In two of these cases, grand corruption was involved, while the one other case entailed political corruption.

Organisations and positions of perpetrators

Close analysis of the 46 cases showed that a substantial number of cases involved the Ministry of Justice, including the police force, the penitentiary, and the immigration department. Eleven (24 per cent) cases concerned decisions regarding permits for immigrants, nine cases were related to drugs, and seven cases involved procurement of goods, including three cases which pertained to the infrastructural sector. In the organisations involved, existing (control and integrity) procedures were not always known to the public officials or not applied. Administrative reports and controls were frequently lacking, as well as clear boundaries between the job descriptions of certain (high level) jobs. In addition, authority was an issue: in several cases the perpetrator ignored requests of – and warnings by – supreme audit and supervisory institutions without being reprimanded. Moreover, the studied organisations generally demonstrated a lack of continuity in execution of policies, as a result of frequent changes in high-ranking staff. The presented cases showed that a change of government often involved an abrupt change in placement of high-ranking government officials leading government organisations.

In the studied cases, the leading officials of the sector or department involved often gave the wrong example by being involved in fraud and corruption themselves. While it has proven impossible to determine the exact rank of each government official involved, more than half of the cases showed the perpetrator as either the head of a ministry, a department, or a team. In eight of the studied cases the perpetrators held the position of minister or commissioner. In other cases, the perpetrators were directors, members of the board, team leaders, or department heads. In the cases where – as far as could be determined – no high-ranking public officials were involved, weak leadership among superiors was rampant. Managerial skills were rarely or never implemented and civil servants were not reprimanded for – or called on – integrity issues. And while fraudulent or corrupt employees were protected from higher up in the organisation, employees who brought abuses of power to the fore were not supported in their aim to purge the organisation of corrupt practices. As far as I could determine, only a small percentage of cases involved a public official working on his/her own. In all other cases there was a conspiracy of several public officials working and plotting together – one case uncovered up to 17 public officials working together – or public officials plotting with outside parties, such as undocumented immigrants, inmates, liaisons, or representatives of commercial businesses.

Discussion

This article has shown that in the time period from 2000–2014, a total of 46 public fraud and corruption cases were brought before the Court of Appeal. In all 46 cases, public officials were tried for using government funds, i.e. tax payers' money, for private ends. In 57 per cent of the cases the primary crime was corruption, in 43 per cent of the cases fraud was the prime transgression. The majority of the selected cases – 65 per cent – was classified at the highest level of grand and political fraud and corruption. The effects of grand and political fraud and corruption cases had a greater impact on the Dutch Caribbean societies' economic and political system, than the petty fraud and corruption cases did. This is due to the large amounts of tax payers' funds involved, the relatively long periods of criminal investigation necessary, and the large amount of (negative) publicity surrounding these cases.

How can these results be viewed in light of international literature or comparative studies on fraud and corruption and to which extent can the results be attributed to a colonial history? What is known concerning public fraud and corruption in international literature on the level of organisations and the rank of positions therein is underscored by the studied cases in the Dutch Caribbean. A large proportion (40 per cent) of the cases took place within the judicial sector, particularly involving law enforcement agencies as well as the penitentiary and immigration departments. Literature shows that the sectors of immigration, law enforcement, diplomacy, public housing, as well as spatial planning and infrastructure, are known to be vulnerable to corruption (De Graaf & Huberts, 2008; Nelen & Nieuwendijk, 2003). This supports the findings yielded by the current study. International literature also shows that organisations that are inflicted with fraud or corruption often lack clear procedures, enhancing unclarity on the separation of duties within an organisation (Huberts, 2014; Lasthuizen, Huberts, & Kaptein, 2005). These findings are also partly confirmed by the results of the current study. In the majority of the organisations, control was inadequate and a corporate culture facilitating or enhancing free communication about integrity issues was lacking. On the other hand, the failing control was not caused by a lack of clear procedures. The procedures were there, including the separation of duties, but were not put into practice by the public officials. Although this by the Dutch created conduct could be improved, the results of the research did not show that the followed legislation was unfit for Dutch Caribbean practice or vulnerable for fraud or corruption.

According to international researchers, good governance and virtuous leadership are essential conditions to prevent corruption and fraud, but are often non-existent in the organisations (Huberts, Six, Van Tankeren, Van Montfort, & Paanakker, 2014). The studied cases show that often the high-ranking official in charge of good governance in the organisation is in fact the perpetrator of fraud and corruption. Moreover, the political fraud and corruption cases showed a great interdependence between the high-ranking official in charge and politics. Family ties and professional roles were often interwoven, decisions often based on personal relationships rather than on good governance principles. As we saw in the favouritism cases, newly appointed ministers appoint officials from their own circle in the public administration and state-owned businesses.

This favouritism may correspond to the tradition of patronage and the theory of the prismatic society of Riggs (1964): the relatives of the ministers expect favours, such as jobs, and the ministers try to expand their power by political appointments. This may also correspond to the root of the colonial history which has formed societies based on gain rather than on the common good. In societies where the idea of the common good remains too abstract, public officials, especially those in high ranks, may feel entitled to now reap the rewards of their position, as so many have done before them. This is because the colonists often acted in their own best interest and did not think of the general interest of the country. It is very difficult to adjust this former practice and to set a new example of desirable behaviour. If fraud and corruption are indeed best prevented by good exemplary behaviour of officials, (former) colonies will indeed encounter more difficulties with preventing these types of behaviour as they often have a long history with bad exemplary behaviour of officials. If public officials do not feel stakeholders in, but instead beneficiaries of, their own government, public fraud and corruption are close by.

Furthermore, international literature on this subject shows that an organisations' internal corporate culture is determinative if the aim is preventing fraud and corruption (Caiden, Dwivedi, & Jabbra, 2001; Lasthuizen, 2008; Punch, 2009). Fraud and corruption are less likely to happen when issues of integrity can easily be discussed and public officials feel free to consult with and also confront each other when colleagues deviate from normal policies and procedures. This, however, did not appear to be the rule across the organisations studied. On the contrary, as was the case in the colonial times where slaves were punished when they expressed their displeasure, the organisational cultural background in several researched cases can be characterised as one of fear and lack of interpersonal trust to express themselves. The public officials felt fear that an assertive attitude would trigger negative consequences and thus these officials overall chose to keep quiet (Marcha & Verweel, 2009; Schotborgh-van de Ven, 2009).

Yet the contemporary culture of fear has other causes beyond the colonial history. In addition, the large-scale fraud and corruption cases in the Dutch Caribbean in recent years appear to have had a negative effect on the public sector. The more negative portrayal of the cases involving Dutch Caribbean politicians in the media greatly influenced political and diplomatic relations within the Dutch Kingdom. Political hardliners about the Dutch Caribbean and their leaders in terms of "corrupted gangs", "mafia practices", and "administrative disorder", published by Dutch Caribbean, Dutch, as well as international media, have contributed to the negative reputation of the Dutch Caribbean as a breeding ground for fraud and corruption. This has also resulted in a situation where terms such as fraud and corruption are easily used in the general discourse for every incident which may not strictly follow prescribed government rules, like handling personal affairs during working hours or engaging in conflicting outside activities. This results in turn in an atmosphere of contraction within government, where public officials are inhibited to take any action at all out of fear of repercussions or public scrutiny. In other words, besides the influence of the colonial past, developments in the latest few decades have led to a situation in which many civil servants show little initiative to tackle or report inconsistent procedures out of fear of stigmatisation and public repercussions.

On top of that, enforcement and judiciary agencies have become quite cautious to investigate and prosecute so-called "big fish" in organised crime rings. This has provided a fertile breeding ground for fraud and corruption in the Dutch Caribbean. In this context, these "big fish" and the lawyers they retain have become exceedingly apt at litigation and introducing legal stalling techniques during court cases. Countering this trend requires an unusually costly and high level expertise, which the law agencies of the small islands in the Dutch Caribbean are not equipped to meet at this time.

Based on the results given above, I conclude that it is too simple to draw a linear relationship between the colonial past of the Dutch Caribbean and the current public fraud and corruption on the islands. This because, first, these types of fraud and corruption also occur in countries without a colonial history. Second, the islands of the Dutch Caribbean have very distinct colonial pasts, resulting in distinct impacts on the islands. Thus, the impact of colonialism and the developments thereafter, was not only different for the Windward and the Leeward islands, but also the impact on the islands of those parts was distinct. Thirdly, the impact of the development of the islands after the colonial period was very different. The islands all developed in various ways and their development was based and dependent on distinct foreign factors, such as the role of the Shell oil refinery in Curacao and of migration in St Maarten. We would deny the strength of the islands and their own development and identity by mainly imputing the current existence of fraud and corruption on the colonial past.

As we have seen, the colonial past indeed had an influence on the functioning of the current society including the occurring fraud and corruption, such as the existence of political patronage, the lack of virtuous leadership, the culture of fear and subservience. Nevertheless, those colonial characteristics have transformed over time into different forms nowadays and cannot be seen as the main stimulant or cause of ongoing public fraud and corruption. The existing literature does show a greater prevalence of fraud and corruption across countries with a colonial past, but other possible explanatory influences, such as small scale, geographic location, political system, and inequality must not be forgotten and, moreover, further researched.

Notes

1 Aruba: Landsverordening administratieve rechtspraak, A.B. 1993, no. 45; Curaçao: Landsverordening materieel ambtenarenrecht, A.B. 2010, no. 86 en no. 87; Sint Maarten: Landsverordening materieel ambtenarenrecht, A.B. 2010, GT no. 1 en A.B. 2010, GT no. 30; BES: Wet administratieve rechtspraak BES, Stb. 2010, 510.
2 Worldbank, Retrieved 24 March, 2017, from http://info.worldbank.org/governance/wgi/#home.
3 Charter for the Kingdom of the Netherlands, 2010, No. 775.
4 Transparency International, Retrieved 8 January, 2016, from www.transparency.org/glossary.
5 Transparency International, Retrieved 23 September 2015 from www.transparency.org/glossary.
6 De Rechtspraak. [The Jurisprudence]. Case No. H 119/2009. Date verdict: 6 January, 2010. Retrieved July 26, 2015, from http://deeplink.rechtspraak.nl/uitspraak?id=ECLI:NL:OGHNAA:2010:BM1438.
7 De Rechtspraak. [The Jurisprudence]. Case No: H 21/2008. Date verdict: 8 July, 2010. Retrieved July 25, 2015, from http://deeplink.rechtspraak.nl/uitspraak?id=ECLI:NL:OGHNAA:2010:BN4464.
8 Amigoe (2000). *Kroongetuige laat het afweten in LGO-suikerfraudezaak*, No. 13 April 13, 2000. Amigoe (2003), "Godett en Monte nog langer vast", No. April 23, 2003.

9 Amigoe (2002). *Administratieve organisatie oude Girobankdirectie faalde*. No. 7 January, 2002. Amigoe (2001). *Topfunctionarissen verdacht van verduistering Setel-geld*, No. 2 November, 2001.
10 Databank Public Prosecutor. Case No: H 7/2009. Date verdict: 5 February, 2009.
11 Databank Openbaar Ministerie. Zaaknummer: H -3/12. Datum uitspraak: 15 March, 2012.
12 De Rechtspraak. [The Jurisprudence]. Case No: EJ-2240/10-H-134/11. Date verdict: January 17, 2012. Retrieved July 29, 2015, from http://deeplink.rechtspr46aak.nl/uitspraak?id=ECLI:NL:OGHACMB:2012:BY09.
13 Amigoe (2003). *'Progressive Design' was dekmantel Middelhof*, 19 August, 2003.

References

Blickman, T. (1997). The Rothschilds of the mafia on Aruba. *Transnational Organized Crime*, *3*(2), 50–89.

Blockman, W. (1988). Patronage, brokerage and corruption as symptoms of incipient state foundation in the Burgundian-Hapsberg Netherlands. In A. Maczak (Ed.), *Klientalelsysteme in Europa der Fruhen Neuzeit* (pp. 117–126). Munich: Oldenbourg.

Blundo, G., & Sardan, J.P.O. (2006). *Everyday corruption and the state: Citizens and public officials in Africa*. New York: Zed.

Caiden, G.E., Dwivedi, O.P., & Jabbra, J.G. (2001). *Where corruption lives*. Bloomfield, CT: Kumarian Press.

Campbell, J.K. (1989). Village friendship and patronage. In A.J. Heidenheimer, M. Johnston, & V.T. Le Vine (Eds.), *Political corruption: A handbook* (2nd ed., pp. 327–337). New Brunswick, NJ: Transaction Publishers.

Central Bureau of Statistics. (2005). *Perceptie van corruptie Bonaire en Curacao 2004 [Perception of corruption Bonaire and Curacao 2004]*. Curacao: Central Bureau of Statistics, Fort Amsterdam.

Central Bureau of Statistics. (2008). *Slăchtofferenquête [Crime victim survey]*. Curacao: Central Bureau of Statistics, Fort Amsterdam.

Collier, M.W. (2005). *Political corruption in the Caribbean basin: Constructing a theory to combat corruption*. New York: Routledge.

De Graaf, G., & Huberts, L.W.J.C. (2008). Portraying the nature of corruption: Using an explorative case-study design. *Public Administration Review*, *68*(4), 640–653.

De Wit, C.W. (2015). *National integrity system assessment Sint-Maarten 2015*. Retrieved from Transparency International www.transparency.org/whatwedo/publication/st._maarten_national_integrity_system_assessment_2015.

De Zwart, F. (2010). Corruption and anti-corruption in prismatic societies. In G. Graaf, P. Maravić, & P. Wagenaar (Eds.), *The good cause: Theoretical perspectives on corruption* (pp. 36–46). Opladen: Barbara Budrich Publishers.

Goede, M. (2013). Transnational Organized Crime (TOC) and the relationship to good governance in the Caribbean. *International Journal of Development Issues*, *12*(3), 253–270.

Gurgur, T., & Shah, A. (2005). *Localization and corruption: Panacea or Pandora's box*. (World Bank Policy Research Working Paper 3486). Retrieved from http://econ.worldbank.org.

Hoetjes, B.J.S. (1977). *Corruptie in het openbare leven van ontwikkelingslanden: Een verkenning van theorie en onderzoek, in het bijzonder gericht op India sinds 1947 [Corruption in public life in developing countries: An exploration of theory and research, particularly focusing on India since 1947]*. Leiden: Leiden University.

Hollinger, R.C., & Davis, J.L. (2006). Employee theft and staff dishonesty. In M. Gill (Ed.), *The handbook of security* (pp. 203–228). Retrieved from http://vm3.ehaus2.co.uk/macmillan/resources/Product-Page-Downloads/G/Gill-Handbook-of-Security-2e/0230006809_10_ch09.pdf.

Huberts, L.W. (2003). *Mag het ietsje meer zijn? Integriteitsonderzoek in het mijnenveld van de moraal [May it be a little more? Research Integrity in the minefield of morality].* Amsterdam: Faculteit der Sociale Wetenschappen, Vrije Universiteit Amsterdam.

Huberts, L.W. (2005). *Integriteit en integritisme in bestuur en samenleving: Wie de schoen past [Integrity and integritism in governance and society: Who fits the shoe. . .].* Amsterdam: Vrije Universiteit Amsterdam.

Huberts, L.W.J.C. (2014). *Integrity of governance: What it is, what we know, what is done and where to go.* Houndsmill, Basingstoke, Hampshire: Palgrave Macmillan.

Huberts, L.W.J.C., Six, F., Van Tankeren, M., Van Montfort, A., & Paanakker, H. (2014). What is done to protect integrity: Policies, institutions, and systems. In L.W.J.C. Huberts (Ed.), *The integrity of governance: What it is, what we know, what is done and where to go* (pp. 167–197). Houndsmill, Basingstoke, Hampshire: Palgrave Macmillan.

Huiskamp, R. (1991). Een corruptiezaak in de achttiende-eeuwse Meierij van 's Hertogenbosch [A corruption case in the eighteenth century Meierij of's Hertogenbosch]. *Tijdschrift voor Sociale Geschiedenis, 17*(1), 73–97.

Ilegems, D., & Sauviller, R. (1995). *Bloedsporen: Een reis naar de mafia [Bloodstains: A trip to the Mafia].* Amsterdam: Atlas.

Killias, M., Mugellini, G., Isenring, G.L., & Villettaz, P. (2016). Administrative reform in the public sector and their impact on the level of corruption: A systematic review. *The Campbell Collaboration.* Retrieved from www.campbellcollaboration.org/library/administrative-reforms-in-the-public-sector-impact-on-level-of-corruption.html.

Lasthuizen, K. (2008). *Leading to integrity: Empirical research into the effects of leadership on ethics and integrity.* Enschede: Printpartners Ipskamp.

Lasthuizen, K., Huberts, L.W.J.C., & Kaptein, M. (2005). Analyse van integriteitsopvattingen [Analysis of opinions on integrity]. In L.W.J.C. Hubert, & J. Naeyé (Eds.), *Integriteit van politie* (pp. 69–93). Apeldoorn/Zeist: Kerckebosch.

Levi, M. (2006). The media construction of financial white-collar crimes. *The British Journal of Criminology, 46*(6), 1037–1057.

Marcha, V., & Verweel, P. (2009). *De cultuur van de angst, de paradoxale culturele ketenen van angst en zwijgen (3rd ed.) [The culture of fear, paradoxical cultural chains of fear and silence].* Amsterdam: SWP.

Mesu, S., Stoffers, E., & Harrigan, B. (2011). *Criminaliteitsbeeldanalyse Sint-Maarten. Een onderzoek naar georganiseerde en commune criminaliteit [Crime analyses St. Maarten: An investigation into the organized and communal criminality].* Zoetermeer: KLPD-Dienst IPOL.

Mooij, A., Tijssens, I., & Van der Mark, J. (2013). *Veiligheidsbeeld BES-eilanden 2013: Criminaliteit, regelovertreding en overlast op Bonaire, Sint-Eustatius en Saba [Security image BES islands 2013: Crime, law violation and nuisance on Bonaire, St. Eustatius and Saba].* Zoetermeer: Dienst Landelijke Informatieorganisatie.

Nauta, O. (2011). *Goed bestuur in de West. Institutionele en maatschappelijke beperkingen voor goed bestuur in de Caribische rijksdelen [Good governance in the West. Institutional and social constraints to good governance in the Caribbean overseas territories].* Oisterwijk: Uitgeverij BOXPress.

Nederlof, M. (2008). *Eerlijckman 1680–1713 in dienst van het Staatse leger en de West-Indisiche Compagnie, 2008.* Curacao: De Curaçaosche Courant.

Nelen, J.M., & Nieuwendijk, A. (2003). *Geen ABC: Analyse van rijksrechercheonderzoeken naar ambtelijke en bestuurlijke corruptie [No ABC: Analysis of research of the royal criminal investigation department on official and administrative corruption].* Den Haag: Boom Juridische uitgevers.

Oostindie, G. (2010). *Postcolonial Netherlands: Sixty-five years of forgetting, commemorating, silencing.* Amsterdam: Amsterdam University Press.

Oostindie, G., & Sutton, P. (2006). *Small scale and quality of governance: A survey of the scholarly literature, with special reference to the Caribbean.* The Hague: Royal Netherlands Institute of Southeast Asian and Caribbean Studies (Leiden), & Ministerie van Binnenlandse Zaken en Koninkrijksrelaties (Den Haag).

Paula, J. (2003). *Ontkend verleden, verzwakte toekomst [Denied past, weakened future].* In R.M. Allen, C. Heijes, & V. Marcha (Eds.), *Emancipatie & acceptatie, Curaçao en Curacaoënaars: Beeldvorming en identiteit honderdveertig jaar na de slavernij* (pp. 111–116). Amsterdam: SWP.

Price, J.M. (1975). New time series for Scotland's and Britain's trade with the thirteen colonies and states, 1740 to 1791. *The William and Mary Quarterly, 32*(2), 307–325.

Punch, M. (2009). *Police corruption: Deviance, accountability and reform in policing.* Cullompton, Devon: Willan Publishing.

Raad voor de Rechtshandhaving. (2012). *Het opsporingsproces op Curaçao: Inspectieonderzoek van de Raad voor de Rechtshandhaving naar het opsporingsproces van veel voorkomende misdrijven op Curaçao [The investigation process in Curacao: Inspection research of the Law Enforcement Council on the investigation process of common crimes in Curacao].* Retrieved from http://bearingpointcaribbean.esimg.net/wp-content/uploads/2014/08/rapport_inspectie_opsporingsproces_cur.pdf.

Riggs, R.W. (1964). *Administration in developing countries: Place of publication not identified.* Boston: Houghton Mifflin.

Römer, R. (2003). *René Römer als inspirator. Actualisering van zijn gedachtegoed [René Romer as inspiration. Updating of his ideas].* Curacao: Universiteit van de Nederlandse Antillen.

Rose-Ackerman, S. (2010). The institutional economics of corruption. In G. Graaf, P. Maravić, & P. Wagenaar (Eds.), *The good cause: Theoretical perspectives on corruption* (pp. 46–63). Opladen: Barbara Budrich Publishers.

Rupert, L.M. (2012). *Creolization and contraband: Curacao in the early modern Atlantic world.* Athens: University of Georgia Press.

Schotborgh-van de Ven, P.C.M. (2009). *De 'verwijtenroute': Over de achtergronden van fraude en corruptie in het Caribische deel van het Koninkrijk: De Nederlandse Cariben [The "route of reproach": On the origins of fraud and corruption in the Caribbean Part of the Kingdom].* 35(5), 84–98. Den Haag: Wetenschappelijk Onderzoek-en Documentatiecentrum. Boom Juridische uitgevers.

Schotborgh-van de Ven, P.C.M., & Van Velzen, S., (2013). *National Integrity System Assessment Curacao.* Retrieved from Transparency International www.transparency.org/whatwedo/pub/national_integrity_system_assessment_curacao_2013.

Schrills, J. (2003). Emancipatie en onze politieke cultuur [Emancipation and our political culture]. In R.M. Allen, C. Heijes, & V. Marcha (Eds.), *Emancipatie & acceptatie, Curaçao en Curacaoënaars: Beeldvorming en identiteit honderdveertig jaar na de slavernij* (pp. 117–127). Amsterdam: SWP.

Serra, D. (2006). Empirical determinants of corruption: A sensitivity analysis. *Public Choice, 126*(1–2), 225–256.

Verhoeven, M., Bokhorst, R., Leeuw, F., Bogaerts, S., & Schotborgh-van de Ven, P. (2007). *Georganiseerde criminaliteit en rechtshandhaving op St. Maarten [Organized crime and law enforcement in St. Maarten].* Den Haag: Wetenschappelijk Onderzoek en Documentatiecentrum/Boom Juridische uitgevers.

Verton, P. (2006). Deugdelijk bestuur en politieke patronage [Good governance and political patronage]. In R.M. Allen, *René Römer als inspirator. Actualiseringen van zijn gedachtegoed* (pp. 202–218). Curacao: Universiteit van de Nederlandse Antillen.

Wagenaar, P., Van der Meij, O., & Van der Heijden, M. (2005). Corruptie in de Nederlanden, 1400–1800 [Corruption in the Netherlands]. *Tijdschrift Voor Sociale En Economische Geschiedenis, 2*(4), 3–21.

Weenink, A.W., & Brug, J.I.M. (2009). *Criminaliteitsbeeldanalyse Curaçao 2008 [Crime-analyses Curaçao].* Zoetermeer: KLPD, Politie, Korps landelijke politiediensten.

Weenink, A.W., Klein Haarhuis, C.M., Bokhorst, R.J., & Smit, M. (2011). *De staat van bestuur van Aruba: Een onderzoek naar de deugdelijkheid van bestuur en de rechtshandhaving [The state of governance of Aruba: An investigation into the adequacy of governance and law enforcement].* Den Haag: Boom Juridische uitgevers.

World Bank Group. (1997). *Helping countries combat corruption: The role of the World Bank.* Retrieved from www1.worldbank.org/publicsector/anticorrupt/corruptn/corrptn.pdf.

4 Ethnicity and crime victimisation in Trinidad and Tobago

Randy Seepersad and Scot Wortley

Introduction

This chapter examines the relationship between ethnicity and crime victimisation in Trinidad and Tobago and tries to determine whether specific ethnic groups are over-represented among victims of crime. Very little is known about this in the Caribbean and indeed, most countries have not collected data that would allow for an examination of this issue. While Trinidad and Tobago has recently begun to collect data on ethnicity and crime, these data have not been examined. The issue of ethnicity and crime is a sensitive one which governments of the region have avoided. Part of the reason stems from the fear that the findings from such data may fuel racist stereotypes and could encourage discrimination. However, for many Caribbean countries, other issues such as understanding the nature and extent of crime, understanding crime trends and understanding which factors are the most important for the purposes of interventions take precedence, as many countries are still struggling to understand the level of crime which is occurring and are under pressure to bring crime to more manageable levels. That said, an understanding of the relationship between ethnicity and crime can assist with these endeavours.

Ethnicity and crime

While very little research has been done on ethnicity and crime in the Caribbean, this line of research has a long tradition in other countries. The majority of studies which have looked at ethnicity have focused on the perpetrators of criminal offences and have concentrated on crime rates and on discriminatory practices in the criminal justice system. For example, researchers have focused on racial biases in police practices (Taylor, Holleran, & Topalli, 2009; Warren, 2011; Weitzer & Tuch, 1999), sentencing decisions (Freiburger & Hilinski, 2013; Wang, Mears, Spohn, & Dario, 2013), processing and treatment of minorities in the criminal justice system (Georges-Abcyie, 1992; Hawkins, 1986; Newburn, Shiner, & Hayman, 2004), and the commission of criminal offences (Henry, Hastings, & Freer, 1996; Hipp, 2007; LaFree, Drass, & O'Day, 1992; Sampson, 1985; Stolzenberg, Eitle, & Alessio, 2006).

Much less research on ethnicity has focused on the victims of crime. Lauritsen and Heimer (2010) found, using data from the 1973 to 2005 US National Crime Victimization Survey, that economic deprivation during times of economic downturn and recession was more closely associated with crime victimisation for Blacks and Latinos than for Whites. Krivo, Peterson, and Payne (2009) and Sampson and Wilson (1995) have argued that higher levels of economic deprivation among minorities lead to social disorganisation and cultural adaptations, which are associated with higher levels of crime victimisation. These processes apply regardless of whether there are economic downturns. Eisler and Schissel (2004) found, using a sample of youths from Canada, that poor Aboriginal youth experienced lower rates of non-criminal victimisation than non-Aboriginal youth, but that the level of criminal victimisation was higher for Aboriginal youth than for non-Aboriginal youth. Biafora and Warheit (2007) found that there were no differences in the levels of victimisation of recently immigrated ethnic minorities compared to similar minorities who had lived in the US for some time. They did, however, find that victimisation rates for Blacks were higher than for other minority groups, regardless of whether these comparison groups had recently immigrated. The research on ethnicity and crime victimisation is sparse and has not focused with any consistency on specific issues. To date, researchers have not examined the relationship between ethnicity and criminal victimisation in the Caribbean.

Like Trinidad and Tobago, many Caribbean countries are hesitant to publish statistics on ethnicity and crime. While some commentators argue that the relationship between ethnicity and crime is unimportant or even non-existent, others feel that such statistics may fuel stereotypes and prejudices. Wortley (1999) argued that generally there are three reasons given for not publishing race-crime statistics: (a) the poor quality of crime statistics, (b) difficulties in classifying ethnicity, and (c) the use of such data to justify discrimination and fuel prejudices. Wortley (1999) also noted, however, that a number of reasons have been advanced for the publication and use of race-crime statistics. He noted that such information can be used to find out whether minorities receive differential treatment in the criminal justice system, it can also be used to challenge racial explanations of crime, and finally, a ban on race-crime statistics will not prevent racist ideas. Such data may, in fact, be used to challenge stereotypes and prejudices.

In Trinidad and Tobago, the quality of crime data has improved substantially over the last decade. This is due in large measure to the Crime and Problem Analysis (CAPA) branch of the Trinidad and Tobago Police Service (TTPS). This is a state-of-the-art data management facility which is linked via secure communication channels to each police station. Crime report data which are entered at the police stations are uploaded, collated, and analysed at CAPA. This is not to say that official crime data are without problems. Indeed, data at CAPA represent crimes reported to the police. Other sources of crime data such as victimisation surveys have consistently shown that police statistics underestimate the true extent of criminal offending (Wortley & Seepersad, 2013). Quite apart from this, if there are racial prejudices, persons may be more likely to report crimes committed by minorities (Shah & Pease, 1992). These same prejudices, if they exist, may affect police activities in such a way that they may translate to higher arrest rates for minorities (Rosenfeld, Rojek, & Decker, 2011). If this occurs, official crime data may be misleading when it comes to understanding the relationship between ethnicity and crime. One strength of the current chapter is that it will examine police data as well as victimisation survey data in order to understand the relationship between ethnicity and crime. As such, the current chapter will be able to determine whether there is concordance between official crime data and other sources of data.

The concepts of race and ethnicity in Trinidad and Tobago

The classification of race and ethnicity also poses special challenges in Trinidad and Tobago. In the distant past when persons of East Indian descent came to work as indentured labourers on the sugar cane plantations, there were distinct racial and ethnic groups which interacted only infrequently. Newly freed African slaves were culturally and racially distinct, as were the plantation owners and aristocracy who were of European origin. This led authors such as Smith (1965) to describe Trinidad and Tobago as a *plural society*. More recently, authors have argued that distinct ethnic groups no longer exist in Trinidad and Tobago. They have explained that processes of acculturation and interculturation have resulted in a *Trinbagonian* culture which applies regardless of phenotypical differences. As such, while there are distinct racial groups in Trinidad and Tobago, some authors have argued that there is only one culture. At the same time, however, others have argued that the continuance of different cultural practices by different racial groups (e.g. adherence to specific religions, types of cuisine) imply that there are several distinct ethnic groups in Trinidad and Tobago. As such, while phenotypical differences may allow researchers to identify different races (though even this may also be difficult) the classification of ethnicity is even more complex as there is no clear agreement on the issue of ethnicity in Trinidad and Tobago.

In Trinidad and Tobago, it is also not clear if there is an alignment of ethnicity and race. This may have been the case shortly after Indian indentured labourers came to the country more than a hundred and fifty years ago but does not apply today. As such, it may not be possible to make inferences about ethnicity from the race of a person. It is also doubtful that there is only one distinct culture/ethnicity in Trinidad and Tobago. The colonial leaders of the past segregated persons of East Indian and African descent into different communities. This segregation still persists today partly because of land ownership and inheritance patterns. The system of schooling, with religious and state schools, also serves to segregate persons by race. Race is still closely aligned with religion in Trinidad and Tobago, and where schools are governed by specific religious boards, the majority of students tend to be of one race. Despite this, persons of different races interact in the society at large, but not to the extent that it could be said that there is only one ethnicity. The observation that crime patterns have exhibited spatial stability, with some areas consistently having high crime rates and others low crime rates (Maguire, Willis, Snipes, & Gantley, 2008; Seepersad, 2015), suggests that cultural/ethnic differences may play a role in the stability of crime patterns. It should be noted however, that this has not been empirically tested, and indeed, other factors such as the spatial distribution of poverty, unemployment patterns and the like could also plausibly account for the observed patterns of crimes in different communities.

In order to understand the relationship between ethnicity and crime one must first be able to measure ethnicity. There are several challenges in doing so in Trinidad and Tobago, and these must be understood within the current context as they create potential limitations for data analysis and the interpretation of findings. As indicated earlier, there is no agreement on which ethnicities exist in Trinidad and Tobago, with some authors arguing that there is only one ethnicity. Despite this, other authors have argued that the persistence of distinct cultural practices by specific racial groups (e.g. adherence to specific religions) signals that there is still some level of overlap between race and ethnicity, that there are distinct ethnic groups in Trinidad and Tobago and these could be distinguished in a fairly reliable way based on the race of the persons concerned (England, 2010; Warikoo, 2005). In contrast, others have argued that there need not be an overlap between race and ethnicity and that specific communities may exhibit specific cultural traits and practices which support the possibility that distinct ethnic groups may exist in specific communities. Seepersad and Williams (2016) have made this argument by drawing on subcultural theories of crime to explain higher levels of criminal offending in communities with the presence of criminal gangs.

Without clear and agreed upon definitions of ethnicity, measurement becomes problematic. Researchers and data collection agencies which attempt to collect data on ethnicity have adopted an approach where they allow respondents to self-identify to which ethnic group they belong. The Central Statistical Office, for example, uses the categories of African, East Indian, Mixed (one parent of African and the other of East Indian descent), Mixed (other), Indigenous, Chinese, Caucasian, Syrian/Lebanese, Portuguese, and Other racial groups. In addition to the categories listed above CAPA has included the classifications of *Dougla*, *Mulatto*, and *Spanish*, along with several nationalities such as German, English, and Columbian. It should be noted that the term Spanish in Trinidad and Tobago is usually used to denote a person of African descent who has a light skin colour or a person who has South American ancestry. The many classifications listed above, coupled with the idiosyncratic use of various terms, may lead to a situation where there is a lack of clarity regardless of whether the classification is done by an agency or via self-report. In addition to this it is also unclear whether respondents and victims are reporting on their race or ethnicity when they respond to items intended to measure their ethnicity.

The present chapter is exploratory in nature and aims to examine official as well as victimisation survey data to determine whether there is a relationship between ethnicity and crime victimisation in Trinidad and Tobago. If such differences are found to exist, potential explanations for such differences will be offered. It is important to point out here that this chapter does not look at the relationship between ethnicity and the perpetration of criminal offences. Indeed, with the exception of murder, the TTPS does not collect data on the ethnicity of the perpetrator. While the majority of international literature has focused on racial disparities in criminal offending, much fewer studies have focused on racial disparities in criminal victimisation. In this regard, while the explanations for observed racial disparities in criminal offending are well-known, there is less certainty about the reasons for racial disparities in crime victimisation.

Data and method

The present chapter examined official crime data for murder, woundings and shooting, robbery, sexual offences, burglaries and break-ins, larceny and larceny of motor vehicles, and domestic violence. Official crime data contain only crimes which were reported or known to the police. Ethnicity data for murder were available from 2001 to 2013, while for domestic violence data were available from 2012 to 2014. Data for all other crimes were available from 2010 to 2014. Data from the 2012 United Nations Development Programme (UNDP) and 2014 American Barometers victimisation surveys will also be examined. Official crime data were sourced from the Trinidad and Tobago Police Service (TTPS), and like the victimisation survey data, contained details of each offence, including the ethnicity of the victim. Both types of data will be used to compute victimisation rates and a comparison of the findings from official data and victimisation survey data will be made. The present chapter is exploratory and hopes to determine whether some ethnicities are over-represented among victims of specified crimes. The chapter will also attempt to determine whether there are systematic patterns of over-representation and will offer explanations for the observed differences among ethnicities.

Results

Murder

CAPA has collected data on the ethnicity of the victims for several serious crimes, and in the case of murder, has also collected data on the ethnicity of the alleged offender. Almost three-quarters (73.7 per cent) of all murder victims for the 2001 to 2013 period were of African descent. Persons of East Indian descent made up the next largest group of victims (17.7 per cent) followed by persons of Mixed descent (6.6 percent) and Other ethnicities (2 per cent). Persons of Caucasian (19 or 0.4 per cent), Chinese (15 or 0.3 per cent), and Spanish descent (11 or 0.2 per cent) were the numerically largest groups within the Other category. In contrast to this, the 2011 census indicated that persons of African descent account for 34.2 per cent of the population, while persons of East Indian descent make up 35.4 per cent, persons of Mixed descent 22.8 per cent, and persons of Other ethnicities 7.6 per cent. Figure 4.1 shows the trends in ethnicity of murder victims for the period from 2001 to 2013. For this period there has been a gradual increase in the proportion of victims who were of African descent. During the same period there was a gradual decrease in the proportion of victims who were of East Indian and Mixed descent.

Arrest rates also differed according to the ethnicity of the victim. For the period from 2001 to 2013, an arrest was made in 22.8 per cent of all murders. With respect to the ethnicity of the victim, detection rates were lower for victims of African descent, compared to victims of Other ethnicities. Arrests were made in 19.1 per cent of all murders where the victim was of African descent. This compared to a

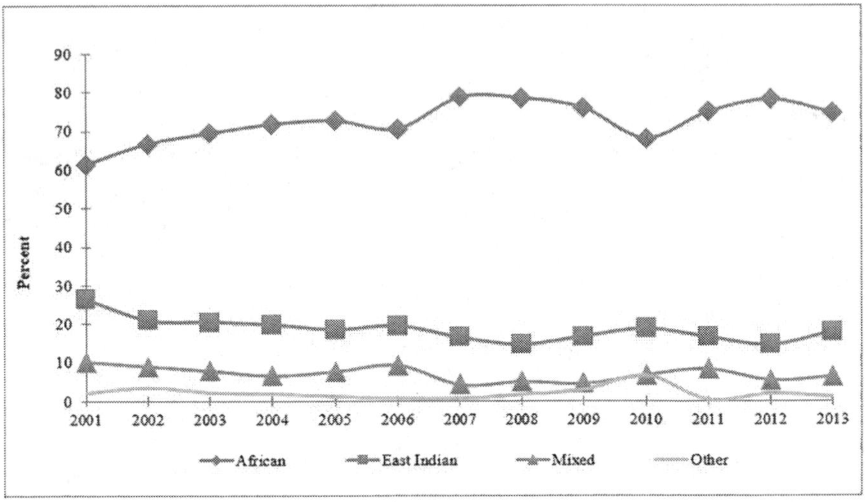

Figure 4.1 Ethnicity of murder victims (2001–2013)

Table 4.1 Cross tabulation of gender and ethnicity of murder victims (2001–2013)

	Victim ethnicity			
	African	*East Indian*	*Mixed*	*Other*
Male	92.4%	81.2%	85.3%	82.6%
Female	7.6%	18.8%	14.7%	17.4%

Note: Data Source: TTPS.

detection rate of 37.7 per cent for victims who were East Indians, 24.4 per cent for victims of Mixed ethnicity and 28.6 per cent for victims of Other ethnicities. These differences were statistically significant; $F(3,4.52) = 44.1, p < .001$.

Table 4.1 shows a cross-tabulation of the ethnicities and gender of all murder victims for the period from 2001 to 2013. The data indicated that where victims were of African descent, the disparity between males and females is larger than when the victims were of Other ethnicities. More specifically, when the victims were of African descent, 92.4 per cent were male while 7.6 per cent were female. In contrast, 81.2 per cent of victims of East Indian descent were male, while 85.3 per cent of victims of Mixed ethnicity were male and 82.6 per cent of victims of Other ethnicities were male. Overall these findings indicated that where victims are of African descent there was a greater likelihood that they would be male compared to if they were of Other ethnicities.

Analysis of variance (ANOVA) indicated that murder victims of different ethnic backgrounds had significantly different ages; $F(3, 4286) = 32.6, p < .001$. When

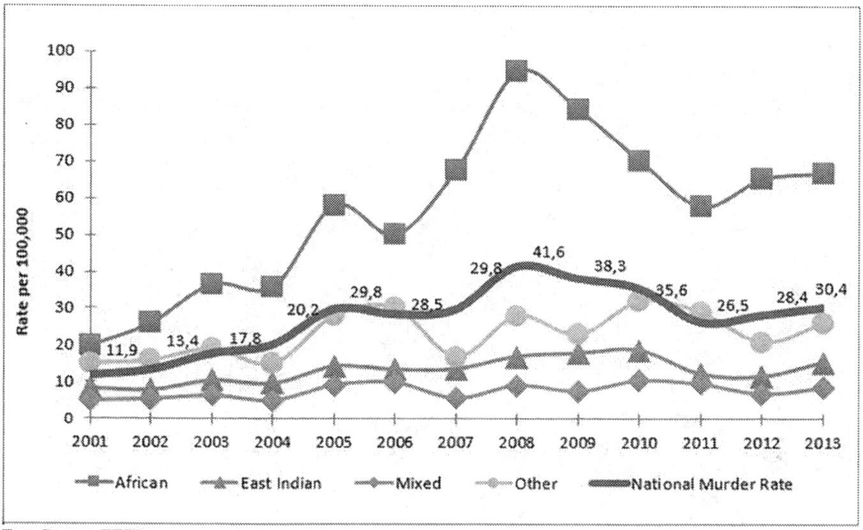

Data Source: TTPS.

Figure 4.2 Murder rates, by ethnicity of the victim (2001–2013)

all murders for the period from 2001 to 2013 were considered, victims of African and Mixed ethnicities had a younger average age than persons of East Indian or Other ethnicities. More specifically, victims of African descent had an average age of 32.0 years (*SD* = 12.9), while persons of Mixed descent had an average age of 32.3 years (*SD* = 14.1). In contrast, victims of East Indian descent had an average age of 36.9 years (*SD* = 14.9), while persons of Other ethnicities had an average age of 39.6 years (*SD* = 17.6).

Figure 4.2 compares the murder rates of persons of various ethnicities to the national murder rate for the period from 2001 to 2013. By far, persons of African descent had the highest murder rates, with the rate approaching 100 murders per 100,000 persons in 2008. Persons of East Indian and Mixed descent had murder rates which were below the national rate for the entire period under consideration. While persons of Other ethnicities experienced a comparably lower number of murders, their murder rate was higher than that of persons of East Indian and Mixed descent for each year of the period under consideration, and was comparable to the national rate for most years.

Woundings and shootings

Data on the victims of wounding and shooting were available from 2010 to 2014. During this period, 2,837 woundings and shootings were recorded. In these incidents, 3,218 victims were involved. The largest proportion of victims was of African descent (66.6 per cent). This was followed by persons of East Indian descent (15.6 per cent), Mixed (10.9 per cent), and Other ethnicities (7 per cent).

The distribution of victims in the Other category was as follows: Dougla (1.9 per cent), Spanish (0.4 per cent), Chinese (0.2 per cent), Caucasian (0.1 per cent), and Mulatto (0.1 per cent). The ethnic distribution of victims was similar for each year under consideration (Figure 4.3).

Figure 4.4 shows wounding and shooting rates according to the ethnicity of the victim for the period from 2010 to 2014. Persons of African descent very consistently

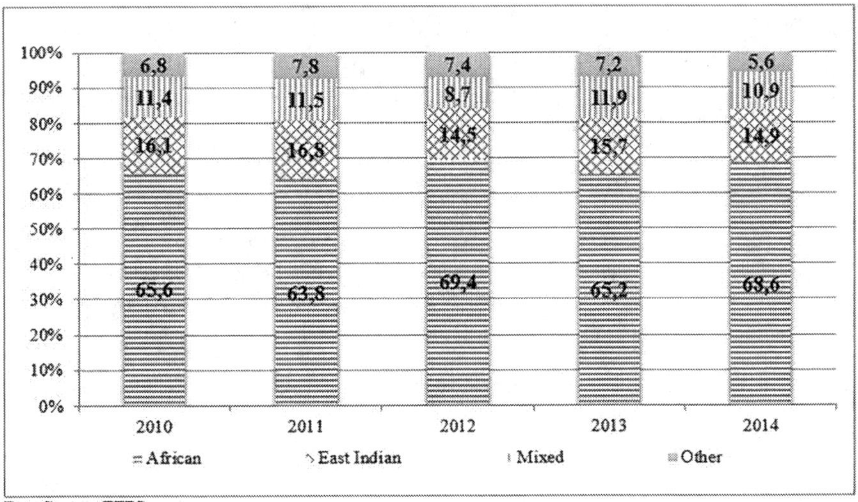

Data Source: TTPS.

Figure 4.3 Ethnicity of wounding and shooting victims (2010–2014)

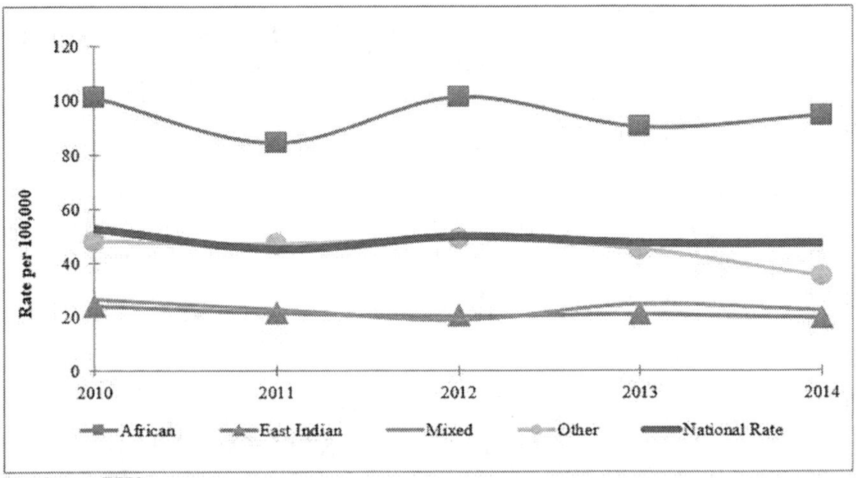

Data Source: TTPS.

Figure 4.4 Wounding and shooting rates, by ethnicity of the victim (2010–2014)

had the highest rates for all years under consideration. The average wounding and shooting victimisation rate for persons of African descent during this period was 94.3 incidents per 100,000 persons. This compares to a national rate of 48.5 per 100,000. Persons of East Indian and Mixed descent had the lowest rates for the period under consideration. The average rate for persons of East Indian descent for the 2010 to 2014 period was 21.3 incidents per 100,000 persons while the average rate for persons of Mixed descent was 23.1. Persons of Other ethnicities had rates which were very close to the national rate (48.1 incidents per 100,000 persons).

Robbery

Data on the victims of robbery were available for the period from 2010 to 2014. During this period, there were 18,859 robberies recorded with 22,875 victims. The victims experienced a range of crimes including assault with intent to rob (3.3 per cent of the victims), attempted robbery (0.1 per cent), robbery (3 per cent), robbery with aggravation (58.6 per cent), and robbery with violence (34.9 per cent). With respect to ethnicity, 40.4 per cent of all victims were of African descent, 38.2 per cent were of East Indian descent, 13.3 per cent were of Mixed descent, and 5.2 per cent were of Other ethnicities. The distribution of victims within the Other category was Caucasians (1.4 per cent), Dougla (1.4 per cent), Chinese (1.2 per cent), and Spanish (0.8 per cent). The ethnicities of 2.9 per cent of the victims were unknown. The ethnic distribution of victims was similar for each year of the period under consideration (Figure 4.5).

Figure 4.6 shows the robbery rates by ethnicity of the victim for the 2010 to 2014 period. Persons of African, East Indian, and Other ethnicities had rates which

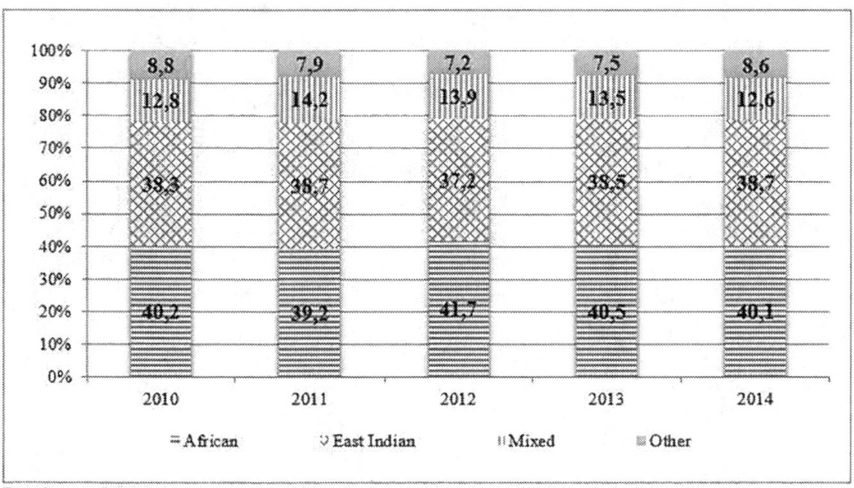

Data Source: TTPS.

Figure 4.5 Ethnicity of robbery victims (2010–2014)

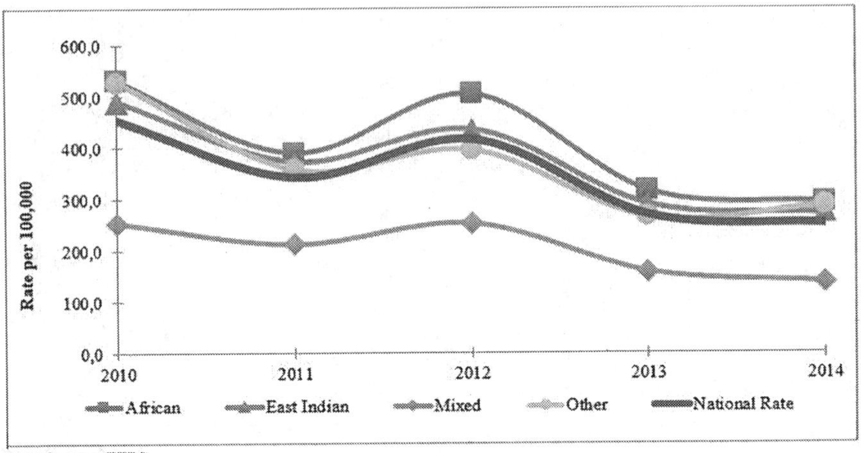

Data Source: TTPS.

Figure 4.6 Robbery rates, by ethnicity of the victim (2010–2014)

were very similar to the national rates. On average, the national robbery rate for the entire period under consideration was 344.5 incidents per 100,000 inhabitants. Persons of African descent had an average rate of 406.6, while persons of East Indian descent had an average rate of 371.5 and persons of Other ethnicities had an average rate of 365.4. Persons of Mixed ethnicity, in contrast, had a rate which was lower than the national average (202.6 incidents per 100,000 persons).

Cross-tabulation of the gender and ethnicity of all robbery victims for the period from 2010 to 2014 indicated that where victims were of African and East Indian descent, a larger proportion were males, compared to where victims were of Mixed or Other ethnicities. More specifically, where victims were of African descent, 70.6 per cent were male while 72.9 per cent of East Indian victims were male. In contrast, 63.8 per cent of Mixed victims were male, while 67.5 per cent of victims of Other ethnicities were male. Cross-tabulation of the type of offence and ethnicity of the victim indicated that regardless of ethnicity, persons were equally likely to become victims of different types of robbery. For example, 3.3 per cent of all victims for the 2010 to 2014 period were victims of assault with intent to rob. When assault with intent to rob was disaggregated by ethnicity, 3.3 per cent of victims were of African descent, 3 per cent were East Indian, 3.5 per cent were Mixed, and 4.9 per cent were of Other ethnicities. Similar equity applies to the other types of robbery.

Sexual offences

Detailed incident data for sexual offences were available for the period from 2010 to 2014. During this period there were 3,361 incidents recorded of which the most prevalent were sex with a female between the ages of 14 to 16 (30.1 per cent of all incidents), rape (27.4 per cent), grievous sexual assault (19.3 per cent) and sex with a female under the age of 14 (11.3 per cent). Less prevalent sexual offences included serious indecency (3.9 per cent), incest (3.7 per cent), and buggery (2.7 per cent). One point six per cent of the incidents were comprised of a range of other offences including attempted rape (0.6 per cent), sex with an adopted minor (0.4 per cent), sexual assault (0.2 per cent), failing to report a sexual offence (0.1 per cent), and sex with a mentally subnormal person (0.1 per cent).

For the period from 2010 to 2014, the largest proportion of incidents involved victims of African descent (43.9 per cent), followed by persons of East Indian descent (26.2 per cent), Mixed ethnicity (19.5 per cent), Dougla (2.6 per cent), Caucasian (0.7 per cent) and Spanish descent (0.2 per cent). The remaining 6.9 per cent of the incidents involved victims of other ethnicities. Figure 4.7 shows the ethnic distribution of the victims of all sexual offence incidents for each year of the period under consideration. While there was some fluctuation from year to year, persons of African descent consistently comprised the majority of victims for each year from 2010 to 2014. Persons of East Indian descent made up the next largest group of victims with the exception of 2011 where there were a larger proportion of victims of Mixed ethnicity (24.9 per cent) than persons of East Indian descent (23.9 per cent). Persons of Mixed descent, on average, were the third largest group, followed by persons of Other ethnicities.

Figure 4.8 shows the sexual offence rates according to ethnicity of the victim for each year of the 2010 to 2014 period, and compares these rates to the national rates. Persons of African and Other ethnicities very consistently had victimisation rates which were somewhat higher than the national rate for each year of the period under consideration. In contrast, persons of East Indian and Mixed ethnicities had

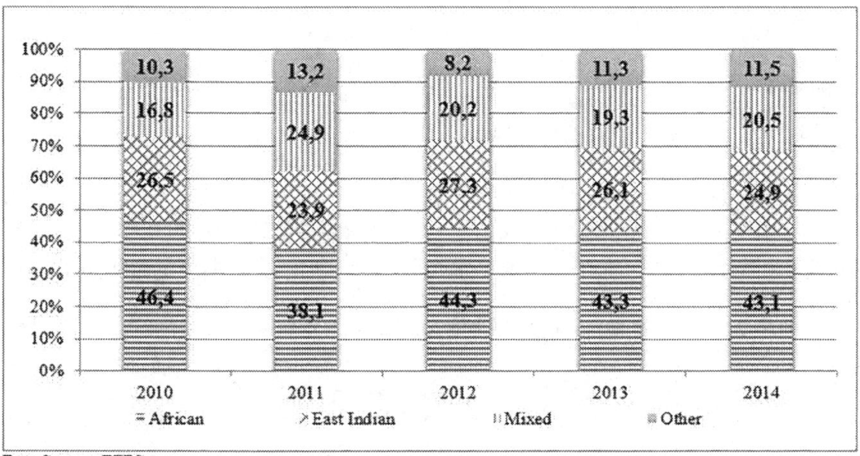

Data Source: TTPS.

Figure 4.7 Ethnicity of sexual offence victims (2010–2014)

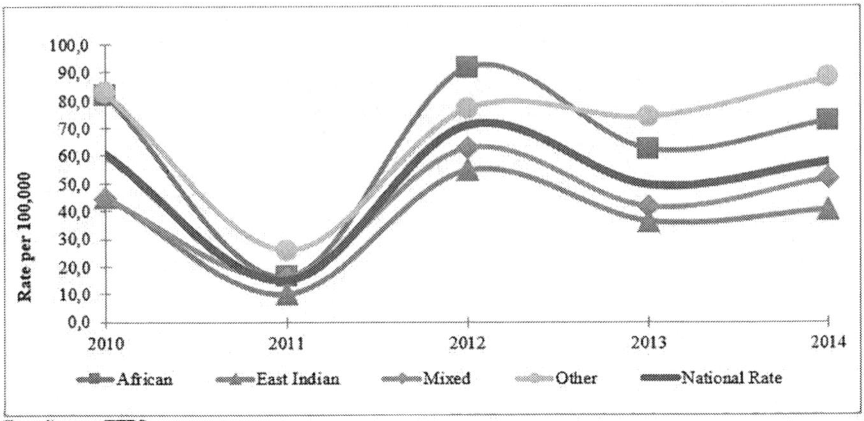

Data Source: TTPS.

Figure 4.8 Sexual offence rates, by ethnicity of the victim (2010–2014)

Table 4.2 Per cent of victims of specified sexual offences, by ethnicity (2010–2014)

	African	*East Indian*	*Mixed*	*Other*
Buggery	41.8	33.0	23.1	2.2
Incest	57.6	20.8	18.4	3.2
Serious indecency	40.8	30.0	26.2	3.1
Sex with female under 14 years	52.0	31.7	0.0	16.4
Grievous sexual assault	46.3	28.6	22.3	2.8
Rape	49.3	25.8	21.1	3.7
Sex with female 14–16 years old	32.4	22.3	23.3	22.0
Other sexual offences	62.3	28.3	5.7	3.8
Total	**43.9**	**26.2**	**19.5**	**10.4**

Note: Data Source: TTPS.

rates which were somewhat lower than the national average for each year. Overall, persons of African and Other ethnicities experienced the highest victimisation rates for sexual offences while persons of East Indian descent experienced the lowest rates.

Table 4.2 shows the proportion of victims of various ethnicities for specified sexual offences for the period from 2010 to 2014. Persons of African descent very consistently accounted for the largest proportion of victims for each of the sexual offences which are listed. For example, 49.3 per cent of all rape victims were of African descent, compared to 25.8 per cent who were East Indian, 21.1 per cent who were Mixed, and 3.7 per cent who were of Other ethnicities. Table 4.3 shows the rates for specified sexual offences according to the ethnicity of the victims.

Persons of African descent had the highest victimisation rates for six of the eight offences listed. In contrast, persons of Other ethnicities had the highest rates for sexual intercourse with a female under the age of 14 and within the 14 to 16 age range. Cross-tabulation of the ethnicity and gender of victims of sexual offences showed that regardless of ethnicity, females comprised the majority of victims. For example, when persons of African descent were considered, 97 per cent of the victims were female and when persons of East Indian descent were considered, 94.8 per cent of victims were female.

Burglary and break-ins

Detailed data on burglary and break-ins were available from 2010 to 2014. During this period, 19,307 incidents were recorded. Detailed data were available for 18,348 incidents or 95 per cent of all incidents. During this time the most prevalent offences were house break-ins and larceny (61.3 per cent of all incidents), burglary (10.4 per cent), shop break-ins and larceny (6.7 per cent), store break-ins and larceny (5.1 per cent) and house break-ins with intent (4 per cent). Persons of African descent represented the majority of victims during 2010 to 2014, accounting for 46 per cent of all victims. This was followed by persons of East Indian descent (32.1 per cent), Mixed descent (13.4 per cent), Caucasians (2.2 per cent) and Chinese (1.1 per cent). Figure 4.9 shows the ethnicity of victims of burglaries and break-ins for each year for the period from 2010 to 2014. These

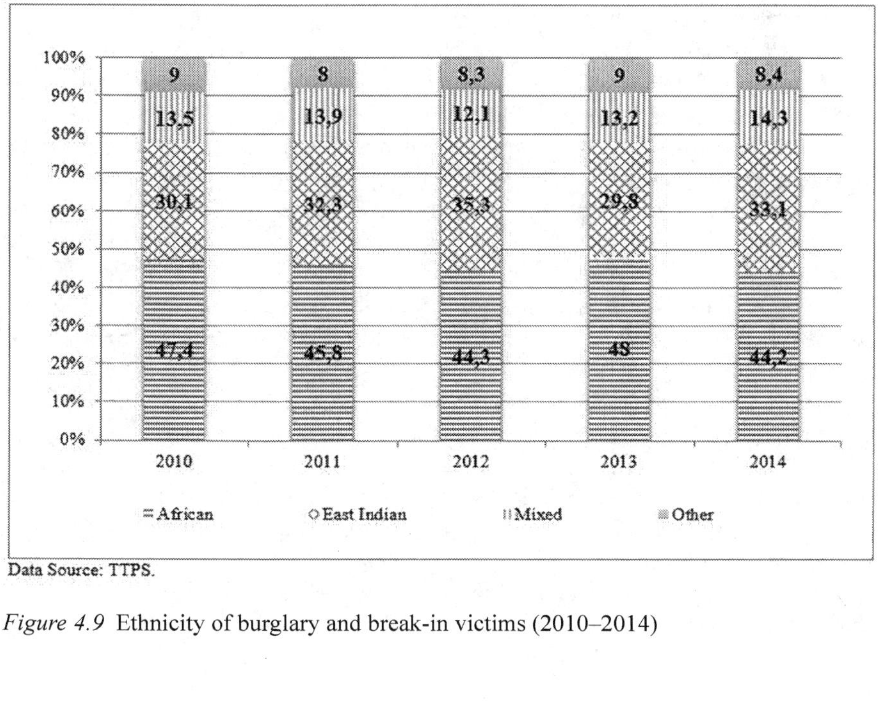

Data Source: TTPS.

Figure 4.9 Ethnicity of burglary and break-in victims (2010–2014)

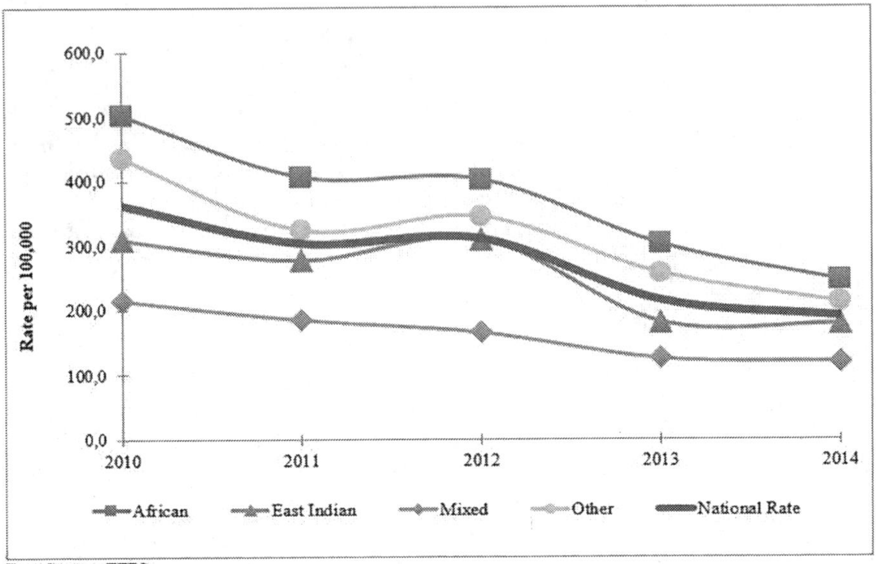

Data Source: TTPS.

Figure 4.10 Burglary and break-in rates, by ethnicity of the victim (2010–2014)

data indicated that the proportion of persons of each ethnicity was stable for all years of the period under consideration.

Figure 4.10 shows the burglary and break-in victimisation rates according to the ethnicity of the victim for each year of the period from 2010 to 2014. Persons of African and Other ethnicities had rates which were consistently higher than the national average for each year under consideration, whereas persons of East Indian and Mixed descent had rates which were lower than the national average. As is consistent with the overall national trends, the victimisation rates of all ethnic groups have declined from 2010 to 2014. It is noteworthy, however, that the ethnic disparity among victimisation rates has declined from 2010 to 2014. More specifically, the difference in victimisation rates among different ethnic groups was very clear in 2010 with persons of African descent having a rate of 502 incidents per 100,000 persons, compared to a rate of 434 for persons of Other ethnicities, 308 for persons of East Indian descent, and 214 for persons of Mixed descent. In 2014, in contrast, the rates for all ethnic groups were much more similar. More specifically, in 2014 the victimisation rate for persons of African descent was 245 incidents per 100,000 persons, compared to a rate of 211 for persons of Other ethnicities, 178 for persons of East Indian descent, and 120 for persons of Mixed descent.

Table 4.3 shows the average annual victimisation rates for specified burglary and break-in offences according to the ethnicity of the victim for the period from

Table 4.3 Average annual rates for specified sexual offences, burglary and break-in offences, and larceny and larceny of motor vehicle offences by ethnicity of the victim (2010–2014)

	African	*East Indian*	*Mixed*	*Other*
Sexual Offences				
Buggery	1.7	1.3	1.4	0.4
Incest	3.2	1.1	1.5	0.8
Serious indecency	2.3	1.7	2.2	0.8
Sex with female under 14 years	8.7	5.1	0.0	12.4
Grievous sexual assault	13.2	7.9	9.6	3.6
Rape	20.0	10.1	12.9	6.8
Sex with female 14–16 years old	14.4	9.6	15.6	44.4
Other sexual offences	1.5	0.6	0.2	0.4
Total rate	**65.0**	**37.4**	**43.4**	**69.6**
Burglary and Break-in offences				
School breaking and larceny	1.9	1.0	0.8	1.6
Storeroom breaking and larceny	1.7	1.4	1.1	1.2
Sacrilege	2.9	1.9	0.5	1.8
Attempted breaking with intent	2.9	1.8	2.6	3.6
Breaking with intent	3.4	3.0	1.1	3.8
Pavilion breaking and larceny	4.8	5.5	3.0	8.4
Office breaking and larceny	7.5	6.8	3.8	11.8
Warehouse breaking and larceny	10.3	13.4	5.3	14.4
House breaking with intent	16.8	7.8	6.7	12.4
Store breaking and larceny	12.7	18.5	6.9	20.2
Shop breaking and larceny	25.0	18.5	6.7	26.0
Burglary	37.8	24.5	18.9	37.2
House breaking and larceny	240.7	144.0	102.4	168.2
Other	2.7	2.2	1.9	3.0
Total Rate	**371.3**	**250.5**	**161.7**	**313.6**
Larceny and larceny of motor vehicles offences				
Larceny	233.6	191.4	113.8	198.4
Larceny motor vehicle	95.9	77.5	45.8	63.2
Larceny from motor vehicle	5.9	3.1	2.6	7.2
Larceny from the person	41.8	27.5	23.7	26.8
Tampering with motor vehicle	0.4	0.5	0.3	0.2
Total rate	**377.5**	**300.1**	**186.2**	**295.8**

Note: Data Source: TTPS.

2010 to 2014. When all offences were considered simultaneously, persons of African descent had the highest overall rate (371.3 incidents per 100,000 persons per annum). They were followed by persons of Other ethnicities (313.6), East Indian descent (250.5), and Mixed descent (161.7). When individual offences are considered, persons of African descent had the highest rates for six of the 14 offences listed while persons of Other ethnicities had the highest rates for eight offences. Persons of East Indian and Mixed descent did not have the highest rates for any offence listed. When all victims of burglaries and break-ins for the 2010 to 2014 period were considered simultaneously, 58.6 per cent were male while 41.4 per cent were female. Cross-tabulation showed that this gender disparity held regardless of ethnic background of the victim, though persons of East Indian and Other ethnic backgrounds had a somewhat larger gender disparity than persons of African or Mixed ethnicity.

Larceny

Detailed incident data were available for 19,939 larceny and larceny of motor vehicle offences for the period from 2010 to 2014. This represented 95.6 per cent of all such offences during this period. These data indicated that the largest proportion of offences within this crime category was larcenies, which accounted for 62.8 per cent of all offences. This was followed by larceny of motor vehicles (25.1 per cent) and larceny from the person (10.5 per cent). For the period from 2010 to 2014 the majority of victims of larcenies were of African descent (43 per cent). They were followed by persons of East Indian (35.4 per cent), Mixed (14.2 per cent), Caucasian (2.1 per cent), Dougla (1 per cent), Chinese (0.7 per cent), and Spanish (0.6 per cent) ethnicity. Figure 4.11 shows the ethnicity of larceny and larceny of motor vehicle victims for each year of the period from 2010 to 2014. There was relative stability in the proportion of victims of different ethnic backgrounds for each year under consideration. Figure 4.12 shows the average annual rates for larceny and larceny of motor vehicles according to the ethnicity of the victim for each year of the period from 2010 to 2014. The national rates are also shown. The data indicated that persons of African descent had the highest rates while persons of Mixed descent consistently had the lowest rates. Persons of

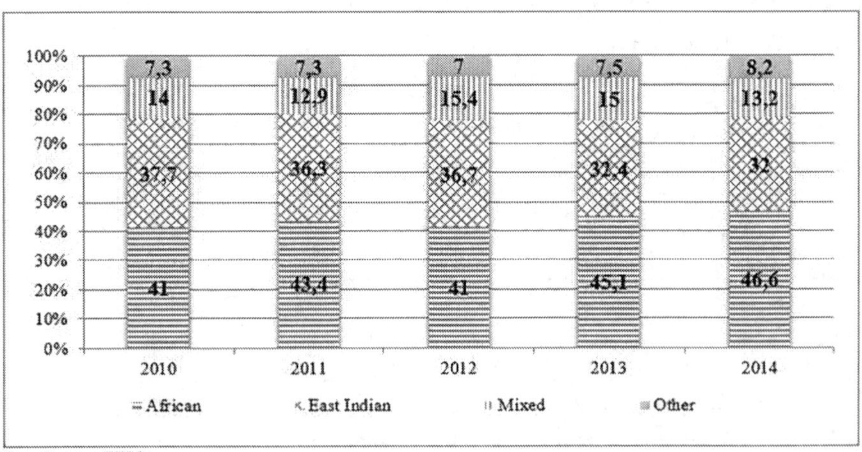

Figure 4.11 Ethnicity of larceny and larceny of motor vehicle victims (2010–2014)

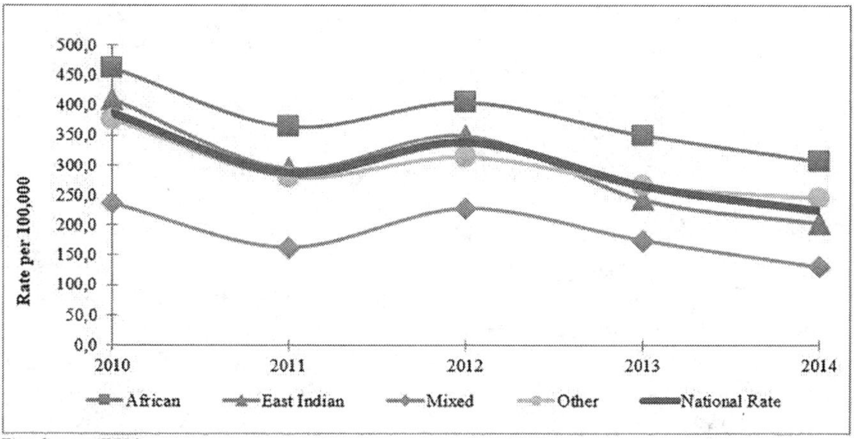

Data Source: TTPS.

Figure 4.12 Larceny and larceny of motor vehicle rates, by ethnicity of the victim (2010–2014)

East Indian and Other ethnicities had rates which were very close to the national average for all years under consideration.

Table 4.3 shows the average annual victimisation rates according to the ethnicity of the victim for specific larceny offences. When all offences were considered simultaneously, persons of African descent had the highest rates (377.5 incidents per 100,000 persons), followed by persons of East Indian (300.1), Other (295.8), and Mixed ethnicity (186.2). When separate offences were considered, persons of African descent had the highest rates for three of the five offences (larceny, larceny of motor vehicles, and larceny from the person). In contrast, persons of East Indian and Other ethnicities had the highest rates for one offence each. Persons of Mixed ethnicity did not have the highest rates for any offence. It is noteworthy that larceny and larceny of motor vehicles made up the bulk of offences (62.8 per cent and 25.1 per cent, respectively). This indicates that persons of African descent were disproportionately affected by two of the most frequently occurring and serious crimes listed in Table 4.3. When all victims of larceny for the period from 2010 to 2014 were considered, 72.1 per cent were male and 27.9 per cent were female. Cross tabulation revealed that this gender disparity held regardless of the ethnicity of the victim.

Domestic violence

Detailed data for reported cases of domestic violence were recorded by the Crime and Problem Analysis branch of the TTPS as of 2012. During the period from 2012 to 2014, 5,407 incidents of domestic violence were recorded. Of these 2,713 cases (50.2 per cent) were assaults and beatings. This was followed by threats (36.6 per cent), breach of protection orders (7.8 per cent), verbal abuse (2.1 per cent), psychological abuse (2.1 per cent), malicious woundings (1.1 per cent), and acts against children (0.1 per cent). It should be noted here that several reports of victimisation could be made by the same person. The data provided by CAPA, however, did not contain personally identifying information so it was not possible to avoid a potential *double counting* issue which could occur when examining the relationship between ethnicity and domestic violence victimisation. As such, the findings here should be considered with appropriate caution as they assessed the relationship between ethnicity and reports of domestic violence incidents, but did not assess the relationship between ethnicity and the proportion of victims who experienced domestic violence within any given year. It is also important to note that the data contained only incidents of domestic violence which were reported to the police. If specific racial groups are less willing to report such incidents, then by itself this could result in racial differences in victimisation levels. Finally, murder was not included in the data supplied by CAPA as incidents of domestic disputes which result in the death of any party is classified as a murder. For the period from 2000 to 2013, 329 murders (6.9 per cent of all murders) were due to domestic violence.

When all incidents of domestic violence for the period from 2012 to 2014 were considered, persons of East Indian descent were victims in 41.9 per cent of cases. This was followed by persons of African (38.4 per cent), Mixed (16.3 per cent), Spanish (0.5 per cent), Caucasian (0.3 per cent), and Chinese (0.1 per cent) descent. Figure 4.13 shows the ethnicity of victims for each year of the period from 2012 to 2014. The proportion of victims of various ethnicities was similar for each year under consideration. Figure 4.14 shows the

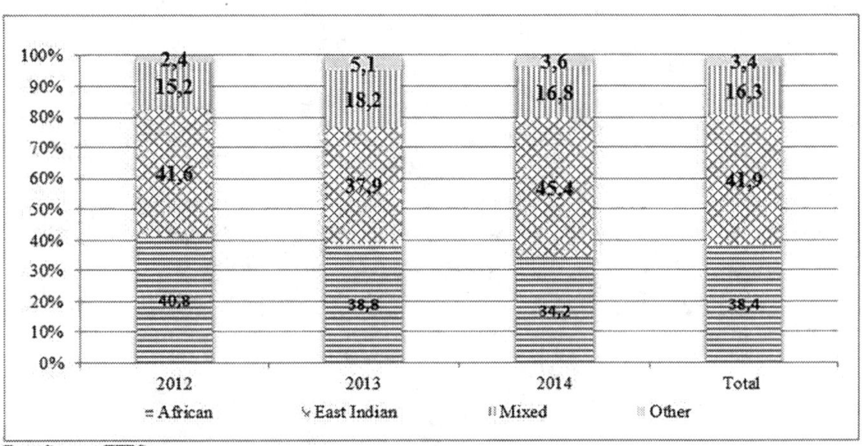

Data Source: TTPS

Figure 4.13 Ethnicity of domestic violence victims (2012–2014)

domestic violence victimisation rates according to the ethnicity of the victim for each year of the period under consideration. The national rate is also shown. When all incidents of domestic violence for the period from 2012 to 2014 were considered, the average national victimisation rate was 135.7 incidents per 100,000 persons. Persons of East Indian descent had the highest victimisation rate (160.5 per 100,000 persons). The only other group with a victimisation rate higher than the national average was persons of African descent, who had a victimisation rate of 152.2. Persons of Mixed descent had a victimisation rate of 97.2. This was followed by persons of Caucasian (60) and Chinese (25.1) descent. Figure 4.14 indicates that persons of African and East Indian descent had similar victimisation rates for 2012 and 2013, but persons of East Indian descent surpassed persons of African descent in 2014. Persons of Mixed and Other ethnicities had victimisation rates which were lower than the national rate for all years under consideration, with persons of Other ethnicities consistently having the lowest rates.

Table 4.4 shows the annual average rates for specific domestic violence offences for the period from 2012 to 2014. Persons of East Indian descent had the highest rates for breach of protection orders, threats, and verbal abuse. In contrast, persons of African descent had the highest rates for assault and beating, malicious wounding, and psychological abuse. Persons of Other ethnicities had the highest rates for offences against children. When all domestic violence offences for the period from 2012 to 2014 were considered, 75.4 per cent of victims were female while 24.6 per cent were male. Cross tabulation showed that this disparity held regardless of the ethnicity of the victim, though the disparity is somewhat larger for persons of Mixed ethnicity.

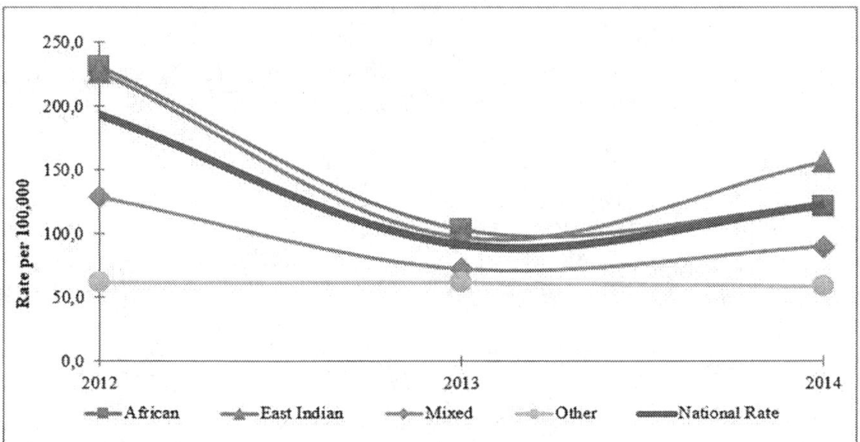

Data Source: TTPS.

Figure 4.14 Domestic violence rates, by ethnicity of the victim (2012–2014)

Table 4.4 Average annual rates for specified domestic violence offences, by ethnicity of the victim (2012–2014)

	African	*East Indian*	*Mixed*	*Other*
Assault and beating	81.0	72.0	54.9	31.0
Breach of protection order	8.5	16.0	7.4	4.7
Children act offences	0.1	0.0	0.0	0.7
Malicious wounding	2.0	1.3	1.3	0.3
Psychological abuse	3.3	3.2	2.0	1.3
Threats	54.4	63.3	30.6	22.3
Verbal abuse	2.9	4.5	1.1	0.7
Total rate	**152.2**	**160.5**	**97.2**	**61.0**

Note: Data Source: TTPS.

Table 4.5 summarises the findings from the official crime data which were examined and shows the per cent of victims and victimisation rates by ethnicity of the victim for specified serious crimes in Trinidad and Tobago. Data for all offences were based on reported crimes for the period from 2010 to 2014, except for murder which was based on offences from 2001 to 2013 and domestic violence which was based on data from 2012 to 2014.

The 2011 census indicated that 34.2 per cent of the population were of African descent, while 35.4 per cent were East Indian, 22.8 per cent were Mixed, and 7.6 per cent were of Other ethnicities. Invariably the data in Table 4.5 show that persons of African descent were victimised at rates which were substantially higher than their representation in the population. This over-representation applies to all seven crimes that were considered, but is especially pronounced for murder and wounding and shooting. Persons of East Indian descent were over-represented as victims of robbery and domestic violence. Persons of Mixed ethnicity were not over-represented as victims of any crime while persons of Other ethnicities were over-represented as victims of sexual offences and burglaries and break-ins.

Concerning the victimisation rates, the average national murder rate for the period from 2001 to 2013 was 27.1 murders per 100,000 inhabitants. The only ethnic groups with rates above the national average were persons of African descent with a rate of 56.4 and persons of Chinese descent with a rate of 30.1. The average wounding and shooting rate for the period from 2010 to 2014 was 48.5 incidents per 100,000 inhabitants. Persons of African descent had a rate of 94.3, while all other ethnic groups had a rate which was below the national average. The average robbery rate for the period from 2010 to 2014 was 344.5 incidents per 100,000 inhabitants. Persons of Chinese descent had the highest rate (1,381 incidents per 100,000). Persons of Caucasian, African, and East Indian descent also had rates which exceeded the national average. The average rate for sexual offences for the period from 2010 to 2014 was 50.6 offences per 100,000 inhabitants. Persons of African and Caucasian descent had rates which exceeded the national rate. The average burglary and break-in rate for the period from 2010 to 2014 was 276.3

Table 4.5 Per cent of victims, and victimisation rates by ethnic background of victims

	National	*African*		*East Indian*		*Mixed*		*Other*		*Caucasian*		*Chinese*	
	Rate	*%*	*Rate*	*%*	*Rate*	*%*	*Rate*	*%*	*Rate*	*%*	*Rate*	*%*	*Rate*
Murder	27.1	73.3	56.4	17.7	13.1	6.6	7.6	2.0	5.0	–	19.1	–	30.1
Wounding and shooting	48.5	66.6	94.3	15.6	21.3	10.9	23.1	6.9	48.1	–	10.2	–	40.2
Robbery	344.5	40.4	406.6	38.2	371.5	13.3	202.6	5.2	276.7	–	842.4	–	1380.5
Sexual offences	50.6	43.9	65.0	26.2	37.4	19.5	43.4	10.4	70.5	–	58.7	–	0.0
Burglary and break-ins	276.3	46.0	371.3	32.1	250.5	13.4	161.7	8.5	216.8	–	1044.0	–	1019.1
Larceny	300.3	43.0	377.5	35.4	300.1	14.2	186.2	7.4	216.8	–	1090.0	–	672.7
Domestic violence	135.7	38.4	152.2	41.9	160.5	16.3	97.2	3.4	62.7	–	60.0	–	25.1

Note: Data Source: TTPS; Percentages and victimisation rates for murder were computed using data from 2001 to 2013, while figures for all other crimes (except for domestic violence) were computed using data from 2010 to 2014; Domestic violence figures were computed using data from 2012 to 2014; Percentages refer to the per cent of victims who were of specified ethnicities; Percentages were not available concerning Caucasian and Chinese victims; Rates are per 100,000; As per the 2011 Census Report, 34.2 per cent of the population were of African descent, 35.4 per cent were East Indian descent, 22.8 per cent were Mixed, and 7.6 per cent were of Other ethnicities.

offences per 100,000 inhabitants. Persons of Caucasian and Chinese descent had the highest rates (1,044 and 1,019 offences per 100,000 respectively). Persons of African descent also had rates which exceeded the national average. The average rate for larceny and larceny of motor vehicles for the period from 2010 to 2014 was 300.3 offences per 100,000 inhabitants. Persons of Caucasian descent had the highest rate (1,090). Persons of Chinese and African descent also had rates which exceeded the national rate. The average rate for domestic violence for the period from 2012 to 2014 was 135.7 offences per 100,000 inhabitants. Persons of African and East Indian descent had the highest rates (152.2 and 160.5 respectively).

When all crimes are considered simultaneously, persons of African descent were victimised at rates which exceeded the national average for all seven crimes listed in Table 4.5. Persons of East Indian descent had rates which exceeded the national average for robbery and domestic violence. Persons of Mixed descent consistently had rates below the national average for all crimes which were considered. Persons of Caucasian descent had rates which exceeded the national average for robbery, sexual offences, burglary and break-ins, larceny and larceny of motor vehicles. Persons of Chinese descent had rates which exceeded the national average for murder, robbery, burglary and break-ins, larceny and larceny of motor vehicles.

Survey data

Official crime data represent reported crimes or crimes which are "known" to the police. Self-report and victimisation surveys have consistently demonstrated that many crimes are underreported. Such surveys thus provide an alternative – and some argue more accurate – means of assessing the true extent of crime in a given society. Unfortunately, victimisation surveys have not been carried out with any regularity in Trinidad and Tobago. One of the most representative surveys, conducted by the UNDP (2012), utilised a random sample of 1,595 adults in Trinidad and Tobago. This was part of a larger study that collected similar data from seven Caribbean countries with a total sample size of 11,155 persons. The UNDP sample was self-weighted by regional and gender distribution and was configured to be representative of the target population. With respect to ethnicity in the Trinidad and Tobago sample, 46.3 per cent of the respondents were of African descent, 28.5 per cent of East Indian descent, 21.3 per cent of Mixed descent, and 3.9 per cent of Other ethnicities. Self-reported victimisation survey data from the UNDP (2012) indicated that the rate of assault with a weapon was 11.9 times higher than reported in official crime statistics while the rate of financial crimes/scams was 7.2 times higher. Sexual assault and/or rape was found to be 6.6 times higher while domestic violence was 6.3 times higher. Robbery was 4.6 times higher while burglaries and break-ins were 4.1 times higher.

Table 4.6 shows the proportion of the sample that was victimised within the last 10 years for 18 specific offences. The most frequently occurring crime was robbery at gunpoint (5.6 per cent of the sample), followed by robbery with other types of weapons (3.8 per cent), break-ins in homes during the day (3.4 per cent), break-ins at night (2.5 per cent), assault with a weapon (2.3 per cent), theft from a motor

Table 4.6 Per cent of persons victimised within the last 10 years and within the last year in Trinidad and Tobago

Offence type	*Victimisation within the Last 10 Years*					*Victimisation within the Last Year*				
	Total	*African*	*East Indian*	*Mixed*	*Other*	*Total*	*African*	*East Indian*	*Mixed*	*Other*
Attempted murder	0.8	0.5	0.7	1.5	–	0.3	0.3	0.2	0.3	–
Assault with a weapon	2.3	2.6	1.5	2.6	3.2	1.1	1.5	0.4	1.2	1.6
Robbery at gunpoint	5.6	5.3	6.2	5.3	6.5	1.0	0.8	1.8	0.6	–
Robbery with other types of weapons	3.8	3.1	3.3	5.9	4.8	1.1	0.7	1.3	1.8	–
Sexual assault and or rape	0.4	0.3	0.7	0.6	–	0.4	0.1	0.4	1.2	–
Extortion/protection	0.3	0.1	0.4	0.6	–	0.2	–	0.2	0.6	–
Domestic violence involving a partner	0.9	1.2	0.2	1.2	–	0.6	0.8	–	0.9	1.6
Family violence	0.8	0.5	0.9	0.6	4.8	0.4	0.1	0.9	0.3	1.6
Break-in at your house in the day	3.4	2.7	2.9	4.4	9.7	1.8	1.9	1.3	2.1	3.2
A break-in at your house at night	2.5	2.2	2.4	2.4	8.1	0.2	1.1	1.1	1.2	3.2
Motor vehicle theft	1.1	1.1	0.4	1.8	3.2	0.3	0.1	0.4	0.6	–
Theft from motor vehicle	1.9	1.5	1.3	2.6	6.5	0.8	0.5	0.2	1.5	3.2
Kidnapping (for ransom)	0.1	–	0.2	–	–	–	–	–	–	–
Abduction	0.1	0.1	–	0.3	–	0.1	–	–	0.3	–
Financial crime/scam	0.6	0.3	0.9	0.9	–	0.3	0.3	0.4	0.3	–
Praedial larceny	0.9	1.1	1.1	0.6	–	0.9	1.1	0.9	0.6	–
Threat on your life (with a weapon)	0.9	1.1	0.2	0.9	4.8	0.4	0.3	0.4	–	3.2
Threat on your life (without a weapon)	0.5	0.3	0.4	0.6	3.2	0.2	0.1	0.2	–	1.6
Total victimisation level	**22.6**	**20.6**	**20.4**	**27.4**	**35.5**	**9.4**	**9.2**	**7.9**	**10.9**	**14.5**

Note: Data Source: UNDP 2012.

vehicle (1.9 per cent), and motor vehicle theft (1.1 per cent). For 11 other crimes that respondents reported, prevalence rates of victimisation were less than 1 per cent. Table 4.6 also disaggregates victimisation rates according to the ethnicity of the victim. Persons of Other ethnicities comprised the majority of victims for nine of the 18 crimes listed. Persons of Mixed ethnicity were in the majority for four crimes, while persons of East Indian descent were in the majority for two crimes. Three other crimes (domestic violence, financial crimes, and praedial larceny) had more than one ethnic group sharing the top spot where victimisation levels were concerned. Overall, 20.6 per cent of respondents of African descent were victimised within the last 10 years, compared to 20.4 per cent of East Indian, 27.4 per cent of Mixed, and 35.5 per cent of persons of Other ethnicities. ANOVA indicated that there were no ethnic differences in victimisation levels when persons of African and East Indian descent were compared, though persons of Mixed descent had higher levels of victimisation than persons of Other ethnicities ($F(2,1.53) = 3.51, p < .03$).

Respondents in the UNDP (2012) survey were also asked to indicate whether they were victimised within the last year (this refers to crimes committed in 2009 – see Table 4.6). It was discovered that 9.4 per cent of the sample were victims of a crime within the last year. With respect to ethnicity, 9.2 per cent of persons of African descent were victimised within the last year, compared to 7.9 per cent of East Indians, 10.9 per cent of Mixed persons, and 14.5 per cent of persons of Other ethnicities. When crimes within the last year were considered, persons of Other ethnicities had the highest victimisation levels for eight of the crimes listed in Table 4.6, while persons of Mixed ethnicity had the highest victimisation levels for five offences. In contrast, persons of East Indian descent had the highest levels for three crimes, while for one other crime, persons of East Indian and African descent held the top position. ANOVA indicated that overall there were no ethnic differences in victimisation levels when total crime victimisation within the past year was considered ($F(2,1.53) = 1.02$, *ns*).

Respondents were asked to indicate whether other persons in their households (i.e. not including themselves) were victims of crime within the last year (see Table 4.7). Within the last year, 11.5 per cent of households had one person other than the respondent who was victimised, 3.6 per cent had two persons who were victimised, 0.9 per cent had three persons who were victimised, and 0.6 per cent had more than three persons who were victimised. Overall, 16.6 per cent of households were victimised within the last year. When the ethnicity of the respondent was considered, 15.2 per cent of households with a respondent of African descent were victimised within the last year, compared to 17.6 per cent of households with East Indian respondents, 17.6 per cent of households with Mixed respondents, and 19.4 per cent of households with respondents of Other ethnicities. Households with respondents of African descent had the highest levels of victimisation for four of the 13 crimes listed in Table 4.7, while households with respondents of East Indian descent had the highest levels of victimisation for five crimes. In contrast, households with Mixed respondents and respondents of Other ethnicities each held the top spot for two crimes. ANOVA indicated that overall there were no ethnic differences in total household victimisation ($F(2,1.53) = 0.63$, *ns*).

Table 4.7 Per cent of households victimised in 2009

Offence type	*Total*	*African*	*East Indian*	*Mixed*	*Other*
Murder	1.4	0.8	1.8	2.4	–
Attempted murder	1.4	1.6	1.5	0.9	–
Assault with a weapon	3.9	4.3	4.4	2.9	1.6
Robbery	11.5	10.2	12.1	13.2	14.5
Sexual assault and/ or rape	1.1	1.2	1.5	0.3	–
Extortion and/or protection rackets	0.6	0.8	0.4	0.6	–
Domestic violence involving a partner	1.9	2.0	2.2	1.2	1.6
Other family violence	1.3	0.8	2.4	1.2	–
A threat on their life	2.6	2.6	2.9	2.6	–
Abduction	0.5	0.7	0.2	0.6	–
Kidnapping	0.6	0.8	0.4	0.6	–
Motor vehicle theft	2.7	1.9	2.6	4.4	3.2
Theft from motor vehicle	2.5	1.4	1.8	5.3	6.5
Total	**16.6**	**15.2**	**17.6**	**17.6**	**19.4**

Note: Data Source UNDP 2012 Victimisation Survey.

The 2014 American Barometers Survey was based on interviews with 49,738 respondents in 27 countries. As part of the broader project, 4,206 interviews were conducted with a representative sample of Trinidad and Tobago residents 18 years of age or older. Population estimates based on this sample were deemed to be accurate plus or minus 1.6 per cent, 99 times out of a hundred.

All respondents were asked to indicate whether they had been the victim of six different crimes in the past five years (see Table 4.8). The results indicated that Mixed ethnicity and Afro-Trinidadian respondents experienced a higher rate of criminal victimisation than East Indian respondents. Overall, 22.6 per cent of Mixed ethnicity and 21.6 per cent of respondents of African descent reported that they were victimised in the past five years, compared to only 15.8 per cent of East Indian respondents. This difference was statistically significant ($\chi^2(2) = 22.59, p < .001$). Respondents of African descent reported the highest rate of motor vehicle theft, physical assault, and threats. Mixed ethnicity respondents, on the other hand, reported the highest rates of burglary, robbery, and theft while East Indian respondents reported the lowest rates across all crimes. Statistical analyses, however, revealed that the ethnic differences with respect to motor vehicle theft and threats were not statistically significant.

Respondents were also asked whether they had experienced these six types of criminal victimisation in the past 12 months (see Table 4.8). The results suggested that one in seven Mixed ethnicity respondents had been victimised in the past year

Table 4.8 Per cent of respondents who have been a victim of crime within the past five years and past year, by ethnicity

Offence type	*Victimisation within past five years*					*Victimisation within past year*				
	African	*East Indian*	*Mixed*	*χ2*	*p*	*African*	*East Indian*	*Mixed*	*χ2*	*p*
Motor vehicle theft	5.4	3.7	4.1	5.55	.062	1.6	0.9	1.5	2.71	.258
Burglary/ Break and enter	6.5	4.6	7.6	10.20	.006	3.6	2.7	4.0	3.27	.202
Robbery	3.5	1.2	4.5	24.50	.001	1.8	0.4	1.7	15.07	.001
Theft	7.3	5.9	8.6	6.58	.032	3.5	2.7	5.1	9.40	.009
Physical assault	6.6	4.3	5.5	8.24	.016	3.4	1.7	2.9	9.13	.010
Threats of assault	4.7	3.6	4.2	2.10	.350	1.7	1.3	2.1	2.61	.272
Any victimisation	21.6	15.8	22.6	22.59	.001	11.8	7.5	14.5	30.74	.001
Household member a crime victim	–	–	–	–	–	8.2	5.6	6.2	9.67	.008
Sample size	**1,735**	**1,405**	**985**	–	–	**1,735**	**1,405**	**985**	–	–

Note: Data Source: 2014 American Barometers Survey.

(14.5 per cent), compared to 11.8 per cent of respondents of African descent and 7.5 per cent of East Indian respondents. This difference was statistically significant ($\chi^2(2) = 30.74, p < .001$). In terms of victimisation incidents which took place over the past year, respondents of African descent reported the highest rates of motor vehicle theft, robbery, and physical assault. Mixed respondents reported the highest rate of break and enter, theft, and threats. Statistical analyses, however, revealed that the ethnic differences with respect to car theft, break and enter, and threats were not statistically significant. Finally, respondents were asked if they knew whether any other member of their household had been the victim of a crime in the past year. Similar to the findings on personal victimisation, the data indicated that Mixed ethnicity (14.5 per cent) and respondents of African descent (11.8 per cent) were more likely to report the victimisation of other household members than East Indian respondents (7.5 per cent). This difference was also statistically significant ($\chi^2(2) = 9.665, p < .008$).

Discussion

The issue of ethnicity and crime is a troubling one internationally, as well as in the Caribbean. In the case of Trinidad and Tobago where the colonial past created a sense of distrust among different ethnic groups, this issue takes on special significance. Racial distrust could affect perceptions of various ethnic groups, leading to the possibility that some groups could be perceived as more crime-prone than other groups. Crime-proneness could be seen both in terms of perpetration and victimisation. Racial distrust could lead to prejudice as well as discrimination in the society at large, and in the criminal justice system in particular (Wortley, 1999). If law enforcement efforts and the access to justice are affected by racial biases, regardless of whether the population recognises that such bias exists, then some ethic groups could be denied the rights which are due to them and could be victimised by a justice system which was designed to protect. The present chapter has looked at the relationship between ethnicity and crime victimisation in an attempt to determine whether different ethnicities are over-represented as victims of crime. While over-representation is suggestive of the possibility of bias in the criminal justice system, other explanations for such over-representation are also possible.

Official crime data in Trinidad and Tobago gave a very different picture of the relationship of ethnicity and crime victimisation compared to victimisation survey data. Official crime data indicated that persons of African descent were victimised far more frequently than persons of any other ethnicity. The only exceptions to this pattern occurred with crimes with a property motive (robberies and burglaries and break-ins) where Caucasians and Chinese persons had comparably higher rates than persons of other ethnicities, though even here the rate for persons of African descent exceeded that of persons of East Indian or Mixed ethnicity. Victimisation survey data, in contrast, indicated that there is a more equitable distribution of crime victimisation. This is more readily apparent in the UNDP (2012) data but is also evident in the 2014 American Barometers Survey. In the case of the UNDP survey, each ethnic group was victimised to approximately the same extent within the past year and within the past 10 years, though persons of Mixed ethnicity were victimised to a slightly greater extent than other persons. In the American Barometers Survey the level of victimisation of persons of African and Mixed ethnicity were similar, with persons of East Indian descent having slightly lower levels of victimisation than these other groups.

The over-representation of persons of African descent as victims in official crime data presents a troubling finding. Several explanations may be offered to make sense of such findings. One possibility may relate to differences in reporting practices. If persons of African descent are more willing to report incidents of victimisation, or persons of other ethnicities are less willing to report, then this could translate into racial disparities in crime data. It is well-known in Trinidad and Tobago, for example, that families of East Indian descent are very unlikely to report incidents of domestic violence. It is not known, however, whether such systematic differences exist with respect to other crimes. The UNDP (2012) data, however, allow for a test of this issue. This data indicated that of all persons who were victims of violent crime in 2009, 68.1 per cent reported the crime to the police. When this was disaggregated by ethnicity, it was discovered that 74.6 per cent of persons of African descent reported the crime to the police, compared to 62.8 per cent of East Indians and 61.9 per cent of persons of Mixed ethnicity.

With respect to property crimes which occurred in 2009, 50.7 per cent of persons of African descent reported the crime to the police compared to 30.2 per cent of East Indians and 38.1 per cent of persons of Mixed ethnicity. Unfortunately, the UNDP study did not ask respondents to give their reasons for not reporting crimes to the police. It is also interesting to note that the police were less likely to take action on the reports made by persons of African descent (they took action in 36.8 per cent of reported cases) compared to persons of East Indian (55.2 per cent) and Mixed (42.9 per cent) ethnicity. Persons of African descent were also somewhat less satisfied with the response of the police (15.8 per cent indicated that they were satisfied or very satisfied) compared to persons of East Indian (27.6 per cent) and Mixed ethnicity (17.9 per cent).

Another possibility is that persons of African descent may be more likely to be the victim of serious violence (e.g. homicide, shootings), while incidences of less serious violence and property crimes are more equally common among people, regardless of ethnic background. Alternatively, it may be that persons of African descent perceive that they are victimised to a greater extent, or perceive that they are victims of more serious crimes compared to persons of other ethnicities. This perception may be driven by actual rates of murder and shooting victimisation which are highest among the African population. If this is generalised to other crimes, then persons of African descent may be more willing to report crimes to the police relative to persons of other ethnicities.

Quite apart from the seriousness of the offence, people fail to report incidents of victimisation for many other reasons. For example, where they feel that the police will be unable to solve the crime, where they are afraid of reprisals from the offender, where the offender is a family member or someone known to them, or where they do not trust the police (UNDP, 2012). If such factors apply more to persons of other ethnicities compared to persons of African descent, then this can also result in disparities in reporting. While these findings indicate that persons of African descent are more likely to report crimes to the police, it seems unlikely that this disparity alone could account for the large over-representation of persons of African descent as victims of crime in official police statistics.

Another explanation relates to police practice. It is possible that policing efforts may be focused on specific populations which are perceived to be more criminogenic. It is not being said here that this is the case or that this represents a deliberate attempt to discriminate against any one ethnic group. Instead, if racial stereotypes do exist, the police as part of the public may also be affected by such stereotypes (Wortley, 1999). If this is so, policing practices may be affected by these biases and could translate into policing which focuses relatively more attention on persons of African descent. While greater focus on any particular ethnic group could translate into higher rates of offending for the affected group, victimisation rates could also be affected since the police will interact more frequently with persons of the specified ethnic group and would be more likely to detect crimes when they occur. Greater frequency of interaction with the police also implies greater accessibility for victims of crime. Such victims may be more likely to report incidents of victimisation because of the ease of accessibility to the police.

The UNDP (2012) collected data which suggest that the above arguments may have some merit. In administering their survey, the UNDP asked respondents to rate the performance of the police on 18 specific areas. Persons of African descent offered the most negative ratings for seven areas. Interestingly, every one of these areas related to the way police officers treat people (e.g. treating people equally, respect for persons' rights, courtesy, fairness). In contrast, persons of East Indian descent offered the most negative ratings for eight areas, and of these seven were for crime control. Persons of Mixed descent offered the most negative ratings for one area (i.e. control of rape), while persons of other ethnicities offered the most negative ratings for two areas. These findings suggest that persons of African descent have more negative experiences when they interact with the police. While the reasons for this are unclear, one possibility may be that the police have more negative opinions of persons of African descent, and thus may treat them differently from persons of other ethnicities. This type of discrimination could also affect policing practice as it relates to crime control and the surveillance of specific ethnic groups (Wortley, 1999).

Another possibility which may explain the over-representation of persons of African descent in official crime data relates to the policing of specific communities which have an over-representation of such persons. In Trinidad and Tobago many communities are racially homogenous. This is a legacy of the country's colonial past where the British kept the main races separated to avoid conflict and to reduce the possibility that they would unite against what some saw as a common oppressor (Smith, 1965). Land ownership patterns today are based on inheritance and as such, racial/ethnic segregation still persists. Some of the communities with higher crime rates, and particularly those with criminal gangs, are populated almost exclusively by persons of African descent (Seepersad & Williams, 2016). The police service utilises sophisticated crime mapping techniques and focuses their efforts on communities which are considered to be crime hotspots. While it is possible that some proportion of the higher crime rates in such communities may be a result of over-policing, it is not necessarily the case that an argument can be made that crime levels are high in such communities because they are composed mainly of persons of African descent. Indeed, there are many other communities in which the majority of residents are of African descent, yet such communities have comparatively low crime rates (Seepersad & Williams, 2016). A more plausible explanation for the higher crime rates in some of the communities upon which the police focus their efforts relates to economic deprivation and social exclusion (UNDP, 2012). Poverty rates in such communities are comparatively high and it is well-known that persons from such communities are systematically discriminated against in terms of access to employment and opportunities for upward social mobility (Seepersad & Williams, 2016). Ironically, while these conditions may have influenced the high crime rates in these communities, the crime rates are now used as a justification for such discrimination and social exclusion. The focus of the police on specific communities with an over-representation of persons of African descent may translate into an over-representation in the official crime statistics.

Summary and conclusion

This chapter has investigated the relationship between ethnicity and crime victimisation in Trinidad and Tobago. Official crime data from the Trinidad and Tobago Police Service show that persons of African descent are over-represented as victims compared to persons of other ethnicities. In contrast, victimisation survey data indicate that there is much more equity in the levels of victimisation experienced by persons of various ethnicities. Several explanations were offered to make sense of these observations. It was suggested that differences in reporting practices could help to explain the observed differences in victimisation levels. It could also be that persons of African descent are the victims of more serious crimes, or perceive that they are the victims of more serious crimes, and are thus more likely to report incidents of victimisation to the police. Policing practices which relate to over-policing of one ethnic group or to higher levels of surveillance of communities with a higher proportion of residents of African descent may also lead to the observed disparities.

This chapter represents a preliminary look at the relationship between ethnicity and crime victimisation in Trinidad and Tobago and provides a starting point for the discussion of other issues. One such issue relates to the difficulties in conceptualizing and measuring ethnicity. In this regard future studies should attempt to operationalise and measure ethnicity in a way which is culturally relevant. Another issue relates to the question of whether it is race or ethnicity which is important in understanding crime victimisation. While the literature has moved away from the use of race as an explanatory construct for the perpetration of criminal offences, it is possible that race (as opposed to ethnicity) could still be important for understanding differences in victimisation levels. For example, if two Trinidadian persons, one of African and the other of East Indian descent move to a foreign country where discrimination exists, despite the fact that both persons may be culturally similar, they may be treated differently based on their race. Still, even here persons in the receiving country may accord different types of treatment to each person based on their perceived ethnicity, not on their race (Wortley, 1999). Organisations and researchers which collect crime data should also make a concerted effort to include the race/ethnicity variable when data are collected. Such data are absent in court and prison statistics, and with the exception of alleged perpetrators of murder, such data are also absent from official crime data on perpetrators. The assessment of the relationship between ethnicity and crime should also go beyond victimisation and should look at offending patterns. In addition, other potentially useful causal variables such as poverty, marginalisation, educational levels, and other such factors should be included in the models which attempt to assess the relationship between ethnicity and crime. Several organisations such as the Police Service, Central Statistical Office (which administers the National Census) and the Ministry of Social Development and Family Services (which administers the Survey of Living Conditions) have all begun to collect geo-coded data for a range of variables. This allows for the utilisation of multiple data sources in analyzing the relationship between race/ethnicity and other variables including crime. Another important question for Trinidad and Tobago is whether some ethnicities receive harsher treatment within the criminal justice system. While such a finding could potentially undermine the legitimacy of the criminal justice system, it will signal the need to put measures in place to redress such inequities.

Data on ethnicity and crime in Trinidad and Tobago should be treated with care and sensitivity to ensure that it is not used to increase racial prejudice and justify discriminatory treatment of some ethnic groups. An initial step in this regard relates to a discussion on the merits of collecting and analyzing ethnicity-crime data in Trinidad and Tobago. While there are arguments against the use of such data, there are many good reasons for its use. Ultimately the collection of such data ensures transparency and signals that attempts are being made to systematically understand the relationship between ethnicity and crime. Potential benefits include finding out whether there is racial equity in treatment by the police, courts, and corrections. Race-ethnicity data could also facilitate the advancement of knowledge with respect to the causes of crime and criminal victimisation and could be used to identify emerging crime problems and help with the development of effective crime prevention programs. Race-ethnicity data could also be used to identify which neighbourhoods should be targeted for crime prevention programming. Such data could thus lead to a more efficient allocation of limited crime prevention resources. In addition, race-ethnicity data could lead to the development of culturally sensitive rehabilitation programs within the Trinidad and Tobago prison system. Race-ethnicity data could be used to evaluate the effectiveness of programs designed to improve police-community relations and public trust in the broader justice system. Finally, such data could help ensure that criminal justice professionals (e.g. police officers, judges, lawyers, correctional officials) reflect the racial-ethnic diversity found within the general population of Trinidad and Tobago.

References

Biafora, F., & Warheit, G. (2007). Self-reported violent victimization among young adults in Miami, Florida: Immigration, race/ethnic and gender contrasts. *International Review of Victimology*, *14*(1), 29–55.

Eisler, L., & Schissel, B. (2004). Privation and vulnerability to victimization for Canadian youth: The contexts of gender, race, and geography. *Youth Violence and Juvenile Justice*, *2*(4), 359–373.

England, S. (2010). Mixed and multiracial in Trinidad and Honduras: Rethinking mixed-race identities in Latin America and the Caribbean. *Ethnic and Racial Studies*, *33*(2), 195–213.

Freiburger, T., & Hilinski, C. (2013). An examination of the interactions of race and gender on sentencing decisions using a trichotomous dependent variable. *Crime & Delinquency*, *59*(1), 59–86.

Georges-Abcyie, D. (1992). Defining race, ethnicity, and social distance: Their impact on crime, criminal victimization, and the criminal justice processing of minorities. *Journal of Contemporary Criminal Justice*, *8*(2), 100–113.

Hawkins, D. (1986). Race, crime type and imprisonment. *Justice Quarterly*, *3*(3), 251–269.

Henry, F., Hastings, P., & Freer, B. (1996). Perceptions of race and crime in Ontario: Empirical evidence from Toronto and the Durham Region. *Canadian Journal of Criminology*, *38*(October), 469–476.

Hipp, J. (2007). Income inequality, race, and place: Does the distribution of race and class within neighborhoods affect crime rates? *Criminology*, *45*(3), 665–697.

Krivo, L., Peterson, R., & Payne, D. (2009). Segregation, racial structure and neighborhood crime. *American Journal of Sociology*, *114*(6), 1765–1802.

LaFree, G., Drass, K., & O'Day, P. (1992). Race and crime in post-war America: Determinants of African-American and white rates, 1957–1988. *Criminology*, *30*(2), 157–188.

Lauritsen, J.L., & Heimer, K. (2010). Violent victimization among males and economic conditions: The vulnerability of race and ethnic minorities. *Criminology & Public Policy*, *9*(4), 665–692.

Maguire, E., Willis, J., Snipes, J., & Gantley, M. (2008). Spatial concentrations of violence in Trinidad and Tobago. *Caribbean Journal of Criminology and Public Safety*, *13*(1–2), 48–92.

Newburn, T., Shiner, M., & Hayman, S. (2004). Race, crime and injustice? Strip search and the treatment of suspects in custody. *British Journal of Criminology*, *44*(5), 677–694.

Rosenfeld, R., Rojek, J., & Decker, S. (2011). Age matters: Race differences in police searches of young and older male drivers. *Journal of Research in Crime and Delinquency*, *49*(1), 31–55.

Sampson, R.J. (1985). Race and criminal violence: A demographically disaggregated analysis of urban homicide. *Crime and Delinquency*, *31*(1), 47–82.

Sampson, R.J., & Wilson, W.J. (1995). Toward a theory of race, crime and urban inequality. In J. Hagan, & R.D. Peterson (Eds.), *Crime and inequality* (pp. 37–54). Stanford, CA: Stanford University Press.

Seepersad, R. (2015). *Crime and violence prevention in Trinidad and Tobago: Baseline mapping report*. Washington: Inter-American Development Bank.

Seepersad, R., & Williams, D. (2016). *Crime and security in Trinidad and Tobago*. Jamaica: Ian Randle Publishers.

Shah, R., & Pease, K. (1992). Crime, race and reporting to the police. *The Howard Journal*, *31*(3), 192–199.

Smith, M.G. (1965). *The plural society in the British West Indies*. Berkeley and Los Angeles: University of California Press.

Stolzenberg, L., Eitle, D., & D'Alessio, S.J. (2006). Race, economic inequality, and violent crime. *Journal of Criminal Justice*, *34*(3), 303–316.

Taylor, T.J., Holleran, D., & Topalli, V. (2009). Racial bias in case processing: Does victim race affect police clearance of violent crime incidents? *Justice Quarterly*, *26*(3), 562–591.

United Nations Development Programme. (2012). *Caribbean human development report: Human development and the shift to better citizen security*. New York: UNDP.

Wang, X., Mears, D.P., Spohn, C., & Dario, L. (2013). Assessing the differential effects of race and ethnicity on sentence outcomes under different sentencing systems. *Crime & Delinquency*, *59*(1), 87–114.

Warikoo, N. (2005). Gender and ethnic identity among second-generation Indo-Caribbeans. *Ethnic and Racial Studies*, *28*(5), 803–831.

Warren, P. (2011). Perceptions of police disrespect during vehicle stops: A race-based analysis. *Crime & Delinquency*, *57*(3), 356–376.

Weitzer, R., & Tuch, S.A. (1999). Race, class, and perceptions of discrimination by the police. *Crime and Delinquency*, *45*(4), 494–507.

Wortley, S. (1999). A Northern taboo: Research on race, crime, and criminal justice in Canada. *Canadian Journal of Criminology*, *41*(2), 261–274.

Wortley, S., & Seepersad, R. (2013). *The Jamaica national crime victimization survey 2012–13*. Jamaica: The Ministry of National Security.

5 Child domestic slavery in Haiti

Benedetta Faedi Duramy

Introduction

Organisations and scholars have increasingly drawn attention to the practice of *restavèk*, a form of child domestic slavery, which affects an estimated 300,000 children in Haiti (United Nations International Children's Emergency Fund, 2006). *Restavèk* children live in appalling conditions: they work extremely long hours without compensation, are often deprived of education, health care, and adequate food, and are vulnerable to abuse and sexual violence. In particular, the chapter acknowledges the struggle of *restavèk* girls, who represent the majority of Haitian child domestic workers, and are especially at risk of experiencing sexual abuse and sexual violence by their own employers. This chapter describes the practice of *restavèk*, gives an overview of some existing empirical findings, profiles the international and domestic legal instruments aimed at eradicating child domestic slavery, and discusses the few civil society organisations currently working with *restavèk* children.

The findings included in this chapter draw from an extensive empirical study conducted in the cities of Port-au-Prince, Gonaive, and Cap-Haitien in Haiti between early June 2006 and late December 2008. The study investigated the incentives, conditions, and decision-making processes behind the involvement of some Haitian rape victims in the armed groups responsible for violence, drug and firearms trafficking, kidnapping, and other illicit activities within their communities. In-depth face-to-face interviews, focus group sessions, and participant observation were utilised among a heterogeneous sample of informants comprised of girls and women who either had been victims of sexual violence or had been members of the armed groups; representatives of international and civil society organisations; as well as members of the judicial, enforcement, and institutional systems working on these issues. Within the scope of the broader research study, findings related to *restavèk* children were also collected and some have already been published elsewhere (Faedi Duramy, 2014). The remainder of this chapter analyses the international and domestic legal instruments addressing child domestic slavery, discusses the practice of *restavèk* affecting many Haitian children by examining some existing empirical findings; and it provides examples of civil society efforts aimed at eradicating the practice and freeing children from slavery in Haiti.

Child slavery under international law

Slavery is prohibited by Article 4 of the Universal Declaration of Human Rights, to which Haiti is a party, stating that "no one shall be held in slavery or servitude; slavery and the slave trade shall be prohibited in all their forms". In addition, Article 23 states that everyone has the right to just and favourable conditions of work and remuneration, and to equal pay without discrimination, and Article 24 stipulates that everyone has the right to rest and leisure, including the right to reasonable working hours and periodic holidays. According to Article 8 of the International Covenant on Civil and Political Rights, ratified by Haiti in 1991, slavery, the slave trade, servitude, and forced labour shall be prohibited. Article 8 further states that no one shall be required to perform forced or compulsory labour. The right to just and favourable conditions of work is protected under the International Covenant on Economic, Social and Cultural Rights, ratified by Haiti in 2013. Article 6 calls all the States Parties to recognise the right to work, including the right of everyone to the opportunity to gain his living by work freely chosen, and to take appropriate steps to safeguard this right. Article 7 protects the right of everyone to the enjoyment of fair work conditions by ensuring in particular:

(a) Remuneration which provides all workers, as a minimum, with:

  (i) Fair wages and equal remuneration for work of equal value without distinction of any kind, in particular women being guaranteed conditions of work not inferior to those enjoyed by men, with equal pay for equal work;
  (ii) A decent living for themselves and their families in accordance with the provisions of the present Covenant;

(b) Safe and healthy working conditions; and
(c) Rest, leisure and reasonable limitation of working hours and periodic holidays with pay, as well as remuneration for public holidays.

Further protection of children from economic exploitation and hazardous work is accorded by the UN Convention on the Rights of the Child, which also clarifies that work must not interfere with children's education, or be harmful to their health or physical, mental, spiritual, moral, or social development (Article 32). Ratified by Haiti in 1995, the UN Convention on the Rights of the Child further calls for States Parties to specify a minimum age for admission to employment, provide appropriate regulation for work hours and conditions as well as penalties or other sanctions to ensure the effective enforcement of such regulations (Article 32). Other provisions under the UN Convention on the Rights of the Child urge State Parties to protect children from all forms of sexual exploitation and sexual abuse (Article 34); and

> take all appropriate legislative, administrative, social and educational measures to protect the child from all forms of physical or mental violence, injury or abuse, neglect or negligent treatment, maltreatment or exploitation,

> including sexual abuse, while in the care of parent(s), legal guardian(s) or any other person who has the care of the child.
>
> 2. Such protective measures should, as appropriate, include effective procedures for the establishment of social programmes to provide necessary support for the child and for those who have the care of the child, as well as for other forms of prevention and for identification, reporting, referral, investigation, treatment and follow-up of instances of child maltreatment described heretofore, and, as appropriate, for judicial involvement.

Moreover, under Articles 28 and 29 the UN Convention on the Rights of the Child recognises the right of children to have education be provided progressively and on the basis of equal opportunity, by ensuring, *inter alia*, that primary education is compulsory and available free of cost to all, and that appropriate measures are taken to encourage regular attendance at schools and the reduction of drop-out rates. States Parties agree that the children's education shall be directed to the development of their personality, talents, and mental and physical abilities to their fullest potential; and their preparation for responsible life in a free society.

In 2014, Haiti also ratified the Optional Protocol to the Convention on the Rights of the Child on the Sale of Children[1], Child Prostitution and Child Pornography requiring the State to criminalise and punish the sale, trafficking, and sexual exploitation of children. In particular for girls, the Convention on the Elimination of all Forms of Discrimination against Women, ratified by Haiti in 1981, calls States Parties to ensure to them equal rights and opportunities in the field of education in rural as well as in urban areas (Article 10). Furthermore, they shall take all appropriate measures to protect health and safety in working conditions. Right on point, under the UN Supplementary Convention on the Abolition of Slavery, ratified by Haiti in 1958, States Parties "shall take all practical and necessary measures legislative and other measures to bring about progressively and as soon as possible the complete abolition or abandonment" (Article 1) of:

> Any institution or practice whereby a child or young person under the age of 18 years, is delivered by either or both of his natural parents or by his guardian to another person, whether for reward or not, with a view to the exploitation of the child or young person or of his labour.
>
> (Article 1 (d))

Also ratified by Haiti in 1958, the ILO Convention No 29 on Forced Labour requires the State to suppress the use of forced or compulsory labour in all its forms for the benefit of private individuals (Article 4). Finally, the ILO Convention No 182 on the Worst Forms of Child Labour, ratified by Haiti in 2007, defines the worst forms of child labour to comprise *inter alia*:

> all forms of slavery or practices similar to slavery, such as the sale and trafficking of children, debt bondage and serfdom and forced or compulsory

> labour . . . [and any] . . . work which, by its nature or the circumstances in which it is carried out, is likely to harm the health, safety or morals of children.
> (Article 3)

To the end of eradicating the worst forms of child labour, States Parties "shall take all necessary measures to ensure the effective implementation and enforcement of the provisions [under the Convention] including the provision and application of penal sanctions" (Article 7). Furthermore,

> Each Member shall, taking into account the importance of education in eliminating child labour, take effective and time-bound measures to:
>
> (a) prevent the engagement of children in the worst forms of child labour;
> (b) provide the necessary and appropriate direct assistance for the removal of children from the worst forms of child labour and for their rehabilitation and social integration;
> (c) ensure access to free basic education, and, wherever possible and appropriate, vocational training, for all children removed from the worst forms of child labour;
> (d) identify and reach out to children at special risk; and
> (e) take account of the special situation of girls.

Finally, in 2009, Haiti ratified the ILO Convention No 138 on Minimum Age setting the minimum working age to 14 years and advocating for stronger national legislation and enforcement mechanisms within States Parties to eradicate the illegal employment and exploitation of younger children. To be noted that The Haitian Constitution stipulates that international obligations undertaken by the Government are binding and enforceable. Its Article 276–2, in fact, expressly provides that "once international treaties or agreements are approved and ratified in the manner stipulated by the Constitution, they become part of the legislation of the country and abrogate any laws in conflict with them".

Domestic legislations on child domestic work

On September 12, 1961, Haiti adopted the Labour Code (*Code du Travail*) updated by Decree on February 24, 1984. Under Chapter 9 of the Labour Code, Article 341 prohibited the employment of children under the age of 12 as domestic workers. The Labour Code further specified that children older than 12 performing domestic work were entitled to receive decent accommodations, clothing, adequate and healthy nutrition, recreational time, and to be enrolled in school or other vocational training programs (Articles 345–346). Moreover, children could not be required to work during school hours, Sunday afternoons, at night, or on public holidays; and they were entitled to 10 hours of uninterrupted rest daily (Article 347). Finally, from the age of 15, children in domestic service had to be regarded as regular domestic workers, and be paid accordingly (Article 350). Violations of these provisions were subject to a fine of up to 3,000 gourdes (Article 355).

In order to comply with the international obligations undertaken by Haiti under the treaties mentioned above, in 2003 the Haitian parliament passed the Act on the Prohibition and Elimination of All Forms of Abuse, Violence, Ill treatment or Inhumane Treatment against Children, which prohibits child servitude, forced or compulsory labour, sexual exploitation, as well as the recruitment of children into criminal activities and armed conflict. In particular, Article 1 annuls Chapter 9 of the Labour Code in its entirety making illegal any forms of child domestic work. The following Article 2 prohibits any form of abuse and violence against children, including, *inter alia*, slavery, forced labour and services, and any other forms of work, which may harm children's health, safety, and dignity because of the type of work or the working conditions. Article 3 further specifies that children may be entrusted to a host family within the context of a relationship based on aid and solidarity. However, such children must enjoy the same privileges and rights accorded to the other children of the family, and thus must be considered as family members. Finally, the Ministry of Social Affairs is responsible for alerting the enforcement system against the actors of any reported abuse, maltreatment, or violence against children (Article 4).

In accordance with the recommendation of the Committee on the Rights of the Child, the adoption of the 2003 Act on the Prohibition and Elimination of All Forms of Abuse, Violence, Ill treatment or Inhumane Treatment against Children aimed specifically at eradicating the restavèk system. Indeed, as mentioned above, Article 1 annulled Chapter 9 of the Labour Code, which previously regulated children in domestic service. However, this amendment has created a gap in the legislation because the new Act does not provide any measures to address the phenomenon of restavèk nor sanctions for offenders. Furthermore, the provision under Article 3 above, which does not clarify the concept of *relationship based on aid and solidarity*, may, in fact, allow the perpetuation of the restavèk practice.

Methods

Some of the findings discussed in this chapter draw from a much broader empirical study conducted by the author in Haiti between early June 2006 and late December 2008. The scope of the research was to investigate the incentives, conditions, and decision-making processes that motivated some girls and women who had been victims of rape and other forms of sexual abuse to join the armed groups and participate in violent attacks against other rival groups or civilians, kidnapping operations, and firearms and drug trafficking. The ultimate goal of the study was to suggest effective measures to free girls and women from violence, to encourage their participation in effective forms of community reconciliation, and to improve their reintegration and rehabilitation into society.

The study was informed by a longitudinal fieldwork conducted during 12 months in the three Haitian cities most affected by armed violence: Port-au-Prince,

Cap-Haitien, and Gonaives. In-depth face-to-face interviews, focus group sessions, and participant observation were held with a heterogeneous sample of 100 informants composed of girls and women, who either had been victims of gender-based violence or had been involved with the armed groups. Representatives of international and civil society organisations as well as members of the judicial, enforcement, and institutional systems working on these issues were also interviewed. Given the prevalence of sexual abuse experienced by *restavèk* girls, relevant findings were also collected and are included in this chapter. In addition, existing findings from other studies and organisations as well as scholarly works, reports, and working documents on child domestic labour in Haiti are discussed in this chapter.

The practice of *restavèk*: findings and discussion

The practice of *restavèk* is deeply connected to the general economic and social contexts as well as, specifically, to children's living conditions and their role within the Haitian society. Considered the poorest country in the Latin American and the Caribbean region, Haiti is also the most disadvantaged of the Western Hemisphere (World Bank, 2006). In 2012, approximately 50 per cent of the Haitian population of over 10 million lived below USD 2.41 a day and about 25 per cent were living below the national extreme poverty line of USD 1.23 a day (World Bank, 2014). The Haitian government has recently reported that almost 6.3 million people cannot meet their basic needs, and, 2.5 million of them cannot satisfy their nutritional needs. Poverty is disproportionally affecting rural areas, where more than 80 per cent of the poor live, and 38 per cent of them cannot cover their food needs compared with 12 per cent in urban areas and 5 per cent in the metropolitan area. Poverty is also concentrated in the North of the country, where the North-East and North-West regions register 40 per cent extreme poverty rate compared with 4.6 per cent in the city of Port-au-Prince (World Bank, 2014).

Poverty hampers progress in education and the utilisation of health care services. According to the most recent household survey conducted in multiple countries, poverty is the reason for not enrolling children in school in 83 per cent of cases and for not consulting a doctor when children are ill in 49 per cent of cases (Pedersen & Lockwood, 2001). Children are particularly vulnerable in Haiti: of the total 2.1 million children between the age of five and 17, approximately 19 per cent of them live in households without their birth parents (Sommerfelt, 2002, p. 33). The World Bank reported that in 2012 87 per cent of Haitian children between the ages of six and 14 living in poor households were enrolled in school contrary to 96 per cent of children living in non-poor households (World Bank, 2015). Lack of education perpetuates poverty: heads of poor households have an average of three times fewer years of education and 61 per cent of them are illiterate, compared with 34 per cent heads of non-poor households (World Bank, 2015). The poor in Haiti are particularly vulnerable: 95 per cent of them experience at least one economically damaging shock per year, including a natural disaster, violence, a health-related event, or other. In response to a shock, between 23 and 56 per cent of poor households change their nutritional behaviours and are likely to withdraw their children from school.

In addition to poverty, Haitian children's condition and roles inside the household explain the origin of the *restavèk* practice. It is indeed the household that represents the first domain where power, authority, and conflict define the contours of relations between adults and children (Maternowska, 2006, p. 44). Cultural beliefs, lack of resources, and violence lead to unequal and imbalanced relationships between family members, which often degenerate into patterns of abuse. Living and "sleeping in Haiti is dangerous" (Maternowska, 2006, p. 46) inside poor and cramped shanties, which often count only one or two rooms, shared by adults and children alike, and easily accessible to neighbours or strangers. Representatives of civil society organisations interviewed for the purpose of the larger study dealing with sexual violence against women and girls in Haiti reported that children's sexual initiation occurs around the age of five or six, primarily with relatives or neighbours. A psychologist working for a rape victims' rehabilitation program also revealed the lack of boundaries among family members and the prevalence of gender-discrimination, neglect, and concealed incest affecting children in the family home.

A professor at the University in Port-au-Prince declared that in the Haitian social hierarchies, women are ranked as second-class citizens and children are, in turn, "so at the very bottom of the society that they are not even regarded as such". Participants of the study recalled the popular Haitian proverb "*ti moun se riches pòv malèrè*" – children are the wealth of the poor – stressing the purpose of children to promote the economy of the household. They are expected to carry water, prepare food, wash dishes and clothes, help selling in the markets, and go on errands for their families. Representatives of the Ministry for the Status of Women interviewed for the purpose of this study, declared that even poverty in Haiti is gendered. Girls are fed less than their brothers, forced to work harder, given less education opportunities, and denied equal access to health care. While parents toil outside the house and brothers are given preferential opportunities to attend school or do apprenticeships, girls as young as seven years old are responsible for watching younger siblings and working inside the home.

Early authors have described arrangements of children's relocations and child domestic labour in Haiti as early as in 1830 (Mackenzie, 1971 [1830]); (Herskovits, 1964 [1937]) and (Simpson, 1942, p. 648 ff., 1942, pp. 666–667). Melville Herskovits, who conducted fieldwork in Mirebalais in the 1930s, referred to such practices as forms of adoption (Herskovits, 1964, pp. 103–104):

> No discussion of the development of the child . . . can neglect to mention the widespread institution of a form of quasi-adoption . . . By this is not meant legal adoption, though that, too, is known and at times occurs. Quasi-adoption involves children who are called "*ti moun qui 'reté à caille 'oun'* – small folk who stay at your house", or, more briefly, "*ti moun*". They are the children, often of peasants, "given" to friends who live in a town or . . . to friends or acquaintances living in the capital . . . To "give" a person a child in this

> manner . . . is regarded as a token of friendship, and such children as were observed, though poorly clothed, were fed not much differently from the children of the families with which they were sent to live. When the "*ti moun*" grows older, he leaves and returns to his own home, though the relationship between foster-father and child may continue friendly if the young person has been well treated.

He also admitted that "to what extent this relationship offers a means for the exploitation of *ti moun* – children – . . . cannot be said, though tales of abuses of it, especially in Port-au-Prince, are heard (Herskovits, 1964, p. 104).

The combination of extreme poverty and the patriarchal misconception of children as property contributed to the development of the practice of exploitation – *restavék* – meaning "to stay with" in Creole, which currently engages around one out of 10 children from 10 to 17 years old in providing domestic work away from their own families (UNICEF, 2006). Generally considered to be a modern form of child slavery, the practice of *restavék* has been connected by some scholars to the historic legacy of slavery, recalling the violence and abuses perpetrated against young slaves at the time of French colonisation (Cadet, 1998). Geographically, the department of Ouest, which includes the greater Port-au-Prince metropolitan area, accounts for a large proportion of children *restavék* (Sommerfelt, 2002, p. 39). Families, especially in rural areas, who barely eke out a subsistence living on the economic margins and are unable to feed or educate their numerous offspring, resolve to send their children to wealthier families living in urban communities (Arbouet, 2015, p. 6).

Girls account for 75 per cent of the approximate 300,000 Haitian child workers sent by indigent parents out of desperation to work as domestic helpers in richer households (Coulter, 2011, p. 10). In 2000, the UN Special Rapporteur Ms Radhika Coomaraswamy conducted a mission on violence against women, its causes, and consequences. In her report, of serious concern were the violence and sexual abuse committed against the young children sent to work as domestic help in households to contribute to the family income. The report denounced that these young girls were frequently at the mercy of their employers and, reportedly, the incidence of physical and sexual violence, resulting in pregnancy, was high (UN, 2000). Findings from a random survey of 1,260 households in Port-au-Prince estimated that, between 2004 and 2006, 35,000 women were sexually assaulted, half of whom were under the age of 18. This study also revealed that 36.2 per cent of female *restavèks* had been victims of sexual violence, 9.6 per cent had been sexually abused, and overall female *restavèks* had a 4.5 times greater chance of being sexually assaulted than non-*restavèks* girls (Kolbe & Hutson, 2006).

A report on child domestic labour in Haiti prepared for UNICEF, ILO, Save the Children UK and Canada reported the story of Jean Luc, who facing economic hardship, resorted to send his two daughters away to perform domestic services in Port-au-Prince (Sommerfelt, 2002, p. 20). One of the girls, who is 10 years old, lives with a non-relative (*etranger).* Jean Luc reported that one of his friends went to see the child during the holidays, and "felt pity for her" (*Li wè kè-l fè-l mal*).

She does not go to school, works in the house, and takes care of three children, of whom two are older than her. Jean Luc has never been able to visit her, and does not know the address of the receiving family. His other girl, who is eight years old, lives instead with one of his brothers. She also does not go to school, and performs domestic tasks like laundry, cleaning, and fetching water. "She is only a small child (*se pa yon gran timoun*)", Jean Luc said (Sommerfelt, 2002, p. 20). When asked what he thinks about the fact that his girls are not attending school, Jean Luc responded that "if they do not go to school, they will neither learn to read nor write. But they know other things, like doing the laundry, and cooking" (Sommerfelt, 2002, p. 20). Despite missing his girls, Jean Luc believes that they are better off in Port-au-Prince given his poor income and how much he is struggling to support his other four children currently living with him. A more recent report reported the story of Nathalie, who is 15 years old, lives in Port-au-Prince and attends a day centre for children who live under difficult circumstances (Sommerfelt, 2015, p. 67).

> Nathalie is originally from Grand'Anse. Her mother died when she was three years old and her father was killed in the 2010 earthquake. Until that time, Nathalie had been living with her father and going to school. When her father died, Nathalie went to live with her Godsister (i.e., the daughter of her Godfather). The Godsister works in the informal sector selling second-hand clothes. The sister's partner, who is employed by the state, also lives in the same house. There are three other children (aged nine, five and two years) in the house. Only the oldest is in school but the five-year-old will start next year, on time, tells Nathalie. Nathalie stopped going to school when she came to live here. Nathalie tells she is suffering (*map pase mizè*) in the house of her Godsister. She says that her Godsister "doesn't give me anything". Nathalie sweeps the floors and does the washing up. The Godsister gives clothes to her children but not to her, in spite of her selling second-hand clothing, Nathalie remarks. When her Godsister cooks meals, and Nathalie is at home, she is usually given food. However, she is often in the day centre, and takes classes there, and when she returns home, food is not put aside to her. When the Godsister is out doing her commerce, and no food is cooked at home, the Godsister gives money to her children to buy food "in the streets" (i.e., snack), but she does not leave money for Nathalie to do the same. Nathalie comments that they do not care about her, and do not mind that she is hungry.

Prospective employers typically visit the birth parents and promise to feed, educate, and care for their *restavéks* in exchange of domestic help. However, in most cases, these children end up being exploited and sexually abused, as well as constrained into further poverty, slavery, and overwork, given meagre food rations, and with limited possibilities for receiving an education. Contrary to their birth parents' hope and expectations, in many cases, *restavéks* end up enduring neglect, exploitation, abuse, and lack of education opportunities. In the end, "poverty begets child labour begets lack of education begets poverty" (UNICEF,

1997). A report published in 1998 by the Institut Psycho-Social de la Famille (IPSOFA) in collaboration with UNICEF indicated that 77 per cent of *restavék* children reached the age of 15 or older without ever attending school (IPSOFA, 1998, p. 43). The same report also described the *restavéks'* tasks (IPSOFA, 1998, pp. 37–38):

> there [is no] . . . labor contract for the unpaid juvenile domestic worker. She is there to perform all the work demanded by the employers. In addition to domestic chores that include cleaning the house, the courtyard, the outbuildings and the sidewalk, the domestic is charged with fetching and transporting the water necessary for the needs of the household. She is often sent to the market, to the neighborhood grocery store or elsewhere depending on the needs of the homeowner and all others, for the child domestic is expected to be of service to the entire household and sometimes even to the neighbors. In addition, she can be asked to watch the children, care for them, take them to school, do the laundry, fetch charcoal, light the stoves, cook, clean dishes and kitchen utensils, take out the trash, clean up human and animal waste, and otherwise do a whole series of tasks that are not asked of the overseer's children, whether girls or boys.

More recently, the National Coalition for Haitian Rights, which focuses on human rights violations perpetrated in the country, has shed light on the some of the hazardous and exploitative conditions that child domestic workers are facing daily (McCalla, 2002, p. 12):

> Fetching water often means balancing a five-gallon bucket (weighing approximately 25 pounds) on the child's fragile head and neck and carrying it over rough and unpaved terrain on plastic sandals or even barefoot. Cooking usually takes place over an open fire in a small grill, leaving the child susceptible to burns, eye irritation, and severe respiratory problems from the smoke of the fire, not to mention the discomfort of squatting or bending over the cooking area for long periods. Walking the household children to school may involve crossing busy and dangerous streets unattended by an adult and carrying a heavy book bag for the other child, even though he or she might be older and stronger. The work generally requires rising before dawn, remaining "on duty" throughout the day, and then continuing to perform tasks late into the night – a work day that can be 12 to 14 hours long.

The parish priest of a Catholic church in a slum of Port-au-Prince, Martissent, who is the director of a specific program providing educational and vocational programs for *restavéks*, reported that *restavéks* "are treated like dogs, sometimes even worse than dogs in Haiti". They often sleep on the floor or standing up if they have misbehaved, eat the leftovers, and wear old shreds of clothing. Still, he acknowledged that a further challenge is the fact that most of these children come from such poor communities that they do not even have birth certificates. The lack of identification documents inevitably facilitates their exploitation and sometimes, disappearance. The situation often degenerates when child *restavéks* reach the age of 15. Indeed, although according to the current law they should then be employed and paid for their services, the hosting families usually either abandon them on the street or continue to keep them working for free (Sommerfelt, 2002).

The story of Alexandre below describes the abuse, hardship, and exploitation that child domestic workers endure (Sommerfelt, 2002, p. 45). Originally from a village in the North-East, Alexandre, who is 12 years old, lost both his parents when he was only 2 years old. After that, he lived with his grandmother until she died, and then moved with his uncle, who eventually got married, and had two daughters and one son by his wife. Alexandre reported that his three cousins attended school when they reached the proper age, but Alexandre did not. He once asked his uncle to send him to school, but his uncle refused, arguing that:

> You have to work. You will [have to] earn money to pay for your schooling (*Se pou ale travay. Wa fè lajan pou peye lekol ou*)". Alexandre tells that while with his uncle, he carried water, brought the cattle to the pastures, went to the market, and had some other tasks as well. Alexandre describes the relationship to his uncle's wife as difficult. He was beaten and maltreated ("*maltrete*") for the smallest thing. The uncle's wife would complain to her husband, who in turn would beat Alexandre "some more". On one occasion, his uncle beat him to a point where a neighbour intervened. Alexandre quotes his neighbour, who said that: "This boy was living with you before your wife. You love your wife much more than him (*Ti gason an te avèk ou anvan fanm lan. Ou pi renmen fanm nan pase li*)". Alexandre tells that the uncle and his wife bought many things for their children and nothing for him. He would walk barefoot and dirty in the village.

To escape this situation of abuse and maltreatment, Alexandre decided to run away but ended up with another family for whom he was performing household chores, including carrying water and looking after a little boy.

> Alexandre tells that one day . . . while having a meal, the "mother" ordered him to clean her son, who had defecated on the floor. Alexandre stopped eating, cleaned the boy, and picked up the excrements from the floor. Alexandre explains that he . . . lost his appetite and could not eat the rest of his food. When he refused to eat, the "mother" beat him. The next day, Alexandre ran away. While living with the various families in Cap-Haitien, running errands and going to the market place, Alexandre had gotten to know children who lived in the streets. Alexandre . . . joined them. However, as it was difficult to earn enough to eat, he and some friends in the streets, who were familiar with Port-au- Prince, decided to go to Port-au-Prince on the back of a bus. Since then, Alexandre has lived in the Portail Léogâne area of Port-au-Prince. For some time now, he has been frequenting an educational centre for street children.

Another recent report reported the story of Joane who is 14 years old. Her mother, who lives in a rural area, sent her to live with a woman in Port-au-Prince three years ago (Sommerfelt, 2015, pp. 69–70).

> "She sent me to get a better life, but that didn't happen (l al chache yon vi miyòo pou mwen, m pa jwenn)". Joane no longer has any contact with her mother and she has no father. She went to school from the age of six to eight and she reached the third year of primary school. She thus started school on time but dropped out before coming to Port-au-Prince. "I'd like to go to school", she says, 'but [if I don't] when I'm bigger I'll sell things in the market". The woman she is living with is elderly. She sells food in the morning but for the past week she hasn't done this. She tells Joane that she has no money to sell food, but Joane says that "it's just for me that there's no money". There are two other children in the household, who are older than Joane. . . . In her current home, Joane says, "I do a lot of work: I wash up, and wash clothes, I cook". Sometimes she is allowed to play with other children, but not when she has got work to do. "I cry when I see them go to school because I can't go", she says. She tells that sometimes, she is beaten for a long time . . . "She treats me badly (mizè l fe m pase)". When we ask why she is beaten, Joane answers, "because I'm not her child". And to illustrate, she adds: "I'm hungry and they don't give me food". The family eats, she says, but they do not give her proper meals . . . She mentions that she sleeps on a sheet on the floor and that the others have beds.

Advocates of the specific program mentioned above for child *restavéks* at the Catholic church of Martissent shared that a culture of neglect and abuse toward children informs the Haitian society, and practices of violence are widely employed as methods of imparting education and discipline. "*Restavék* children are mistreated because [Haitian] children are mistreated, because most parents have a repressive mindset shaped by the political environment they were raised in . . . It is the *macoute* mentality" (McCalla, 2002, p. 16). The anthropologist George Eaton Simpson, who studied sexual and familial institutions in Northern Haiti in the 1940s recounted that at the time (Simpson, 1942, pp. 665–666):

> children in the country were strictly disciplined. Children were punished for playing without the permission [of] their parents, for returning late for an errand, for stealing and lying, and for other offenses. Whippings were common. For some offense, often a slight one, a child was made to kneel for three hours, sometimes on salt or a piece of rough iron, with his arms outstretched. For more serious offenses a child was beaten until he bled, kept prisoner in a room, sent to jail, to the army, or to the "central house of correction" at Port-au-Prince, or thrown out of the house.

A recent study conducted by the Haitian Institute for Childhood – *Institut Haïtien de l'Enfance* – revealed that nine out of 10 adults favour the use of corporal punishments on children as a form of discipline. This number also includes many of the 33 per cent of the Haitian women who have been victims of domestic violence beyond the age of 15 (Cayemittes, Placide, Barrère, Mariko, & Sévère, 2001). Poverty and the lack of solidarity toward indigent families as well as the widespread culture of exploitation represent the primary root causes of the practice of *restavék*. While traditionally the families of destination were relatively wealthy and educated, nowadays only the modest and disadvantaged households rely on the domestic help of *restavéks* (McCalla, 2002, p. 16). A 1992 UNICEF report estimated the average monthly income of US$166 for households employing a *restavék*, but that figure has been decreasing in the last decade (McCalla, 2001, p. 17).

In June 2009, the Special Rapporteur on Contemporary Forms of Slavery paid an official country mission visit to Haiti to engage in a dialogue with national institutions in order to identify the challenges in addressing the situation of *restavék* children. The Special Rapporteur, who held consultations with various NGOs, government officials, children, and United Nations agencies, defined the *restavék* practice as a "severe violation of the most fundamental rights of the child – the foundation of society – and reinforces a vicious cycle of violence" (UN human rights expert condemns child slavery in Haiti, 2009). She further stated that:

> [the *restavék* system] . . . deprives children of their family environment and violates their most basic rights such as the rights to education, health, and food as well as subjecting them to multiple forms of abuse including economic exploitation, sexual violence and corporal punishment, violating their fundamental right to protection from all forms of violence.

The Special Rapporteur also noted that the majority of the demand for young domestic servants has shifted from wealthier and more educated families to poor ones, who otherwise would not be able to afford help and probably may not have the means to send their own children to school, much less their *restavéks* (UN, 2009). Another concerning recent change in the *restavék* system is the emergence of recruiters or *koutchye*, who have replaced the old direct arrangements between birth and host families and are paid to recruit children from rural areas to work for urban families (Special Rapporteur, 2009, p. 7). This new tendency, which could be classified as trafficking, has in fact created an increased number of children being placed with strangers rather than friends or relatives and with little or no ongoing contact with their parents (Smucker & Murray, 2004).

Extreme poverty in the rural areas, the overall demographic expansion, and the migratory movements toward urban communities entrap birth families and children into a downward spiral of slavery, abuse, and sexual violence. The former director of the ILO International Program on the Elimination of Child Labour (IPEC) office in Haiti declared that the practice of "*restavék* is very deeply rooted in the Haitian culture and 99 per cent of the people considered it normal" (Hoag, 2001). The story of Rosefa below describes the motivations behind the recruitment of children from domestic services by their employing family (Sommerfelt, 2002,

p. 78). Rosefa is a single woman in her mid-fifties, who lives in a small two-room house in Les Cayes with three children who are not her own.

> [She] lives from renting out rooms in a neighbouring house, and from selling bananas and coconuts she cultivates in the garden. Rosefa and the children live well, but simple . . . Until this day, Rosefa has had ten children staying with her . . . Originally, Rosefa started inquiries for children because she needed assistance from girls for housework, and from boys to work in the garden and sell produce in the market. . . . She has enrolled all the children to school. . . . According to Rosefa, many adults abuse children. She holds that children have to go to school, and "you know", she says: "they are children, not animals". If you only make them work and give them nothing in return, they will not be satisfied. And she adds, children will cry if they are not sent to school. . . . Andresia, the youngest girl who stays with Rosefa is now 11 years old. She came at the age of approximately six. Rosefa guesses her age, as Andresia did not have a birth certificate. In order to enroll Andresia to school, she needed "papers", and Rosefa found a godmother and godfather for her, baptised her, and thus got the necessary papers for school enrolment. Andresia is now in evening school, and performs household duties in the mornings. . . . Rosefa tells about the first girl she had staying with her with affection. She came at the age of 16, and is now an adult woman. She works in Port-au- Prince,. . . . [S]she has done well, says Rosefa, as she is working as a servant for nuns, and earns 150 Haitian dollars per month, and has no expenses for room or board as she stays in the convent in which she works. She does not spend her money for living, says Rosefa, but instead sends her salary to her parents in the countryside.

The example of Rosefa is unfortunately not representative of the many host families that employ children into domestic servitude in Haiti. Enduring overwork, lack of adequate nutrition and rest, hazardous tasks, and sexual abuse, most of *restavéks* end up experiencing stunted growth, depression, and emotional distress (McCalla, 2002, p. 20). To escape their desperate situations many of them resort to living on the street, begging for food, and eventually being recruited into the gangs. Girls often end up getting trapped into prostitution and sex-trafficking, or sexually enslaved by armed groups. A recent study by the *Coalition Haïtienne pour la Defense des Droits de l'Enfant* (COHADDE) found that the number of street children in Haiti has tripled since 1991; and most of them were former *restavék*, orphans, or children escaping violent and abusive homes (COHADDE, 2002). A pastor drew a comparison between the

> zombies, [that] according to voodoo legend, have no more will[,] [t]hey can't communicate[,] [t]hey can only obey . . [and the] . . . young domestics, [who] once grown, are just like zombies, mute, passive, prepared for nothing but to join the great mass of our marginalised society.
>
> (McCalla, 2002, p. 20)

Responses to child domestic slavery in Haiti

Despite the recent legislative efforts, the provisions under the 2003 Act on the Prohibition and Elimination of All Forms of Abuse, Violence, Ill treatment or Inhumane Treatment against Children are seldom enforced and the *restavèk* practice continues largely unchecked. Cases of sexual and physical abuses against *restavèk* children are first handled by the Brigade for the Protection of Minors, a police corps dealing specifically with children. Once in custody of the Brigade for the Protection of Minors, *restavèk* children are then transferred to the care of the Institute for Social Welfare and Research (Institut du bien-être social et de la recherche or IBESR), whose mandate is to protect vulnerable children. However, due to scarce financial and human resources, the Institute for Social Welfare and Research largely relies on charities' shelters to provide temporary housing for these children and, to date, does not provide any reinsertion programs to them. Although the Brigade for the Protection of Minors refers all cases of abuse against children, including *restavèks*, to the Prosecutor's office, a system of impunity often allows offenders to escape prosecution.

To address the plague of child domestic slavery, the Haitian Ministry of Social Affairs and Labour is developing a national plan to eradicate *restavèk* in Haiti by 2030. Meanwhile, a few civil society organisations have provided assistance to *restavèk* children during the last decade. The Foyer Maurice Sixto (the Maurice Sixto Home), located in Carrefour, a poor neighbourhood in the southwest of Port-au-Prince, provides meals, basic education, and vocational training as well as recreational activities to *restavèk* children. One of the directors of the organisations reported that:

> [their] long-term goal is to stop the exodus of children from rural areas to urban centers where they become easy prey for all forms of exploitation . . . [and the] short-term objectives are to help the children to overcome the trauma caused by separation from their families; acquire reading and writing skills; discover their talents, abilities and creativity; learn a manual trade such as carpentry, metalwork, basketwork, cooking or sewing; become complete human beings with fully-developed personalities aware of their rights and responsibilities; and gain a sense of self-worth through love and encouragement.
>
> (McCalla, 2002, p. 29)

Similarly, The Fondasyon Limyè Lavi provides basic education to *restavèk* children living as in and around the city of Les Cayes. Another organisation, L'Escale, seeks instead to remove the children from the *restavèk* arrangement, by providing psychological support and helping them to reunite with their parents.

Conclusion

In September 14, 2015 the High Commissioner for Human Rights highlighted that "priority attention should be given to the vulnerability of children, especially those unaccompanied, to contemporary forms of slavery, including forced child begging, taking their best interests as a primary consideration" (Special Rapporteur, 2015). This chapter has discussed specifically the practice of *restavèk* in Haiti, which enslaves around 300,000 children to forced domestic work, sexual and physical abuse, preventing them from connecting with and returning to their original families as well as from having access to education, health care, and adequate nutrition. The chapter has described the legislative efforts undertaken by Haiti to comply with its international obligations. However, shortcomings in the enforcement system determine little application of the law and allow the perpetuation of the practice. To date, only a few organisations are working to bring relief to *restavèk* children. Further international and domestic efforts should be made to ensure the eradication of the practice and the enforcement of the law as well as to provide adequate support to organisations working towards such goals.

Note

1 Optional Protocol to the Convention on the Rights of the Child on the sale of children, child prostitution and child pornography, General Assembly Resolution A/RES/54/263. May 25 2000, Retrieved from www.ohchr.org/EN/ProfessionalInterest/Pages/OPSCCRC.aspx

References

Act on the Prohibition and Elimination of All Forms of Abuse, Violence, Ill treatment or Inhumane Treatment against Children [Loi relative à l'interdiction et à l'élimination de toutes formes d'abus, de violences, de mauvais traitements ou traitements inhumains contre les enfants]. Le Moniteur N° 41 du jeudi 5 juin, 2003.

Arbouet, P. (2015). Restavèk and access to justice. *International Human Rights Internship Working Paper Series*, *3*(8), 1–30.

Cadet, J.-R. (1998). *Restavec: From Haitian slave child to middle class American.* Austin: Texas University Press.

Cayemittes, M., Placide, M.F., Barrère, B., Mariko, S., & Sévère, B. (2001). "*Enquête Mortalité, Morbidité et Utilisation des Services 2000"–EMMUS-III, 2002.* Haiti: Institut Haïtien de l'Enfance; Calverton, Maryland (USA): ORC Macro. Retrieved from https://dhsprogram.com/pubs/pdf/FR121/FR121.pdf.

Coalition Haïtienne pour la Défense des Droits de d'Enfant (COHADDE). (2002). *Rapport Alternatif au Comité des Droits de l'Enfant, Section 6.1.2.* Haiti: COHADDE. Retrieved from www.crin.org/en/docs/resources/treaties/crc.32/Haiti_ngo_report.pdf.

Constitution de la République d'Haïti, La République d'Haïti. 1987.

Convention on the Rights of the Child, General Assembly Resolution 44/25, 20 November 1989. Retrieved from www.ohchr.org/Documents/ProfessionalInterest/crc.pdf.

Coulter, M.A. (2011). *Aftershock: A journey of faith to Haiti.* Bloomington, IN: WestBow Press.

Faedi Duramy, B. (2014). *Gender and violence in Haiti: Women's path from victims to agents.* New Brunswick, NJ: Rutgers University Press.

Haitian Labour Code 1961 updated in 1984.

Herskovits, M.J. (1964). *Life in a Haitian valley.* New York: Octagon Books.

Hoag, C. (2001, September 24). Where slaves revolted, slavery thrives. *Businessweek*. Retrieved from www.businessweek.com.

IPSOFA. (1998). *Restavek, La domesticité juvénile en Haïti*. Port-au-Prince: IPSOFA.

Kolbe, A.R., & Hutson, R.A. (2006). Human rights abuse and other criminal violations in Port-au-Prince, Haiti: A random survey of households. *The Lancet, 368*(9538), 864–873.

Mackenzie, C. (1971). *Notes on Haiti, made during a residence in that republic* (Vol. 1). Beaverton, OR: International Scholarly Book Services.

Maternowska, M.C. (2006). *Reproducing inequities: Poverty and the politics of population in Haiti*. New Brunswick: Rutgers University Press.

McCalla, J. (2002, April). Restavek no more: Eliminating child slavery in Haiti, National Coalition for Haitian Rights. Retrieved from https://jmcstrategies.com/wp-content/uploads/2008/08/rnm20021.pdf.

Optional Protocol to the Convention on the Rights of the Child on the sale of children, child prostitution and child pornography, General Assembly Resolution A/RES/54/263. May 25 2000, Retrieved from www.ohchr.org/EN/ProfessionalInterest/Pages/OPSCCRC.aspx.

Pedersen, J., & Lockwood, K. (2001). *Determination of a poverty line for Haiti*. Oslo: Fafo Institute of Applied International Studies.

Simpson, G.E. (1942). Sexual and familial institutions in Northern Haiti. *American Anthropologist, 4*(4), 665–666.

Smucker, G.R., & Murray, G.F. (2004). *The uses of children: A study of trafficking in Haitian children*. Port-au-Prince, Haiti: USAID/Haiti Mission.

Sommerfelt, T. (2002). *Child domestic labour in Haiti: Characteristics, contexts and organisation of children's residence, relocation and work*. Retrieved from www.haitinow.org/wp-content/uploads/2012/08/Life-as-a-Child-Domestic-Worker-in-Haiti-FAFO-2005.pdf.

Sommerfelt, T. (2015). *Child fosterage and child domestic work in Haiti in 2014: Analytical report*. (Fafo-report, 2015:54). Retrieved from Fafo website www.fafo.no/index.php/nb/zoo-publikasjoner/fafo-rapporter/item/child-fosterage-and-child-domestic-work-in-haiti-in-2014-analytical-report.

Special Rapporteur. (2015, September 14). *Statement by the Special Rapporteur on contemporary forms of slavery, including its causes and consequences at the 30th session of the United Nations Human Rights Council*. Retrieved from www.ohchr.org/EN/NewsEvents/Pages/DisplayNews.aspx?NewsID=16440&LangID=E.

UN. (2000). *Integration of the human rights of women and the gender perspective violence against women, Report of the Special Rapporteur on violence against women, its causes and consequences, Ms. Radhika Coomaraswamy, submitted in accordance with Commission on Human Rights resolution 1997/44 Addendum Report on the mission to Haiti, 2000*. (E/CN.4/2000/68/Add.3). Retrieved from www.ijdh.org/wp-content/uploads/2000/01/Violence-Against-Women.pdf.

UN. (2009). *Promotion and protection of all human rights, civil, political, economic, social and cultural rights, including the right to development, Report of the Special Rapporteur on contemporary forms of slavery, including its causes and consequences, Gulnara Shahinian*. (A/HRC/12/21). Retrieved from www2.ohchr.org/english/bodies/hrcouncil/docs/12session/A-HRC-12-21_E.pdf.

UN human rights expert condemns child 'slavery' in Haiti (2009, June 10). UN News Centre. Retrieved from www.un.org/apps/news/story.asp?NewsID=31089#.WR7IQ2iGO71

UNICEF (1997). The state of the world's children 1997. Oxford: Oxford University Press. Retrieved from: https://www.unicef.org/sowc97/download/sow1of2.pdf.

UNICEF. (2006). *Child Alert: Haiti.* Retrieved from www.unicef.org/childalert/haiti/content/Child%20Alert%20Haiti%20(En).pdf.

World Bank. (2006). Social resilience and state fragility in Haiti: A country social analysis. (Report no. 36069). Retrieved from the World Bank website http://documents.worldbank.org/curated/en/533491468257084108/Haiti-Social-resilience-and-state-fragility-in-Haiti-a-country-social-analysis.

World Bank. (2014). *Investing in people to fight poverty in Haiti: Reflections for evidence-based policy making.* (Report No. 94430). Retrieved from the World Bank website http://documents.worldbank.org/curated/en/222901468029372321/Reflections-for-evidence-based-policy-making.

World Bank. (2015). *Haiti: Can non-public schools fill the gap for poor children? From evidence to policy.* World Bank, Washington, DC. Retrieved from https://openknowledge.worldbank.org/handle/10986/21577.

6 The language of partner violence in the Caribbean

A decolonial feminist analysis

Halimah A.F. DeShong

Introduction

The language of violence in intimate relationships has been the subject of much critical analysis with several scholars (particularly feminist social scientists) calling attention to the gendered relations of power such narratives reveal (Adams, Towns, & Gavey, 1995; Anderson & Umberson, 2001; Boonzaier & De le Rey, 2003, 2004; DeShong, 2015; DeShong & Haynes, 2016; Dobash & Dobash, 2004; Sukhu, 2012). In the English-speaking Caribbean, qualitative studies on narratives of intimate partner violence (IPV) have demonstrated how gendered inequalities and gendered ideologies (re)produce the conditions under which this violence is sustained (DeShong, 2011, 2015; DeShong & Haynes, 2016; Hadeed & El-Bassel, 2006; Lazarus-Black, 2007; Sukhu, 2012). In their respective work on legislative, policy, and community responses to intimate partner violence (IPV) in the Caribbean, Tracy Robinson (2004) and Mindie Lazarus-Black (2003, 2007, 2008) described how both the heterosexist and gender-normative posturing of Caribbean nation-states have become enshrined into laws and policies. Caribbean scholarship has usefully challenged the historically masculinist orientation of studies of crime and violence, very similar to feminist studies of crime and violence in North America and Europe from the 1980s onwards (Chesney-Lind & Pasko, 2013).

In this chapter, I will analyse the narratives produced about IPV in 34 in-depth interviews with survivors/victims and perpetrators. The research is based on fieldwork conducted in St Vincent and the Grenadines during two periods between 2007 and 2008. Three main themes are addressed in this analysis: (a) gendered depictions of violence, (b) strategies for explaining IPV and, (c) discourses of provocation and blame. While tangible acts of violence are not reducible to language, the explanations of violence mobilised in interviews are saturated with a colonialist gender logic. In fact, participants (particularly men's) commitment to these scripts is the context within which such violence is justified, rationalised, supported and perpetuated. In short, they deploy narratives produced within what Maria Lugones (2010, 2016) has referred to as the *colonial/modern gender system/logic*.

A decolonial feminist approach to the study of IPV

In post-colony societies, we often miss that the invention of race is coterminous with the emergence of colonialism itself, so that while it may be obvious to focus on the man/woman distinction, the centrality of the human/nonhuman distinction is often left unaddressed (Lugones, 2010, 2016; Méndez, 2015; Wynter, 2003). Drawing on the theoretical works of Sylvia Wynter (2003); Maria Lugones (2010, 2016); and Xhercis Méndez (2015), insights from decolonial feminist analysis are applied and reveal how IPV is overwhelmingly produced as an effect of challenges to a dichotomous and hierarchical gender order. Decolonial feminism displaces the focus on the man/woman distinction so prevalent in much of Northern feminist analyses. Instead, its proponents historicise the creation of the colonial/modern gender logic/system (Lugones, 2010, 2016) demonstrating how gender and race are produced through the genre *Man* – read as European, white, bourgeois *Man* – within colonial relations of power, and comes to epitomise The Human (Lugones, 2010, 2016; Méndez, 2015; Wynter, 2003). For instance, men who use violence often reproduce this logic when they position themselves as victims of women's irrationality and disobedience.

(Re)constructions of violence in interviews about IPV were often imbued with harmful and overlapping assumptions about gender, race, class, and sexuality. For example, men frequently cited the need to regulate women's sexuality as a rationalisation for their violence, even while admitting to expectations of their own sexual freedom (DeShong, 2011). However, given the lack of focus on the socio-political and socio-historical context within which Caribbean gender systems are created and sustained in the research on IPV, frameworks that centre the production of gender and its attendant relations of power, in explanations of violence, predominate in Caribbean research. While this work is useful for pointing to the salience of gendered scripts, actions, beliefs, and institutions in undergirding the practice of violence, there remains a need to consider what Xhercis Méndez (2015, p. 49) described as destabilizing the "colonial logic" of gender and account for the "dehumanizing and racializing work that [it] performed". Far from any attempt to dispense with the concept of gender itself, in her articulation of a decolonial feminist methodology, Mendez proposed a historicisation of gender away from this focus on social relations between a generic Man and a generic Woman. Instead, there is need to account for how one set of bodies have come to epitomise the Human in colonial relations of power, while others have been produced as degenerate. In other words, gender does not operate away from the colonial/modern logic of race and racialisation. I propose that rather than thinking about the colonial/modern logic of race and racialisation as intersecting other social relations of power such as class, sexuality, and ability (as is often the case in reductionist (mis)applications of Black feminist scholarship on intersectionality), the theoretical import of a decolonial feminist analysis is its focus on how race and racialisation *organise* social relations in an attempt to produce normative bodies/citizens and systems of power. In other words, race and racialisation overdetermines the production of gender, (hetero) sexuality, class domination and citizenship in post-colony societies.

It is worth noting here, that in spite of a general tendency to mobilise dichotomous and hierarchical assumptions about gender created as part of this colonial/modern system/logic, Afro-Caribbean and African American women's experiences of IPV are often interpolated within broader institutions of the nation-state in racialised ways that place Afro-Caribbean women, in particular, outside of its white European bourgeois gendered logic. For instance, in early studies by Danns and Parsad (1989) and Brice-Baker (1994), as well as more recent research by O'Neal and Beckman (2017), they all documented the experiences of racism of Afro-Caribbean, African American and Latina women who sought the assistance of state officials. The former noted that whereas Indo-Guyanese women were defined as experiencing "violence against women", Afro-Guyanese women were defined as "fighting with their partners" (Danns & Parsad, 1989). Similarly, African American and Afro-Caribbean women in the United States were constructed as strong black emasculating matriarchs who did not require any state intervention since they were not only adept at defending themselves, but were also responsible for the violence they experienced (Brice-Baker, 1994). Latina women have been found to experience similar barriers (O'Neal & Beckman, 2017). In other words, African American, Afro-Caribbean and Latina women in the United States and Caribbean were defined as failing to conform to the ideological trappings of Woman racialised as white; or (as in the case of the Guyana) conforming to the reductionist and colonist constructions of Indo-Guyanese women as submissive/passive victims. It becomes even more urgent to assess gender as a system (Barriteau, 2001) and as a set of racialised practices bequeathed us, when considering the state and social response to IPV in the Caribbean. A decolonial feminist analysis centres the extent to which re-constructions of IPV hinges on colonial/modern gender logic and what exposing these might mean for changing the conditions under which such violence is produced.

Methods

Procedures

Data collection for this paper was conducted between 2007 and 2008 as part of doctoral research on the language of gender and intimate partner violence. Ethics approval was sought and granted from the University of Manchester Ethics Committee before fieldwork began, and the Family Court, Family Services, Her Majesty's Prison for male offenders and one community police station in St. Vincent and the Grenadines all granted permission to conduct the study. Officials at these entities solicited participation on my behalf. These official received a written project description sheet, and I followed up with verbal explanations about the research. They were told that I was conducting qualitative research on domestic/intimate partner violence that focused on how people make sense of these experiences. Once participants agreed to do the interviews, this process was repeated and informed consent was sought.

Sample

A purposive sample of persons who had perpetrated and experienced violence was selected from the above entities. IPV was operationalised as inclusive of physical harm and a range of controlling and coercive acts in intimate relationships. Thus, selection was based on a person's direct experience of IPV with the intention that the researcher would interpret the meanings attached to such violence.

Thirty-four persons (including 19 women and 15 men) were interviewed. Contact was made with 19 (12 women and seven men) interviewees through the Family Court, seven (four men and three women) through the Family Services, three men were interviewed at Her Majesty's Prisons, and a further four women and one man were contacted with the assistance of a senior officer at a community police station. The sample also included eight couples. Of the 34 persons interviewed, 27 identified as black, four persons identified as mixed (black and Kalinago), two person identified as mixed (black and East Indian), and one person identified as white. Pseudonyms are used in order to protect the identity of respondents, and also to differentiate among them.

Analysis

In-depth interviews covered the following themes: social networks, image of self and of their partner, their experiences in their relationships, history of family violence and violence in their intimate relationships. This paper focused solely on those areas of the interviews in which we discussed violence in their intimate relationships. Verbatim transcripts of interviews were produced and these were read several times before any close analysis began. The most recent reading of these interviews involved a critical application of decolonial feminist insights (as previously discussed) in order to contextualise the heavily saturated 'gendered' narratives produced about violence. Unlike previously cited works in which the operation of race can be observed in state responses to violence (Brice-Baker, 1994; Danns & Parsad, 1989; O'Neal & Beckman, 2017), its centrality is not as obvious in these interviews where participants discussed women and men as take-for-granted categories. A decolonial feminist approach centres how a colonial/modern gender logic is constantly mobilised to explain/excuse/rationalise violence, and the possibilities for change that might exist if we begin to think about gender analysis in more historically accurate ways.

Gendered portrayals of violence

Interviews about violence are key sites for the production of dichotomous and hierarchical gendered narratives rooted in a colonial/modern logic. However, these are often taken-for-granted assumptions that appeal to notions of normalcy and nature. For instance, there was a marked difference between women's and men's presentations of violence. Women reported more violent acts perpetrated against them and were described by both partners as suffering greater injuries. Whereas men's violence was presented as effective, women's use of violent acts was often trivialised and rendered ineffective. In their analysis of men's accounts of IPV, Anderson and Umberson (2001, p. 363) observed that "men depicted their violence as rational, effective, and explosive, whereas women's violence was represented as hysterical, trivial, and ineffectual". Similarly, men in the current study regard violence enacted in relationships as having differential effects. On the one hand, men's narratives are tied in significant ways to definitions of *Western Man*, particularly as they emphasise the efficient and "controlled" use of violence to regulate/eliminate their partners' recalcitrance and secure deference. However, as will be demonstrated in the next broad theme, narratives on the efficient use of violence should be read against men's attempts at externalizing violence. Colonialism created the conditions under which white bourgeois Man was required to be efficient in his use of violence against groups racialised as black, brown, and mixed. However, regional and global activism, and state action have led to increased public loathing of violence against women, particularly in the context of intimate relationships. Given the creation of white bourgeois Woman as the epitome of Woman (understood as the incomplete negation of Western Man), how these narratives of gender are mapped on to the bodies of white, black, mixed, brown, and indigenous women in post-colony societies requires greater interrogation.

In this first example, Lionel presented his partner as audacious for enacting violence: "she had the nerve to pick up her hand and hit me". He said:

> I said "who you really talking to?". "Nobody". "What do you mean nobody? How could you be on the phone for so long talking to no fucking one?" I said to her "come off the damn phone". The person called back. I said "what the fuck?" I took the phone and smashed it on the ground. I destroyed her phone, you know. Then she had the nerve to pick up her hand and hit me. That was her mistake. Man I gave her two hard lashes, man. I told her to chill out. Man, I took the broomstick and just gave her a hard blow and I broke it on her, because as God [*"as God" is a shortened version of "as God is my witness".*], I didn't really want to hit her. I gave her a hard slap in her face man, you know. Afterwards, I told her that I was sorry because it hurt me too because I know that I have my mother and my sister too and I have my daughter too and I don't really want to hit her . . . I think she got a mark on her face because she felt the slap.
>
> (Lionel)

Lionel was more forthright about the nature and extent of his violence than most men in this study. His actions are depicted as decisive. The first part of the account acts as a justification of his right to use of violence to destroy her property and, later, to "tame"/subdue her. He positions himself as in control, while at the same dismissing her actions. Implicit in the extract are notions of men's physical superiority in relation to women. His is a dominant masculine performance that disciplines insubordination, and her implied irrationality in the situation. There are contrasting accounts on what it means to be a woman in his explanation. In some public discourses, women are esteemed as mothers, daughters, and sisters in a colonialist scripting of gender, imbued with respectability politics. In fact, public service announcements (PSAs) for ending IPV against women in the Caribbean often mobilise the mother/daughter/sister archetypes in their advocacy to end violence. Images of the "bearer of life" and nurturer are felt to bestow an elevated status on women (DeShong, 2012). This colonialist-religious archetype of the virtuous Woman – the Madonna figure – is assigned to mothers, sisters, and daughters as undeserving of violence (DeShong, 2012). However, it would appear that within this same colonial/modern gender logic, a masculinity that punishes women's insubordination dominates.

Lionel also addressed the issue of provocation (a theme I shall return to later) – the act of striking him, and her decision to disobey him and continue her telephone conversation. In short, his partner's supposed departure from ideas about acceptable behaviour for women in the context of a relationship was used to justify his reaction when he destroyed her phone in anger. His religious invocation "as God" is meant to speak to his intentionality in this situation. This reference to God, the one who knows what is really inside each of us, is invoked to convince the listener of Lionel's "true" intentions, that is, "I didn't really want to hit her". In short, his violence is portrayed as a decisive means of subduing her. These appeals to the rational/irrational hierarchal dichotomy in violent narratives demonstrate the ways in which colonialist scripts on gender, personally and socially predominate and form the basis for, not only how violence is understood, but continues to be supported.

In contrast, Giselle, Lionel's partner, rejected the notion of his physical superiority, and in so doing disrupts the primacy of the colonial/modern gender logic. She stated "well when he broke up my phone, he got the better of me because he had a weapon, because he had a stick, right". She acknowledged that he was able to overpower her in the situation, but complicated the subordinate position created for her in Lionel's account. In her view, it was the weapon and not his physical strength that accounted for his dominance.

In the next example, Roger's account echoed that of Lionel.

> Well it's obvious the man would get the upper hand right . . . When me and her argue it would lead to a fight. In order for me to get her to humble [*calm*] herself I have to get the upper hand. Let me tell you, she's bigger than me, you know. She's bigger than me, but her bigness don't fool me. I would make sure she get on the ground, not box her down or anything of that sort, you know. I would squeeze her; fight with her like a man, right. I would squeeze her off; choke her off. When I say choke her off, not in a way to like kill her, but just so she could humble herself, you know, because the way she behaves; she behaves as if she could beat me. She can't beat me, regardless of what. I would hold her around her neck [*He performs the action as he explains*] like I would hold her like so and if I really put pressure on her that would fuck her up. No, but I wouldn't do that. I would do that just so she could humble herself. But she would want to box me, pull a knife at me and I would be like "humble yourself, you can't beat me, you can't this, you can't that", but she insists.
>
> (Roger)

Men's effective use of violence is again emphasised here as universal. Roger implied that fighting is something men do, so his decision to fight her like a man functions to remind her that if she assumes perceived masculine traits then she will receive the extreme effects of male aggression. Violence is used to discipline and remind women of their inherent physical inferiority relative to men.

In addition, Roger's account reinforced the value of examining violence within the context it occurs. The acts of pulling a knife or striking someone with a fist can be considered extreme threats and acts of violence. However, in Roger's accounts these acts were dismissed as her unsuccessful response to his use of violence and threats of violence against her. Although he presented his violence as having a decisive effect, he also implied that his actions should not be considered extreme forms of violence. Instead his violence is meant to subdue, rather than harm. His actions were depicted as a form of controlled violence, so that his partner is never in any fatal danger. Men constantly made claims central to a colonial/modern gender logic, in their constant reference to a rational, decisive, and assured self as they described their violence. Conversely, appeals to this logic was observed as they explained violence as a result of them losing control – a theme explored in greater detail in the next section. Moreover, the ranking of difference in favour of men, whether based on intellectual/rational or physical capabilities, is central to the gender systems bequeathed us as part of this colonial/modern logic, and though this is often complicated by lived experiences, it is institutionalised within our social and political systems, affecting the personal ways in which such markers of identity are mobilised.

Some women concurred with these dichotomous depictions of violence in their relationships. I asked Dawn "have you ever set out to hit him first?" She responded "Me? I can't beat him because all he talks about is killing and killing". Her fear of using violence as a response was underpinned by what she presented as his constant threats of fatal violence. Her belief in the effectiveness of his violence accounted for her decision to avoid its use in their relationship. Likewise, Deidre described her unsuccessful attempts to defend herself against the attacks of her partner: "In the last part of the relationship, normally he would hit me, but I would try to fight back, but he is bigger than me so obviously I ain't going to get anywhere". Her attempt to defend herself was presented as futile. The effectiveness of his violence was presented as a consequence of his greater physical strength, a point alluded to by other men and women in the study.

However, not all women responded to their partners' threats and acts of violence by accepting the idea of men's greater physical strength in relation to women. Rose, whose partner admitted that he hit her because she would always visit friends when, in his view, she should be at home, talked about a violent episode:

Int.: Could you tell me how the fight started then? What did each of you do?
Rose: It's words, words. He tell me something, and I tell him back something and he slap me, and I don't like it and we wrestle up.
Int.: So when he slapped you –
Rose: I slapped him back, yeah, you expect I would take a slap?! We end up and wrestle and then we just cool it.

In her recollection of events, Rose unsettled the archetype of the "submissive" and "subdued" Woman, so central to the colonial/modern gender system/logic, and she presented her use of violence as effective as that of her partner. Her reckoning of the events is counter-discursive as rhetorically, she asked, "you expect I would take a slap?!" This couple was atypical when compared to other participants in this study. Even though the acts described could imply equal perpetration of violence in the relationship, hers was presented as an act of retaliation against his violence. Although the tendency in these accounts is to dismiss women's violence as ineffective and men's violence as achieving real ends, a few women, (but no men) debunked these claims, and thus, subverted the dominant narratives within this colonial/modern gender complex.

It is worth reiterating the relevance of early analyses provided by Danns and Parsad (1989) and Brice-Baker (1994), and how they help to situate this tendency to mobilise colonialist scripts of gender. Afro-Caribbean and African American women's experiences of IPV are often interpolated within broader institutions of the nation-state in racialised ways that place these women outside of its white European bourgeois gendered logic. Similarly, O'Neal and Beckman (2017) emphasised the need to situate the IPV experiences of Latina women in the United States within the context of institutional racism and sexism. The current analysis builds on these existing bodies of work, which seek to expose how the colonial/modern "normativity" of gender creates the condition under which IPV is produced and sustained personally, socially, and institutionally for women in post-colony societies in the Caribbean, as well as for women from racialised minority groups in other regions.

Strategies for explaining violence

Participants engaged a number of strategies in their portrayals of violent events in the relationship. Men offered far less details about these events when their accounts were compared to those of women. This is similar to findings of qualitative research conducted by Anderson and Umberson (2001) in the United States and Sukhu's (2012) study of men in Trinidad and Tobago. Men often used language to create distance between themselves and their violence. They avoided the use of the first person when naming violence, and used other techniques of language to rationalise, justify, and even minimise these events. The use of the passive voice allowed men to externalise and depict violence as disembodied acts. Women were more expansive about the nature of violence and its effects, whereas men focused on their motivations, offering far less information about the nature and consequences of their actions. Men's linguistic strategies have an overall effect of legitimizing their use of violence against women.

In this first example, Lenny explained that he used violence against his partner because she confronted him about treating his children from a previous relationship better than their shared biological children.

Int.: Ok what was the worst time you'll had an argument and you hit her?
Lenny: I don't even know [*long pause*]. Roughly about the same kind o' talk she bring to me about kids and stuff like that and then I just lose control and she would get a hard pound [*a pound is a blow delivered with one's fist folded*]. I never try to carry it so far because when she cry I know how it feels, eh. When she cry I really enter her feelings.

Evident in the above is Lenny's use of the passive to distance himself from violence. He described the outcome of his actions and avoided implicating himself directly as a perpetrator. Responsibility for his actions was assigned to his partner as "instigator". In the previous section, reference was made to violence as a rational choice made by men to maintain order, but Lenny's violence was presented as occurring as a consequence of the loss of a stable, self-assured coherent self. Paradoxically, his admission that "I never try to carry it too far because when she cry I know how it feels, eh. When she cry I really enter her feelings" conveyed a sense of control. It conveyed the impression that he is in command of his bodily functions and can decide how much force to use so she is not "seriously" hurt. Men moved between notions of violence as a rational choice and as a consequence of loss of a rational self. Notwithstanding this tension, both explanations were grounded within the very same colonial/modern gender logic.

This tendency to externalise violence is illustrated in the following examples. Randy said "I'm not a violent person", and later he claimed "most of the times when she gets hurt it's when she tries to run from me and end up damaging herself". Likewise, Lenny suggested that "you see, I'm not really a violent person". Scott insisted "I didn't really abuse her like that much". Scott's statement implied that there are degrees of violence and abuse. Moreover, these examples suggested that for the men in this study the use of violence was not a reflection of their embodied identity, but the result of particular external factors.

In the presentation of violence, couples differed on how each partner discussed this issue. Of the eight couples interviewed a pattern emerged. Women disclosed more acts of violence perpetrated against them and they offered more details of these events. It is only in the case of Randy and Janet that there was concurrence in the reports of the frequency and nature, but their rationalisations varied. In the accounts of Bruce and Lance, both men reported that there was only one incident in which they used violence in their relationships. However, their partners, Angie and Linda reported the opposite. They described their partners' violence as regular and in some instances extreme. The following is a comparison of the differences in the reporting of violence.

Int.: Could you tell me about the first time you'll had an argument and there was a fight?

Lance: It was just that one time. We never fought before that time when she get hurt.

By comparison, Linda says

Int.: What usually happens when you'll argue?

Linda: Well we would fight because he would lash me and I wouldn't take it, you know, but then because he was stronger than me, I used to sustain a lot o' hard lashes, eh.

The accounts of the couple, Angie and Bruce, betrayed a similar discrepancy in terms of their presentation of the frequency as well as the severity of Bruce's violence. Angie describes her experience in the last year of their relationship:

Int.: In the last year, how often has he hit you?

Angie: Well that is the worst part of the whole relationship, probably mostly every weekend when we argue.

Int.: Why do you think he hits you?

Angie: He doesn't just come out and hit me. When we argue it does just get to that, but probably because he feels that I don't have anybody to back me up in a sense because the neighbour, she does so much things, nobody don't deserve to be hit eh, but the guy who she is with, he can't go and make any move to like hit the girl because she has her family around her.

In my interview with Bruce, he described his violence as a response to his partner's insistence on going out without telling him where she was going. Later in the interview I asked Bruce "Could you tell me about the worst time that you had an argument with your partner and you hit her?" He responded "that was the only time, so it's not like to say that me and she does be fighting, fighting, fighting". He separated their experience of conflict in the relationship from the image of battering or sustained violence. In contrast, Angie depicted Bruce as regularly inflicting violence. Comparing the accounts of couples about men's violence, Dobash, Dobash, Cavanagh, and Lewis (1998) noted that men and women tend to provide considerably different versions of these events. Angie's response that he hits her almost every weekend when they argue positioned Bruce as a batterer. Her reference to the neighbours also presented violence as a mechanism through which men attempted to restore order based on colonialist framing of gender present in post-colony societies.

Participants also categorised violence into lesser and more extreme forms. Regina described the moment in which her partner began to use violence against her:

> You see from when I had my son, there is where he really started to hit me and so. We never had an excessively violent relationship, you know, but he would choke me and hit, but he never kicked or hit me in any excessive way. So I wouldn't say that relationship was violent, but it had violence in it both with words and hitting and so. I won't say he ever kicked me or beat me down, but he hit me already . . . That is the most he used to do me choke me down. He used to do that a lot. I feel he knew that was my weak spot or something because when he choked me he never used to let go.
>
> (Regina)

She categorised violence in terms of degrees of seriousness. In this instance, the acts of choking and hitting were described as less extreme than kicking or what is, in her view, an excessive strike. Choking was presented as an immobilizing act, with the intent of restraining her rather than creating an adverse physical effect. Her partner, Roger, concurred that this was his intent for using violence: "I would squeeze her off, choke her off. When I say choke her off, not in a way to like kill her, but just so that she could humble herself". These statements conveyed the impression that her experiences should not be likened to the worst excesses of IPV. What are the socio-political and socio-historical conditions under which violence used to subdue and/or to ascertain compliance is rationalised in the above ways? In addition to a colonial/modern gender system, which permits violence as a strategic move available to men, the violence inflicted on groups racialised as non-white, and the contemporary ways in which this violence resonates politically, socially, and personally requires much further interrogation.

A comparison of men's and women's accounts of violence in this study reinforced previous research done on the gendered differences in reports of violence (Boonzaier & De la Rey, 2004; Dobash et al., 1998; Lazarus-Black, 2008; Sukhu, 2012). Men created distance between themselves and their violence through language. Whereas they admitted to engaging in the use of violent acts, several men attempted to separate themselves from the image of the batterer. They often avoided statements that would tie them directly to the violence they perpetrated. Conversely, women were more expansive about the nature and consequences of their partners' violence. Often, there were different meanings attached to the same violent acts by different respondents. In short, several strategies for making sense of violence are used in these accounts, with an overall effect of minimizing, justifying, excusing, legitimizing, and condemning men's violence in intimate relationships. Antonio de Moya's (2004) reference to the elevated levels of IPV against women during cuckolding festival (*La Fiesta de Cuernos*) in the Dominican Republic, and Alissa Trotz's (2004) discussion of the linkages between colonial inheritances and contemporary violence in Guyana, revealed how the infrastructure of colonial race and gender create the conditions under violence against women is reproduced, sustained, and justified.

Discourses of provocation and blame

Discourses of provocation were animated by the very same colonial/modern gender logic, as men constantly referred to women's irrationality and disobedience. The source of violence was presented as something external to the individual, something outside of his control. In some instances, men reported being overcome by rage or some external or embodied evil. In contrast, women placed the responsibility for their violent victimisation with their partners. However, there were moments in some women's accounts in which they too endorsed the idea that women provoked violence. These rationalisations were both supported and rejected by women, who moved between feeling responsible for – and victims of – violence.

Randy's account exemplified the theme of violence as a consequence of women's provocation:

> If I could just tell you the story about how everything happened, you would understand. It's not that I am a violent person . . . The things she says to me gets me in a rage. I does just get a flash back of what my family did to me and I does just lose it, you know. I would just end up and start, I would hit her . . . Everything would just go blank . . . I come to court because she bring me here because I've been hitting her and stuff like that, right, but most of it's her fault. I wouldn't just go, look I would be a crazy man to just go and start beating her like that, right. She did things to me. She knows I get angry . . . I explained to her if I want to go down the road let me go and cool off my head

> and come back. Don't block me and then she bring me hear and telling people I just come and – I'm not that kind a crazy person who would just come and start beating her like that, so honestly it's not my fault really, but then I take the blame because I ain't supposed to really do that.
>
> (Randy)

In this dual depiction of self, Randy described a person enraged by his partner's provocation, the memory of difficult childhood experiences and the loss of self, "everything would just go blank". These all point to loss of control and of an essential self that is non-violent. This allowed him to externalise violence, and to maintain some semblance of rationality so esteemed in colonialist constructions of Western Man. Men's justifications indicated an awareness that violence against women is loathed in public discourses, that it is not in keeping with celebrated publicly scripts of masculinity in official spaces, and that there are state sanctions against such violence. The reference to childhood violence appeared as a rationalisation. In other words, his violence and subsequent loss of control were presented as the result of some outside stimulus. His centring of a rational self can be observed in the statement, "I would be a crazy man to just go and start beating her like that". In his reckoning, the external trigger absolved him of responsibility and placed it with his partner who is presented as "provoking" him into violence. Again, female irrationality was used as justification.

Provocation is one of the most widely mobilised ways in which IPV is framed, personally, socially, and politically. For example, provocation as a mitigating circumstance is afforded to persons charged with homicide and other violent offences involving an intimate partner. The overwhelming majority of the accused in such cases are men, both in the Caribbean and globally. Dobash et al. (2004) challenged the assumption that men who kill an intimate partner are not the usual violent offender but are ordinary men provoked into fatal violence. Instead, these men have a history or "specialise" in violence against their intimate partners (Dobash et al., 2004). The emphasis on provocation in our social understanding of IPV can be traced to the creation of Western Man as otherwise rational, save for Western Woman's ability to destabilise this usually coherent self. Attempts to access entrance into The Human has meant that the vast majority of persons in post-colony societies have sort to emulate the standard as residing in white bourgeois man.

Similarly, Scott engaged the notion of being provoked into violence:

> Yeah, the first time me and her had a thing [a violent event] I did, it's a piece o' wire I got and gave she [he beat her with a piece of electrical cable] . . . The first time me and her did get in anything my mother used to come, well she and my mother used to get along well and my mother used to tell her a whole set of lies about me and all kind o' stuff . . . Then she used to discuss all kind o' things with my mother about me and the next thing, it was like she go up by the neighbours and do the same thing, and I used to get upset because it used to be people say and people say and people say, so I got piece o' wire now and gave her a couple strokes.

Int.: You mean you beat her with the wire?
Scott: Yeah. Piece o' wire.

Scott's statement that "the first time me and her had a thing" served to deflect attention away from him by suggesting that there was mutual perpetration of violence and thus mutual responsibility. Disobedience and disloyalty were cited as his explanation for using violence. His talk on violence draws on ideas about what is acceptable behaviour across the public/private divide within Vincentian society.

His account also reinforced popular assumptions about women as too concerned with idle gossip. Several women mentioned their preference for male friends giving women's love of "comes" [gossip] as the reason for this choice. In a few instances, when describing their partners' social network, men also confirmed this. Idle gossip was often cited as a feature idiosyncratic to women, which men needed to regulate. Scott alluded to this, in his warning to his partner to desist from discussing issues about him with persons outside of their household. His violence can be read as a means of punishing this putative female "vice".

Understandings of violence as a function of women's recalcitrance and, by extension, provocation, were further highlighted in following account:

> I could be nice or I could be hard sometimes, and when I'm nice sometimes she usually wants to try to be harden [stubborn]. I mean I allow her. I don't want to get into anything with her. She usually wants to play a more, ok, you know some girls now would be more humble [reserved/obedient]. She wouldn't want to humble. She would more likely say "no", this/that, answer, back talking, you understand, behaving badly, so I would leave her, but a man might say "he's soft", "he's foolish". No. If I follow my mind and I plan [to plan someone is to hit her/him with the flat side of a machete] her, what would happen to me now because she might provoke me. She might tempt me so bad that I might have to give her some plans, next thing the police come and I end up with the worst of it.
>
> (Lionel)

There is an overall impression that power resided with him in allowing her to be as rebellious as she is. He lamented the fact that, for him, she lacks the humility of most women. His reference to "humble" women alludes to notions of the reserved woman who avoids confrontation by deferring to her partner. Lionel's narrative exemplified the extent to which participants adhered to this dichotomous and hierarchical logic of gender that produces the differential valuing of women and men. The genealogy of gendered assumptions and arrangements is often distilled of its colonial legacy. A closer analysis revealed how the very creation and evolution of gender is based on a racialised binary ranking order to which these participants subscribe.

In this regard, participants cited men's dissatisfaction with women's ability to complete domestic chores as one of the reasons for men's violence. In this example, Floyd documented a violent episode during which time his partner lost a baby:

Int.: What were you'll fighting about?
Floyd: I don't know if you remember this movie, 'Generation'?
Int.: Mm hmm.
Floyd: I tell her don't watch that movie. Don't, don't encourage that.
Int.: You mean the soap opera?
Floyd: Yeah.
Int.: Why didn't you want her to watch it?
Floyd: Because like, like it causing people's relationship to go astray. I say to her don't watch it. I come home, nothing to eat. What I mean, like ok, she just start to cook because everything is just the movie, so I, I, I start to make noise [*argue*] and, and, this is the thing, every time you start to make noise with her, she's always first to square up at you [*to be confrontational*], and I lashed her, and she is the kind o' person when you lash and tell her to listen, she doesn't stop. She feels she must get her revenge.

Men exercised power in relationships by positioning women as nurturers and homemaker. Expectations about domestic responsibilities, childcare, and men's desire to restrict women to spaces marked as private, are at odds with a history of women's work/labour, and economic activities in general. In mobilizing an idealised version of women as mothers and wives, men are wont to confront the lived experiences of women for whom work has always been experienced in its multiple forms (paid and unpaid) in the Caribbean. The emphasis on domesticity in men's accounts illustrated the paradox characteristic of a colonial/modern gender system, in which women are expected to manage the home space even as the survival of families requires women's income, especially, in a context where women head a significant proportion of Caribbean households. Similarly, his preoccupation with the soap opera as having the capacity to corrupt "feminine virtues" and "family values" is undergirded by a similar logic.

Women's accounts also featured men's attempt to restrict them to the confines of domesticity. In the next example, Chantal discussed her partner's use of violence when she fails to prepare meals for him after work:

Int.: In terms of housework, how did you'll get along deciding how you would share the chores?
Chantal: Me. He's not sharing. He doesn't want to do anything. He just wants to sit down whole day watching TV or on the phone whole day with women. If he goes out and comes back and doesn't meet food he would want to lash you.

Chantal's account is indicative of men's attempt to sustain particular arrangements of power in violent intimate relationships. There is an expectation of women's domesticity. In spite of the historical participation of large groups of Caribbean women in the public paid labour force (Hodge, 2002), there remains the tendency to situate these women within British colonialist middle-class values of femininity bequeathed by a history of colonialism in the Anglophone Caribbean. This explains men's expectation of their evening meal upon arrival. These examples emphasise unequal relations of power between men and women in the context of intimate relationships and the family. Colonialist discourses on gender are used to justify violence against women who, in men's view, fail to satisfy the ideals of domesticity. These discourses are also used to blame women for men's use of violence.

Conclusion

The work produced about violence in intimate relationships in the Caribbean has been critical in pointing to the gendered discourse, practices, relations of power, and systems that support and sustain such violence. However, the socio-political, historical, and socio-cultural context for the production of such gendered practices of violence require further examination. In this chapter, I used an archive of interview data to show how narratives of IPV are imbued with a colonial/modern gender logic, as defined in the works of Maria Lugones (2010, 2016) and Xhercis Méndez (2015). Méndez (2015) extolled the salience of Sylvia Wynter's (2003) work in making visible how the invention of race, through the human/nonhuman distinction, created under colonialism, continues to organise social and political relations in post-colony societies. A decolonial feminist analysis of intimate partner violence exposes how the normative framing of white European bourgeois Man as The Human, is mobilised in service of rationalisations of – and support for – violence. Whether it is to explain the use of violence, to deflect blame, or to present violence as the preserve of men, these accounts must be read as part of larger systems of inequality that are historically, socially, and politically produced. Further work that focuses on the production of and responses to violence by the state and its attendant officials, policies, practices, and laws should also frame the discussion within broader socio-political, socio-cultural, and socio-historical contexts. Moreover, this work should consider how scripts on violence coalesce, are ruptured and/or subverted across various sites within a colonial/modern gender logic/system.

References

Adams, P.J., Towns, A., & Gavey, N. (1995). Dominance and entitlement: The rhetoric men use to discuss violence towards women. *Discourse and Society*, *6*(3), 387–406.

Anderson, K.L., & Umberson, D. (2001). Gendering violence: Masculinity and power in men's accounts of domestic violence. *Gender & Society*, *15*(3), 358–380.

Barriteau, V.E. (2001). *The political economy of gender in the twentieth-century Caribbean*. Houndsmill: Palgrave Macmillan.

Boonzaier, F., & De la Rey, C. (2003). "He's a man and i'm a woman": Cultural constructions of masculinity and femininity in South African women's narratives of violence. *Violence against Women*, *9*(8), 1003–1029.

Boonzaier, F., & De la Rey, C. (2004). Woman abuse: The construction of gender in women's and men's narratives of violence. *South African Journal of Psychology*, *34*(3), 443–463.

Brice-Baker, J.R. (1994). Domestic violence in African-American and African-Caribbean families. *Journal of Social Distress and the Homeless*, *3*(1), 23–38.

Chesney-Lind, M., & Pasko, L. (2013). *The female offender: Girls, women & crime*. Thousand Oaks: Sage Publications.

Danns, G.K., & Parsad, B.S. (1989). *Domestic violence in the Caribbean: A Guyana case study*. Georgetown: Women's Studies Unit, University of Guyana.

De Moya, A. (2004). Power games and totalitarian masculinity in the Dominican Republic. In R.E. Reddock (Ed.), *Interrogating Caribbean masculinities: Theoretical and empirical analyses* (pp. 68–99). Kingston: University of the West Indies Press.

DeShong, H.A.F. (2011). Gender, sexuality and sexual violence: A feminist analysis of Vincentian women's experiences in violent heterosexual relationships. *Journal of Eastern Caribbean Studies, 36*(2), 65–96.

DeShong, H.A.F. (2012). What does it 'really' mean to be a woman? Narratives of gender by women and men. In V.E. Barriteau (Ed.), *Love and power: Caribbean discourses on gender* (pp. 107–147). Kingston: University of the West Indies Press.

DeShong, H.A.F. (2015). Policing femininity, affirming masculinity: Relationship violence, control and spatial limitation. *Journal of Gender Studies, 24*(1), 85–103.

DeShong, H.A.F., & Haynes, T. (2016). Intimate partner violence in the Caribbean: State, activist and media response. *Global Public Health, 11*(1–2), 82–94.

Dobash, R.P., & Dobash, R.E. (2004). Women's violence to men in intimate relationships: Working on a puzzle. *British Journal of Criminology, 44*(3), 324–349.

Dobash, R.P., Dobash, R.E., Cavanagh, K., & Lewis, R. (1998). Separate and intersecting realities: A comparison of men's and women's accounts of violence against women. *Violence against Women, 4*(4), 382–414.

Dobash, R.E., Dobash, R.P., Cavanagh, K., & Lewis, R. (2004). Not an ordinary killer just an ordinary guy: When men murder an intimate woman partner. *Violence against Women, 10*(6), 577–605.

Hadeed, L.F., & El-Bassel, N. (2006). Social support among Afro-Trinidadian women experiencing intimate partner violence. *Violence against Women, 12*(8), 740–760.

Hodge, M. (2002). We kind of family. In P. Mohammed (Ed.), *Gendered realities: Essays in Caribbean feminist thought* (pp. 474–485). Kingston: University of the West Indies Press.

Lazarus-Black, M. (2003). The (hetero)sexual regendering of a modern state: Criminalizing & implementing domestic violence law in Trinidad. *Law & Social Inquiry, 28*(4), 979–1008.

Lazarus-Black, M. (2007). *Everyday harm: Domestic violence, court rites, and cultures of reconciliation*. Urbana: University of Illinois Press.

Lazarus-Black, M. (2008). Vanishing complainants: The place of violence in family, gender work & law. *Caribbean Studies, 36*(1), 25–51.

Lugones, M. (2010). Toward a decolonial feminism. *Hypatia, 25*(4), 742–759.

Lugones, M. (2016). The coloniality of gender. In W. Harcourt (Ed.), *The Palgrave handbook of gender and development* (pp. 13–33). Houndsmill: Palgrave Macmillan.

Méndez, X. (2015). Notes toward a decolonial feminist methodology: Revisiting the race/gender matrix. *Transcripts, 5*, 41–59.

O'Neal, N., & Beckman, L. (2017). Intersections of race, ethnicity and gender: Reframing knowledge surrounding barriers to social services among Latina intimate partner victims. *Violence against Women, 23*(5), 643–665.

Robinson, T. (2004). An analysis of legal change: Law & gender-based violence in the Caribbean. *Caribbean judicial colloquium on the application of international human rights law at the domestic level*. Nassau: The Bahamas.

Sukhu, R. (2012). Masculinity and men's violence against known women in Trinidad whose responsibility? *Men and Masculinities, 16*(1), 71–92.

Trotz, A. (2004). Between despair and hope: Women and in contemporary Guyana. *Small Axe, 8*(1), 1–20.

Wynter, S. (2003). Unsettling the coloniality of being/power/truth/freedom: Towards the human, after man, its overrepresentation an argument. *CR: The New Centennial Review, 3*(3), 257–337.

7 Participatory action research

Identifying and addressing sexual violence in St Lucia

Rebecca Hayes, Christina DeJong, Souyenne Dathorne and Velika Lawrence

Introduction

International research continues to demonstrate the highly prevalent, yet largely ignored, crime of sexual assault (e.g. Contreras, Bott, Guedes, & Dartnall, 2010; Krahe, Tomaszewska, Kuyper, & Vanwesenbeeck, 2014; Le Franc, Samm-Vaughan, Hambleton, Fox, & Brown, 2008; Planty, Langton, Krebs, Berzofsky, & Smiley-McDonald, 2013). Sexual assault is a crime that tends to be more prevalent among women/girls than among men/boys. In an examination of 113 studies of the sexual aggression of young people in Europe, researchers found lifetime prevalence rates of female sexual victimisation ranged from 9 to 83 per cent while male rates ranged from 2 to 66 per cent (Krahe et al., 2014). In the United States, one report suggests that one in five women and one in 71 men will have been raped at some point during their lives (Black et al., 2011). Even though research continues to demonstrate high prevalence rates globally, there still remains a lack of research in some countries. With sexual assault having long-term negative psychological effects for victims of sexual assault, particularly for child sexual assault victims (Yuan, Koss, & Stone, 2006), it is important to have an idea of how prevalent it is in all countries, including those in the Caribbean.

Official sexual assault statistics are available in many countries, but these are largely considered unrepresentative as underreporting persists for this crime (Belknap, 2010). Reluctance to report may be due to gender expectations which encourage victim blaming: those victimised could fear retaliation, feel guilt, lack support from family and friends, or fear how law enforcement will respond (Contreras et al., 2010). With the underreporting and long-lasting negative impacts of sexual assault, it is important to identify the specific gaps in the existing research. To our knowledge, one such gap in sexual violence research concerns the Caribbean island of St Lucia which is located in the lower Antilles. Recently, an exploratory study (Hayes, Dathorne, & Taylor, 2016) examined help-seeking behaviour of sexual violence survivors on the island and found that survivors were hesitant to come forward. However, those that did come forward reported the need for resources for dealing with the effects of the attack.

With official statistics in St Lucia demonstrating a low prevalence rate, it is difficult to attain resources for the prevention of – and responses to sexual assault.

An understanding of both the prevalence of sexual violence and the cultural gender roles that support it are integral in order to properly address this social problem. The effects of sexual victimisation can be both immediate and long-term. The immediate effects could hinder a woman's ability to function normally in her everyday life, which may lead to long-term impacts. For example, due to different responses to trauma she may be vulnerable to loss of employment, housing, and relationships. Ongoing effects are also common such as psychological trauma, substance abuse, re-victimisation (Tapia, 2014; Ullman, Filipas, Townsend, & Starzynski, 2005, 2006), and the hindered ability to lead a productive life, especially for those who have experienced child sexual abuse (Finkelhor, 1990; Gladstone et al., 2004; Tapia, 2014; Yuan, Koss, & Stone, 2006). Other Caribbean countries, such as Trinidad and Tobago and Jamaica, have created specific rape response programs to aid victims who have experienced sexual assault (see www.hands.org.gy/crisiscntre, n.d.). However, St Lucia continues to lack specific support for sexual assault programming. Therefore, the current exploratory study sought to assess the rates of sexual assault in St Lucia.

Prevalence rates of sexual violence in the Caribbean

Gender-based violence research is available in the Caribbean; however, less research is available from the smaller islands such as St Lucia (see Arscott-Mills, 2001; Contreras et al., 2010; Hadeed & El-Bassel, 2006; Le Franc et al., 2008). Recently a synthesis of over 200 unpublished and published sexual violence studies was compiled in order to assess the magnitude of sexual violence in Latin America and the Caribbean. This report demonstrated that in Latin America and the Caribbean "forced sex by an intimate partner ranges from 5% to 47%" and sexual abuse by non-partners ranged from 8 to 27 per cent (Contreras et al., 2010, p. 8). However, half of the studies for this report were conducted in Brazil and Mexico while the Caribbean islands that they specifically mentioned included: the Dominican Republic, Haiti, Jamaica, and Cuba (Contreras et al., 2010). With research collectively synthesizing the Caribbean islands, it makes it difficult to examine the cultural nuance amongst the islands, or to conduct cross-country comparisons.

Another methodological consideration impacting these statistics is the broad or narrow definitions for sexual abuse utilised by different studies, which impedes comparison across countries and even regions. Furthermore, the use of narrow definitions limits the assessment of the scope of sexual violence, especially as many studies only ask a few questions. Even when definitions used in studies are similar, cultural differences could be used to (partially) explain the different rates. For example, in one study, Jamaican women reported higher rates of sexual violence than did women in Trinidad and Tobago or Barbados (Le Franc et al., 2008). Samms and Cholewa (2014) argue that there are theoretical explanations regarding cultural expectations in Jamaica that can be used to explain high rates of sexual abuse among children. According to the United Nations Children's Fund (2006), there was a study conducted in Jamaica that reported that some males believed that they were allowed to have sex with any female in their household regardless of age if they were under his care/protection (Le Franc, 2002). Another posited an explanation related to a belief that young girls are not as likely to contract a sexually transmitted disease as women (Samms & Cholewa, 2014). These gendered cultural expectations could be demonstrative that females are viewed as property and therefore lack agency. If women/girls are property then their consent is not necessary, and therefore rape goes unacknowledged.

While research demonstrates that sexual violence is a problem in the Caribbean for women/girls, there is, to our knowledge, no published academic research on sexual assault in the island country of St Lucia. This could be due to the small population of St Lucia (172,000 people) compared to other Caribbean countries where research has been conducted on sexual violence.[1] Therefore, official statistics are the only manner in which to estimate the prevalence of sexual assault in St Lucia and these do not demonstrate that sexual violence is an issue. The official estimates, as reported by governmental organisations, of sexual violence in St Lucia are low. In 2010, 69 rapes were reported to the police, 66 of them were "accepted",[2] and 25 were investigated with 14 resulting in arrests (Sudderth, 2013). Official statistics may not be accurate as there are inconsistent and often illogical definitions of sexual violence in St Lucia. For example, from 2000 to 2004, rape and incest were not listed as a crime against the person but as a crime against public morality, while crimes such as defilement of an inmate or mental person were listed under prostitution (Division of Human Services & Family Affairs, 2011; Royal St. Lucia Police Force, 2011; S. Dathorne, personal communication, December, 2010). Additionally, it was only in 2009 that attempted rape was also recorded as a crime, with 11 cases reported and three closed (Royal St. Lucia Police Force, 2009).

Defining, reporting, and handling of sexual violence in St Lucia

Due to lack of research on sexual violence in St Lucia, we have to assume that some of the cultural influences that impact occurrences of sexual violence in other Caribbean countries are also pertinent in St Lucia. However, a culturally specific observation that likely influences sexual violence statistics is the manner in which it is defined, recorded, and responded to in St Lucia. Reports on the Caribbean region assert that there are discrepancies in terminologies in many countries, especially when defining child sexual abuse (The United Nations Children Fund, 2006). First, the different agencies in St Lucia which record sexual violence (e.g. Department of Gender Relations, St Lucia Crisis Center, Vulnerable Person's Unit) use varying definitions of sexual assault, and this influences how these behaviours are counted in official statistics. Generally speaking, the crisis centre uses a broad definition which allows the victim/survivor to call in and define for herself/himself whether an assault occurred. However, the victim/survivor has to make the contact and from our anecdotal observations it does not seem that people are encouraged by law enforcement or others to seek assistance.

The official St Lucian criminal code has categories such as rape, attempted rape, or unlawful sexual connection to name a few (Royal St. Lucian Police Force, 2000–2012. In the 31 December 2006 Revision of the Laws of Saint Lucia, Criminal Code, rape is classified as:

> (1) any person who has sexual intercourse with another; (a) without their consent, (b) without believing that the other consents to such intercourse or is reckless as to whether the other person consents or not, commits the offence of rape and is liable on conviction on indictment to imprisonment for life. (2) For the purpose of subsection (1), consent is not considered to have been obtained where the complainant submits or does not resist by reason of – (a) the application of force to the complainant or to any other person, (b) threats or fear of the application of force to the complainant or to any other person; (c) the personation of the spouse of the complainant, (d) false and fraudulent representations as to the nature of the act, (e) the use of the accused's position of authority over the complainant; (f) the administration to the complainant of a drug, matter or thing, with intent to stupefy or overpower the complainant; or (g) intimidation of any kind. (3) A husband commits the offence of rape where he has sexual intercourse with his wife without her consent by force, fear or the use of a drug or thing with intent to stupefy or overpower her, where there is in existence in relation to them – (a) a decree nisi of divorce or nullity granted under the Divorce Act; (b) a decree of judicial separation granted under Civil Code, (c) a separation agreement or where the parties are in fact separated, or (d) a peace binding order or an order for the husband not to molest his wife or have sexual intercourse with her including a protection order from the Family Court. (4) The provisions of subsection (3) apply with the necessary modifications to a wife who commits the offence of rape, (5) A husband or wife who commits the offence of rape is liable on conviction to imprisonment for 14 years, (6) A person under the age of 12 years is deemed incapable of committing the offence of rape.
>
> (p. 70)

This long and convoluted official definition of the crime of rape may contribute to the existing research, which says that victims may not report their assault because they are unclear on how to define what occurred (Krebs, Lindquist, Warner, Fisher, & Martin, 2007). Krebs et al. (2007) found among a sample of men and women in the United States, that 35 per cent of victims did not report their assault because they were unsure whether a crime was committed or if inflicted harm was intentional. Questioning whether a crime was committed underlines the importance of a clear definition of sexual assault. For example, Warshaw's (1988) now famous book titled "I Never Called it Rape" demonstrates how complicated defining sexual assault can be to the victim. The question also remains as to how these definitions are interpreted by law enforcement and how this impacts the treatment of potential victims. Terminology matters, and with self-blame and guilt often being experienced by victims of sexual assault, it is unsurprising that victims tend not to report (Contreras et al., 2010; Jewkes, Purna, & Garcia-Moreno, 2002; Ullman, 1996).

If defining the assault is already difficult for victims/survivors (Krebs et al., 2007; Warshaw, 1988), and official definitions in St Lucia are confusing, then the low official statistics could be demonstrative of misinterpreted definitions as a reason for underreporting. In 2012, the St Lucian police department's vulnerable persons' unit recorded 41 rapes, whereas the crisis centre recorded 14. At first glance, this statistic appears counterintuitive compared to research in Western society that demonstrates higher reporting rates for community organisations or academic research (e.g. Breiding et al., 2014; Koss, 1985; Koss, Gidycz, & Wisniewski, 1987; Krahe et al., 2014) as opposed to official governmental organisations (see 2012 Bureau of Justice Statistics for a US comparison). However, there could be culturally nuanced understanding for these differences. Victims in St Lucia may not want to be seen in a crisis centre for fear that friends and neighbours will find out about their victimisation. Also, in St Lucia tardiness to meetings or social events is an accepted cultural practice and if someone is setting up a time to report the sexual assault it can prove difficult when parties are not timely. Given the psychological consequences of rape, such as depression or avoidance behaviour (Cybulska, 2007), the cultural lackadaisical norms on meetings and appointments may discourage reporting. Finally, a recent review on the response to gender-based violence by low- and middle-income countries found that it is common for penal and civil law to be constructed in such a way that discourages reporting and makes convictions unlikely (Morrison, Ellsberg, & Bott, 2004).

Aside from definitional issues in St Lucia, the size and economy of the island also likely impact sexual violence statistics. St Lucia is an English-speaking, largely rural, developing country located in the West Indies with almost 28.8 per cent of inhabitants living below the poverty line (Central Statistics Office, 2012; Kairi Consultants Limited, 2006). Recent longitudinal research in the United States found that between 2005 and 2010 females who lived in lower income households and in rural areas experienced higher rates of sexual violence (Planty, Langton, Krebs, Berzofsky, & Smiley-McDonald, 2013). Regarding higher amounts of sexual violence in rural areas, this is perhaps due to closer social contacts within rural communities, (Lewis & Reed, 2003) as the majority of sexual assaults is committed by an acquaintance (Krebs et al., 2007). A combination of poverty levels, acquaintance-heavy social connections, and cultural beliefs that encourage sexual abuse of young girls (Samms & Cholewa, 2014), offers a potential explanation of the higher prevalence rates in these communities.

Rape myth culture

Along with the definitional issues and higher rates in rural, impoverished areas there is also the theoretical notion of cultural acceptance of sexual violence through a gendered hierarchy (i.e. hegemonic masculinity). In St Lucia there are social norms, traditions and values that underlie the colonial and patriarchal culture of hegemonic male dominance over women's sexuality and the body (Dobash &

Dobash, 1979; Hayes et al., 2016; Jemmott & Maharaj, 2013; Jewkes et al., 2002). As mentioned previously, certain males in Jamaica may feel entitled to have sex with females in their household regardless of age, which as a cultural expectation may influence acts of sexual abuse. While conducting our field research in St Lucia, we heard numerous times of an accepted practice of fathers "breaking in" their daughters. While this evidence is anecdotal and needs to be backed by empirical data, the idea of women/girls as property fits within the post-colonial and patriarchal notions that are still likely a part of St Lucian culture. Historically, women and girls were literal property of the white European settlers and rape largely went unpunished (Jemmott & Maharaj, 2013).

What is still a very common occurrence in the Caribbean and elsewhere is that women's bodies are sexually objectified through advertisements, television, and social media, and yet according to gender roles sexual desires for girls and women are less accepted than those for boys and men. Therefore, if sexual activity does take place, then women/girls may be held accountable due to a double standard. That means, if a woman/girl is perceived as in any way interested in sexual activity, whether through dress or behaviour, she becomes partially culpable if she is sexually violated. Often termed victim blaming, this reinforces the gender inequality that legitimises violence against women (Jewkes et al., 2002). Victim blaming of sexual assault victims is often researched by the acceptance of the Rape Myth Scale (Burgess, 2007; Burt, 1980; Hayes-Smith & Levett, 2010). Rape myths are described by Burt (1980), "as prejudicial, stereotyped or false beliefs about rape, rape victims, and rapists" (p. 217). These ideas are tied into gender roles, norms and expectations. The idea is that "good girls" do not do certain things, and assaults do not happen to "good girls", but to girls who have caused the attack themselves by behaving, dressing, or talking in "bad" ways. This belief is harmful to men and boys as well: in these scenarios, men do not have control over themselves which undermines a man's intelligence and ability. Additionally, these notions leave no room for a male to be a victim of sexual assault as men are not allowed to be victimised.

To elaborate, rape myths are common (yet inaccurate) assumptions about sexual assault (Burgess, 2007; Burt, 1980; Hayes-Smith & Levett, 2010; Lonsway & Fitzgerald, 1994). One such common assumption is that women lie about rape. This assumption easily lends itself to questioning the victim. Another common assumption surrounds the consumption of alcohol (Hayes-Smith & Levett, 2010). When women drink alcohol they are more susceptible to and therefore culpable for their assault, yet men seem to gain a pass if they drink alcohol and are viewed as less culpable as the assaulters. These assumptions encourage questioning of the victims' behaviour. Research in the United States demonstrates that both men and women endorse rape myths, yet the endorsement of rape myths is more pronounced among men (Davies, Gilston, & Rogers, 2012; Lonsway & Fitzgerald, 1994; Hayes, Abbott, & Cook, 2016; Hayes, Lorenz, & Bell, 2013; Hayes-Smith & Levett, 2010; Suarez & Gadalla, 2010). Further research demonstrates how complicated the notions of gender/sexual expectations are within the construction of a victim that leads to victim blaming (such as belief in rape myths) (Davies, Rogers, & Whitelegg, 2009; Davies et al., 2012). In previous studies researchers not only found a higher rate of victim blaming among males, but even more so if the victim was a gay male (Davies et al., 2009 Davies et al., 2012). As rape myth research has largely been conducted in the Western world, whether rape myths exist in the Caribbean (Non-Western), and how gendered sexual expectations impact rape myths is an area for research.

Current study

St Lucia is a country that has been overlooked in studies of sexual violence, and therefore research is needed to understand the issue in this country. As introduced earlier, the current exploratory study sought to assess the rates of sexual assault in St Lucia using a survey methodology, and examined whether there were victim-blaming attitudes (rape myths) that contributed to the low official reporting rate. This research study was conducted in partnership with PROSAF-Surviving Sexual Abuse in the Caribbean and in collaboration with St Lucian Gender Relations to create culturally relevant questions and to assist with future programming/resources. A presentation and report of this study was then provided to St Lucian governmental and non-governmental organisations in order to assist them with addressing the issue on the island. Our exploratory study discussed here is the second in a series that addresses the prevalence of sexual violence, the needs of survivors of sexual violence, and the cultural notions (such as rape myths) that encourage or normalise it. The present study can be used in St Lucia to assist with programming to help with understanding sexual violence. Additionally, this research contributes to the growing literature that exposes sexual violence as a global issue. The current study addresses the question: How prevalent is sexual violence in St Lucia among men and women? The following hypotheses are either based on extant research from other countries on sexual assault or from the qualitative interviews in St Lucia.

H1: Based on commonly stated ratios of sexual violence, we hypothesise that 20 to 25 per cent of women participants will identify as a victim/survivor of sexual assault.
H2: Women will be more likely than men to report sexual assault.
H3: People in working-class neighbourhoods will be more likely to report sexual assault.
H4: Men will be more likely to support rape myths than women in St Lucia.
H5: Female victims will report a greater awareness of laws and resources for victims in St Lucia than male victims.

Methods

Procedure

The current study built on a previous qualitative exploratory study on sexual violence conducted in St Lucia (Hayes et al., 2016). The qualitative study included interviews from women who had experienced sexual violence in St Lucia, and for the current study, the emerging themes from those interviews were used to create the survey. The previous study gained insight as to sexual violence survivors' perspectives on resources on the island and their experiences with informal and formal support providers (Hayes et al., 2016). The semi-structured interview consisted of questions regarding their feelings and reactions to assault disclosure in St Lucia, what the impact of the disclosure was on them, and what kinds of resources (if any) they would like to see in response to sexual violence. This preliminary examination aided in the creation of a meaningful, culturally appropriate survey.

This survey was disseminated in St Lucia during the months of July and August of 2013. A non-probability, cluster sample of houses from four neighbourhoods in the north end of the island was surveyed. Each house in each neighbourhood was included and a team of two researchers went door-to-door to inquire about participation. If there was no answer after two attempts the house was not included. When a potential participant answered the door, he or she, was asked (in English or Patois) if they were over 18 and if they would like to participate in the short survey on sexual assault. If they were not 18, they were asked if anyone in the house was 18 or older. If the person agreed to participate, then the informed consent and survey was administered directly while the team waited for it to be completed. Respondents were informed that they could quit the survey at any time. If the person stated that they did not want to participate, they were thanked for their time.

The survey and corresponding consent forms were approved both by Central Michigan University's Institutional Review Board and St Lucia's Institutional Review Board. All researchers received training for victim advocacy in order to respond appropriately if a victim/survivor felt traumatised by the survey questions. Additionally, training on how to maintain objectivity during the administering of the survey also occurred.

Sample

The total sample of 158 cases consisted of a majority of females (65 per cent, $n = 102$) and working-class respondents (48.7 per cent, $n = 77$), with an average age of 42.8 years ($SD = 16.2$; range 18–79). Social class was indicated by the neighbourhood in which the survey was collected, with 49 per cent of the participants residing in the working-class area, 31 per cent of the participants were located in the middle-class area, and 20 per cent of participants residing in the upper-class neighbourhood. For the purposes of this study, class was defined as the neighbourhood of residence, with one neighbourhood categorised as *working class*, two neighbourhoods classified as *middle class* and one neighbourhood classified as *high class*. These categorisations were chosen after many informal conversations with individuals working in the government and also amongst the citizens residing in the neighbourhoods.

Measures

Prevalence of sexual violence

The measures of sexual violence were adapted from the 2010 US Air Force Assessment of Sexual Violence (Steiger et al., 2010), as well as the widely used Sexual Experiences Survey (SES) (Koss & Gidycz, 1985; Koss et al., 1987). A definition of sexual assault was provided for the participants at the start of the survey, which stated, "by sexual assault, I mean the use of *any* kind of sexual behaviour as a weapon to harm an individual. This can include anything from fondling and groping to insertion of body parts or objects into another person's orifice". We also provided the following information to respondents to assist with their understanding of sexual assault:

> There are three things to consider when deciding whether a sexual act is consensual or a crime: (1) Age – if the person is not over the age of 18 then they cannot consent. (2) Ability to consent – if a person is drunk or drugged, or if they have some disability that prevents them from consenting, and even some elderly may not have the ability to consent. (3) Both people actively agreed – if someone used physical force or threats then there is no consent.

For each item, participants responded *yes, no,* or *I do not wish to answer*. For example, one of the questions was: "Has someone ever had sexual contact without your consent or made you have sexual contact with yourself or another person without your consent?"

A qualitative question provided participants with space to describe any experience that they may have deemed sexual violence. The question asked, "Is there an incident that was not covered above that you are questioning whether it was rape or sexual assault? Please describe below". The questions included for selection in the Experience of Sexual Violence scale were, "Have you ever been raped?", "Has anyone ever forced you to have sex?", "Has someone ever made you engage in a sex act without your consent?", and "Has anyone ever forced you to have anal or oral sex?". The items included in this measure along with their full wording in the survey are included in Appendix 7.1. All four items loaded at .5 or greater in the factor analysis, with a reliability of .84. The items were summed and recoded into a dichotomous (dummy) variable indicating *any prior assaults* or *no prior assault.* Cases that were missing or in which the victim preferred not to answer were coded as *no prior assault.*

Reactions of a support provider

Questions were then asked regarding the reaction of the person who was told, if they told anyone, about the participant's sexual violence. Participants were asked, "Did you ever tell anyone about your assault?" with response categories of *yes, no,* and, *I do not want to answer this question.* Then participants were asked, "About how long after your assault did you tell someone?" with an open ended response. Next, they were asked, "Whom did you tell about your assault?" with response categories, *family, friend, other,* or *I do not want to answer this question.* The follow-up question was then, "How did they react?" with responses of *positive, negative,* or *I do not want to answer this question.* A qualitative question also inquired as to, "How did you feel about their reaction towards your story?"

Resources items

Seven items focusing on resources for assault survivors were administered from those respondents who had reported yes to any of the questions on whether they had been sexually assaulted ($n = 91$). For each item, respondents indicated a value on a 7-point Likert-scale ranging from 1 *strongly disagree* to 7 *strongly agree* concerning the extent to which they were knowledgeable about, and wanted resources on the island. These items were created from themes based on the qualitative interview, as well as recommendations from the St Lucian government. Respondents were asked about their awareness of laws about sexual assault, coping methods, and resources available to sexual assault survivors. Both factor and reliability analysis indicated that this group of items was not measuring a common concept. Consequently, we analysed these items individually and determined residents' knowledge of resources, as well as compared the responses across genders.

Rape Myth Scale

The Rape Myth Scale adapted from Burt's (1980) Rape Myth Acceptance Scale is a previously validated scale. The scale tests hypotheses regarding rape from social, psychological, and feminist theory. The original scale includes 11 statements. We included four additional items. The additional items were taken from prior research (see Hayes-Smith & Levett, 2010) and were meant to capture blaming attributed to alcohol and/or drugs taken by the victim. The items used in this scale are listed in Appendix 7.2 and included items such as "If the victim took drugs/drank alcohol prior to the assault, the rape was partially her fault" and "A healthy woman can successfully resist a rapist if she really wants to". All items were included in a factor analysis to confirm the underlying factors. Based on this analysis, three items were excluded that loaded on separate factors from the rape myth scale namely: "Even if the victim was drunk, the sexual assault was not his/her fault", "I am familiar with 'date rape' drugs", and "Any female can be raped". After eliminating those items, only one remaining item did not load over .5 on the scale: "One reason that women falsely report a rape is that they frequently have a need to call attention to themselves". However, the reliability analysis indicated that overall scale reliability would only improve slightly if removed from the scale (see Appendix 7.2); therefore, this item was retained in the final scale (Cronbach's $\alpha = .85$). An additive scale was created by summing the items and dividing by 12 to scale responses from 1 to 7, with 1 indicating *strongly disagree* and 7 indicating *strongly agree*. Nine cases were omitted due to missing values, and the distribution was positively skewed (skewness = .76, $p < .001$) with a grand mean of 2.88 ($SD = 1.22$).

Results

Victimisation history

Approximately 17 per cent of the sample reported at least one sexual victimisation in their lifetime (19.6 per cent for women, 12.5 per cent for men), with 20 per cent reporting attempted sexual assault (see Table 7.1). A smaller percentage reported forced sexual contact (13.9 per cent), forced sex (9.5 per cent) or rape (8.9 per cent). When asked the question, "Is there an incident that was not covered above that you are questioning whether it was rape or sexual assault? Please describe below", 12 participants provided a qualitative response. One participant said, "Touched in the private area, kissed in an undesirable manner". Whereas another simply stated, "Molestation". When participants were asked how soon after the assault they told someone, 33 participants (20.9 per cent) responded. Of these, nine told someone right away with the remainder of responses ranging from "a week" to "never until now". The questions regarding the initial disclosure of the assault and subsequent reaction were largely left blank. When participants responded to the question as to how they felt regarding the reaction of the person that they told about their assault only 31 responded. Out of these 31, 26 (74 per cent) reported positive responses from the person they told. The word "supported" was a common response. Five participants (14 per cent) reported a negative response with one participant stating, "no one but my elder brother believed me". The final four did not fit neatly into either category.

Hypotheses one and two are partially supported, based on the findings presented in Table 7.1. In partial support of Hypothesis 1, percentage of reporting a

Table 7.1 Proportion of extent of lifetime sexual victimisation, by gender and class (self-reported; $N = 158$)

Type of victimisation	*Overall*	*Females (SD) (n = 102)*	*Males (SD) (n = 56)*	*Working Class (SD) (n = 77)*	*Middle Class (SD) (n = 49)*	*High Class (SD) (n = 32)*
Forced Sexual Contact	.139 (.35)	.186 (.39)	.054 (.23)**	.195 (.40)	.122 (.33)	.031 (.18)
Forced Sex Act	.095 (.29)	.098 (.30)	.089 (.29)	.143 (.35)	.061 (.24)	.031 (.18)
Forced Oral or Anal Sex	.070 (.26)	.049 (.22)	.107 (.31)	.130 (.34)	.000 (.00)	.031 (.18)*
Prevalence: Any report of completed sexual assault	.171 (.38)	.196 (.40)	.125 (.33)	.247 (.43)	.122 (.33)	.063 (.25)*
Attempted Sexual Contact	.203 (.40)	.206 (.41)	.196 (.40)	.182 (.39)	.184 (.39)	.281 (.46)
Attempted Sex Act	.203 (.40)	.206 (.41)	.196 (.40)	.221 (.42)	.184 (.39)	.188 (.40)
Attempted Oral or Anal Sex	.108 (.31)	.088 (.29)	.143 (.35)	.130 (.34)	.102 (.31)	.063 (.25)
Raped	.089 (.29)	.118 (.32)	.036 (.19)*	.143 (.35)	.061 (.24)	.000 (.00)*

Note: *Difference between males and females significant at $p(t) < .05$ (t-test); **$p(t) < .01$. Class differences significant at $p(F) < .05$ (ANOVA).

sexual assault was 19.6 per cent of women which is almost the hypothesised 20 to 25 per cent. Table 7.1 also includes results from independent *t*-tests that were conducted to determine whether significant differences existed between men and women across the included types of sexual victimisation. When sexual victimisation was broken down by gender, women were generally more likely to report victimisation than men, although this difference was only statistically significant for forced sexual contact and rape, which partially supports Hypothesis 2. Eighteen per cent of female respondents indicated they had experienced forced sexual contact compared to 5.4 per cent of men ($t(155.47) = -2.70$, $p < .01$); similarly, 12 per cent of women reported rape victimisation compared to only 4 per cent of men ($t(155.54) = -2.02$, $p < .05$). Finally, while this difference was not statistically significant, the percentage of men in the sample who reported attempted forced oral or anal sex (14.3 per cent) was higher than the prevalence reported by women (8.8 per cent; $t(94.79) = .99$; $p > .05$).

Table 7.1 also includes an analysis of variance for the mean rates of victimisation, breaking down the sample by social class. Two types of victimisation were significantly related to social class; specifically, residents in the working class were more likely to report sexual victimisation (24.7 per cent) and rape (14.3 per cent) than those who resided in the middle-class or high-class neighbourhoods ($F(2) = 3.375$, $p < .05$). For each type of victimisation, the working-class participants reported the highest rates, followed by the middle- and high-class respondents. This finding supports Hypothesis 3.

Table 7.2 contains the items in the survey that measured rape myths. The scale measuring agreement with rape myths compared these attitudes across categories

Table 7.2 Average rating for "Belief in rape myths", by gender ($N = 158$)

Items	*Total N M (SD)*[1]	*Males M (SD)*	*Females M (SD)*
Drinking alcohol blame victim	3.06 (2.19)	3.63 (2.25)	2.80 (2.12)*
Takes drugs blame victim	3.44 (2.18)	3.73 (2.25)	3.30 (2.15)
Going home on first date, willing to have sex	2.74 (1.94)	3.13 (2.15)	2.56 (1.83)
Women report rape falsely for attention	4.14 (2.07)	4.64 (1.91)	3.92 (2.12)
A healthy woman can resist rape	3.31 (2.18)	3.69 (2.26)	3.14 (2.13)
Clothing choices, blame victim	3.24 (2.24)	3.42 (2.18)	3.16 (2.27)
Most rape victims are promiscuous	2.71 (2.06)	3.02 (2.28)	2.57 (1.95)
Necking/petting, blame victim	3.61 (2.20)	3.53 (2.16)	3.65 (2.23)
Hitching women deserve rape	2.15 (1.66)	2.07 (1.44)	2.19 (1.76)
Stuck up women need a lesson	1.70 (1.37)	1.89 (1.53)	1.61 (1.29)
Unconscious desire to be raped	2.27 (1.69)	2.78 (1.93)	2.03 (1.53)*
Drunk women fair game at parties	1.97 (1.66)	2.20 (1.84)	1.87 (1.57)
Overall scale (averaged score)	2.87	3.16	2.73*

Note: $*p(t) < .05$, or $**p(t) < .01$

of sex, class, and location. Male and female respondents significantly differed in their mean scores on rape myth acceptance. Specifically, female respondents (M = 2.73, SD = 1.19) disagreed more with rape myths than male respondents (M = 3.16, SD = 1.24; $t(147) = 2.02$; $p < .05$). Concerning separate item gender comparisons, only two items in the rape myth scale differed significantly across gender. Female respondents were less likely than male respondents to agree with the statements "Even if a victim of sexual assault was drunk at the time of the incident, the sexual assault is not her/his fault" ($t(152) = 2.23$; $p < .05$) and "Women have an unconscious wish to be raped" ($t(92.7) = 2.25$; $p < .05$). It is important to note, however, that these means were low: generally, respondents tended to disagree with these statements but women were more likely to disagree than men. We therefore find partial support for Hypothesis 4: men will be more likely to support rape myths than women.

Finally, Table 7.3 presents t-tests comparing the means of the degree of awareness of laws and resources available to victims of sexual assault with respondent gender. The majority of responses were close to the mean, indicating neither a strong agreement nor disagreement about knowledge of laws and resources. For example, the statement, "I know the laws for reporting the crime of sexual assault in my country" received a mean of 4.53. However overall, participants did indicate a stronger agreement rating for the item stating, "A place with

Table 7.3 Awareness of sexual assault laws and resources in St Lucia, among self-reported victims of sexual assault

Items	*N*	*Overall M (SD)*	*Men M (SD)*	*Women M (SD)*
I know the laws for reporting the crime of sexual assault in my country	91	4.53 (2.01)	5.35 (1.65)	4.20 (2.06)*
I feel that there are laws to help survivors of sexual assault in my country	91	4.26 (2.08)	4.67 (1.84)	4.09 (2.16)
There are adequate resources to help survivors of sexual assault in my country	86	3.31 (1.92)	3.70 (1.67)	3.17 (2.00)
A place with confidentiality is needed for survivors in my country	87	6.31 (1.50)	6.12 (1.64)	6.39 (1.45)
I felt as if the assault was at least partially my fault	79	2.99 (1.96)	3.52 (2.09)	2.77 (1.89)
People often confide in me that they too have been raped or sexually assaulted	80	3.94 (2.20)	4.14 (2.03)	3.86 (2.26)
I used various outlets other than telling someone my story to help me deal with my sexual assault	75	4.09 (1.85)	4.26 (1.96)	4.02 (1.82)

Note: *$p(t) < .05$; Cases missing on these variables responded "I do not want to answer this question". Valid n for men ranges from 21 to 26, valid n for women ranges from 52 to 65.

confidentiality is needed for survivors in my country" ($M = 6.31$). It is worth noting that while other items were normally distributed, this item was highly skewed with 89.6 per cent of respondents stating they *agree* or *strongly agree* with this statement.

Victims indicated neutral ratings for items such as "Awareness of laws", "People confide in me about sexual victimisation" and "I've used outlets other than telling others about my victimisation", but were more likely to agree with statements indicating that "A place with confidentiality is needed for victims". Victims were likely to disagree with statements that "the assault was partially my fault" and "there are adequate resources for victims in my country". *T*-tests between the average scores for men and women indicate that only one item was significantly different by gender. Women were less likely to report awareness of laws for reporting crime than men ($t(57.37) = 2.78$; $p < .05$). Hypothesis 5 was hypothesised in the opposite direction as women were supposed to know more about resources, with few differences between men and women; therefore, this hypothesis is not supported. However, given the low number of valid responses in Table 7.3 (particularly for males), it is difficult to draw strong conclusions from these results.

Discussion

As initially stated, the present study examines prevalence rates of sexual violence in St Lucia and attitudes underlying the incidence of sexual violence, called rape myths. Globally, percentages of sexual violence vary across cultures. Regardless of culture, however, it is continuously determined that sexual violence is a social problem, particularly prevalent among women (Krahe et al., 2014). In St Lucia, about one in five female participants from this sample reported suffering from some form of sexual victimisation during their lifetime. Female participants were also significantly more likely than male participants to report forced sexual contact or rape. However, among this sample about one in eight male participants reported sexual victimisation during their lifetime.

The finding that females reported higher sexual victimisation experiences than males is not surprising; however, the amount of male sexual victimisation reported here *is* surprising. According to the National Violence Sexual Resource Center (2015), one in five women and one in 71 men will be raped at some point in their life. Research on sexual coercion in the Caribbean (particularly Barbados, Jamaica, and Trinidad and Tobago) generally reported higher percentages for women than men. In Barbados sexual coercion by strangers was 3.9 per cent for women and 0.2 per cent for men, and sexual coercion in a relationship was 52.8 per cent for women and 39.6 per cent for men (Le Franc et al., 2008). Yet, the same percentage for both men and women for sexual coercion (53.5 per cent) was reported by participants in Trinidad and Tobago (Le Franc et al., 2008). Therefore, there is evidence of high percentages for male sexual assault in other Caribbean islands and the possible underlying reasons need to be addressed. For these purposes, nevertheless, we turn to a discussion of the possible reasons for female sexual victimisation in St Lucia.

Aspects of masculinity within Caribbean culture might encourage violence against women, including sexual violence of women and girls. "Doing gender" (West & Zimmerman, 1987) in the form of masculinity is often about demonstrating strength or power and dominating, with women often as the object in these exchanges. As Joseph (2015) states, "Men's positioning among each other depends on their power displays in competitive gendered relations, often expressed through actions and words directed towards women" (p. 168). This competition for female attention and sexual conquests can lead to something that is not consensual, i.e. sexual assault. However, it does not explain the high rate of male sexual violence found in this sample. Gender norms and expressions of masculinity often insinuate that only women and girls can be victims (for further reading on gender see Lorber & Farrell, 1991). This research was assessing lifetime sexual violence meaning that the male sexual violence could have been child sexual abuse; however, that is an empirical question that needs to be researched in future studies.

As discussed in the literature review, there are theories regarding the high incidence of child sexual abuse in Jamaica, that focus on male expectations of women and girls who are under the male's care (Samms & Cholewa, 2014; The United Nations Children's Fund, 2006). Even though this theory is related to more female victimisation it is reminiscent of colonisation. During colonisation, women and girls were property of the white European settlers (Jemmott & Maharaj, 2013). Understanding the legacy of colonialism may help unravel cultural differences in sexual assault reporting (such as high male rates). For example, and related to colonisation, there are many countries that still criminalise homosexuality and gender non-conformity (Buist & Lenning, 2016). In countries where homosexuality or gender non-conformity are (or were) illegal, this impacts the level of homophobia experienced within that society (Buist & Lenning, 2016). Homophobia often leads to assault of those who do not fit neatly into the gender/sex expectation.

Another gender/sex expectation derived from post-colonialism is the sexual objectification of black women (hooks, 1992) which is part of the legacy of slavery and the African diaspora. Nonetheless, demonstrating female sexuality through clothes and dance can also be another way to "do gender" (West & Zimmerman, 1987) in Caribbean society. However, this is often used as an excuse to denigrate women as sexual objects (Szymanski, Moffitt, & Carr, 2011). Such objectification reduces an individual to mere body parts, and therefore unable to consent to sexual activity. In addition, women's bodies are viewed as public property further rendering consent unnecessary. This is not to say that women cannot use their sexuality and may enjoy the attention of men. The issue is that the sexual objectification and an overreliance on a women's sexuality, as her only worth, encourages dehumanisation, and subsequently sexual violence.

Potential cultural explanations for sexual violence aside, the manner in which sexual victimisation was defined in this study could have also impacted the rate of reporting. We included inquiry into multiple types of sexual violence. Le Franc et al. (2008) also used multiple definitions of sexual assault that included coercion and within Trinidad and Tobago found that sexual coercion in a relationship was reported by 52.8 per cent of women and 39.6 per cent of men. Even among girls/women the statistics for sexual violence can range, as stated in Contreras et al.'s (2010) review, where the range of sexual violence for women by non-partners was between 8 and 27 per cent while 5 to 47 per cent by intimate partners.

The higher prevalence of sexual assault among working-class participants in the current study supports recent longitudinal research in the United States that showed working-class residents (particularly rural) are more likely to report sexual violence (Lewis & Reed, 2003; Planty et al., 2013). While it is possible that working-class residents experience more sexual violence, it is important to note that in the current study, working-class neighbourhood residents were more responsive to fill out the survey than residents in other neighbourhoods. However, on numerous occasions the team observed the openness of the working-class neighbourhood compared with the other neighbourhoods. More research needs to be conducted on the reasons why working-class neighbourhood respondents were more responsive, and if that impacted their willingness to disclose.

When participants were asked more about their disclosure specifically, many participants left those items blank. Those that did respond reported generally positive experiences with initial support providers, similar to the qualitative interviews that were conducted in an earlier phase of this project (Hayes et al., 2016). While some participants reported that they told someone right away, more reported that it took longer (if they told anyone at all). This is not surprising given, as mentioned previously, that sexual assault is an often underreported crime (Estrich, 1987). It is often underreported due to the victim blaming (i.e. rape myths) that occurs directed at those who experience sexual assault (Belknap, 2010), which is why we examined rape myth acceptance within this sample.

Expectedly, acceptance of rape myths was lower for females than males. This finding is supportive of extant research on the topic (Davies et al., 2009, 2012; Lonsway & Fitzgerald, 1994; Hayes et al., 2016; Hayes et al., 2013; Hayes-Smith & Levett, 2010; Suarez & Gadalla, 2010). We assessed possible cultural differences amongst individual items and found items regarding drug use, women falsely reporting, women's capability to fight off her attacker, and women engaging in kissing/necking had higher agreement rates than other items. Two of these items are indicative of victim blaming, where it is her fault if she was on drugs or she had started to engage in any type of intimate activity. Two other very damaging assumptions about rape contribute to complete disbelief of the victim where "women lie about rape" or that "any healthy woman should be able to fight off her attacker". Both of these beliefs suggest that when a "normal healthy" woman comes forward there might be an automatic reaction that discounts her experience. The view of women as liars is a gendered assumption that not only allows for sexual assault offenders to not be accused, but can also impact intimate partner violence. This cultural trope is very damaging to women and encourages violence against them.

Along with studying the nature of sexual assault, the rape myth attitudes scale should be adapted to address cultural differences. Burt's (1980) scale was a starting point and has been validated in the United States, but there are some cultural expectations surrounding gender norms that are different in St Lucia. For example, hitchhiking is an item in the original scale and in St Lucia it is normal for both males and females to hitchhike rides from passing vehicles. Other attitudes regarding sexual assault likely exist within the Caribbean culture, that might not exist in other cultures and examining those will be important for a better understanding of the differences in prevalence rates.

Knowing the attitudes toward sexual assault may also provide insight as to why (at least in this sample) individuals lack knowledge about resources on the island. It is unsurprising that individuals do not know the laws, as law on the books versus how they are implemented is different, particularly concerning rape laws (see Caringella, 2008). While participants did not know the laws, they indicated a high agreement with the need for a confidential space to report sexual victimisation. With so many barriers standing in the way of reporting, such as fear of retaliation, not being believed, and fear of law enforcement response (Belknap, 2010; Contreras, et al., 2010), wanting a confidential space is predictable. St Lucia is a small, largely rural island where most people know each other, which encourages the need for a confidential safe space for reporting and was identified as a theme in previous research (Hayes et al., 2016). Research could attempt to find specific information regarding resources and reporting among those who experience sexual assault.

Limitations

As this research was exploratory, there are limitations that should be addressed in future research. The relatively small sample size implies that the lack of statistical significance among any findings could be due to a lack of power. Furthermore, restrictions in funding and time limited the amount of time we were able to spend in the field collecting data. Future research should attempt to cover a wider geographical area, spend more time collecting data, and attain (and record) a proper response rate. In our study, our research team included as many St Lucians as Americans when collecting data. Although this was not a limitation, but an asset in the present study, if future research is to be expanded in the area, we strongly suggest the recruitment and training of St Lucian residents. This is a form of cultural victimology, where cultural relativism is used, and in order to understand victimisation experiences (as well as make victims feel comfortable), it is important to include members from the community in all aspects of the project. Another limitation is the limited scope of the survey, which needs to include more culturally appropriate rape myth items, questions on the nature of the incidence, as well as demographics (e.g. race, religion, and income). The original survey was limited because of time constraints and Institutional Review Board suggestions. Future research should include a re-writing of the survey. Finally, another limitation regards response rate: studies should record the houses that participate versus the houses that do not.

Conclusion

Overall, this research has begun the process of understanding sexual assault on the island of St Lucia. As to our knowledge, no previous research on this topic has been conducted in St Lucia. Perhaps the major contribution of this research lies in raising awareness to the sexual assault resources that are currently being constructed from the outcomes of the research. It also provides information about sexual assault to organisations on the island. Nonetheless, more research is needed in order to create sustainable and culturally appropriate resources.

Appendix

Appendix 7.1 Factor loadings for experience of sexual violence ($N = 158$)

	Factor loading	*Alpha if item removed*
Has someone ever had sexual contact without your consent or make you have sexual contact with yourself or another person without your consent?	.841	.796
Has someone ever made you engage in oral sex or anal sex without your consent?	.645	.874
Has someone ever made you engage in a sex act without your consent?	.900	.742
Have you ever been raped?	.891	.749

Note: Cronbach's alpha = .84

Appendix 7.2 Factor loadings for Rape Myth Scale ($N = 158$)

	Factor loading	*Alpha if item removed*
If the victim of a sexual assault was drinking alcohol at the time of the incident, it is partially his/her fault that the sexual assault occurred.	.612	.838
If the victim of sexual assault willingly took drugs at the time of the incident, the sexual assault is partially the victim's fault.	.519	.845
A woman who goes to the home or apartment of a man on their first date implies that she is willing to have sex.	.556	.843
One reason that women falsely report a rape is that they frequently have a need to call attention to themselves.	.302	.858
Any healthy women can successfully resist a rapist if she really wants to.	.566	.844
When women go around braless or wearing short skirts and tight tops, they are just asking for trouble.	.682	.832
In the majority of rapes, the victim is promiscuous or has a bad reputation.	.673	.834
If a girl engages in necking or petting and she lets things get out of hand, it is her own fault if her partner forces sex on her.	.741	.828
Women who get raped while hitching get what they deserve.	.665	.837
A woman who is stuck up and thinks she is too good to talk to guys in the street deserves to be taught a lesson.	.749	.834
Many women have an unconscious wish to be raped, and may then unconsciously set up a situation in which they are likely to be attacked.	.681	.837
If a woman gets drunk at a party and has intercourse with a man she's met there, she should be considered "fair game" to other males at the party.	.700	.835

Note: Cronbach's alpha = .850

Notes

1 Specifically, the population of the Dominican Republic is 10M, with Jamaica at 2.7M, Trinidad and Tobago at 1.34M, and Barbados at 283,000 (The Caribbean Journal, 2013).
2 We were unable to determine the meaning of this term from the police department.

References

Arscott-Mills, S. (2001). Intimate partner violence in Jamaica: A descriptive study of women who access the services of the Women's Crisis Centre in Kingston. *Violence against Women*, *7*(11), 1284–1302.

Belknap, J. (2010). Rape: Too hard to report and too easy to discredit victims. *Violence against Women*, *16*(2), 1335–1344.

Black, M.C., Basile, K.C., Breiding, M.J., Smith, S.G., Walters, M.L., Merrick, M.T. . . . Stevens, M.R. (2011). *The national intimate partner and sexual violence survey: 2010 summary report*. Retrieved from the Centers for Disease Control and Prevention, National Center for Injury Prevention and Control www.cdc.gov/ViolencePrevention/pdf/NISVS_Report2010-a.pdf.

Breiding, M.J., Smith, S.G., Basile, K.C., Walters, M.L., Chen, J., & Merrick, M.T. (2014). Prevalence and characteristics of sexual violence, stalking, and intimate partner violence victimization: National intimate partner and sexual violence survey, United States, 2011. *Surveillance Summaries*, *63*(8), 1–18.

Buist, C.L., & Lenning, E. (2016). *Queer criminology*. New York: Routledge.

Bureau of Justice Statistics. (2012). Retrieved from www.bjs.gov/index.cfm?ty=tp&tid=317.

Burgess, G.H. (2007). Assessment of rape-supportive attitudes and beliefs in college men: Development, reliability, and validity of the rape attitudes and beliefs scale. *Journal of Interpersonal Violence*, *22*(8), 973–993.

Burt, M.R. (1980). Cultural myths and support for rape. *Journal of Personality and Social Psychology*, *38*(2), 217–230.

The Caribbean Journal. (2013). Ranking Caribbean countries by population density. Retrieved from www.caribjournal.com/2013/10/22/ranking-caribbean-countries-by-population-density/#.

Caringella, S. (2008). *Addressing rape reform in law and practice*. New York, NY: Columbia University Press.

Central Statistics Office. (2012). *St. Lucian Central Statistics office*. Retrieved from www.stats.gov.lc.

Contreras, J.M., Bott, S., Guedes, A., & Dartnall, E. (2010). *Sexual violence in Latin America and the Caribbean: A desk review*. South Africa: Sexual Violence Research Initiative.

Cybulska, B. (2007). Sexual assault: Key issues. *Journal of the Royal Society of Medicine*, *100*(7), 321–324.

Davies, M., Gilston, J., & Rogers, P. (2012). Examining the relationship between male rape myth acceptance, female rape myth acceptance, victim blame, homophobia, gender roles, and ambivalent sexism. *Journal of Interpersonal Violence*, *27*(14), 2807–2823.

Davies, M., Rogers, P., & Whitelegg, L. (2009). Effects of victim gender, victim sexual orientation, victim response and respondent gender on judgments of blame in a hypothetical adolescent rape. *Legal and Criminological Psychology*, *14*(2), 331–338.

Division of Human Services and Family Affairs. (2011). *Social issue: Child abuse, January–December, 2010*. Report for Department of Gender Relations, St. Lucia.

Dobash, R.E., & Dobash, R. (1979). *Violence against wives: A case against patriarchy*. New York, NY: Free Press.

Estrich, S. (1987). *Real rape*. Cambridge, MA: Harvard University Press.

Finkelhor, D. (1990). Early and long-term effects of child sexual abuse: An update. *Professional Psychology: Research and Practice, 21*(5), 325–330.

Gladstone, G.L., Parker, G.B., Mitchell, P.B., Malhi, G.S., Wilhelm, K., & Austin, M. (2004). Implications of childhood trauma for depressed women: An analysis of pathways from childhood sexual abuse to deliberate self-harm and revictimization. *The American Journal of Psychiatry, 161*(8), 1417–1425.

Hadeed, L.F., & El-Bassel, N. (2006). Social support among Afro-Trinidadian women experiencing intimate partner violence. *Violence against Women, 12*(8), 740–760.

Hayes, R.M., Abbott, R.M., & Cook, S. (2016). It's her fault: Students drinking behavior and acceptance of rape myths from two college campuses. *Violence against Women, 22*(13), 1540–1555.

Hayes, R.M., Dathorne, S., & Taylor, C. (2016). Silent no more: A qualitative examination of sexual violence in St. Lucia. *International Journal of Rural Criminology, 3*(1), 92–105.

Hayes, R.M., Lorenz, K., & Bell, K. (2013). Victim blaming others: Rape myth acceptance and the just world belief. *Feminist Criminology, 8*(3), 202–220.

Hayes-Smith, R.M., & Levett, L. (2010). Student perception of sexual assault resources and prevalence of rape myth attitudes. *Feminist Criminology, 5*(4), 335–354.

hooks, bell. (1992). *Black looks: Race and representation.* Boston, MA: South End Press.

Jemmott, E.T., & Maharaj, P.E. (2013). Gendered sexual relations and sexualized gender relations. In A. Jones (Ed.), *Understanding child sexual abuse: Perspectives from the Caribbean* (pp. 38–50). London, UK: Palgrave MacMillan.

Jewkes, R., Purna, S., & Garcia-Moreno, C. (2002). Sexual violence. In E.G. Krug, L.L. Dahlberg, J.A. Mercy, A.B. Zwi, & R. Lozano (Eds.), *World report on violence and health* (pp. 147–181). Geneva, Switzerland: World Health Organization.

Joseph, J. (2015). A narrative exploration of gender performances and gender relations in the Caribbean diaspora. *Identities: Global Studies in Culture and Power, 22*(2), 168–182.

Kairi Consultants Limited. (2006). *Assessment of poverty in St. Lucia volume 3.* Retrieved from www.stlucia.gov.lc/.

Koss, M.P. (1985). The hidden rape victim: Personality, attitudinal, and situation characteristics. *Psychology of Women Quarterly, 9*(2), 193–212.

Koss, M.P., & Gidycz, C.A. (1985). The sexual experiences survey: Reliability and validity. *Journal of Consulting and Clinical Psychology, 53*(3), 442–423.

Koss, M.P., Gidycz, C.A., & Wisniewski, N. (1987). The scope of rape: Incidence and prevalence of sexual aggression and victimization among a national sample of students in higher education. *Journal of Consulting and Clinical Psychology, 55*(2), 162–170.

Krahe, B., Tomaszewska, P., Kuyper, L., & Vanwesenbeeck, I. (2014). Prevalence of sexual aggression among young people in Europe: A review of the violence from 27 EU countries. *Aggression and Violent Behavior, 19*(5), 545–558.

Krebs, C.P., Lindquist, C.H., Warner, T.D., Fisher, B.S., & Martin, S.L. (2007). *The campus sexual assault study.* (NIJ Grant No. 2004-WG-BX-0010). Washington, DC: U.S. Department of Justice.

Le Franc, E. (2002). Child abuse in the Caribbean. Adressing the rights of the child. In C. Barrow (Ed.). Children's rights, Caribbean realities (pp. 285–304). Kingston, Jamaica: Ian Randle Publishers.

Le Franc, E., Samm-Vaughan, M., Hambleton, I., Fox, K., & Brown, D. (2008). Interpersonal violence in three Caribbean countries: Barbados, Jamaica, and Trinidad and Tobago. *Revista Panamericana de Salud Pública, 24*(6), 409–421.

Lewis, S.H., & Reed, E. (2003, September). *Sexual assault in rural communities.* Harrisburg, PA: VAWnet. Retrieved from www.vawnet.org/applied-research-papers/print-document.php?doc_id=419.

Lonsway, K.A., & Fitzgerald, L.F. (1994). Rape myths: In review. *Psychology of Women Quarterly*, *18*(2), 133–164.

Lorber, J., & Farrell, S.A. (1991). *The social construction of gender*. Newbury Park, California: Sage Publications.

Morrison, A., Ellsberg, M., & Bott, S. (2004). *Addressing gender-based violence in the Latin American and Caribbean region: A critical review of interventions*. Policy Research Working Paper, No. 3438. Washington, DC: World Bank.

National Violence Sexual Resource Center. (2015). *Statistics about sexual violence*. Retrieved from www.nsvrc.org/sites/default/files/publications_nsvrc_factsheet_media-packet_statistics-about-sexual-violence_0.pdf.

Planty, M., Langton, L., Krebs, C., Berzofsky, M., & Smiley-McDonald, H. (2013). *Female victims of sexual violence, 1994–2010*. (NCJ 240655). Washington, DC: U.S. Department of Justice.

Royal St. Lucia Police Force. (2009). *Crime statistics [Excel spreadsheet]*. St. Lucia: Royal St. Lucia Police Force.

Royal St. Lucian Police Force. (2000–2012). Retrieved from www.rslpf.com.

Royal St. Lucia Police Force. (2011). *Crime statistics [Excel spreadsheet]*. St. Lucia: Royal St. Lucia Police Force.

Samms, K.M., & Cholewa, B.E. (2014). Exploring the context of child sexual abuse in Jamaica: Addressing the deficits. *Journal of Child Sexual Abuse*, *23*(2), 115–127.

Steiger, D.M., Chattopadhyay, M., Rao, M., Green, E., Nemeckay, K., & Yen, E. (2010, December). *Findings from the 2010 prevalence/incidence survey of sexual assault in the Air Force*. Washington DC: Report U.S. Air Force Office of sexual assault prevention and response. Retrieved from www.airforcemag.com/SiteCollectionDocuments/Reports/2011/March%202011/Day29/Gallup_sexual-assault_1210.pdf.

Suarez, E., & Gadalla, T.N. (2010). Stop blaming the victim: A meta-analysis on rape myths. *Journal of Interpersonal Violence*, *25*(11), 2010–20135.

Sudderth, L.K. (2013, October). Services for survivors of sexual assault in St. Lucia. Report submitted: St. Lucian Governmental Officials.

Szymanski, D.M., Moffitt, L.B., & Carr, E.R. (2011). Sexual objectification of women: Advances to theory and research. *The Counseling Psychologist*, *39*(1), 6–38.

Tapia, N. (2014). Survivors of child sexual abuse and predictors of adult re-victimization in the United States: A forward logistic regression analysis. *International Journal of Criminal Justice Sciences*, *9*(1), 64–73.

Ullman, S.E. (1996). Social reactions, coping strategies, and self-blame attributions in adjustment to sexual assault. *Psychology of Women Quarterly*, *20*(4), 505–526.

Ullman, S.E., Filipas, H.H., Townsend, S.M., & Starzynski, L. (2005). Trauma exposure, PTSD, and problem drinking among sexual assault survivors. *Journal of Studies on Alcohol*, *66*(5), 610–619.

Ullman, S.E., Filipas, H.H., Townsend, S.M., & Starzynski, L. (2006). Correlates of PTSD and drinking problems among sexual assault survivors. *Addictive Behaviors*, *31*(1), 128–132.

The United Nations Children's Fund. (2006). *Violence against children in the Caribbean regional assessment: UN Secretary General's study on violence against children*. Retrieved from www.uwi.edu/ccdc/downloads/Violence_against_children.pdf.

Warshaw, R. (1988). *I never called it rape*. New York: HarperPerennial.

West, C., & Zimmerman, D.H. (1987). Doing gender. *Gender and Society*, *1*(2), 125–151.

Yuan, N.P., Koss, M.P., & Stone, M. (2006, March). *The psychological consequences of sexual trauma*. Harrisburg, PA: VAWnet, a project of the National Resource Center on Domestic Violence/Pennsylvania Coalition Against Domestic Violence. Retrieved from www.vawnet.org.

Section C

Causes and risk factors for offending

8 The influence of gender on social capital resources and youth problem behaviour outcomes in Trinidad and Tobago

Alvinelle Matthew

Introduction

Youth problem behaviour remains one of the most urgent concerns among policy makers in the Anglophone Caribbean. Recent statistics have shown that young people contribute significantly to total crime rates, with trends showing that crime is predominately a male problem (Harriott & Jones, 2016; Ryan, Rampersad, Bernard, Mohammed, & Thorpe, 2013; UNDOC, 2007; UNDP, 2012; Williams, 2009). Universally, criminologists agree that women are less likely to commit criminal acts than men, and those females who do offend tend to start later, desist sooner, and are less likely to commit serious offences (Broidy & Agnew, 1997; McCarthy, Felmlee, & Hagan, 2004; Steffensmeier & Allan, 1996; Zimmerman & Messner, 2010). Many studies, ranging from the health field to employment opportunities education to violence, report that gender in the Caribbean acts as a determinant of one's life outcomes (Harriott & Jones, 2016; Lazarus-Black, 2008; Seguino, 2003). In a recent Jamaican-based study, Bourne and McGrowder (2009) reported that gender plays an equally important role as one's socioeconomic status or religious background in influencing one's quality of life. Gender is not only a determinant of criminal behaviours in Jamaica and other Caribbean isles, but also in Trinidad and Tobago, where studies have reported that males between 18 and 25 years report higher rates of criminal involvement than their female counterparts (Ryan et al., 2013; Seepersad, 2016).

Social capital is a contributing factor to youth involvement in criminal activity, as numerous studies have repeatedly demonstrated that higher levels of social capital predict lower levels of offending behaviour. Adolescents who resort to violence often lack close-knit social bonds that provide them with social norms, values, and resources important in regulating normative behaviours. Especially adolescents living in highly disorganised communities, with visible signs of physical decay and social disorder, such as increased drug activity, poverty, and residential mobility, are more likely to experience a heightened degree of social exclusion, which in turn inhibits them from forging instrumental and normative relationships to guide behaviour (Putnam, 1995; Dufur, Hoffmann, Braudt, Parcel, & Spence, 2015; Rosenfeld, Messner, & Baumer, 2001; Weiss, 2011). Despite this burgeoning international research, very few studies have thoroughly analysed social capital impacts in the Latin America and Caribbean region (McIlwaine & Moser, 2001; Reynolds, 2006), with little or no studies examining the gender dimension of social capital and how it may operate differently in predicting problem behaviour between Caribbean males and females.

Therefore, the objective of this study is to analyse the gender gap in social capital resources, by examining whether males, as compared to females, access or possess different amounts of social capital resources in the social contexts of the family, school and community. More specifically, the current study examines whether the social capital resources gained by males as compared to females influence the extent to which either gender group engages in acts of truancy (i.e. painting graffiti, damaging property, smoking cigarettes) and in more serious acts of violence (i.e. physical fights, assault, wounding, and murders). Although prior studies have associated gender differentials in youth offending with a number of individual and contextual risk factors, such as neighbourhood characteristics, socioeconomic background, and aggression (e.g. Zimmerman & Messner, 2010), the results of the current study contribute to the Caribbean literature in further understanding the dynamic relationship between socially based resources and gender as protective factors in reducing the effects of youth problem behaviour.

Defining social capital

Social capital has gained wide appeal in sociological writings, being accredited with producing positive outcomes in health (Kawachi, Kennedy, Lochner, & Prothrow-Stith, 1997), economic development (Dasgupta, 2005), school completion (Teachman, Paasch, & Carver, 1996), community development (Temkin & Rohe, 1998), and positive adolescent outcomes (Furstenberg & Hughes, 1995). Researchers have amassed several definitions in an attempt to adequately describe this concept, with few critics lamenting it has become all things to everyone and hence nothing to no one. Putnam, one of the early contributors to the term, suggested that social capital comprises those "features of social organisation, such as trust, norms and networks that can improve the efficiency of society by facilitating coordinating actions" (1993, p. 167). Putnam (1993) regarded social capital as a public good, which idealises the power of associational activity in generating trust, norms, and values that foster economic development. Coleman (1987, 1990) also honed in on the idea of collective action, but focused on relations in the family and community to generate social capital resources. Coleman and Hoffer (1987) contributed that social capital has both structural and functional components. Structural social capital measures the objective and observable, the types of formal or informal networks which facilitate or prohibit access to meaningful resources (Lau & Li, 2011; Uphoff, 2000). Resources, however, are not transferred by merely knowing someone but depend on the functionality of the relationship, defined by cognitive elements such as shared norms, values, trust, attitudes, and beliefs. It is these subjective and intangible elements that predict the amount of resources accessed and exchanged in any relationship. Accordingly, in many treatises with social capital, scholars have often measured indicators of both structural and cognitive elements to assess whether social capital exists (Goddard, 2003). In this current study, I followed previous studies and utilised Coleman's concept of social capital mainly because of its widespread application in the criminological literature and its intuitive appeal in demonstrating how meso level interactions between families and surrounding communities predict positive outcomes of children and youth (Ferguson, 2006).

Social capital and crime

Burgeoning research has been conducted with social capital as a crime correlate in a number of social environments including – but not limited to – families, schools, communities, and workplaces (Buonanno, Montolio, & Vanin, 2009; Dufur et al., 2015; McCulloch, 2003; Messner, Baumer, & Rosenfeld, 2004). Criminologists have argued that social capital theory presents a better understanding of socially based factors which influence criminality, and also allows for researchers to integrate criminological theory in examining crime rates from one environment to the next (Salmi & Kivivuori, 2006). Previous studies have drawn on attributes of the social disorganisation theory (Shaw & McKay, 1942), general strain theory (Agnew, 1985, 1992), and age-graded informal control (Hirschi, 1969; Sampson & Laub, 1993) to postulate that a lack of social relations, social ties, and trust negatively influence youth offending. Within the family, for example, the affective ties forged between parents and their children may play a role in transmitting normative instructions, monitoring behaviour, fostering social support, and providing quintessential resources that deter young people from engaging in negative situations. Again, the family may also forge external links to community relationships that further reinforce positive behaviour or even supplemental resources that reduce the need for youths to engage in risky behaviours (Furstenberg, 2005). Similar arguments are postulated under the social capital-crime connections, which suggest interdependencies between criminological theory and social capital theory (Nakhaie & Sacco, 2009; Salmi & Kivivuori, 2006). Coleman (1988) for instance, reported that high levels of social disorganisation were found to be equivalent to a lack of social capital.

Although research findings are not always consistent, in general, empirical evidence has supported that social capital indicators produce less unhealthy behaviours as evidenced by a range of offences, from truancy to murder (Crosnoe, 2004; Drewry, Burge, & Driscoll, 2010; Strohschein & Matthew, 2015; Dufur et al., 2015). Fewer studies, however, have investigated the effect of multiple sources of social capital on a wide range of offending behaviour. Wright and Fitzpatrick (2006) investigated the association between family, school, and community social capital on adolescent violent behaviours. Their study data came from the National Longitudinal Study of Adolescent Health, which included 4,834 adolescents attending secondary schools. The results indicated that parental child involvement, parental monitoring, school affiliation, and religious participation decreased youth violence. However, contrary to expectations, they found that sports participation and club participation increased violent behaviour. More recently, Strohschein and Matthew (2015) also explored the relative influence of family, school, and neighbourhood social capital on self-reported violence, property crimes, and substance use in adolescents among a Canadian sample (*N* = 3,180). They reported that social capital in families, schools, and the neighbourhood each contributed independently to youth's self-reported violence, property crime, and substance use, net of controls such as socioeconomic status. All relationships operated in the expected direction, with the exception of a positive association between neighbourhood social capital and substance abuse. This finding points to a potentially negative side of social capital: it may be that stronger neighbourhood ties help adolescents easily procure illicit substances and drugs for personal use and criminal behaviour. Other studies (Dufur et al., 2015; Dufur, Parcel, & McKune, 2008; McNeal, 1999; Parcel & Dufur, 2001; Wright, Cullen, & Miller, 2001) also showed that a lack of social capital in varying social environments was associated with an increased amount of antisocial behaviour; however, they limited their investigations to either one (i.e. family) or two sources of social contexts (i.e. family and school).

Beyond the international research, numerous regional studies in the Caribbean have independently explored varying aspects of social capital in relation to a range of youth outcomes. Lowe et al. (2014) explored the influence of neighbourhood factors on mental health outcomes across four Caribbean countries. In their study, neighbourhood factors were measured through five subscales, namely: social cohesion, neighbourhood attachment, neighbourhood quality, neighbourhood crime, and neighbourhood disorder. They found that for Jamaican students neighbourhood factors were highly associated with depressive symptoms: more so than in other countries (i.e. Bahamas, St Kitts and Nevis, St Vincent). Abdirahman, Bah, Shrestha, and Jacobsen (2012) also conducted a cross-regional study on the association between parental involvement and mental health among students living in Cayman Islands, St Lucia, St Vincent, and the Grenadines, and Trinidad and Tobago. They also reported that students who felt that their parents were understanding and monitored their activities reported fewer mental health issues. In a Bahamian based study, Jones et al. (2012) examined the influence of parental monitoring on risky behaviour, assessing parental monitoring through eight items on parents' knowledge of their whereabouts. They found that adolescents who reported greater parental monitoring reported less involvement in sexual activity, physical fights, and less alcohol consumption.

Despite these contributions, previous research remains limited, as none of these studies have undertaken a gendered analysis to consider whether gender differences in social capital predict different levels of offending behaviour.

Studies within the Caribbean have also examined the independent effects of social capital, with little studies examining the complementary effects of multiple sources of social capital on youth problem behaviours. Additionally, existing studies have also originated predominately from more developed countries; as a result, we are unable to answer whether social capital factors operate in the same pattern in the Caribbean context as they do in more developed countries, especially when we include the gender-crime gap into the equation.

Gender and social capital

In the mainstream literature, there is a dearth of studies on the links between gender and social capital. In those existing, researchers often used measures of social capital that captured individuals' involvement in associational or voluntary activities and examined whether there were any differences in participation by gender (see Burt, 1998; Eriksson, Dahlgren, Janlert, Weinehall, & Emmelin, 2010). For instance, in the education field, several US-based studies concluded that female students were more likely to seek out both parental and institutional support, to get involved in voluntary associations and had higher levels of extracurricular participation than males (Flacks & Thomas, 1998; Kalsner & Pistole, 2003). On the other hand, males were less likely to join extracurricular networks and as such often acquired less social capital resources. Even in instances where males joined organisations, they were more likely to join politically based organisations compared to females, who more likely joined voluntary organisations (Norris & Inglehart, 2003).

In the Caribbean, some have argued that the familial structure within Caribbean societies limits the development of strong social bonds and resourceful networks (Campbell & McLean, 2002; Reynolds, 2008). Reynolds (2008) for example, suggested that Caribbean family relationships are characterised by high individualism, and female-headed households, which inevitability limits participation in civic and community activities. Females inevitability are excluded from social participation because they are preoccupied with the economic responsibility for the household. Of those who participate, women are more involved in civil society or bonding type networks, compared to men who engage in more formal business-type bridging networks (Innerarity, 2003). Similar observations were made in Latin America, as Molyneaux (2002) discussed that women are naturally predisposed to serve their families or communities either because they are less motivated by a self-serving individualism or, more materially, because of their social "embeddedness" in family and neighbourhood ties due to their responsibility for the domain of social reproduction. As much as these studies present explanations on gender differences in social capital resources, the foregoing findings focus on adult populations. Little is known on how young males and females, with less power and responsibility, engage in social connections with others, to an extent that social connections generate beneficial resources.

Morrow (2003) has presented one of the few discussions on how social capital is differentiated by gender in an American school-aged sample. Drawing on children's accounts through qualitative measures, the study showed how gender differences were apparent in reports of trust, social networks, views of local area, and civic participation. They found that social capital for children was not homogenous and experiences of social capital were different for girls than for boys. For example, girls' references to friendships or informal networks were seen as a form of social support, which reflected the cognitive element of social capital, whereas boys saw networks as an avenue for sports and shared activities (i.e. structural social capital). The varied meanings ascribed to social capital also appeared to be influenced by gendered examples provided in the home and in some cases, the social capital experiences differed not only by gender roles but also by age, social stratification, and even neighbourhood characteristics.

This current study is based on Morrow's (2003) contribution by continuing to explore how Caribbean adolescents negotiate and create their own sources of social capital and how these social capital resources are differentiated along gender lines. This study advances the literature by examining how these acquired sources of social capital in multiple social contexts by gender influences male and female offending behaviours. To do this, this study utilised self-reported measures of social capital and youth offences over the past 12 months to investigate: (a) whether females compared to males accumulate higher levels of family, school, and community social capital, and (b) whether social capital resources can explain the gender differences in youth offending behaviour. Accordingly, the study proposes the related hypotheses that females as compared to males will report higher levels of family, school, and community social capital resources. The study also expects that social capital in each social context will exert a positive independent effect in a direction which reduces delinquent and violent behaviour: males and females who report higher levels of social capital will be less involved in problem behaviour.

Methods

Sample and data collection procedures

The current sample was part of a thesis project which assessed the relative influence of family, school, and community social capital on self-reported youth delinquent and violent outcomes, after adjusting for socio-demographic variables and peer delinquency. The Ministry of Education granted approval for the study after reviewing the survey design to ensure these methods and measures avoided harm and met the standards of acceptable research. Approximately three weeks before the actual survey date, consent forms were distributed to students to request parental permission for participation in the survey. The survey was fielded between February 6, 2014 and March 21, 2014. A total of 605 students aged 12–17 at four secondary schools in the urban Arima district of Trinidad and Tobago were randomly approached to fill out an in-school survey. On the survey date for a given school, a systematic selection of one in four students was conducted in each classroom. Selected students were taken to another room and given 45 minutes to complete the questionnaire under the supervision of the researcher and an assigned teacher. The students were advised not to sign the questionnaire. Likewise, if the student did not want to answer a question, they were advised to leave it blank (full questionnaire available upon request). A total of 568 (94 per cent) questionnaires were returned. After listwise deletion, the final sample size for males and females respectively was 209 and 284 for the delinquency models and 203 and 284 for the violence models.

Measures

Youth self-reported delinquency and violence measures

The first dependent variable was assessed with eight items to create a scale of a count of the frequency of behaviours. Youth were asked to indicate whether they had ever engaged in various delinquent behaviours, and if so, how frequently. Delinquent behaviours were: (a) Have you ever smoked a cigarette?; (b) Have you ever smoked illegal drugs (such as marijuana)?; (c) Have you ever sold any (soft or hard) drugs or acted as a middleman or go-between?; (d) Have you ever damaged something on purpose, such as a window, a car, a seat on a bus or in school?; (e) Have you ever stolen something that did not belong to you?; (f) Have you ever broken into a building with the purpose of stealing something?; (g) Have you ever painted graffiti or signs on someone else's property or public place?; and (h) Have you ever carried a weapon, such as a knife, chain etc.? The frequency scale was developed to gauge adolescents' level of frequent involvement in delinquent behaviours. Only those who said yes were included in the frequency scale coded as 1 *1 to 2 times*, 2 *3 to 4 times*, 3 *5 to 6 times*, and 4 *over 7 times*. Total scores were summed to produce a scale ranging from 0 to 28 with higher scores representing increased involvement in delinquent behaviour (Cronbach's alpha = .76; $M = 4.50$, $SD = 4.98$).

The second dependent variable was assessed with six items. Youth were asked to indicate whether they had ever engaged in various violent acts and if so, how frequently (in the past 12 months). The items were formulated as follows: (a) Have you ever threatened somebody with a weapon or threatened to beat them up to get money or other things from them?; (b) Have you ever gotten into a serious physical fight?; (c) Have you ever taken part in a fight where a group of your friends was against another group?; (d) Have you ever intentionally beaten up someone, or hurt them with a stick or knife, so badly that they had to see a doctor?; (e) Have you ever pulled a gun or knife on another person?; and (f) Have you ever shot or stabbed another person? The dependant variables corresponding to violence and the frequency of involvement in violence were constructed using the procedure described in the delinquency section. The total frequency of self-reported violence ranged from 0 to 21 ($M = 2.93$, $SD = 3.92$). The scale was internally consistent as shown by a Cronbach alpha of .81.

Social capital measures

Consistent with prior research, family social capital was assessed in terms of parental supervision, parental involvement, and family attachment. These three scales were utilised in prior assessments of family social capital in previous studies (see Dornbusch, Erickson, Laird, & Wong, 2001; Parcel & Dufur, 2001; Resnick et al., 1997; Strohschein & Matthew, 2015). Parental supervision comprised three items in which the respondent indicated whether he or she *strongly disagreed* (coded 0) to *strongly agreed* (coded 4) with the following: (a) my parents know with whom I spend most of my free time; (b) my parents want to be acquainted with my friends and their parents; and (c) my family pays attention to what I do. Items were summed to produce a scale ranging from 0 to 12, with higher scores representing higher levels of parental supervision (Cronbach's alpha = .66). Parental involvement comprised two items in which the respondent indicated whether he or she *strongly disagreed* (coded 0) to *strongly agreed* (coded 4) with the following (a) my parents follow my educational achievements; and (b) my parents support and encourage me. Items were summed to produce a scale ranging from 0 to 8, with higher scores representing higher levels of parental involvement (Cronbach's alpha = .78). Family attachment comprised three items in which the respondent indicated whether he or she *strongly disagreed* (coded 0) to *strongly agreed* (coded 4) with the following: (a) my family and I have fun together, (b) most of the time I get along fine with my family, and (c) I have a warm relationship with my family. Items were summed to produce a scale ranging from 0 to 12, with higher scores representing higher levels of family attachment (Cronbach alpha = .78).

School social capital was assessed utilizing items from Resnick's et al. (1997) school-connectedness scale used in prior research (Dornbusch et al., 2001; Wright & Fitzpatrick, 2006). The current scale comprised six items in which the respondent indicated whether he or she *strongly disagreed* (coded 0) to *strongly agreed* (coded 4) with the following: (a) feel close to people at the school, (b) feel like a part of the school, (c) feel others are treated unfairly, (d) am happy to be at school, (e) feel teachers treat students fairly, and (f) feel safe at the school. The term of "unfairly" in item 3 was changed from the original word "prejudiced" from the International Youth Survey because results from the pilot test highlighted a lack of clarity by students with the term. The responses to "feel others are treated unfairly" were reverse coded so that along with the other items higher values indicated greater attachment. The six items were summed to produce a scale ranging from 0 to 24, with higher scores representing higher levels of school attachment (Cronbach alpha = .63).

Neighbourhood social capital was assessed with Sampson, Raudenbush, and Earls' (1997) cohesion scale measuring whether respondents *strongly disagreed* (coded 0) to *strongly agreed* (coded 4) with the following (a) people in this neighbourhood generally don't get along with each other; (b) I live in a neighbourhood where people have close relations; (c) people around here are willing to help their neighbours; (d) people in this neighbourhood do not share the same values; and (e) people in this neighbourhood can be trusted. Responses to items (a) and (d) were reversed coded so that along with the other items, higher values represented higher levels of neighbourhood cohesion. Items were summed to produce a scale ranging 0 to 20 (Cronbach's alpha = .57).

Control variables

Age, family structure, residential moves, social and physical disorder, and peer delinquency were included as control variables in the analyses. Age was included as actual age in years at the time of participation. Family structure was coded into four different family types; single family, two biological parents, step family, and a reference category "other family type". Residential mobility was assessed by asking the respondents to indicate how many times they changed residences during their lifetime with responses ranging from 1 *never moved* to 4 *over seven moves*. This item was recoded into a dummy variable with 1 *moved* and 0 *never moved*.

Previous delinquency studies have suggested that youth who associate with delinquent peer groups are more likely to offend (De Coster, Heimer, & Wittrock, 2006; Dufur et al., 2015; Weiss, 2011). As such, two scales were included to control for peer delinquency and violent behaviours.

Friends' delinquent acts comprised seven items, in which the respondent indicated whether they had friends who engaged in the following activities (a) smoked cigarettes; (b) smoked illegal drugs (marijuana); (c) sold hard or soft drugs or acted as the go-between; (d) intentionally damaged public property; (e) broken into a building with the intentions to steal; (f) painted graffiti; (g) carried a weapon. Each item was coded 1 when students responded affirmatively and 0 otherwise and then summed to produce a scale that ranged from 0 to 7 (Cronbach alpha = .84). Peer violent acts was measured with a six-item scale in which the respondent indicated whether they had friends who engaged in the following activities: (a) threatened someone with weapon; (b) participated in a serious physical fight; (c) took part in a group fight; (d) hurt someone badly enough they needed bandages; (e) pulled a gun or knife on someone; (f) stabbed or shot another person. Each item was coded 1 when students responded affirmatively and 0 otherwise and then summed to produce a scale that ranged from 0 to 6 (Cronbach alpha = .84).

Analyses

The analyses were carried out in three stages. The first stage compared the level of social capital resources reported by males and females as well as their scores on the delinquency and violent scales (see Table 8.1). The second stage compared relations between social capital variables and the dependent variables of delinquent and violent behaviour for males and females, respectively. These relationships were tested with Spearman correlations as the data did

Table 8.1 Descriptive statistics on study's variables

Variables	*Male (n = 326)*		*Female (n = 239)*	
	%	*M (SD)*	*%*	*M (SD)*
Age		13.91 (1.50)		13.87 (1.48)
Family structure				
Two biological parents	37.5		37.1	
Single parent	22.5		20.3	
Step family	18.1		13.5	
Other family types	21.9		29.1	
Residential move	33.3		27.8	1.33 (0.59)
Social disorder		6.66 (4.42)		6.31 (4.34)
Physical disorder		7.98(5.00)		8.42 (4.67)
Delinquent friends		2.12 (2.32)		1.99 (2.08)
Violent friends		2.07(2.08)		2.12 (1.89)
Parental monitoring		7.83 (2.60)		8.36 (2.62)
Family attachment		7.79 (3.02)		7.69 (3.15)
Parental involvement		6.19 (1.95)		6.13 (1.99)
School affiliation		13.57 (4.37)		12.82 (4.24)
Neighbourhood cohesion		11.04 (3.47)		10.23 (3.55)
Outcome measures:				
Delinquency		2.35 (1.61)		2.23 (1.98)
Violent behaviour		2.09 (1.76)		1.34 (1.59)

Note: $*p < .05$, $**p < .01$.

not meet the assumption of a normal distribution. The final stage of the analyses investigated the social capital effects on delinquent and violent behaviour for males and females, respectively. OLS analysis holds the assumptions that the dependent variable is a continuous value, normally distributed (i.e. not skewed), and linearly associated with independent variables. However, crime data often represents rare count events with smaller values such as zeros more often reported as the most observed value (Piza, 2012). In the current data, the frequency distributions for the count delinquency and count violent scale found that the most common value was indeed zero (40 per cent and 42 per cent of the respondents), which indicated many adolescents reported no delinquent or violent acts. These high percentages of the score 0 on the outcome variable violate the assumption that the distribution of the dependent variable (and the error terms) is normal. Accordingly, the study used negative binomial regressions which relax the assumption of an equal mean and variance by adding a term for over-dispersion in the data. In these models, regression coefficients are interpreted as the logarithm of the ratio of the expected value before and after a one-unit change in an explanatory variable, with all other terms held constant (Long, 1997; Osgood, 2000). Tables 8.2 and 8.3 present correlational results

Table 8.2 Spearman's correlations between crime covariates, peer deviance and social capital variables for males

	1	*2*	*3*	*4*	*5*	*6*	*7*	*8*	*9*	*10*	*11*
1. Age	1	–.08	.17**	.13*	–.01	.01	.01	–.08	–.07	.15**	.04
2. Family structure		1	.18**	.22**	–.11	–.15**	–.07	.11	–.07	.18**	.15**
3. Friends' delinquent behaviour			1	.76**	–.30**	–.27**	–.35**	–.28**	–.25**	.60**	.46**
4. Friends' violent behaviour				1	–.22**	–.21**	–.25**	–.26**	–.25**	.55**	.55**
5. Parental monitoring					1	.44**	.55**	.30**	.30**	–.31**	–.29**
6. Family attachment						1	.58**	.34**	.31**	–.33**	–.27**
7. Parental involvement							1	.33**	.27**	–.42**	–.32**
8. School affiliation								1	.28**	–.36**	–.32**
9. Neighbourhood cohesion									1	–.29**	–.31**
10. Youth delinquency										1	.68**
11. Youth violence											1

Note: $*p < .05$, $**p < .01$.

Table 8.3 Spearman's correlations between crime covariates, peer deviance and social capital variables for females

	1	*2*	*3*	*4*	*5*	*6*	*7*	*8*	*9*	*10*	*11*
1. Age	1	–.03	.19**	.12	.01	–.09	–.00	–.12	–.11	.07	.01
2. Family structure		1	.02	01	–.01	–.12	–.06	–.05	.03	. .08	.04
3. Friends' delinquent behaviour			1	.76**	–.17*	–.20**	–.25**	–.21**	–.25**	.55**	.42**
4. Friends' violent behaviour				1	–.16*	–.19**	–.24**	–.19**	.09**	.51**	.41**
5. Parental monitoring					1	.43**	.56**	.23**	.17**	–.22**	–.21**
6. Family attachment						1	.57**	.30**	.19**	–.29**	–.23**
7. Parental involvement							1	.26**	.18**	–.41**	–.29**
8. School affiliation								1	.12	–.23**	–.10
9. Neighbourhood cohesion									1	–.24**	–.14*
10. Youth delinquency										1	.56**
11. Youth violence											1

Note: $*p < .05$, $**p < .01$.

Table 8.4 Negative binomial regression models for family, school and community social capital on delinquency

Predictors	*Males (n = 284)*	*Females (n = 209)*
	β(SE)	*β(SE)*
Intercept	.70 (0.59)*	2.23 (0.80)**
Control variables		
Age	.10 (0.03)**	–.02(0.05)
Family Structure[a]		
Two-parent family	–.29 (0.14)	–.19 (0.16)
Single family structure	–.26 (0.16)	–.15 (0.21)
Step-parent household	. 21 (0.21)	. 05 (0.22)
Residential mobility	–.01 (0.12)	.08 (0.15)
Social disorder	. 03 (0.02)	–. 00 (0.02)
Physical disorder	–.01 (0.01)	–.01 (0.02)
Peer delinquency	.16 (0.03)***	.22 (0.04)***
Family Social Capital Indicators		
Parental Monitoring	.00 (0.03)	.02 (0.03)
Parental Involvement	–.10 (0.04)***	–.15 (0.05)***
Family Attachment	–.02 (0.02)	–.01 (0.03)
School Social Capital Indicators		
School Affiliation Index	.00 (0.01)	.00 (0.02)
Neighbourhood Social Capital Indictors		
Neighbourhood Cohesion	–.04 (0.02)*	–.04 (0.02)

Note: $*p < .05$, $**p < .01$, $***p < .001$. Goodness of fit Deviance statistic for the male model was 333.17, and for the female model 224.48.

across gender regarding delinquent and violent behaviour, while Tables 8.4 and 8.5 present the findings of negative binomial regressions for the outcome delinquent behaviours and the outcome violent acts, respectively.

Results

Descriptive and bivariate results

Is there a gender difference in the levels of social capital reported by males and females? Table 8.1 presents the descriptive statistics of the key variables used in the study by gender. Females ($M = 8.36$, $SD = 2.62$) reported higher levels of parental monitoring than did males (males $M = 7.83$, $SD = 2.60$), $t(55) = 2.34$ $p = .02$. However, males ($M = 13.57$, $SD = 4.37$) reported higher levels of school affiliation than did females ($M = 12.82$, $SD = 4.24$), $t(55) = -1.76$ $p = .07$. For the community social capital resources, males ($M = 11.04$, $SD = 3.47$) also reported

Table 8.5 Negative binomial regression models for family, school and community social capital on violent behaviour

Predictors	*Males (n = 284)*	*Females (n = 209)*
	β(SE)	*β(SE)*
Intercept	2.39 (0.80)**	2.08 (1.12)**
Control variables		
Age	–.01 (0.05)	–.09 (0.07)
Family Structure[a]		
Two-parent family	–.38 (0.18)*	.22 (0.25)
Single family structure	–.34 (0.21)	.03 (0.31)
Step-parent household	–.20 (0.28)	.26 (0.33)
Residential mobility	–.05 (0.15)	.18 (0.23)
Social disorder	. 01 (0.02)	. 02 (0.03)
Physical disorder	.01 (0.02)	.02 (0.02)
Peer delinquency	.26 (0.04)***	.21 (0.04)***
Family Social Capital Indicators		
Parental Monitoring	–.03 (0.03)	.03 (0.04)
Parental Involvement	–.08 (0.05)	–.13 (0.06)
Family Attachment	–.03 (0.03)	–.10 (0.04)*
School Social Capital Indicators		
School Affiliation Index	–.02 (0.02)	.02 (0.03)
Neighbourhood Social Capital Indictors		
Neighbourhood Cohesion	–.05 (0.02)*	.01 (0.03)

Note: $*p < .05$, $**p < .01$, $***p < .001$. Goodness of fit Deviance statistic for the male model was 318.43, and for the female model 211.57.

higher levels of social cohesion than did their female counterparts (M = 10.23, SD = 3.55), $t(56)$ = -.2.71, p = .01.

Was the social capital related to delinquent and violent behaviour? Tables 8.2 and 8.3 present correlational results across gender regarding these variables. Correlation analyses among the crime covariates indicated that age was associated with male delinquent behaviour (r = .15, p = .01) but not associated with male violent behaviour (r = .04, p = .54). Among females, age was neither a significant predictor of delinquent (r = .07, p = .26) nor violent behaviour (r = .01, p = .91). Males who associated with delinquent peers reported more delinquent behaviour (r = .60, p = .00) and more violent behaviour (r = .46, p = .00). Among females almost identical results were found with more peer deviance strongly associated with more delinquency (r = .55 p = .00) and more violence (r = .42 p = .00). All measures of social capital indicators across the family, school, and community were inversely associated with delinquency and violent behaviour for both males and females. Thus, more social capital was related with less delinquency and violence across gender.

Multivariate analyses

Model 1 (Table 8.4) shows that among the control variables, older males on average reported more delinquent behaviours ($\beta = .10, p = .01$). Males whose peers were engaged in higher numbers of delinquent activities reported on average a significantly higher count of delinquent acts than males whose peers were engaged in fewer delinquent acts ($\beta = .16, p = .00$). Concerning the family social capital variables, males who reported higher levels of parental involvement reported on average a significantly lower count of delinquent behaviours than males with lower levels of parental involvement ($\beta = -.10, p = .00$). School connectedness did not exert any significant impact on male participation in delinquent behaviours. Males who reported higher levels of neighbourhood cohesion reported on average a significantly lower count of delinquent behaviours compared to males with lower levels of neighbourhood cohesion ($\beta = -.04, p = .04$).

Regarding, the predictors among the girls, peer delinquency was the only significant control variable. Females whose peers were engaged in higher numbers of delinquent activities reported on average a significantly higher count of delinquent acts than females whose peers were engaged in fewer delinquent acts ($\beta = .22$, $p = .00$). Of the social capital variables, females who reported higher levels of parental involvement reported on average a significantly lower count of delinquent behaviours than females with lower levels of parental involvement ($\beta = -.15, p = .00$). Again, contrary to the bivariate analyses, school connectedness did not exert any significant impact on females' participation in delinquent behaviours, neither did neighbourhood (see Table 8.4).

Model 2 examined the effect of social capital variables by gender on violent behaviour and shows that males living in two-parent households engaged in less violent behaviour than males living in other household types ($\beta = -.38, p = .04$). The relationship between deviant peer association also held for violent behaviours: males who associated with violent peers reported on average a significant higher count of violent behaviours ($\beta = .26, p = .00$). Contrary to our expectation, none of the family or school social capital variables had any significant relationship with male violent behaviour when adjusting for controls. However, males who reported higher levels of neighbourhood cohesion reported lower counts of violent behaviour ($\beta = -.05, p = 03$). For the girls, among the control variables only associating with violent peers was a significant predictor of female violent behaviour ($\beta = .21, p = .00$). Furthermore, the female model supported the hypothesis that family social capital played an essential role in controlling violent behaviour among females. Females who reported higher levels of parental involvement reported on average a significantly lower count of delinquent behaviours than female with lower levels of parental involvement ($\beta = -.13, p = .04$). Likewise, females who reported higher levels of family attachment reported on average a significantly lower count of violent behaviours than female youth with lower levels of family attachment (β = -.10, p = .01).

Discussion

Research has amply documented that social capital resources buffer adolescents from engaging in criminal behaviour (Dufur et al., 2015; Rosenfeld et al., 2001; Strohschein & Matthew, 2015). Few studies, however, have explored the gender dimension on the impact of social capital, to assess whether the patterns of anti-social behaviour vary by gender because of accumulated social capital resources (Burt, 1998; Molyneaux, 2002; Morrow, 2003). The current study provides further evidence that family and community social capital resources are instrumental for controlling youth outcomes, but also demonstrate that these resources operate differently in reducing problem behaviours between the genders in the Caribbean context.

Initially, descriptive statistics revealed that males reported slightly higher levels of family attachment and parental involvement than females. On the flipside, females had higher levels of parental monitoring than males. This finding supports the well-established research which demonstrates that parents tend to monitor the activities of girls rather than boys (Giordano & Cernkovich, 1987; Svensson, 2003). This finding also echoes Quinlan's (2006) study which described Caribbean communities as matrifocal, which results in daughter-biased parental care. Strict discipline and protection of females are dominant features in Caribbean socialisation. Quinlan (2006) also reported that this lopsided parenting results in unfavourable outcomes for Dominican males. Concerning school context, although prior studies underscore the importance of school connectedness in predicting less health risk behaviours among Caribbean adolescents (Blum et al., 2003), this study found no significant gender differences in self-reported school connectedness. It may be that school environments are gender-neutral, with Caribbean males and females being exposed to equal amounts of social support and resources. However, teachers and school officials might be overly concerned with completing formal curriculum, while little attention is placed on creating alternative avenues for social support and resources that can be easily tapped into by either gender. Within the community, the results showed that males reported higher levels of neighbourhood cohesion than females. One possible explanation may be that males were more involved in extra familial activities and community groups, which help foster closer-knit ties. This is in line with prior research that found that Trinidadian males participated more in extracurricular activities, athletics, and organised events, whereas females participated in artistic and religious activities (Mello & Worrell, 2008). Accordingly, males are better positioned to develop stronger community social relationships.

These findings offer sufficient evidence on gender differences in the accumulation of social capital resources among school-aged youths in the Trinidad and Tobago context. These findings fit well with prior Caribbean-related research on independent aspects of social capital and gender (Jones et al., 2012; Lowe et al., 2014; Mello & Worrell, 2008; Reynolds, 2006). The current study goes beyond the existing findings by examining three complementary sources of social capital, as opposed to a single social context as done in previous studies. Additionally, the findings add two important contributions. First, the study debunks the findings of prior regional studies (see Innerarity, 2003) that females have stronger social capital networks than males. This may be true for adult populations, but may not be the same for adolescent populations. Second, these results also suggest that males benefit more from structural and cognitive resources gained from two social contexts, the family and the community. Females, however, benefitted more from structural social capital resources developed within the family. This gender difference may be due to Caribbean socialisation practices, in which males are considered to be breadwinners and are given more freedom to develop extra familial associations (Brown, Chevannes, & Scott, 1998). Subsequent research should attempt to clarify characteristics of male-female interactions that allow males' greater access to social capital resources than females, especially in the Caribbean context.

The main focus of the study investigated whether accumulated social capital resources influence male and female offending differently. Using two levels of offending behaviour modelled across gender, the general findings demonstrated that family and community social capital resources were important predictors of youth problem behaviour, net of controls. Male offending, however, was predicted in part both by family and community social capital variables, while in contrast, female offending was only influenced by family-based social capital resources. In line with prior studies that established a crime – age link (e.g. Moffit, 1993), age played a role in predicting male involvement in delinquent behaviours, net of social capital variables. Older males appeared to be more involved in delinquent behaviours compared to younger male students. However, violent behaviour among males and delinquent and violent behaviour among females did not vary by age: at least not for those aged 12 to 17 years old.

Males living in two-parent households also committed less delinquent acts compared to males in other household types, which has been established in the extant literature (Demuth & Brown, 2004; Gault-Sherman, 2012), that argues that adolescents living in two-parent households typically benefit from increased parental supervision and in turn, children may have limited time opportunities to engage in negative behaviours. two-parent households are also better positioned to generate more financial and physical resources than single-parent household types, which buffer any lack in resources, and in turn inhibit crime. This finding on the buffering effect of two-parent households for males is quite important as Caribbean families have been predominately described as matrifocal and children are often "single parented" (Brunod & Cook-Darzens, 2001). In these families, as reported by Quinlan (2006) males are at a higher risk for engaging in alcoholism and other poor behavioural choices. Given that mothers rarely choose to be single parents, and equally accepting the importance that these findings give to the paternal role for fathers, alternative modes should be explored to construct or reconstruct the presence of fathers or "father figures" in the Caribbean family structure. Furthermore, as household type was not predictive of delinquent or violent acts for the female adolescents, future studies need to consider the *gendered* impact of absent fathers within a Caribbean context as well.

By far, the strongest effect among the control variables was the effects between delinquent peer association and male delinquency. The strength of this relationship offers support for the differential association theory which argues that friendship networks play an essential role in predicting male offending behaviours. For females, associating with delinquent peers also emerged as a significant predictor of delinquency. Overall, results demonstrated that association with violent peers was markedly more important than all the hypothesised predictors for both predictors and regardless of gender. This pattern of findings is consistent with the international and regional literature which has demonstrated that deviant peer association is the strongest correlate of youth problem behaviours (Wang et al., 2014; Weiss, 2011; Zimmerman & Messner, 2010; Gough et al., 2015; UNICEF, 2010). For example, Wang et al. (2016) reported on the effects of deviant peers in a Bahamian youth population, demonstrating that adolescents who reported delinquent behaviour of friends also engaged in these nefarious activities themselves.

Being exposed to deviant peers clearly encourages antisocial participation, which possibly explains the heightend rates of gang activity across the Caribbean region (Ryan et al., 2013). For example, a local study identified that the peer group acts as the most immediate and influential mechanism for policing male performance during adolescence, dictating what they choose or choose not to do (Plummer & Geofroy, 2010). This study documented that the peer group demands conformity, and is uncompromising on male gender expectations which are interwoven into the social fabric of Caribbean society. These roles often dictate that real men are tough, risk taking, and dominant; as such, in males' response to these expectations, we can explain the increased rates of male violence. This argument can be equally applied to Caribbean females, as growing evidence (see Seepersad, 2016) has identified increasing involvement of females in gang-related activities. These findings, in part, can explain the observed increase in female delinquency and violence via the influence of peers. Perhaps similar to males, females are assuming traditionally defined male patriarchal gender roles and responding to conflict with toughness, dominance, and self-rewarding behaviours.

Does social capital matter for male delinquency? Parental involvement and community cohesion were found to be inversely related to male delinquent behaviour, which replicated findings in prior studies (Crosnoe, 2004; Dornbusch et al., 2001; Hoffmann & Dufur, 2008; Gault-Sherman, 2012). It may be that parental involvement signals to males, parents' interest in their behaviour and life outcome and therefore, males avoid negative behaviours to keep and win the approval of parents. As with males, instrumental parenting behaviours, in this case involvement in schooling, appears to create opportunities to model pro-social behaviour or transmit normative messages that deter female offending, delinquency, and violent behaviours. It is important to note that parental involvement was a significant predictor of male and female offending, net of controls. Thus emphasizing that parental involvement in children's academic journey does not only have manifest outcomes for academic success, (see Goddard, 2003), but indirectly encourages pro-social behaviour choices as opposed to delinquency. Studies within the Caribbean region have reported that parental involvement is a strong determinant in influencing adolescent choices (Abdirahman et al., 2012). The basic idea that parents engaging and spending time with their children buffers serious and non-serious forms of crime re-emphasises the need to better understand the means by which parents become involved with their children, and in turn utilise them as mechanisms in crime-fighting strategies in the Caribbean context.

Concerning violent behaviour, the importance of living in two-parent families remains a significant predictor of male violent behaviour. Regarding the social capital variables, neighbourhood cohesion reported the strongest protective effect on male violent behaviour. The observed relations between the family type social capital resources and male delinquency disappeared, while the relationships within the community appeared to discourage violence among males instead. This might indicate, that Caribbean males do not seek out social support or resources found in families and schools that typically provide normative instructions to offset violent behaviours. This is an important finding because research that focuses on deterring violent behaviour may overly focus on the family as the primary socialisation unit to deter male violence, while ignoring the prohibitive role of the community.

Violent offending among females appeared to be influenced by family attachment, parental involvement, and deviant peer association. Interestingly, family attachment was not significantly related to delinquent behaviour across gender. It could be argued that because of socialisation practices girls develop stronger emotional attachments with family members, which they can draw on as a social resource to avoid criminal choices. Caribbean males are socialised to be independent, tough, breadwinners, or as Chevannes (2001) phrases it "a man minds but woman cares" (p. 222). From early ages, Caribbean women are socialised to fulfil motherly roles, typified by caring and emotive ties. It is not surprising, therefore, that the study found that only among females, greater levels of emotive closeness (i.e. family attachment) to parents was related to less violent behaviour. These socialisation experiences can also best be amply captured in the Guyanese originated phrase "tie the heifer, loose the bull", in which females are closely monitored and males are allowed greater freedom. Because of these practices, females are inevitably exposed to less social networks outside of the family, and thereby accumulate less social capital resources. These relations do not only inhibit extra familial ties or create strong family bonds, but may also generate effective sanctions for females to adhere to behavioural norms against violent crimes. Further, it is interesting to point out that although the bivariate analyses revealed that males acquired higher levels of cognitive type social capital resources, these resources did not manifest into preventing violent behaviour. Rather, it was the lower stocks of cognitive socially based resources acquired by females that deterred violent behaviours.

Implications

Accordingly, these results have important implications for Caribbean policy makers in utilizing social capital resources in reducing problem behaviour across the gender groups. First, these results establish that crime-fighting interventions should be gender-specific, and adopt targeted strategies that builds community-based social capital resources for males. Public policy strategies should encourage mandatory participation in community-based networks or associations for males. Increased opportunities for social participation can be created by instituting community networks or agencies as a part of secondary school students' curriculum. Expanding the size of males' community networks may not always increase a sense of civicness, but will provide enhanced opportunities for community supervision and behaviour monitoring. Such an idea dovetails and supports previous drafted government initiatives such as mandatory national youth service, as proposed in Trinidad and Tobago by Ryan et al. (2013). Previously existing community interest groups such as 4Hclubs, boy scouts, and cadets, should be also revitalised and reinstituted for compulsory participation during one's schooling years, particularly for males as they seem better positioned to benefit from community-based interactions. With respect to females, these findings highlight the importance of strengthening family ties and parent involvement as effective policy interventions to reduce delinquent and violent behaviour. Since control of family relations are outside of the public sphere, public policy can only supplement resources that ease and improve the interactions in parenting behaviours and family lifestyles. Policy can dictate laws that permit national leave for parents for the purposes of attending Parent Teachers' Association meetings and other important calendar events. Supplemental resources to maximise parental involvement may include parenting workshops, or supplemental resources such as scholarships or that can ease the strain parents' face and they can redirect their attention to successfully managing and supporting children's activities. Particularly for males, increased father involvement can exhibit positive outcomes on pro-social development.

Importantly, these findings stress the need to develop targeted policies that reduce the controlling effect of negative peer influence. In addition to the dominant impact of peers during adolescent years, most Caribbean societies are characterised by high levels of gang activity, whose offenders are young males (Harriot, 2002; Ryan et al., 2013; Seepersad, 2016). This increases the need for strong peer control policies. Unfortunately, policies cannot intervene in adolescences' lives and dictate with whom they associate, rather policies can focus on intentionally building positive peer groups that can infiltrate and dilute the effect of negative peers in different social settings, schools, and communities. This can be accomplished by establishing peer education programs that educate selected peers with skills as conflict resolution skills, that can help reach at risk peers. Along similar lines, policies can also establish peer-mentoring groups that offer an alternative source of belongingness than antisocial groups, particularly gangs. Through these targeted initiatives it is expected that Caribbean adolescents could become increasingly resistant to negative peer influence.

Limitations

Notwithstanding the above contributions, this study has several limitations that must be acknowledged. First, the sample used to explore these associations was an in-school survey in an urban area of Trinidad and as such, the results may not be generalised to different populations. In addition, although the study used comprehensive measures of social capital replicated from prior studies, and crime correlates, other potentially important variables such as one's socioeconomic status and trust were collected but not included in the final models. Third, many of the measures (independent and outcomes) were self-reported by the individual and may be subjected to either under- or overreporting. Fourth, the cross-sectional design of the study makes it difficult to interpret a causal relationship between social capital, gender, and offending behaviour. Although causal effects could not be determined, the findings do suggest that social capital operates differently among males and females in relation to offending behaviour.

Conclusion

Despite the weaknesses outlined, this study demonstrates the varying effects that social capital resources embedded in different social contexts may have on male and female offending behaviours in Trinidad. Social interactions in the family have a strong controlling effect on female offending, across different offending types. School-aged females seem less influenced by social relations in the school and community in making decisions towards or away from crime. Rather, the study suggests that males seem dually influenced by social connections within the family and community. Not surprisingly, the data indicate that associating with delinquent or violent peers has a substantial influence on both male and female criminal behaviours. Collectively, these findings emphasise the importance of including multiple strategies from different social contexts in strategies aimed at reducing male and female problem behaviour, in particular, in a Caribbean context.

References

Abdirahman, H.A., Bah, T.T., Shrestha, H.L., & Jacobsen, K.H. (2012). Bullying, mental health and parental involvement among adolescents in the Caribbean. *West Indian Med Journal*, *61*(5), 504–508.

Agnew, R. (1985). Social control theory and delinquency: A longitudinal test. *Journal of Criminology*, *23*(1), 47–61.

Agnew, R. (1992). Foundation for a general strain theory of crime and delinquency. *Journal of Criminology*, *30*(1), 47–87.

Blum, R., Halcon, L., Beuhring, T., Pate, E., Campell-Forrester, S., & Venema, A. (2003). Adolescent health in the Caribbean: Risk and protective factors. *American Journal of Public Health*, *93*(3), 456–460.

Bourne, P.A., & McGrowder, D.A. (2009). Rural Health in Jamaica: Examining and refining the predictive factors of good health status of rural residents. *Rural Remote Health*, *9*(2), 1116–1130.

Broidy, L., & Agnew, R. (1997). Gender and crime: A general strain theory perspective. *Journal of Research in Crime and Delinquency, 34*(3), 275–300.

Brown, J., Chevannes, B., & Scott, M. (1998). *Why men stay so: An examination of gender socialisation in the Caribbean.* Jamaica: University of the West Indies.

Brunod, R., & Cook-Darzens, S. (2001). Men and the paternal function in Caribbean families. Retrieved from www.ncbi.nlm.nih.gov/pubmed/18253598.

Buonanno, P., Montolio, D., & Vanin, P. (2009). Does social capital reduce crime? *Journal of Law and Economics, 52*(1), 145–170.

Burt, R.S. (1998). The gender of social capital. *Rationality and Society, 10*(1), 5–46.

Campbell, C., & McLean, C. (2002). Ethnic identities, social capital and health inequalities: Factors shaping African-Caribbean participation in local community networks in the UK. *Journal of Social Science and Medicine, 55*(4), 643–657.

Chevannes, B. (2001). *Learning to be a man: Culture, socialization and gender identity in five Caribbean communities.* Kingston: The University of the West Indies Press.

Coleman, J.S. (1987). Families and schools. *Educational Researcher, 16*(6), 32–38.

Coleman, J.S. (1988). Social capital in the creation of human capital. *American Journal of Sociology, 94*, 95–120.

Coleman, J. (1990). *Foundations of social theory.* Cambridge: Harvard University Press.

Coleman, J.S., & Hoffer, T.B. (1987). *Public and private schools: The impact of communities.* New York: Basic Books.

Crosnoe, R. (2004). Social capital and the interplay of families and schools. *Journal of Marriage and Family, 66*(2), 267–280.

Dasgupta, P. (2005). Economics of social capital. *The Economic Record, 81*(1), S2–S21.

De Coster, S., Heimer, K., & Wittrock, S.M. (2006). Neighbourhood disadvantage, social capital, street context and youth violence. *The Sociological Quarterly, 47*(4), 723–753.

Demuth, S., & Brown, S.L. (2004). Family structure, family process and adolescent delinquency. *Journal of Research in Crime and Delinquency, 41*(1), 58–81.

Dornbusch, S.M., Erickson, K.G., Laird, J., & Wong, C.A. (2001). The relation of family and school attachment to adolescence deviance in diverse groups and communities. *Journal of Adolescent Research, 16*(4), 396–422.

Drewry, J.A., Burge, P.L., & Driscoll, L.G. (2010). A tripartite perspective of social capital and its' access by high school dropouts. *Education and Urban Society, 42*(5), 499–521.

Dufur, M., Hoffmann, J., Braudt, D., Parcel, T., & Spence, K. (2015). Examining the effects of family and school social capital on delinquent behaviour. *Deviant Behaviour, 36*(7), 511–526.

Dufur, M.J., Parcel, T.L., & Mckune, B.A. (2008). Capital and context using social capital at home and at school to predict child social adjustment. *Journal of Health and Social Behaviour, 48*(2), 146–161.

Eriksson, M., Dahlgren, L., Janlert, U., Weinehall, L., & Emmelin, M. (2010). Social capital, gender and educational level – impact on self-rated health. *The Open Public Health Journal, 3*, 1–12.

Ferguson, K. (2006). Social capital and children's wellbeing: A critical synthesis of the international social capital literature. *International Journal of Social Welfare, 15*(1), 12–18.

Flacks, R., & Thomas, S.L. (1998). College students in the nineties: Report on a project in progress. *Revision of a paper presented at the Annual Meeting of the American Association for the Study of Higher Education.* Albuquerque, NM, November 6–9, 1997.

Furstenberg, F. (2005). Banking on families: How families generate and distribute social capital. *Journal of Marriage and Family, 67*(4), 809–821.

Furstenberg, F.F., & Hughes, M.E. (1995). Social capital and successful development among at-risk youth. *Journal of Marriage and Family*, *57*(3), 580–592.

Gault-Sherman, M. (2012). It's a two way street: The bidirectional relationship between parenting and delinquency. *Journal of Youth Adolescence*, *41*(2), 121–145.

Giordano, P.C., & Cernkovich, S.A. (1987). Family relationships and delinquency. *Criminology*, *25*(2), 295–318.

Goddard, R.D. (2003). Relational networks, social trust and norms: A social capital perspective on students' chances of academic success. *Educational Evaluation and Policy Analysis*, *25*(1), 59–74.

Gough, H., Longman-Mills, S., De La Haye, W., Mann, R., Brands, B., Hamilton, H., . . . Khenti, A. (2015). Family relations, peer influence, spirituality and drug use among students in one university in Kingston, Jamaica. Retrieved from www.scielo.br/pdf/tce/v24nspe/0104-0707-tce-24-spe-00184.pdf.

Harriott, A.D. (2002). Crime trends in the Caribbean and responses. *Report submitted to the United Nations Office on Crime and Drugs*. University of the West Indies, Kingston, Jamaica.

Harriott, A.D., & Jones, M. (2016). Crime and violence in Jamaica. Inter-American Development bank. Retrieved from https://publications.iadb.org/bitstream/handle/11319/7773/Crime-and-Violence-in-Jamaica-IDB-Series-on-Crime-and-Violence-in-the-Caribbean.pdf.

Hirschi, T. (1969). *Causes of delinquency*. Berkeley: University of California Press.

Hoffmann, J.P., & Dufur, M.J. (2008). Family and school capital effects on delinquency: Substitutes or complements? *Sociological Perspectives*, *51*(1), 29–62.

Innerarity, F. (2003). *Gender dimensions of social capital in the Caribbean*. Kingston: University of West Indies Press.

Jones, G., Chen, X., Stanton, B., Dinaj-Koci, V., Deveaux, L., Lunn, S., . . . Gomez, M.P. (2012). Parental monitoring and risky behaviour among Bahamian youth. *International Journal of Child, Youth and Family Studies*, *3*(4), 376–395.

Kalsner, L., & Pistole, M.C. (2003). College adjustment in a multi-ethnic sample: Attachment, separations-individuation, and ethnic identity. *Journal of College Student Development*, *44*(1), 92–109.

Kawachi, I., Kennedy, B.P., Lochner, K., & Prothrow-Stith, D. (1997). Social capital, income inequality, and mortality. *American Journal of Public Health*, *87*(9), 1491–1498.

Lau, M., & Li, W. (2011). The extent of family and school social capital promoting positive subjective wellbeing among primary school children in Shenzhen, China. *Children and Youth Services Review*, *33*(9), 1573–1582.

Lazarus-Black, M. (2008). Vanishing complainants: The place of violence in family, gender, work and law. *Caribbean Studies*, *36*(1), 25–51.

Long, J.S. (1997). *Regression models for categorical and limited dependent variables*. Thousand Oaks, CA: Sage Publications.

Lowe, G.A., Lipps, G., Gibson, R.C., Halliday, S., Morris, A., Clarke, N., & Wilson, R. (2014). *Neighbourhood factors and depression among adolescents in four Caribbean countries*. Retrieved from www.ncbi.nlm.nih.gov/pmc/articles/PMC3997363/.

McCarthy, B., Felmlee, D., & Hagan, J. (2004). Girls friends are better: Gender, friends, and crime among school and street youth. *Criminology*, *42*, 805–835.

McCulloch, A. (2003). An examination of social capital and social disorganization in neighbourhoods in the British household panel study. *Social Science & Medicine*, *56*(7), 1425–1438.

McIlwaine, C., & Moser, C. (2001). Violence and social capital in urban poor communities: Perspectives from Colombia and Guatemala. *Journal of International Development*, *13*(7), 965–984.

McNeal, R. (1999). Parental involvement as social capital: Differential effectiveness on science achievement, truancy and dropping out. *Social Forces*, *78*(1), 117–144.

Mello, Z., & Worrell, F. (2008). *Gender variation in extracurricular activity participation and perceived life chances in Trinidad and Tobago adolescents*. Retrieved from www.scielo.cl/pdf/psykhe/v17n2/art08.pdf.

Messner, S.F., Baumer, E.P., & Rosenfeld, R. (2004). Dimensions of social capital and rates of homicide. *American Sociological Review*, *69*(6), 882–903.

Moffitt, T.E. (1993). Adolescence limited and life course persistent antisocial behaviour: A developmental taxonomy. *Psychological Review*, *100*(4), 674–701.

Molyneaux, M. (2002). Gender and the silence of social capital: Lessons from Latin America. *Development and Change*, *33*(2), 167–188.

Morrow, V. (2003). *Conceptualizing social capital in relation to children and young people: Is it different for girls?* Paper presented Gender and Social Capital Conference, University of Manitoba, Winnipeg, Canada.

Nakhaie, M.R., & Sacco, F.V. (2009). Social capital, individual disorder and property offences. *International Journal of Law and Psychiatry*, *32*(6), 392–399.

Norris, P., & Inglehart, R. (2003). *Gendering social capital: Bowling in women's league*. Paper presented at St. John's College, University of Manitoba, Winnipeg, Canada, May 2–3, 2003.

Osgood, D.W. (2000). Poisson-based regression analysis of aggregate crime rates. *Journal of Quantitative Criminology*, *16*(1), 21–43.

Parcel, T.L., & Dufur, M.J. (2001). Capital at home and at school: Effects on child social adjustment. *Journal of Marriage and the Family*, *63*(4), 32–47.

Piza, E. (2012). *Using Poisson and negative binomial regression models to measure the influence of risk on crime incident counts*. Retrieved from www.rutgerscps.org/docs/CountRegressionModels.pdf.

Plummer, D., & Geofroy, S. (2010). When bad is cool: Violence and crime as a rite of passage into manhood. *Caribbean Review of Gender Studies*, *4*, 1–17.

Putnam, R.D. (1993). The prosperous community: Social capital and public life. *The American Prospect*, *4*(13), 35–42.

Putnam, R.D. (1995). *Making democracy work: Civic traditions in modern Italy*. Princeton: Princeton University Press.

Quinlan, R. (2006). *Gender and risk in a matrifocal Caribbean community: A view from behavioural ecology*. Retrieved from http://public.wsu.edu/~rquinlan/quinlan-gender-risks.pdf.

Resnick, M.D., Bearman, P., Blum, R., Bauman, K., Harris, K., Jones, J., Tabor, T., Beuhring, R., Sieving, M., Shew, M., Ireland, M., Beringer, L., & Ury, J. (1997). Protecting adolescents from harm: Findings from the national longitudinal study of adolescent health. *Journal of the American Medical Association*, *278*(10), 823–832.

Reynolds, T. (2006). Bonding social capital within the Caribbean family and community, special issue: Ethnicity and social capital. *Journal of Community, Work and Family*, *9*(3), 273–290.

Reynolds, T. (2008). Ties that bind: Families, social capital and Caribbean second-generation return migration. *Families and Social Capital ESRC Research Group Working Paper* (No. 23). Retrieved from www.payonline.lsbu.ac.uk/ahs/downloads/families/familieswp23.pdf.

Rosenfeld, R., Messner, S., & Baumer, E. (2001). Social capital and homicide. *Social Forces*, *80*(1), 283–310.

Ryan, S., Rampersad, I., Bernard, L., Mohammed, P., & Thorpe, M. (Eds.). (2013). *"No time to quit: Engaging youth at risk: Executive report of the committee on young males and crime in Trinidad and Tobago"*. University of the West Indies St. Augustine: Multimedia Production Centre.

Salmi, V., & Kivivuori, J. (2006). The association between social capital and juvenile crime: The role of individual and structural factors. *European Journal of Criminology, 3*(2), 123–148.

Sampson, R. J., Raudenbush, S. W., & Earls, F. (1997). Neighborhoods and violent crime: A multilevel study of collective efficacy. *Science, 277*(5328), 918–924.

Sampson, R.J., & Laub, J.H. (1993). *Crime in the making: Pathways and turning points through life*. Cambridge, MA: Harvard University Press.

Seepersad, R. (2016). *Crime and violence in Trinidad: IADB series*. Retrieved from https://publications.iadb.org/bitstream/handle/11319/7772/Crime-and-Violence-in-Trinidad-and-Tobago-IDB-Series-on-Crime-and-Violence-in-the-Caribbean.pdf?sequence=4.

Seguino, S. (2003). *Is economic growth good for well-being? Evidence on gender effects in Latin America and the Caribbean, 1970–2000*. Working paper, Department of Economics, University of Vermont.

Shaw, C.R., & McKay, H.D. (1942). *Juvenile delinquency in urban areas*. Chicago: University of Chicago Press.

Steffensmeier, D., & Allan, E. (1996). Gender and crime: Towards a gendered theory of female offending. *Criminology, 38*(2), 403–438.

Strohschein, L., & Matthew, A. (2015). Adolescent problem behaviour in Toronto, Canada: Associations with family, school and neighbourhood social capital. *Sociological Inquiry, 85*(1), 129–157.

Svensson, R. (2003). Gender differences in adolescent drug use: The impact of parental monitoring and peer deviance. *Youth and Society, 34*(3), 300–329.

Teachman, J., Paasch, K., & Carver, K. (1996). Social capital and dropping out of school early. *Journal of Marriage and the Family, 58*(3), 773–783.

Temkin, K., & Rohe, W. (1998). Social capital and neighbourhood stability: An empirical investigation. *Housing Policy Debate, 9*(1), 61–88.

United Nations Children Fund (UNICEF). (2010). *Views on juvenile offending Barbados, Dominica and St. Lucia*. Retrieved from www.unicef.org/easterncaribbean/Juvenile_Offing_Study_WEB.pdf.

United Nations Development Programme (UNDP). (2012). *Caribbean human development report 2012: Human development and the shift to better citizen security*. Retrieved from http://hdr-caribbean.regionalcentrelac-ndp.org/images/pdf/caribbean_hdr_2012.pdf.

United Nations Office on Drugs and Crime and World Bank (UNDOC). (2007). *Crime, violence and development: Trends, costs and policy options in the Caribbean*. Report No. 37820. Washington, DC: The World Bank.

Uphoff, N. (2000). Understanding social capital: Learning from the analysis and experience of participation. In G. Parthadas, & S. Serageldin (Eds.), *Social capital: A multifaceted Perspective* (pp. 215–249). Washington, DC: World Bank.

Wang, B., Stanton, B., Deveaux, L., Ximoning; L., Koci, V., & Lunn, S. (2014). The impact of parental involvement in an effective adolescent risk reduction intervention on sexual risk communication and adolescent outcomes. *Aids Education and Prevention, 26*(6), 500–520.

Weiss, H.E. (2011). Adolescents as a source of social control: The utility of adolescent social capital for reducing violent delinquency. *Sociological Spectrum, 31*(5), 54–78.

Williams, I. (2009). *Tackling youth crime and violence in the Caribbean. Presentation on behalf of the CARICOM at WHO meeting*. Retrieved from www.who.int/violence_injury_prevention/violence/4th_milestones_meeting/williams.pdf.

Wright, D., & Fitzpatrick, K.M. (2006). Social capital and adolescent violent behaviour: Correlates of fighting and weapon use among secondary school students. *Social Forces*, *84*(3), 14–35.

Wright, J.P., Cullen, F., & Miller, J.T. (2001). Family social capital and delinquent involvement. *Journal of Criminal Justice*, *29*(1), 1–9.

Zimmerman, G.M., & Messner, S. (2010). Neighbourhood context and the gender gap in adolescent violent crime. *American Sociological Review*, *75*(6), 958–980.

9 Trouble in paradise? Pathways to prison among Caribbean women incarcerated in the Netherlands

Katharina J. Joosen

Introduction

In the Netherlands, Dutch Caribbean women are over-represented in official crime statistics. While Caribbean women represent less than 2 per cent of the total population of women in the Netherlands, in 2015 they represented 4.2 per cent of female crime suspects (Central Bureau of Statistics [CBS], 2016a). Dutch Caribbean women also make up over 10 per cent of the female prison population, being one of the largest ethnic minorities across female prisons in the Netherlands (CBS, 2016b; Joosen & Slotboom, 2015). Furthermore, involvement in criminal activity appears to take place from a young age, as Dutch Caribbean women are twice as likely to be persistent offenders by the age of 22 when compared to native Dutch women (Blokland, Grimbergen, Bernasco, & Nieuwbeerta, 2010). A similar over-representation of Caribbean women in prison can be found, for example, in the United Kingdom where Afro-Caribbean women comprise a quarter of female prisoners, while accounting for only 1 per cent of the general population (Sudbury, 2013).

However, it is likely that this over-representation in registered crime and prison populations is due – at least in part – to practices of ethnic or racial profiling by the Dutch police (Çankaya, 2015) and criminal justice system (Weenink, 2009). Such practices could lead to inflated rates of Caribbean crime suspects and could negatively impact on their sentencing outcomes as well. For example, one study investigating the sentencing of cocaine smugglers showed that, while defendants born in the Netherlands were more likely to receive a shorter sentence than the guidelines would dictate, the reverse was true for those born in the Dutch Caribbean. Caribbean defendants were more likely to receive a sentence higher than expected based on the weight they smuggled into the country (Boone & Korf, 2010). As around two-thirds of incarcerated women in the Netherlands have children (e.g. Alberts, Joosen, Slotboom, Kruttschnitt, & Bijleveld, 2016), and Caribbean women are often single mothers (Blank, 2013; Kibbelaar, 2010), their high incarceration rate also has a relatively large impact on societies both in Europe and across the Caribbean. Nonetheless, there is little known about specific pathways to offending and incarceration among Caribbean women who end up in the Dutch prison system.

Drug-connected women: a gendered typology?

What we do know from available international and Dutch literature is that the majority of incarcerated Caribbean women has been convicted of a drug-related offence (e.g. Bailey, 2013; Clement, 2008; Maduro, 2014; Morris, 2008; Sudbury, 2013). At first sight this seems not that gender-specific as a large majority of male Caribbean offenders is also involved in drug-related offending across various levels of organised crime networks related to worldwide drug economies (e.g. Figueira, 2006; Wallace, 2017). However, for women these offences consist mainly of involvement in the international trafficking of drugs either as a mule or in a more facilitating role, for example, through stashing drugs, preparing mules for departure, or the packaging of drugs (Fleetwood, 2014; Van San, 2011). Nonetheless, examples of more active roles such as setting up one's own networks for drug dealing have also been reported across studies (e.g. Bailey, 2013, Fleetwood, 2014). Furthermore, the large percentage of women *incarcerated* for drug offences does not mean that Caribbean women are mainly *committing* drug offences. In fact, in 2015 the majority of female Dutch Caribbean defendants was suspected of a property crime (62 per cent) or a violent offence (19 per cent), compared to a much smaller minority of 6 per cent that was registered as a suspect of a drug-related offence (CBS, 2016c). Apparently, these property and violent offences do not lead to the more severe sentences involving actual incarceration. For example, a qualitative analysis of 90 court files of Dutch Caribbean women and girls showed that they were most likely in court due to shoplifting, tax fraud, or violent offences related to romantic partners or friends, often ignited by jealousy, cheating, or other acts of perceived disrespect (Althoff, 2013). The over-representation of (Afro) Caribbean women in European prisons, therefore, seems particularly related to drug-related crimes. This is a phenomenon that Sudbury (2013) has described as the result of a transnational war on drugs that has especially affected poor, racialised, and criminalised communities.

Across international studies, definitions of subgroups or typologies of (female) prisoners have often been based in part on the type of offence committed (e.g. Joosen et al., 2016). Daly's (1994) qualitative analyses of presentence investigation reports was one of the first studies to describe both male and female typologies based on offence type, background characteristics, and risk factor exposure. She defined five pathways into lawbreaking for female offenders, namely, (a) street women, (b) harmed-and-harming women, (c) battered women, (d) drug-connected women, and (e) other women. The first three categories were characterised by lives with exposure to multiple risk factors such as early instability, victimisation, parental deviancy, running away from home, partner violence, substance abuse, and psychopathology. However, the typology of female drug-connected offenders was merely described as women who "used or sold drugs with boyfriends or family members" (p. 56). Although Daly also indicated that these drug-connected women only had minimal criminal histories and that their offending seemed linked to the men in their lives, the descriptions of these five drug-connected women gives us little additional insight into their specific pathways to offending. Furthermore, as a recent study showed a considerable overlap in background characteristics of female and male drug-connected offenders in the Netherlands (Joosen et al., 2016) – as did Daly's (1994) original description – we know little about gendered motivations and risk factors for drug-connected offending, even less so in the Caribbean.

Gendered pathways to offending in a Caribbean context

Several – mainly qualitative – studies have examined and described specific gendered motivations for – and pathways into – drug-related crimes such as drug smuggling. In her review on international studies on women involved in cocaine trafficking, Fleetwood (2014) discussed three potential motivations for involvement in drug smuggling. Most female drug smugglers cited financial motivations in combination with the fact that drug smuggling is perceived as a type of crime that is preferred over other (more harmful or violent) types of crimes. Other women cited their relationships with partners to be the leading cause or motivation for drug smuggling. Some of these women agreed "willingly" in order to save the relationship or the potential future together, others were (violently) coerced into smuggling by partners or other men in their social networks. These descriptions seem in line with the description of heterogeneity within a group of Afro-Caribbean female prisoners in the UK. For these women comparable motivations of money, deception, or coercion were described by Sudbury (2013), who added on to this description by emphasizing that in the case of violent coercion by drug dealers the children and family of women are often also threatened with harm.

Another qualitative study described the motivations of 12 female drug smugglers incarcerated on the island of Barbados (Bailey, 2013). In addition to the motivations related to poverty and emotional dependency on partners, an alternative motivation for material possessions was highlighted in one of the interviews. Although the focus on greed as a motivation for drug-related crimes is rarely articulated in studies on female offenders, Van San, De Boom, and Van Wijk (2007) described a similar motivation in their study among Dutch Caribbean women incarcerated for drug trafficking. Among 15 incarcerated Curacaoan women, some voiced dreaming of the "big money" and being confronted from an early age with such "easy ways" to make money. For them drug trafficking was preferred over property offending as the pay-out is substantially larger and they were confronted with success stories from other women in their immediate environment.

Overall, it appears that the strong focus on childhood victimisation that is apparent in much of the international gendered pathways literature on female offending and experiences of female prisoners (e.g. Widom, 2014), has been less clearly related to the crime of drug smuggling. Bailey (2013) did describe experiences with physical and sexual childhood victimisation reported by some of the incarcerated drug traffickers in Barbados. However, these experiences seem to be less dominant in paving pathways to incarceration among female drug offenders when compared to, for example, Daly's description of street women. When looking at the lives of other types of Dutch Caribbean defendants, a study of their court files did reveal violence to be predominantly present in the lives of these girls and women – both in the family situation where they grew up as later with romantic partners (Althoff, 2013). Thus, it is not to say childhood victimisation has less impact on the lives of female drug smugglers or among Caribbean offenders in general. However, there have been no studies statistically testing the direct or indirect impact of these and other known criminogenic factors, on the risk for offending and incarceration among Caribbean women. What does come across from the various qualitative studies is the gendered impact of poverty and romantic involvement with potentially deviant partners, on the lives of Caribbean women who end up incarcerated for drug smuggling.

The impact of matrifocality and relationships

Across the Caribbean, single-parent female-headed households have been known to be a prevalent and normalised family structure. For example, a report by UNICEF (2002 as cited in Bailey, 2013) reported that almost six out of 10 children in the Caribbean are raised by single mothers. Furthermore, in Curacao, around 40 per cent of women grow up without a father present in the household (Van Brummen-Girigori, Buunk, Dijkstra, & Girigori, 2016), while 30 per cent of children in Aruba grow up in single-parent households (UNICEF, 2013). Matrifocality is used as the construct to describe such families in which the mother is the head of the household and fathers are often absent from the family residence and/or not involved in the parenting of children (Allen, 2009 as cited in Kibbelaar, 2010). Some duality exists in Caribbean cultures on this dominant role of women as head of the household. On the one hand, she is in control of decision making, which provides her with agency and power within the family context. On the other hand, these women do not have a partner with which to share emotional and financial burdens. This has led to the view of Caribbean women as independent, yet overburdened, "superwomen" who emasculate and exclude men from the household (Dagenais, 1988 as cited in Momsen, 2012; Kibbelaar, 2010; Momsen, 2012). Furthermore, a paradox exists between the prevalent matrifocal family structure and Caribbean societies based on patriarchal (family) values dictating a double sexual standard, unequal pay, and limited political power (Momsen, 2012).

The concept of the *feminisation of poverty* has been proposed as one of the explanations for female involvement in the international drug trade (Fleetwood, 2014). According to Sudbury (2013), across the Caribbean, neo-liberal economic reforms (i.e. privatisation, reducing social security policies) have especially impacted single-parent *female*-headed households as these women carry the double burden of daily childcare, as well as financial responsibilities within their families. The combination of the Caribbean's ideal location for the trade in drugs, with the trend towards the acceptance of *informal economies* in response to the economic marginalisation of (Afro)-Caribbean women, has propelled many of these women into the claws of international drug trafficking networks (Fleetwood, 2014; Sudbury, 2013).

In addition, according to Bailey (2013) "Female lawbreakers are viewed by Caribbean society not as criminals, but as mothers who are struggling" (p. 118). This view is also in line with the description of one of two types of Dutch Caribbean female drug smugglers: struggling housewives from lower socioeconomic neighbourhoods where involvement in the drug trade is not stigmatised but normalised. However, according to Van San (2011), this group of women includes both financially marginalised women and those who just like easy money. Thus, it appears from the extant qualitative literature that matrifocality, through the feminisation of poverty, might form a risk factor for crime involvement – particularly with drug-related offences – among (Dutch) Caribbean women.

As stated above, in addition – and interlinked with poverty – authors have discussed the impact of intimate partners on the risk for drug trafficking among (Caribbean) women (e.g. Bailey, 2013; Daly, 1994; Fleetwood, 2014; Sudbury, 2013). More generally, across the international literature, deviant or criminally involved partners have been found to increase the risk of offending and incarceration among women (e.g. Cauffman, Monahan, & Thomas, 2015; Joosen & Slotboom, 2015; Salisbury & Van Voorhis, 2009). Furthermore, the experience of intimate partner violence is highly prevalent across the Caribbean (e.g. Le Franc, Samms-Vaughan, Hambleton, Fox, & Brown, 2008; Van Wijk & De Bruin, 2012), including among incarcerated women (e.g. Browne, Miller, & Maguine, 1999). For women involved in drug trafficking, romantic partners are often the key players to introduce the option of drug trafficking to economically and emotionally vulnerable women. In a way it seems that the literature suggests that Caribbean women are equally at risk without (i.e. matrifocality and feminisation of poverty), as they are in some cases with partners.

However, within the Caribbean, the role of partnerships seems to point to another paradox. On the one hand, (Dutch) Caribbean women are known as strong and independent and have even been portrayed by some as leaving little room for men in the household and upbringing of children (Kibbelaar, 2010; Marcha & Verweel, 2009). On the other hand, men play dominant roles in women's lives. This is particularly so in lower social classes where there is much rivalry between women over men. Furthermore, status and respect from the community are also achieved by materialistic gains from partnerships with men (Van Brummen-Girigori & Buunk, 2016; DeShong, 2011; Van San, 2011). For example, a study among Dutch Caribbean families involved in the drug trade discussed the role of the so-called *gangster girlfriend*, who benefitted from their boyfriend's criminal endeavours and sometimes even pressured their men to persist on their illegal career paths (Van San, 2011). As these men often have multiple simultaneous relationships with the mothers of their children, they move around between homes with these women attending to their physical and practical needs. In return, these women facilitate their men's criminal activities by spending illegal earnings, providing alibies to the police, or stashing drugs at home. Thus, their introduction as accomplices to these drug offences seems neither coerced, tricked, nor out of dire economic hardship. These various studies do, however, underline the complex and cultural-specific impact that relationships have on the risk for offending and incarceration among (Dutch) Caribbean women. Nevertheless, quantitative studies have yet to demonstrate the precise relationship between poverty, partner deviancy, and offending among Caribbean women statistically.

Current study

As the use of drugs in itself is not a criminal offence in the Netherlands, all women incarcerated for a drug-related offence are convicted or charged with either drug smuggling, or the production, sale, and/or possession of illegal drugs. Since the 1990s the crime of drug smuggling has become a normalised informal way to secure financial survival, especially among lower income single mothers in the (Dutch) Caribbean (e.g. Bailey, 2013; Van San, 2011). However, this does not mean that all Caribbean women in poverty naturally opt for a life as a drug mule. Nonetheless, very few quantitative studies – internationally, or in the Netherlands – have statistically examined the impact of life experiences and exposure to potentially criminogenic risk factors on the risk for offending and incarceration among (Dutch) Caribbean women. Therefore, in the current study I will investigate which factors increase the risk for periods of incarceration among Caribbean women in Dutch prisons. In doing so, I will focus in particular on indicators of financial hardship (i.e. financial debts and (un)employment), (single) motherhood, and intimate partner deviancy. Furthermore, I will investigate the potential different impact of life experiences among Caribbean women in comparison to an age-matched group of native Dutch incarcerated women.

Methods

Sample

For the current study a subsample was selected from the VIP project, which is a large Dutch study that investigated the lives of incarcerated women in the Netherlands (see Joosen & Slotboom, 2015; Joosen et al., 2016). During the period from June 2012 to September 2013, (newly) incarcerated women across each of the four Dutch female prison sites were personally approached and asked to participate in the study, which resulted in a response rate of 80.3 per cent. Women who did not want to participate mainly stated that they did not want to talk about their lives, did not have time, or had too much on their minds. Of the 512 women who initially agreed to participate, a total of 397 women were interviewed during their time in prison. Most of the 115 women, who agreed to participate but were not interviewed, had already been released from prison before the interview could take place (due to short sentences, longer but ending sentences, or transferrals to different sites).

A total of 102 women was selected from the overall sample, of whom 51 were born in the Caribbean, and 51 were age-matched native Dutch controls. The subgroup of Caribbean women was born in Curacao (58.8 per cent), the Dominican Republic (21.6 per cent), Aruba (13.7 per cent), or St Maarten (5.9 per cent). The subgroup of native Dutch women was born in the Netherlands and also had two biological parents who were born in the Netherlands. The age-matching for both groups was determined based on age in months (including two decimal points). The average age at the time of interview was 32.8 years (*SD* = 10.4, range 18–55). Most of the Caribbean women were incarcerated for a drug-related offence (74.5 per cent), three (5.9 per cent) for a violent offence, another three (5.9 per cent) for a property offence, and seven (13.7 per cent) for another type of offence. Among the native Dutch female prisoners, most were incarcerated for either a violent offence (37.3 per cent) or a property offence (31.4 per cent), while only two (3.9 per cent) were incarcerated for a drug-related offence and 14 (27.8 per cent) for another type of offence.

Procedure

Trained research assistants approached participants personally. Potential participants received information on the aim and importance of the study. They were told that participation was voluntary and the decision not to participate would have no effect on their trial, sentence, or treatment in prison. Prior to the start of the interviews consent forms were signed, which emphasised confidentiality of the data and the right to withdraw participation at any time during or after the interview. Interviews took place in private settings without the presence of guards or other prison staff. Interviews consisted of a life history calendar focusing on the following domains: namely, (a) work, income, and living situation, (b) victimisation, (c) partner relationships, (d) motherhood, (e) mental health treatment, (f) addiction, and (g) self-reported offending. Furthermore, an additional Computer Assisted Personal Interview (CAPI) was administered including more detailed information on childhood variables. All respondents received compensation for their interview in the form of a phone card with a value of 5 euros. The Ethics Committee of the Faculty of Law (CERCO) of the VU University Amsterdam approved the study design, including interviewer protocols.

Measures

Life history calendar

Retrospective data was collected through Life History Calendars ([LHC] e.g. Freedman, Thornton, Camburn, Alwin, & Young-DeMarco, 1988; Laub & Sampson, 2003), a known method to help record the lives of respondents by allocating events and transitions on a biographical timeline using one year segments (see also Roberts & Horney, 2010). When recording events on a LHC, easily remembered events (e.g. birth of children) act as a reference for other connected memories, thereby enabling the complete chronological recording of respondents' lives. The LHC's were filled out by hand during semi-structured interviews using standardised codes that were used to compute both the outcome measure of *incarceration* and the following predictors variables: *living with both parents prior age 16, teenage motherhood, debts, employment, daily childcare, single, single motherhood, substance-abusing partner, criminal partner*, and *violent partner.*

For the current analyses incarceration was measured through a *time-variant* dichotomous variable, which implies that even within the group of incarcerated respondents, individual variation across the observed time period is measured. In other words, for each year segment a score for incarceration (yes/no) is observed as individuals who reported one or more periods of incarceration at a certain age were generally not incarcerated during the entire time period observed (18–55 years). The time-variant variables debts, daily childcare, and single were dichotomously recorded on the calendar per year as 0 *no* or 1 *yes.* The time-variant variable employment was computed from two separate variables for temporary and regular employment, therefore, reflecting any type of work in a given year coded as 0 *no* or 1 *yes*. For the time-variant variable single motherhood, the variables for single and daily childcare were aggregated into a new variable reflecting whether in any given year women were both single and responsible for the daily care of (at least one of) their child(ren). For the variable substance-abusing partner, separate codes for excessive alcohol use, any type of soft drug use, or any type of hard drug use were merged into a new dichotomous time-variant variable reflecting per year whether or not women reported involvement in a relationship (i.e. steady, cohabiting, or married) with a substance-abusing partner. Codes for the type of criminal involvement of a partner (i.e. property, violent, or drug offending) were combined into a time-variant variable reflecting any criminal activity of a partner in any given year. Similarly, codes for either incidental or regular psychological, physical, and/or sexual partner violence victimisation were aggregated into one time-variant variable for having a violent partner/relationship.[1] Living with both parents prior to the age of 16 and teenage motherhood were both used as *time-invariant* dichotomous variables. Living with both parents prior age 16 was coded as 1 *yes* when respondents had lived with both their biological mother and father in each of the years from age 0 to age 15. Teenage motherhood was coded as 1 *yes* when women had given birth to a first child prior age 20.

Computer Assisted Personal Interview (CAPI)

The administered CAPI was originally designed for the Dutch Prison Project (Dirkzwager & Nieuwbeerta, 2015) and later adapted for the VIP study. The following variables were measured dichotomously referring to the period prior age 16 with answer categories for 0 *no* and 1 *yes*, namely childhood psychological abuse, childhood physical abuse, childhood sexual abuse, parental divorce, witnessing family violence, running away from home, early first alcohol use, and early first drug use. The variable for parental health problems was a composite measure of two dichotomous variables for severe parental psychological symptoms and/or severe physical illness. The measurement of parental deviancy was created from five dichotomous variables: namely, excessive parental alcohol or drug use, parental arrest, parental conviction, and parental incarceration. These five variables were separately filled out for biological mothers, fathers, and alternative caregivers, and were combined into a single rating to reflect any exposure to these forms of parental/caregiver deviancy prior to the age of 16. Being institutionalised was measured through four sub-questions asking respondents whether prior to the age of 16 they ever spent any time in (a) supervised living homes, (b) foster care (c) institutions of Child Protective Services, (d) psychiatric treatment centres or (e) juvenile detention. When respondents reported at least one of these five living situations the composite measure for institutionalisation prior age 16 was coded as 1 *yes*. Last, low educational levels were measured with a dichotomous variable with a score of 1 indicating that respondents had only finished primary school. Only one respondent had missing values on several of the dichotomous variables; these were not filled up.

Analyses

First, separate chi-square tests were conducted for each of the included predictor variables to analyse whether prevalence rates between Caribbean and native Dutch women were significantly different. Furthermore, for the analysis of *multivariate* outcomes a person-year file was constructed based on the age of the individuals. This file contained a separate record for each year observed between ages 18 and 55, and included two types of variables: (a) time-variant – changing their value throughout the observed years (e.g. incarceration, employment); (b) time-invariant – recording the same value in all years pertaining to the same person (e.g. teenage motherhood). A logistic model was required as our outcome variable (incarceration) was dichotomous. When choosing between a random or fixed effects model, the latter has the advantage of exclusively analyzing within-individual variations while controlling for stable (un)observed personal characteristics (without adding these as variables to the model). This is especially advantageous when power for adding variables to the model is limited due to smaller sample sizes (Rabe-Hesketh & Skrondal, 2008).

To answer our research questions, we first analysed the effects of the time-variant factors measured at AGE_t (i.e. daily childcare, single) on the likelihood of incarceration in the same year. Separate models were run for having a substance-abusing partner, having a criminal partner, and having a violent partner as overlap between various aspects of partner deviancy would have caused multicollinearity in the model. In the first three models I estimated the impact of daily childcare and being single as two separate variables on the likelihood of incarceration in the same year (see Table 9.1). In the next three models I analysed the combined impact of being a single mother (see Table 9.2). Analyses were run separately for both subgroups of Caribbean and native Dutch women. In addition, maturation effects were accounted for using second order polynomials for age in all our models. Last, we repeated the models with the above-mentioned predictors as lagged variables (a certain characteristic registered in the previous year; AGE_{t+1}) to investigate the temporal order of events. Across subgroups, cases with all negative or all positive outcomes were excluded from the analyses (see Tables 9.1 and 9.2 for exact *n* per model).

Table 9.1 Prevalence of potential risk and protective factors for offending and incarceration among Caribbean and Dutch incarcerated women in the Netherlands

Variables	*Dutch (n = 51)*	*Caribbean (n = 51)*			
	%	*%*	*OR*	*χ2*	*P*
Lived with both parents < 16	39.2	23.5	0.48	2.51	.088
Parental divorce	41.2	30.0	0.61	1.38	.241
Parental health problems < 16	58.8	29.4	0.29	8.95	.003
Parental deviancy < 16	51.0	39.2	0.62	1.43	.233
Childhood psychological abuse < 16	45.1	29.4	0.51	2.68	.101
Childhood physical abuse < 16	39.2	21.6	0.43	3.75	.053
Childhood sexual abuse < 16	31.4	19.6	0.53	1.86	.173
Witness of family violence	35.3	16.0	0.35	4.92	.027
Runaway < 16	45.1	22.0	0.34	6.03	.014
Institutionalised < 16	29.4	8.0	0.21	7.58	.006
First alcohol use < 16	56.9	27.5	0.29	9.05	.003
First drug use < 16	45.1	11.8	0.16	13.92	.000
Low educational level	32.0	21.6	0.58	1.40	.236
Teenage motherhood	19.6	47.1	3.64	8.65	.003
Debts – 18+	74.5	68.6	0.75	0.43	.510
Employment – 18+	80.4	70.6	0.59	1.33	.250
Daily childcare – 18+	56.9	74.5	2.22	3.52	.061
Single – 18+	66.7	82.4	2.33	3.30	.069
Single motherhood – 18+	25.5	52.9	3.29	8.06	.005
Substance-abusing partner – 18+	60.8	31.4	0.30	8.88	.003
Criminal partner – 18+	66.7	27.5	0.19	15.74	.000
Violent partner – 18+	66.7	49.0	0.48	3.26	.071

Table 9.2 Variables related to periods of incarceration across the life span for Caribbean and Dutch female inmates

Variables	*Caribbean women (n = 47)*			*Dutch women (n = 49)*		
	OR (SE)	*P*	*95% – CI*	*OR (SE)*	*P*	*95% – CI*
Model 1						
Age	0.99 (0.17)	.946	[0.71–1.38]	2.35 (0.64)	.002	[1.37–4.01]
Age*age	1.00 (0.00)	.129	[1.00–1.00]	1.00 (0.00)	.203	[0.99–1.00]
Daily childcare	0.34 (0.17)	.027	[0.13–0.88]	0.18 (0.12)	.013	[0.05–0.70]
Employment	0.74 (0.29)	.437	[0.34–1.59]	0.10 (0.06)	.000	[0.03–0.31]
Debts	2.96 (1.36)	.019	[1.20–7.31]	0.95 (0.54)	.927	[0.31–2.88]
Single	2.92 (1.06)	.003	[1.44–5.94]	0.58 (0.29)	.283	[0.21–1.57]
Substance-abusing partner	0.05 (0.06)	.009	[0.01–0.48]	1.56 (0.82)	.400	[0.55–4.39]
Model 2						
Age	0.95 (0.16)	.752	[0.68–1.33]	2.36 (0.64)	.002	[1.38–4.02]
Age*age	1.00 (0.00)	.086	[1.00–1.01]	1.00 (0.00)	.193	[0.99–1.00]
Daily childcare	0.35 (0.17)	.034	[0.13–0.92]	0.17 (0.12)	.011	[0.04–0.67]
Employment	0.85 (0.32)	.662	[0.40–1.79]	0.10 (0.06)	.000	[0.03–0.32]
Debts	2.60 (1.20)	.039	[1.05–6.41]	0.94 (.914)	.914	[0.31–2.89]
Single	2.90 (1.05)	.003	[1.43–5.90]	0.55 (0.28)	.235	[0.20–1.48]
Criminal partner	1.03 (0.71)	.961	[0.27–3.94]	1.68 (0.74)	.243	[0.70–3.99]
Model 3						
Age	1.04 (0.18)	.806	[0.75–1.45]	2.34 (0.64)	.002	[1.36–4.01]
Age*age	1.00 (0.00)	.243	[1.00–1.01]	1.00 (0.00)	.219	[0.99–1.00]
Daily childcare	0.32 (0.17)	.030	[0.12–0.89]	0.18 (0.12)	.012	[0.05–0.68]
Employment	0.80 (0.31)	.564	[0.37–1.71]	0.07 (0.04)	.000	[0.02–0.24]
Debts	2.57 (1.14)	.033	[1.08–6.13]	0.97 (0.54)	.960	[0.33–2.89]
Single	2.48 (0.89)	.011	[1.23–5.01]	0.61 (0.31)	.328	[0.22–1.65]
Violent partner	0.35 (0.21)	.077	[0.11–1.12]	2.29 (1.11)	.087	[0.89–5.92]

Note: Model 3 Caribbean group *n* = 45.

Results

Life experiences and exposure to criminogenic factors

Prevalence rates for lifetime exposure to potential risk and protective factors showed that overall the incarcerated native Dutch group appeared to report a greater exposure to various risk factors across the life course. Regarding the time-invariant variables, incarcerated native Dutch women reported significantly higher percentages of parental health problems, witnessing family violence, running away from home, institutionalisation, and early drug and alcohol use compared to incarcerated Caribbean women.

Table 9.3 Variables related to periods of incarceration across the life span for Caribbean and Dutch female inmates: the impact of single motherhood

Variables	*Caribbean women*			*Dutch women (n = 49)*		
	OR (SE)	*p*	*95% – CI*	*OR (SE)*	*p*	*95% – CI*
Model 1			*(n = 47)*			
Age	0.95 (0.16)	.732	[0.68–1.31]	1.91 (0.49)	.011	[1.16–3.16]
Age*age	1.00 (0.00)	.078	[1.00–1.01]	1.00 (0.00)	.641	[0.99–1.01]
Employment	0.65 (0.24)	.248	[0.31–1.35]	0.12 (0.06)	.000	[0.04–0.34]
Debts	2.30 (1.04)	.066	[0.95–5.57]	0.86 (0.45)	.768	[0.31–2.40]
Single mother	0.69 (0.34)	.444	[0.27–1.79]	0.45 (0.34)	.293	[0.10–1.98]
Substance-abusing partner	0.07 (0.07)	.015	[0.01–0.59]	1.83 (0.92)	.228	[0.68–4.92]
Model 2			*(n = 46)*			
Age	0.92 (0.15)	.603	[0.66–1.27]	1.91 (0.49)	.011	[1.16–3.14]
Age*age	1.01 (0.00)	.055	[1.00–1.01]	1.00 (0.00)	.637	[0.99–1.01]
Employment	0.74 (0.28)	.417	[0.35–1.54]	0.12 (0.07)	.000	[0.04–0.36]
Debts	1.97 (0.89)	.132	[0.81–4.78]	0.84 (0.45)	.739	[0.29–2.38]
Single mother	0.63 (0.30)	.326	[0.24–1.60]	0.41 (0.31)	.246	[0.09–1.84]
Criminal partner	0.59 (0.41)	.451	[0.15–2.35]	1.78 (0.77)	.186	[0.76–4.17]
Model 3			*(n = 45)*			
Age	1.02 (0.17)	.928	[0.73–1.41]	1.87 (0.48)	.015	[1.13–3.09]
Age*age	1.00 (0.00)	.182	[1.00–1.01]	1.00 (0.00)	.717	[0.99–1.01]
Employment	0.68 (0.26)	.302	[0.32–1.42]	0.08 (0.05)	.000	[0.03–0.27]
Debts	2.16 (0.95)	.080	[0.91–5.12]	0.93 (0.48)	.889	[0.34–2.56]
Single mother	0.56 (0.27)	.225	[0.22–1.44]	0.61 (0.47)	.552	[0.13–2.78]
Violent partner	0.24 (0.14)	.013	[0.08–0.74]	2.12 (0.98)	.107	[0.85–5.26]

However, the subsample of incarcerated Caribbean women reported a significantly higher percentage of teenage motherhood. Concerning the time-variant factors, the native Dutch subsample reported higher prevalence rates for relationships with either a substance-abusing or criminal partner, while the Caribbean women were significantly more likely to report single motherhood during adulthood. All prevalence rates for the included child- and adulthood factors are presented in Table 9.1 separately for Caribbean and native Dutch women including chi-square statistics and odds ratios.

Variables related to periods of incarceration

First, the models are discussed in which being single and having daily childcare responsibilities were entered separately (see Table 9.2). These logistic fixed effects models showed that for Caribbean women who were responsible for daily childcare, the likelihood of periods of incarceration in those years was decreased across models (Model 1 $OR = 0.34$, $p = .027$; Model 2 $OR = 0.35$, $p = .034$; Model 3 $OR = 0.32$,

$p = .030$). Furthermore, for Caribbean women with debts, the likelihood of incarceration in any given year was two and a half to three times higher across each of the three models (Model 1 $OR = 2.96, p = .019$; Model 2 $OR = 2.60, p = .039$; Model 3 $OR = 2.57, p = .033$), which was also the case when Caribbean women reported being single in any given year (Model 1 $OR = 2.92, p = .003$; Model 2 $OR = 2.90, p = .003$; Model 3 $OR = 2.48, p = .011$). Regarding partner deviancy, Caribbean women were significantly less likely to have a substance-abusing partner in the years they were incarcerated ($OR = 0.05, p = .009$). In addition, a trend was found for having a violent partner ($OR = 0.35, p = .077$), which was (almost) significantly related to a decreased likelihood of incarceration in any given year. For the native Dutch women different factors appeared to play a role. Across all three models the likelihood of incarceration for these women was decreased when they were employed (Model 1 $OR = 0.10, p = .000$; Model 2 $OR = 0.10, p = .000$; Model 3 $OR = 0.07, p = .000$), or had daily childcare responsibilities (Model 1 $OR = 0.18, p = .013$; Model 2 $OR = 0.17, p = .011$; Model 3 $OR = 0.18, p = .012$). Moreover, the variable age was only significant among the native Dutch women (Model 1 $OR = 2.35, p = .002$; Model 2 $OR = 2.36, p = .002$; Model 3 $OR = 2.34, p = .002$), implying that only for the Dutch subsample the likelihood for incarceration increased with age.

When examining the models that included the composite variable of single motherhood the logistic fixed effects models for both groups of women showed that this variable was not significantly related to periods of incarceration (see Table 9.3). However, for Caribbean women, having a substance-abusing partner ($OR = 0.07, p = .015$), or a violent partner ($OR = 0.24, p = .013$) decreased the likelihood of being incarcerated in any given year. Among the native Dutch women periods of incarceration continued to be decreased when women were employed (Model 1 $OR = 0.12, p = .000$; Model 2 $OR = 0.12, p = .000$; Model 3 $OR = 0.08, p = .000$) and increased as women aged (Model 1 $OR = 1.91, p = .011$; Model 2 $OR = 1.91, p = .011$; Model 3 $OR = 1.87, p = .015$). Thus, for the native Dutch women none of the partner deviancy factors appeared to be significantly related to periods of incarceration as opposed to the Caribbean group. Important to note is, however, that the direction of effect does seem to be significantly different across subgroups.

Predictors of periods of incarceration

All models were re-estimated using lagged variables, which enabled the examination of the impact of these variables on the risk for incarceration one year later. Among Caribbean women, having a substance-abusing partner in any given year significantly decreased the likelihood of incarceration one year later (Model including single/daily childcare: $OR = 0.13, p = 0.23$; Model including single motherhood: $OR = 0.12, p = 0.19$). In the full models none of the other previously significant factors remained significant when examining the impact on incarceration one year later. However, when entered separately into the model only controlling for age, the lag variables debts, being single, and daily childcare were not significantly related to the likelihood of incarceration one year later either; signalling that the significance of these variables could also be consequences of – as opposed to risk factors for – incarceration. For the native Dutch women, the impact of employment and daily childcare continued to significantly decrease the likelihood of incarceration one year later across models (statistics are available upon request).

Discussion

In order to distinguish more insight into specific pathways to prison for Caribbean women, the current study focused on whether Caribbean women incarcerated in the Netherlands reported differences in exposure to criminogenic life experiences compared to native Dutch incarcerated women. Furthermore, I examined whether these life experiences had a different impact on the risk of periods of incarceration among these two groups of female prisoners. Results showed that the group of native Dutch women reported more exposure to both childhood and adulthood criminogenic factors, such as parental health problems, family violence, running away and institutionalisation, early substance use, and later relationships with substance-abusing or criminal partners. The group of Caribbean women were (almost) 3.5 times as likely to be teenage and/or single mothers throughout their lives prior to incarceration as compared to the native Dutch women. Both groups did not differ significantly regarding experiences with parental divorce, parental deviancy, childhood abuse, low educational levels, debts, and employment.

The fact that the native Dutch group reported more risk exposure overall could be related to the differences in types of crime that led to the incarceration of these two subgroups of female prisoners. While the Caribbean women were mainly incarcerated for drug offences, the native Dutch women were mainly imprisoned for violent offences. Another study conducted on the total sample of incarcerated women in the VIP study has in fact shown that prisoner typologies based on background characteristics are in part defined by types of offences. Whereas incarcerated violent offenders' lives were characterised by exposure to multiple criminogenic factors, the typology of incarcerated drug-related offenders was merely characterised by debts, relationships, and children (Joosen et al., 2016).

When examining which experiences were related to periods of incarceration, the results showed that daily childcare and relationships with substance-abusing partners lowered the likelihood of periods of incarceration in the same year. When the subgroup of Caribbean women had debts or were single, they were more likely to experience incarceration in any given year. Being a single mother was not significantly related to the likelihood of incarceration in any given year. However, across the models in which the variable single mother was entered, the impact of debts appeared lowered and was no longer significant. In fact, combining two variables with opposite effects on the likelihood of incarceration – daily childcare and being single – might have negatively affected the overall model (i.e. cancelling out of effects). For the Dutch women we found a somewhat different picture across models with employment and daily childcare both decreasing the likelihood of incarceration in any given year. When examining the delayed impact of these variables on the risk of incarceration one year later, among the Caribbean women only a substance-abusing partner seemed to predict a lower risk of incarceration one year later. At first sight it appears that for the Caribbean women having debts and being single are more strongly related to the risk of incarceration than is the case for facing single motherhood. Especially, as even a deviant partner troubled by substance abuse seems to have a more positive influence regarding the likelihood of incarceration than when women are without a relationship.

How can this protective effect for incarceration of relationships with a substance-abusing partner be explained? First of all, it is important to note that this effect was found within a high-risk group of incarcerated women. Across international literature on female prisoners it has been found that the social stigma associated with female offending and incarceration limits the possibilities for female offenders to find pro-social partners (e.g. Lanctôt, Cernkovich, & Giordano, 2003). As being single does seem to be a risk for offending, a partner with substance abuse might in fact be preferred above a violent or otherwise criminal partner. Second of all, perceptions of female prisoners on their partners and relationships can be much more complex and fluid than the quantitative "evidence" might suggest (Leverentz, 2006). As literature has shown a high similarity of deviancy and substance abuse between partners – known as assortative mating – (Boutwell, Beaver, & Barnes, 2012), being happy with an antisocial partner might account for the positive impact on the risk for incarceration found in the current study. Furthermore, substance abuse in the current study was measured through excessive alcohol use and *any* type or frequency of drug use, implying that partners with occasional soft drug use were also included among the group of substance-abusing partners. It is therefore possible that this variable reflects the positive influence of not being single, which for these partners at least outweighed any potential negative impacts associated with their substance (ab)use.

The delayed effect of debts on incarceration one year later was not significant, although it did approach significance. Thus, the effect was less clear than when examined within the year of incarceration itself. This can be interpreted in two ways, namely (a) the impact of debts and being single increases the risk for (drug) offending and subsequent incarceration over a short period (within the same year), (b) the risk of becoming single and in debt is increased by the periods of incarceration. Both these interpretations can be supported by existing empirical evidence. Across international studies having debts has been found as a significant risk marker for female offending and subsequent incarceration (Aaltonen, Oksanen, & Kivivuori, 2016). Furthermore, this would be in line with the empirical qualitative studies describing the impact of the feminisation of poverty in which single Afro-Caribbean *women* are most vulnerable for economic marginalisation (e.g. Sudbury, 2013). However, incarceration can also increase women's debts when they cannot afford rent or other bills during their imprisonment and nobody is there to take care of such affairs (McIvor, Trotter & Sheehan, 2009). Regarding this subgroup of Caribbean women, insignificant results could also be due to lack of power as the direction of the effect was risk increasing and approached significance levels in most of the lagged models.

Limitations

Several limitations of the current study are important to take into consideration while interpreting these results. First, by using extensive life history calendars we were able to map out the respondents' life course in one year segments, which enabled a multi-level analysis with a broad range of risk and protective factors. However, we did not have information on the monthly sequencing of events within any given year. Therefore, it was not possible to establish what the chronological order of events was for the models investigating the variables related to periods of incarceration; this does not allow for any interpretation of causality. To truly establish causality, it would have been better to measure these domains through a longitudinal prospective design, as opposed to retrospectively filling out the LHC. The fact that the LHC's were filled out in retrospect implies that the suggested causality is also dependent on the quality of respondents' memories and the level of disclosure of events. Third, the sample sizes of both the Caribbean and native Dutch subgroups were relatively small for the type of analyses conducted and the number of variables included in each model. Replication in larger samples is highly recommended, even though challenging considering the small number of (Caribbean) women incarcerated in the Netherlands. Lastly, as we did not have a control group of Caribbean non-criminal women and all of the included women were in fact already incarcerated, it remains difficult to interpret how these variables can be translated into insights on risk factors for offending and incarceration among the general population of (Dutch) Caribbean women.

Conclusion

The current study has shown that in particular, financial struggles and (the absence of) to a lesser extent, partnerships, affected the likelihood of incarceration among Dutch Caribbean women incarcerated in the Netherlands. While having a substance-abusing partner kept women out of prison, being single and in debt seemed to rather increase the risk for periods of incarceration across the life course of criminally active Caribbean women. Although causality of the latter risk-increasing factors was difficult to establish due to limited statistical power, it did seem that being single as opposed to single motherhood was the more salient factor for predicting incarceration risk. This could be due to the fact that daily childcare responsibilities seemed to decrease as opposed to increase the risk for periods of incarceration. However, for the incarcerated Caribbean women this protective effect might have been less strong than for the incarcerated native Dutch women, as delayed effects were not proven.

In addition, although comparable data among Caribbean male prisoners was not collected, it could be reasoned that, especially, the impact of being single might be differently related to periods of incarceration across gender: in particular, when considering the theoretical notions of the feminisation of poverty across the Caribbean as well as the dominant presence of matrifocal family structures, and what these might imply for the salience of (the absence of) romantic relationships as predictor of criminal involvement among Caribbean men and women. Thus, future quantitative studies are necessary to unravel the precise causal impact of motherhood on the risk of offending across different contexts and gender. Especially, the (gendered) meaning of context variables such as relationships (with deviant partners), debts, and being single within matrifocal Caribbean cultures deserves more attention in order to shape policies that help eradicate the occurring racialised process of feminisation of poverty across the Caribbean and decrease incarceration risk among Caribbean women.

Note

1 Partner violence was not recorded as violent offending under criminal activity of a partner; overlap in recording these events was avoided as such.

References

Aaltonen, M., Oksanen, A., & Kivivuori, J. (2016). Debt problems and crime. *Criminology, 54*(2), 307–331.

Alberts, S., Joosen, K.J., Slotboom, A.-M., Kruttschnitt, C., & Bijleveld, C. (2016). *Only the lonely? Contextual impacts of motherhood on periods of incarceration among female prisoners in the Netherlands*. Paper presented at the annual meeting of the American Society of Criminology, New Orleans, November 16–19.

Althoff, M. (2013). Multiple identities and crime: A study of Antillean women and girls in the Netherlands. *European Journal of Criminology, 10*(4), 394–407.

Bailey, C. (2013). Exploring female motivations for drug smuggling on the island of Barbados: Evidence from Her Majesty's Prison, Barbados. *Feminist Criminology, 8*(2), 117–141.

Blank, S. (2013). An historical and contemporary overview of gendered Caribbean relations. *Journal of Arts and Humanities, 2*(4), 1–10.

Blokland, A., Grimbergen, K., Bernasco, W., & Nieuwbeerta, P. (2010). Criminele carrières van autochtone en allochtone jongeren uit het geboortecohort 1984 [Criminal carreers of native and ethnic minority youth from the birth cohort 1984]. *Tijdschrift voor Criminologie, 52*(2), 31.

Boone, M., & Korf, D.J. (2010). Bestraffing van cocaïnesmokkelaars: Richtlijnen, rechters, rechtbanken en de persoon van de dader [Sentencing of cocaine smugglers: Guidelines, judges, the court and the person of the offender]. *Tijdschrift voor Criminologie, 53*(3), 239–257.

Boutwell, B.B., Beaver, K.M., & Barnes, J.C. (2012). More alike than different: Assortative mating and antisocial propensity in adulthood. *Criminal Justice and Behavior, 39*(9), 1240–1254.

Browne, A., Miller, B., & Maguin, E. (1999). Prevalence and severity of lifetime physical and sexual victimization among incarcerated women. International *Journal of Law and Psychiatry, 22*(3–4), 301–322.

Çankaya, S. (2015). De politiële surveillance van ras en etniciteit [The police surveillance of race and ethnicity]. *Cahiers Politiestudies, 2*(35), 13–33.

Cauffman, E., Monahan, K.C., & Thomas, A.G. (2015). Pathways to persistence: Female offending from 14 to 25. *Journal of Developmental and Life-Course Criminology, 1*(3), 236–268.

Central Bureau of Statistics. (2016a). *Verdachten; geslacht, leeftijd, land van herkomst en generatie allochtonen [Suspects; sex, age, country of origin and generation]*. Retrieved from http://statline.cbs.nl/Statweb/publication/?DM=SLNL&PA=81959NED&D1=0,3&D2=2&D3=0&D4=0–1,19,42,44,61,66&D5=0&D6=l&HDR=G5,G2,G1,G4,T&STB=G3&VW=T.

Central Bureau of Statistics. (2016b). *Gedetineerden; geslacht, leeftijd en herkomstgroepering [Prisoners; sex, age and ethnic group]*. Retrieved from http://statline.cbs.nl/Statweb/publication/?DM=SLNL&PA=82321NED&D1=a&D2=2&D3=0&D4=0-1,5-8&D5=l&HDR=G1,G2,G4&STB=T,G3&VW=T.

Central Bureau of Statistics. (2016c). *Verdachten; delictgroep, geslacht, leeftijd en herkomstgroepering [Suspects; offense type, seks, age and country of origin]*. Retrieved from http://statline.cbs.nl/Statweb/publication/?DM=SLNL&PA=81947NED&D1=54-55,57,59&D2=2&D3=0&D4=0-1,6&D5=15-16&HDR=G4,G3,G1,G2&STB=T&VW=T.

Clement, F.I. (2008). *Mamma's en bolita's. Een verkennend onderzoek naar de criminaliteit van vrouwen op Curaçao [Mamma's and bolita's: An exploratory study into criminality of women on Curacao]* (Unpublished master thesis). University of Groningen. Groningen.

Daly, K. (1994). *Gender, crime, and punishment*. New Haven: Yale University Press.

DeShong, H. (2011). Gender, sexuality and sexual violence: A feminist analysis of Vincentian women's experiences in violent heterosexual relationships. *Journal of Eastern Caribbean Studies, 36*(2), 63–97.

Dirkzwager, A.J.E., & Nieuwbeerta, P. (2015). *Prison project: Codebook and documentation*. Leiden and Amsterdam: Universiteit Leiden/NSCR.

Figueira, D. (2006). *Cocaine and heroin trafficking in the Caribbean: The case of Haiti, the Dominican Republic and Venezuela* (Vol. 2). Lincoln, NE: iUniverse.

Fleetwood, J. (2014). *Drug mules: Women in the international cocaine trade*. London: Palgrave Macmillan.

Freedman, D., Thornton, A., Camburn, D., Alwin, D., & Young-DeMarco, L. (1988). The life history calendar: A technique for collecting retrospective data. *Sociological Methodology, 18*, 37–68.

Joosen, K.J., Palmen, H., Kruttschnitt, C., Bijleveld, C., Dirkzwager, A., & Nieuwbeerta, P. (2016). How "gendered" are gendered pathways into prison? A latent class analysis of the life experiences of male and female prisoners in The Netherlands. *Journal of Developmental and Life Course Criminology, 2*(3), 321–340.

Joosen, K.J., & Slotboom, A.-M. (2015). Terugblikken op de aanloop: Dynamische voorspellers van criminaliteit en detentie gedurende de levensloop van vrouwelijke gedetineerden in Nederland [The prelude in retrospect: Dynamic predictors of offending and incarceration across the life course of female prisoners in the Netherlands]. *Tijdschrift voor Criminologie, 57*(1), 84–98.

Kibbelaar, P. (2010). *Vrouwen van de Nederlandse Antillen en Aruba [Women from the Dutch Antilles and Aruba]*. Retrieved from Rijksoverheid website www.rijksoverheid.nl/documenten/rapporten/2010/04/20/onderzoek-vrouwen-van-de-nederlandse-antillen-en-aruba.

Lanctôt, N., Cernkovich, S.A., & Giordano, P.C. (2007). Delinquent behavior, official delinquency, and gender: Consequences for adulthood functioning and well-being. *Criminology, 45*(1), 131–157.

Laub, J.H., & Sampson, R.J. (2003). *Shared beginnings, divergent lives: Delinquent boys to age 70*. Cambridge, MA: Harvard University Press.

Le Franc, E., Samms-Vaughan, M., Hambleton, I., Fox, K., & Brown, D. (2008). Interpersonal violence in three Caribbean countries: Barbados, Jamaica, and Trinidad and Tobago. *Revista Panamericana de Salud Pública, 24*(6), 409–421.

Leverentz, A.M. (2006). The love of a good man? Romantic relationships as a source of support or hindrance for female ex-offenders. *Journal of Research in Crime and Delinquency, 43*(4), 459–488.

Maduro, E. (2014). Gedetineerden in Curaçao [Prisoners in Curacao]. *Modus, 12*(1–2), 53–60.

Marcha, V., & Verweel, P. (2009). *De Curaçaose vrouw. . .moet je ontdekken [You have to discover the Curacaoan woman]*. Amsterdam: SWP Publishers.

McIvor, G., Trotter, C., & Sheehan, R. (2009). Women, resettlement and desistance. *Probation Journal, 56*(4), 347–361.

Momsen, J.H. (2012). Patriarchy in absentia: Women and development in the Caribbean. In A. Buang, & J.H. Momsen (Eds.), *Women and empowerment in the NAM world:*

Different contexts, different facets (pp. 71–86). Kuala Lumpur: NAM Institute for the Empowerment of Women.

Morris, P.K. (2008). Imprisoned in Jamaica: An exploratory study of inmate experiences and differential responses to prison life in a developing country. *International Criminal Justice Review*, *18*(4), 435–454.

Rabe-Hesketh, S., & Skrondal, A. (2008). *Multilevel and longitudinal modelling using stata* (2nd ed.). College Station, Texas: Stata Press.

Roberts, J., & Horney, J. (2010). The life event calendar method in criminological research. In A.R. Piquero, & D. Weisburd (Eds.), *Handbook of quantitative criminology* (pp. 289–312). New York, NY: Springer.

Salisbury, E.J., & Van Voorhis, P. (2009). Gendered pathways: A quantitative investigation of women probationers' paths to incarceration. *Criminal Justice and Behavior*, *36*(6), 541–566.

Sudbury, J. (2013). Mules, "yardies", and other folk devils: Mapping cross-border imprisonment in Britain. In J. Sudbury (Ed.), *Global lockdown: Race, gender, and the prison-industrial complex* (pp. 167–184). London and New York: Routledge.

Van Brummen-Girigori, O., & Buunk, A.P. (2016). Intrasexual competitiveness and non-verbal seduction strategies to attract males: A study among teenage girls from Curacao. *Evolution and Human Behavior*, *37*(2), 134–141.

Van Brummen-Girigori, O., Buunk, A.P., Dijkstra, P., & Girigori, A. (2016). Father abandonment and jealousy: A study among women on Curacao. *Personality and Individual Differences*, *96*, 181–184.

Van San, M. (2011). The appeal of 'dangerous' men: On the role of women in organised crime. *Trends in Organized Crime*, *14*(4), 281–297.

Van San, M., De Boom, J., & Van Wijk, A. (2007). *Verslaafd aan een flitsende levensstijl: Criminaliteit van Antilliaanse Rotterdammers*. Rotterdam: RISBO.

Van Wijk, N.P.L., & De Bruijn, J.G.M. (2012). Risk factors for domestic violence in Curacao. Journal of Interpersonal Violence, 27(15), 3032-3053.

UNICEF. (2013). *The situation of children and adolescents in Aruba*. Retrieved from www.unicef.nl/media/1389252/aruba_sitan_public_version__28english_29.pdf.

Wallace, W.C. (2017). *An exploratory study on the impact of organized crime on societies in Small Island Developing States: Evidence from five (5) Caribbean countries*. Retrieved from http://chds.dodlive.mil/files/2017/03/Perspectivas_March-2017.pdf.

Weenink, D. (2009). Explaining ethnic inequality in the juvenile justice system: An analysis of the outcomes of Dutch prosecutorial decision making. *British Journal of Criminology*, *49*(2), 220–242.

Widom, C.S. (2014). The 2013 Sutherland address: Varieties of violent behavior. *Criminology*, *52*(3), 313–344.

10 Constructing crime in Antigua

Perceptions of structural explanations of crime in post-colonial era

Janeille Z. Matthews

Introduction

David Garland (1996, 2000, 2001) has argued that high rates of property crime and violent crime have become a standard feature of the late modern social experience. Although crime typically has an uneven social distribution and high-risk victimisation is a concentrated phenomenon, high crime rates and the threat of crime have seeped into the modern consciousness and have become a "taken for granted" element of late modernity (Garland, 1996). While Antigua may not be what Garland envisioned as a late modern society, it does share features with such societies (e.g. globalisation), and thus is not excepted from this development. In Antigua, increased rates of property and violent crime are no longer an anomaly and crime is viewed as the "most serious challenge facing the country" (Maertens & Anstey, 2007, p. 1). A UNDP crime survey (2012, p. 19) found that 54 per cent of respondents feel insecure because of crime and security. However, these property and violent crime rates should not be separated from Antigua's history or its socioeconomic context. As Reiner (2000) argues, examining a country's socioeconomic context can facilitate a broader understanding of (a) the circumstances in which offenders have acted and (b) their experience of these circumstances as pressures and temptations to commit crimes. According to Reiner (2000), a country's socioeconomic context can shed light on shifts in the availability of means and opportunities to commit crimes and associated social controls. But beyond Reiner's rationale, Antigua's history of slavery and British colonialism is of particular importance as this legacy necessarily affects contemporary definitions of crime, crime patterns, and mechanisms of crime control. As such, this research aims to contribute to post-colonial crime discourse in its attempt to move away from the *ahistoricism* that post-colonial scholars suggest is all too prevalent in establishment criminological analysis (see Oriola, 2006). Additionally, this research intends to contribute to an empirical justification for future crime policy interventions in Antigua.

Theoretical background

Strain theory

Merton (1938, 1957) famously redefined anomie as a structural disjunction between culturally prescribed goals and socially prescribed means of attaining those goals. The thrust of Merton's argument is that anomie ensues when wealth and material gain are communicated to all members of society as cultural symbols of success yet legitimate opportunities to achieve these goals are not available to everyone. The consequence of this structural disjunction, according to Merton (1938), is a *definite pressure*, or what he (1968) and subsequent theorists would later characterise as *strain*, exerted upon persons in the society (e.g. Agnew, 1992). To adjust to this pressure or strain, persons employ one of five possible *modes of adjustment* (Merton, 1938, p. 676), which comprise *conformity*, *ritualism*, *rebellion*, *innovation* and *retreatism*. Only the latter two modes of adjustment – innovation and retreatism – however, are closely associated with criminal behaviour and thus germane to the crime discourse in Antigua. Innovation occurs when an individual has subscribed to the virtues of achieving wealth and material gain without equally internalizing the institutional norms governing the means for their attainment. As such, in a society that places a high premium on these goals and social ascent, when legitimate channels of vertical mobility are closed or narrowed, the individual logically responds by employing illegitimate or illegal means to achieve them. Retreatism on the other hand is an escape mechanism that allows individuals to be "in the society but not of it" (Merton, 1938, p. 677).

Building on Merton's work, Agnew (1992) argued that strain may result not only from the failure to achieve positively valued goals but also from the failure to achieve legitimate expectations and the failure to achieve an equitable outcome. According to Agnew, the frustration and disappointment that an individual may feel when he or she is somehow blocked from achieving the goals of wealth and material gain may be the same or even greater if that individual's past experience or knowledge of similarly situated persons suggests that he or she should have achieved those goals. Similarly, the frustration and disappointment may be the same or greater if an individual fails to achieve wealth and material gain and also feels that his or her failure is unfair or unjust. Additionally, Agnew (1992) more precisely specified the relationship between strain and delinquency by pointing out that strain is likely to have a cumulative effect on delinquency after a certain threshold level is reached.

Although Merton developed his theories with particular regard to the United States and did not assume that they automatically applied elsewhere, general strain theory and anomie are critical to understanding some of the messages that are identified in Antigua's historical and contemporary news media and public crime discourse – messages that posit that crime stems from such strains as poverty, unemployment, poor education, bad housing, and class discrimination. And, like Merton's quintessential innovator, youth from economically depressed areas turn to crime when they are constrained in their opportunities for legitimate work. This explanation for crime implies a crime solution that lies in creating more opportunities for disadvantaged young people.

Social disorganisation

Of similar importance to understanding messages in Antigua's crime discourse is the notion that crime stems from a breakdown of the traditional family and traditional community. This explanation of crime can be traced back to social ecology and urban mapping research (Downes & Rock, 2011; Rock, 2012; Williams, 2012), which theorises that the city is not just a set of buildings in a particular geographic area but a living ecological environment in which the residents of the city and the city's institutions are so inextricably connected that they tend to interact as a whole (Williams, 2012). In addition, *social disorganisation theory* holds that crime is associated with neither individual pathologies nor poverty but with rapid social change within urban communities. According to Shaw and McKay (1942, 1969), in the central areas of a city where there are very rapid shifts in population, residents see themselves as transient and do not take an interest in their surroundings or form bonds with their community. Where contacts are extended, heterogeneous groups mingle, neighbourhoods disappear, and people, deprived of local and family ties, are forced to live under the loose, transient, and impersonal relations that are characteristic of cities. As a consequence, social institutions such as Church, school, and family may be weakened. This social change or *disorganisation* allows for moral dissensus, which in turn allows for criminality (Downes & Rock, 2011; Williams, 2012; Wirth, 1931, 1940).

Over time, criminologists would refine social disorganisation theory and expand its parameters. For example, Sampson, Raudenbush, and Earls (1997) argued a more nuanced version of social disorganisation theory asserting that it is actually *collective efficacy*, or social cohesion among neighbours combined with their willingness to intervene on behalf of the common good, that is associated with reduced violence (Reisig & Cancino, 2004). In addition, it has been posited that social disorganisation and collective efficacy can be generalised to nonmetropolitan and rural areas as well (Reisig & Cancino, 2004; Osgood & Chambers, 2000). For all of these theorists, treating or severely punishing individual offenders would not remedy a community's crime problem. The solution ought to lie in a bottom-up approach focused on social organisation and community stability known as *community crime prevention* (Williams, 2012).

Social control

In addition, the notion that crime stems from a breakdown of the traditional family and traditional community can also be linked to *social control theory* (Hirschi, 1969), which holds that all people have the potential to violate the law, but not all people break the law because internal and external forces control their behaviour. Such forces include attachment and commitment to conventional institutions, individuals, and processes (Siegel, 2011). Building on the core assumptions of control theory, Braithwaite (1989) argued that crime rates are correlated with a community's ability to attach shame to an offender's actions. To the extent that community ties weaken over time, offenders care less and less about how they are perceived by the community and are less and less ashamed of their actions. When offenders are not made to feel shame for their actions, they are not deterred from further offending. When combining these theoretical perspectives to interpret Antigua's crime trends and patterns, it is important as well to place these perspectives against a backdrop of slavery and emancipation, British colonialism, tourism, development, inequality, poverty, and criminal deportation.

Social and economic backgrounds of informal economies in Antigua

On 1 August 1834 slaves in Antigua became free men and women. However, as Natasha Lightfoot (2015) explains, there were significant restraints on this newfound freedom. Antiguans were emancipated into poverty, social regulation, disenfranchisement, and a culture of violence that the de jure end of slavery failed to mitigate. From a social and cultural perspective, existing constructs of Antiguan family life were under siege. As Christian churches, through their missionaries, sought to create an orderly society in which ex-slaves would become pliant law-abiding subjects and obedient sugar labourers, they endeavoured to restructure black Antiguan family life in ways that would reflect the intended order of the society (Lightfoot, 2015). Matrifocal constructions of family that encompassed extended family, informal unions, and multiple intimate partnerships – constructions of family that resulted from African cultural tradition and the disruptive nature of slavery – were discouraged while patriarchal constructions of the nuclear family characterised by monogamous partnerships and wedlock were promoted in their stead (Lightfoot, 2015, p. 143). Women disproportionately bore the brunt of this sexual regulation (Lightfoot, 2015).

From an economic perspective, endogenous and exogenous pressures on the island's economy created an unprecedented economic crisis. The Sugar Duties Act of 1846, which effectively ended protective tariffs imposed on sugar produced outside the British Empire, caused the price of sugar to fall precipitously. As the price of sugar fell, so too did the wages of the labourers. Antiguan planters began importing white European and Madeiran contract labourers, who they felt would be more compliant workers. The additional supply of workers increased competition for limited jobs, further suppressing wages and increasing the cost of living because legislators increased the price of essential goods to meet the costs associated with importing of labour. Additionally, in 1848 a hurricane devastated much of the island causing 90,000 pounds of damage (Lightfoot, 2015).

The economic turmoil of the late 1840s persisted into the next decade, contributing to the 1858 uprising (Lightfoot, 2015). During this four-day uprising, hundreds of black Antiguan workers violently attacked Barbudan labourers, who were perceived as taking jobs away from capable Antiguans in very difficult economic times. This violence has been described as a tool that black Antiguan workers employed to chip away at the perceived barriers to their progress (Lightfoot, 2015, p. 230). The socioeconomic conditions that gave rise to the 1858 revolt would persist well into the twentieth century.

But, by the late 1960s sugar, Antigua's cash crop, could no longer sustain the economy. As such, the country focused on developing small farmers and small-scale food production for the local market. As a supplement to this restructured agriculture sector, the country looked to tourism, related construction, and light manufacturing as a way to diversify its economy (Caribbean Development Bank

[CDB], 2007; De Albuquerque & McElroy, 1999; Knight, 1989). Most of this diversification occurred during the 1980s when the total number visitors to the island, as well as hotel rooms doubled. By extension, the international airport became a service point for aircrafts serving the region thus creating employment and income growth in the transportation sector. Indeed, by 1993 agriculture's share of the country's GDP had fallen to 3.7 per cent while tourism simultaneously grew to account for 50 per cent (CDB, 2007; De Albuquerque & McElroy, 1995), making Antigua one of the better-off countries in the Caribbean and the developing world (CDB, 2007).

In the 1990s tourism growth declined to less than half of the 1980s growth rate, leaving the country with high debt and growing arrears. Economic difficulties were further exacerbated by five major hurricanes, and a volcanic eruption in neighbouring Montserrat. Furthermore, a ruling by the World Trade Organization (WTO) threatened the banana industry in Dominica, which affected the very stability of Antigua's Eastern Caribbean Dollar. Fiscal imbalance widened and declining credit worthiness prevented access to regular financing. The practical implications of these new economic realities included the postponement of necessary public investment, labour market distortions that made government the single largest employer in the country, and an overreliance on tourism as the mainstay of the economy (De Albuquerque & McElroy, 1999; Sahay, Robinson, & Cashin, 2006).

These new economic realities also served to restructure the nature of poverty in the country as a growing number of women and new immigrants became dependent for employment on seasonal low-skilled and low-paying jobs in the hotel and restaurant sectors. These low-paying jobs were hypersensitive to such exogenous events as natural disasters and fluctuations in European and North American economies. For example, after hurricane Luis in 1995 approximately 15 to 25 per cent of the hotel and tourism jobs were lost (Griffith, 2004). Because government became a significant employer for the poorest segment of the population, once public sector cuts began, it was the poorest segment of the population that was disproportionately affected (CDB, 2007). As in other parts of the region (e.g. Harriott, 2000), the face of poverty in Antigua was rapidly becoming that of a low-skilled worker with full-time employment in the formal labour market.

Rather than turn to the IMF for assistance, the government developed and implemented its own voluntary "home-grown" structural adjustment (e.g. Government of Antigua, 1995, 1997), which was designed to diversify the economy, rein in spending, cut public sector employment, and raise revenues through indirect taxation. However, according to reports and assessments, this structural adjustment program never fully achieved intended results (e.g. CDB, 2007). Raising revenue through indirect taxation also proved problematic as this had the effect of further entrenching inequality – the gap between the middle class and the poor – which persisted into the 2000s (CDB, 2007). By 2007, 28.3 per cent of Antiguans were estimated to be vulnerable (10 per cent), poor (14.6 per cent) or indigent (3.7 per cent) and the vast majority of this population was employed in the formal economy (CDB, 2007).

Though inequality and poverty were hardly foreign to Antigua as a former slave colony, the way in which people navigated their condition evolved with the country's growth and development. While black working people in post-1834 Antigua wielded rumour and seditious speech, theft, spiritual practices, and physical violence, among other things, to subvert the perceived limitations to their freedom (Lightfoot, 2015), in twentieth- and twenty-first century Antigua, similar coping strategies were employed albeit by more sophisticated means. Some of the same conditions that facilitated economic prosperity in the 1980s simultaneously facilitated the flourishing of a nascent underground economy built around drug running, prostitution, and human trafficking. Through its international connections, this underground economy eventually became attractive and rewarding enough to serve as a counterpoint to participation in the formal economy (see Bowling, 2010). Moreover, evidence suggests that there is no longer a social stigma associated with participation in this underground economy and a growing number of people – especially marginalised young people – move fluidly between these two economies. Not only have young people admitted to running drugs to survive, a 2001 survey discovered that 20 per cent of secondary school students would engage in the sale of drugs if given the opportunity (CDB, 2007).

Furthermore, from 1998 to 2006 Antigua had a higher rate of criminal deportation than Trinidad and Tobago and Guyana. While the data does not support theories that deported criminal offenders are primarily responsible for most of the country's increase in serious crime, a 2008 CARICOM[1] study on criminal deportation in the Caribbean found that even small numbers of deported criminal offenders might result in a disproportionately negative effect on the society to which they returned (Barnes, Seepersad, Simpson, & Community, 2008), most likely by introducing new ways of offending, such as hi-tech fraud crimes (e.g. Barnes et al., 2008) and increasing the sophistication of Antigua's home-grown criminal offenders. Thus, in contemporary Antigua it seems that a flailing formal economy facilitated the pervasiveness and institutionalisation of illegal acts that served to subvert the perceived barriers to progress. The unfulfilled promises of emancipation, growth and development, tourism, inequality, poverty, and criminal deportation then seem to be the backdrop to Antigua's crime trends and patterns. However, it is not clear that the country's contemporary crime discourse acknowledges any of this.

Perceptions of socioeconomic causes of crime in Antigua

For many people living in Antigua, the country's history and socioeconomic context seem divorced from its perceived crime problem. Similarly, the newspaper media appear only rarely to speak about crime in the context of the structural impediments that are inextricably linked to the country's history and socioeconomic background. However, overlooking Antigua's historical and socioeconomic realities has significant implications because it is widely acknowledged that the dominant social crime narrative actually directs criminal justice policy (e.g. Gamson, 1992; Loseke, 2003; Sasson, 1995). That is, the most widely shared understanding of crime will establish the contours of Antigua's crime problem: its sources, trends, definitions, and policy responses (Surette, 2015). In other words, the crime reality that people believe to be true will influence legislation and the allocation of government resources. This will also communicate implicit value judgments: which members of society are virtuous or dangerous, who deserves attention and protection, and which actions should be rewarded or penalised (Sasson, 1995).

To the extent that a discussion of structural impediments is absent from popular and media crime discourse, it will likely be absent from policy considerations as well. To the extent that popular and media crime discourse fails to acknowledge the historical and socioeconomic backdrop against which crime occurs in Antigua, policies may be imported wholesale from other jurisdictions without any consideration of narrowly tailored imperatives, that are more in keeping with a post-colonial developing island nation. Combining the theoretical underpinnings of anomie, strain, disorganisation theory, and social control, this research uses *frame analysis* to examine the extent to which the popular and media crime discourse in Antigua employs traditional socioeconomic explanations of crime in discussing the country's perceived crime problem.

Methods

The methodology employed in this research is frame analysis, a methodology widely attributed to Goffman (1974), commonly used to conduct research in the constructionist paradigm (Sasson, 1995). The methodology is premised on the idea that we are active assemblers of meaning and in constructing accounts of public issues we draw upon the resources at our disposal, including popular wisdom, our personal experiences, and media discourse. In using these resources to create coherent and meaningful accounts of public issues, we select from a range of interpretive frameworks available in the culture in order to create meaning (Sasson, 1995). These interpretive frameworks, or frames, are the *schemata of interpretation* and typically include a diagnostic component that identifies a condition as intolerable and attributes blame or causality, as well as a prognostic component that prescribes a course of ameliorative action (Borah, 2011; Goffman, 1974; Sasson, 1995). Additionally, frame analysis presupposes that meaning created through the use of frames occurs in various contexts including mass media and everyday conversation.

This study relied on a documentary analysis comprised of newspaper articles, political manifestos, government speeches, political speeches, parliamentary debates, criminal law judicial opinions and annual crime reports. Understanding that documents are not firm evidence of what they report, but construct particular kinds of representations, these documents help to establish a catalogue of culturally available frames pertaining to crime in Antigua (Atkinson & Coffey, 2011; Sasson, 1995). Additionally, this research relied on nine focused interviews (Kvale, 2009) with key stakeholders[2] and 10 peer group discussions comprised of 52 members of the public. Participants were recruited for the peer group discussions using such convenience sampling techniques as email and word of mouth because I was cognisant of the fact that I was not asking participants to merely complete a survey or to participate in a peer group discussion at a neutral location, but rather to allow me into their intimate social spaces, including their homes (Gamson, 1992). Understanding Antiguan culture, I suspected I would be met with suspicion and hesitation if I approached random people unfamiliar with me in a shopping centre or other public space. Sacrificing random selection, I instead strove for heterogeneity with respect to key demographics such as race, age, and ethnicity.[3]

The discussions held were not traditional focus groups but were peer group conversations, which are smaller than traditional focus groups, held in the participants' own environment, conducted with participants who are already familiar acquaintances and conducted with little interference or intervention by the facilitator. This method was chosen because focus groups have two significant weaknesses that cannot be overlooked. First, there is always some uncertainty about the accuracy of what the participants say given that the researcher creates and directs the groups, often in an unfamiliar environment, making focus groups less naturalistic than other qualitative methods. Second, the reliance on interaction in the group to produce the data can be problematic because there may be a tendency toward both conformity – participants withholding things that they might say in private – and polarisation, participants expressing more extreme views in the group than those they may express in private (Morgan, 1997). The peer group discussions consisted of at least three participants who were already familiar with each other. Because I wanted them to meet in a familiar space where they might have spontaneously engaged in a conversation about crime had I not been present, I met the participants in locales as disparate as the beach, a restaurant, participants' homes, and participants' workplaces.

My qualitative data analysis involved coding the data, dividing the text into small units, assigning a label to each unit and then grouping the codes into themes (Creswell & Plano Clark, 2011). I analysed the qualitative corpus of this study – all of the collected qualitative data – with two goals in mind: (a) to track the frequency of selected crime frames and (b) to capture frames that spontaneously emerged in the documents. I first read and reread the corpus in order to gain intimate familiarity with its contents. With respect to the documents and focused interviews, I coded the text as displaying a positive version of a particular frame if it expressed at least one component of that frame to characterise Antigua's crime situation or as a solution (Sasson, 1995). Because each discussion rather than individual is the unit of analysis, in analyzing transcripts of peer group discussions, where participants expressed unanimous support for a frame, I coded that frame's performance as *strong*. Where participants disagreed with one another over a frame's merits, I coded that frame's performance as *mixed* and where participants were unanimous in their rejection of a frame, I coded that performance as *weak*. While I first coded the data manually, I later used NVivo software in order to exploit the benefits of computer-assisted qualitative data analysis. NVivo made the coding and retrieval process faster and more efficient, it allowed me to relate coded text to demographic information, and it enhanced the transparency of my analysis (Bazeley, 2009; Bryman, 2012). Additionally, using NVivo allowed me to quantify my data corpus and count the frequency of themes and codes thus helping me to recognise patterns and idiosyncrasies, document analytic moves, and verify interpretations (Sandelowski, Voils, & Knafl, 2009, p. 3).

Results

This research focuses on two of the culturally available frames that emerged from my investigation, *Blocked Opportunities* and *Social Breakdown*, which can be distilled to the following:

> Blocked Opportunities: Crime stems from poverty, unemployment, poor education, bad housing, and class discrimination. Kids come from [economically depressed] places like Gray's Farm and Point turn to crime when they don't see any opportunities for legitimate work. If we're serious about fighting crime, we need to create more opportunities for disadvantaged kids. We'll only make progress in the fight against crime when we begin to seriously address these "root causes".
>
> Social Breakdown: Crime stems from a breakdown of the traditional family and traditional community. In the past there was less crime because neighbours looked out for one another and parents supervised and disciplined their children. The best way to fight crime is for neighbours, in partnership with the police, to band together to restore order to their communities.

Blocked Opportunities in the news

Components of the Blocked Opportunities frame appeared in only 7.4 per cent of newspaper articles. Where this frame was evident, none of the articles explicitly argued that crime stems from poverty unemployment, poor education, bad housing, or class discrimination. Rather, these articles drew on the frame in order to reject its fundamental premise. For example, a 1995 article registered "alarm" that:

> even in the nation's best schools, pupils from privileged backgrounds are turning up armed with handguns, knives and ice picks at the ready, to do serious injury to their schoolmates and the wider public at the slightest provocation and sometimes without any provocation at all.
>
> ("Commentary on Crimes of Violence", 1995).

Although the surprise articulated in this example suggests an underlying assumption that criminal behaviour is the domain of those who do not have access to the best schools and are not from privileged backgrounds, it is an assumption that is directly being challenged.

Where components of the Blocked Opportunities frame were explicitly refuted, the suggestion was that crime is not related to poverty and other social conditions. One editorial explained, "in bygone days . . . without affluence, nay, even amid excruciating poverty and oppression, children were raised to become decent and law-abiding citizens of the land" ("Stemming the Rising Tide", 1998). Here, the writer appeared to argue against a causal relationship between poverty, oppression, and crime. This is a common retort that Merton (1938) himself addressed in his argument that poverty and limited opportunities alone are not sufficient to induce high rates of criminal behaviour. Similarly, in discussing the validity of strain theory, scholars such as Reiner (2012) and Braithwaite (1979) acknowledged that the relationship between economic deprivation and crime is complex and cannot be reduced to a simple causal formulation. This rebuttal argument, which was prevalent throughout the peer group discussions, highlights the need for a more nuanced understanding of the relationship between crime and poverty as perceived by society.

Blocked Opportunities in peer group discussions

Across all group discussions, the performance of the Blocked Opportunities frame was weak. In half of the peer group discussions there was a mixed reaction to the Blocked Opportunities frame, meaning that in these discussions, at least one group member articulated a cogent position contrary to the other group members when discussing the merits of the frame. In the remaining half, there was a "weak" reaction to the Blocked Opportunities frame. In these discussions there was unanimous rejection of the frame. None of the peer group discussions gave a strong, or even unanimous, support for either the idea that crime stems from poverty, unemployment, poor education, bad housing, and class discrimination, nor that young people from economically depressed communities turn to crime when they do not see any opportunity for legitimate work. However, in discussions where at least one participant articulated a cogent position in favour of the frame, they did so by making one of three arguments below.

Supportive argument 1: crime is born of necessity

When asked who they thought were committing the crimes, peer group participants constructed the offender in clear Mertonian terms in the four out of five discussions in which at least one participant supported the Blocked Opportunities frame. Participants focused on those who they believed may be "desperate" and "unemployed" or people who are simply, "frustrated and do not know what to do". As Sasson (1995) found, the easiest way to understand this construction of offending is that sometimes crime is simply born of necessity.

Supportive argument 2: stressful life events have a cumulative impact on a person

Agnew (1992) expanded the parameters of Merton's theory in part by pointing out that strain is likely to have a cumulative effect on delinquency after a certain threshold level is reached. Many participants spoke in language reminiscent of Agnew's general strain theory. They constructed the offender as an otherwise law-abiding person who works, cannot support his or her family, and finally reaches a breaking point. Alluding to the recent difficulties in the Antiguan economy and alleged exploitation of undocumented immigrants, those who work do not always receive compensation, for example, when the government cannot pay workers promptly or when undocumented immigrants who are getting paid in the informal economy do not receive the compensation due to them.

Supportive argument 3: the ends justify the means

According to Merton's (1938) redefinition of anomie, when there is a higher premium on success than there is on the way in which it is attained, some members of society are likely to resort to achieving success by any means necessary. Put simply, the ends will always justify the means. Of those peer group discussions that showed support for the frame of Blocked Opportunities, three out of five were infused with talk of anomie, emphasizing the premium placed on the cultural symbols of success or the inability to achieve success through socially prescribed means. With regard to the socially prescribed means of attaining success, participants made one of three points: (a) that the educational system has failed to serve as an effective vehicle for success, (b) opportunities do exist but because they are inaccessible or culturally stigmatised they are effectively non-existent, or (c) there is a cultural bias as to what types of opportunities are created.

Rebuttal argument 1: if you look for opportunities they're there – they are there

Despite the few supportive arguments, however, the Blocked Opportunities frame was heavily contested. More than half of all participants argued that there are plenty of opportunities for those less fortunate, including opportunities for them to create their own opportunities. However, participants who made this argument did so in two slightly different ways. Merton (1938) contended that cultural stigmatisation of manual labour coupled with the prestige of white-collar work can create a strain towards criminality. According to Merton (1938, p. 67), the low income associated with manual labour cannot compete "in terms of conventional standards of achievement" with the high income associated with white-collar work. For slightly different reasons, one-third of all peer group participants proffered an argument similar to Merton's. According to these participants, the cultural stigmatisation of manual labour coupled with the prestige of white-collar work forces some native-born Antiguans to eschew potentially lucrative opportunities involving manual labour. Unable to gain access to more prestigious jobs, some are said to turn to crime in order to support themselves. Arguing from a slightly different perspective, some participants held the view that a lot of young people simply do not wish to work. In short one participant summed up this version of the rebuttal argument insisting that there are other reasons for the crime situation but not lack of opportunity as she said:

> as an employer I know what I'm talking about – employing young people who want a salary and not a job. It's not because they can't get a job. They got the job. But it's not the job they want it's the money.

Rebuttal argument 2: poverty and deprivation do not inevitably lead to crime

Although very few participants decried the contention that poverty inevitably manifests in criminality, this contention aroused strong feelings. Given Antigua's history as an agrarian slave colony and the country's recent transition to a service economy, much of the growth of the Antiguan middle class has occurred within the past 35 years (e.g. De Albuquerque & McElroy, 1995). As such, many Antiguans are not that far removed from the experience of living on very little means. Using herself as an example, one peer group participant argued in part that:

> by and large most of us come out of the same cramped small circumstances because most of us come from villages . . . We are one generation away from the village. And the villages – the houses – were small and cramped and your fence was abutting your neighbour's fence . . . I find that we have given people again another set of excuses. I listen sometimes to the music that comes out of Jamaica and they talk about the down pressed and the sufferer . . . Big deal. Plenty people born poor . . . It doesn't mean that you have to stay poor. And you can be poor in pocket but not poor in spirit and I think that the spirit that took most of us up and out is what is lacking now . . . Poverty is a state of mind . . . It's not the amount of dollars you have in your pocket. I know there are times when if anybody attack me they would beat me for wasting their time to mug me because I never had enough. But, I was never poor in spirit, never.

Although empirical data casts doubt on the claim that crime was not prevalent in Antigua in the past (Matthews, 2014), participants making this argument are employing the theme of what scholars call relative deprivation – it is not poverty per se that causes crime but inequality (Siegel, 2011).

Rebuttal argument 3: it's not only kids from Gray's Farm and Point . . .

In half of the discussions, some participants argued that it is not only youth from economically depressed areas who commit crime. Additionally, participants argue that middle-class people commit crimes also but have the resources to either keep the matter quiet or out of the formal criminal justice system. In four discussion groups, participants explained further that offenders often apprehended in Gray's Farm or Point are not actually from these communities, but seek refuge there because it is more densely populated. Furthermore, the people in these communities tend not to cooperate with police investigations and/or these communities are already stigmatised as "bad areas". Moreover, in these discussion groups there was general unease surrounding the implicit definition of crime as street crime. For these participants, white-collar crime and domestic violence are often overlooked in the country's crime discourse.

Social Breakdown in the news

Components of the Social Breakdown frame appeared in slightly more than one-third of the newspaper articles included in this study. In each article, these components were not contested. Writers seemed unanimously to support the fundamental premise that crime stems from a breakdown of the traditional family and traditional community. In these articles writers supported the contention that in the past there was less crime because neighbours looked out for one another and parents supervised and disciplined their children. Proposed solutions took three main forms. The first solution called for collective action by residents, churches, the police, the public, and private sectors. However, notwithstanding this call to collective action, most articles proposing this solution specifically implored parents to get involved. In calling for schools, churches, and families to work together to fight crime, a 1998 editorial places particular emphasis on the need for a "partnership between parents and children" because "family is the strongest and most powerful instrument for social change" ("Stemming the Rising Tide", 1998). In another article the then Youth Affairs Minister Winston Williams is described as "reprimanding" parents when he said, "adults should . . . play a more active role parenting their children if they want to effectively address the problem. Government cannot rear your children" (Richards, 2007, p. 24). Thus, in singling out parents, calls for collective action still seem laden with a fundamental message of personal responsibility and better parenting.

The second proposed solution called for interventions that include mentoring, counselling, and various programs aimed at at-risk youth. For example, a 2005 editorial argued that at-risk youth need to be subjected to programs that allow them to experience prison life, "to see how being on lockdown breaks the backs of bullies and street heroes and learn that, contrary to the lore, there is no honour in thug life" ("Time to Take Our Country Back", 2005). Reminiscent of Shaw's Chicago Area Project (Shaw & McKay, 1942, 1969), another article proposed a range of programs intended to provide educational support, develop parenting skills, assist with substance abuse and gang prevention, and strengthen community relations with the police force. The article also revealed government plans to open a multi-functional community centre in the heart of one economically depressed community. Sasson (1995) rightly pointed out that these interventions all share in common the tacit claim that crime stems from inadequate supervision or a failure of moral integration. While one article called for collective action invoking imagery of more communal living and interdependent village life, the article rejected the need for government programs designed to provide structure and discipline for at risk youth. The argument is that "government does not need to set up a boot camp to discipline wayward youngsters, but rather, that parents need to play a more active role in their children's lives" (*The Daily Observer*, 2/2/1998, 24).[4]

Consistent with a growing body of literature in the United States that focuses on the importance of faith in rehabilitative interventions, the final proposed solution called for greater reliance on religion. For example, in the 1998 editorial that refuted the claims of the Blocked Opportunities frame, the writer embraced the

Social Breakdown frame arguing that, "The churches too must get their act together. They must recapture the ground lost to the influence of television in directing the proper socialisation of children" ("Stemming the Rising Tide", 1998). Similarly, the writer of a 2006 article described the efforts of the inter-denominational police group called Cops for Christ quoting the president who said, "we feel apart from our duties as police officers, we can do more as Christians . . . With the prayers of the nation along with support, I believe we can see the best come out of all of our youths" (Richards, 2006a, p. 5).

In the articles that conjured the Social Breakdown frame to explain the causes of the country's crime problem, most did so by comparing contemporary times to a more genteel time of yesteryear where "children were raised to become decent and law-abiding citizens of the land" ("Stemming the Rising Tide", 1998), when "police used to do foot patrol and not just be mobile" (Richards, 2006b, p. 4). In the writers' historical imaginations, neighbours looked out for one another, the extended family was paramount, and social institutions were strong. Collectively, the articles paint a dystopian portrait of an Antigua currently in the midst of social crisis. The excerpt below illustrates the point:

> It is clear that an alarming plague of social dry rot has set in. The plague is upon our homes and families; it is upon our churches and upon our schools. Indeed, it is upon our Government, which is deemed to be one of the most corrupt in the whole wide world.
>
> ("Stemming the Rising Tide", 1998)

Against this dystopian backdrop, writers attributed crime to family breakdown and poor parenting as well as community disintegration and weakening social institutions. The perception that family breakdown and poor parenting cause crime is not surprising considering the various calls for parents to get involved in crime fighting efforts by partnering with schools, their children, churches, and government. With respect to this line of argument, a 2009 editorial aptly summarised the sentiment, "the biblical admonition of training up a child in the way he ought to go and when he is old he will not depart from it, still holds true" ("When Mothers Cry, 2009").

Social Breakdown in the peer group discussions

The overall performance of the Social Breakdown frame in peer group discussions was strong. Seven of the 10 peer group discussions showed strong support for the frame as participants unanimously agreed with the contention that crime stems from a breakdown in traditional family and traditional community. Across all discussion groups, slightly more than two-thirds of participants endorsed this view. In two discussions there was a mixed reaction to the frame meaning at least one group member articulated a cogent position contrary to the other group members when discussing the merits of the frame. Only in one discussion, participants had a weak reaction to the Social Breakdown frame by rejecting it unanimously.

Like the newspaper articles previously discussed, peer group discussants favouring the Social Breakdown frame presented a dystopian view of contemporary Antigua. Contrasting present-day contemporary society to that which they remembered from their childhoods, participants claimed that neighbours no longer know the other residents in the community, crime is much more prevalent, parents no longer discipline their children, and people no longer care about their environment. In Antiguan parlance, life in Antigua is not like "before time". In the peer group discussions where at least one participant articulated a cogent position in favour of the Social Breakdown frame, the participants showed their support for the frame by arguing either there has been a shift in cultural values, parents are not raising their children as they should, or the solution to the country's crime problem lies in collective or community anticrime activism or other types of interventions. In some cases, participants made all of these arguments.

Supportive argument 1: there has been a shift in cultural values over time

Whether it be the waning influence of church or of shame, or a diminishing sense of civic duty, participants arguing in this way claimed that there has been a shift in cultural values over time. In language reminiscent of Pearson's (1984) *Hooligan*, participants argued that the erosion of people's connection with church and similar social institutions has led to deviant behaviour. In one discussion group a participant argued more pointedly:

> What I find has changed is that people don't have shame like they used to have shame. Because when I was growing up committing a crime, or a police have you even for questioning – that was big shame for your family. It didn't just involve you it shamed your whole family . . . what we used to know as shame no longer is shameful.

This argument is reminiscent of John Braithwaite's (1989) classic work on reintegrative shaming in which he argues that crime rates are correlated with a community's ability to attach shame to an offender's actions. To the extent that community ties weaken over time, offenders care less and less about how they are perceived by the community and are less and less ashamed of their actions. Also underlying these arguments is a sense of increasing individualism – a shift away from interdependence.

Interestingly, two peer group discussions made a more nuanced argument with respect to this shift towards individualism. In ways that Sampson et al. (1997) refined the work of earlier social disorganisation theorists by arguing from a perspective of collective efficacy, participants in these two groups presented more refined arguments than those in other groups. For these participants, the key difference between how Antiguans used to live and how they now live is not only interdependence and social cohesion among neighbours but neighbours' willingness to intervene on behalf of the common good. These two groups point to child rearing to make their point. In the past, child rearing was the responsibility of the entire community. The most common referent in these discussions is the African adage, it takes a village to raise a child. Neighbours had the authority to intervene and discipline each other's children.

Supportive argument 2: parents are not raising their children as they should

Most participants supporting this frame argued that crime resulted from parents inadequately supervising, disciplining, and instilling proper values in their children. The nexus between crime and negligent parenting articulated in the public discourse is rooted in social control theory. More specifically, these insights are reminiscent of parental efficacy, a contribution to control theory that argues that effective parenting can help neutralise the effect of both individual and social forces that promote delinquent behaviour (Siegel, 2011). Similarly, other participants suggested that parents are not transmitting correct values to children, in part because they are young themselves.

In most of the peer group discussions in which participants argued that parents are not adequately supervising and disciplining their children, participants attempted to explain this lax parenting by pointing to what they perceived as an increase in young girls having children and/or the increased need for single mothers to hold more than one job. Additionally, participants raised a profound point made by Hirschi and other control theorists – children who hurt, hurt others. These participants unknowingly supported Hirschi's claim that family detachment, including intra-family conflict, child abuse, lack of affection, and lack of supervision, are predictive of offending and reinforce Van Voorhis, Cullen, Mathers, and Garner's (1988) conclusion that "bad homes" place youth at risk. Echoing sentiments expressed in 2007 by the Youth Affairs Minister (see Richards, 2007, p. 24), some participants argued that parents are not only negligent in raising their children, but are, in some circumstances, complicit in the children's wrong doing.

Supportive argument 3: community solutions are needed for community problems

Three of the four discussion groups that advocated community-based interventions suggested community programs in the vein of Shaw's Chicago Area Project (Shaw & McKay, 1942, 1969). These participants observed that young people are idle today in ways they were not idle in the past. For these participants, structured programs with adequate supervision are needed to fill the void left by negligent parents and neighbours who increasingly mind their own business. The focus for some participants is the length of the school day for the average young person who attends a government school. This is a popular topic in the country's public discourse, as many have argued over the years that the school day should extend to at least 3:00pm rather than the current 1:00pm. The remaining group argued for both this type of community program as well as a coordinated neighbourhood watch. In this latter group the idea of self-help and community-led activism was strongest: the community must band together, work with the police, and restore order to their communities.

Rebuttal argument 1: single-parent homes do not cause crime

Notwithstanding the popularity of the Social Breakdown frame, a fifth of all participants rejected various components of the frame. One main objection was that there is no causal relationship between single-parent households and crime. What is interesting about this rebuttal is that it reveals unspoken assumptions as to what the traditional family might mean. At no point does the Social Breakdown prompt define "traditional family" but discussion participants and newspaper writers seemed to imagine the "traditional family" as a two-parent household. Although she wholeheartedly agreed with the frame, one participant cautioned against using a two-parent nuclear family as the default reference point when speaking about the "traditional family" in a Caribbean context. While she agreed that crime is caused by a breakdown in traditional family, this participant argued:

> the fact of the matter [is] we're a slavesome society and what you have were parents . . . a father and a mother who in as much as they didn't live together, respected one another up to a point and by and large the father attempted to support his children . . . the relatives of both sides would look out for the children in one way or the other. Those of us who grew up in families where you had that sort of extended family and so on we still get caught in that kind of setting and we love it dearly and we sorry for all the people who don't have it. But it is not a very common thing to see anymore.

Here, the breakdown of traditional family means not an increase in the prevalence of single mothers but an increase of parental responsibilities falling solely on the shoulders of that single mother as a result of a breakdown of the extended family.

Caribbean sociologists and anthropologists have issued this same warning by arguing, for example, that "research and policy on family in the Caribbean got off to a poor start in the post-World War II colonial period, with culturally inappropriate conceptions of what constitutes 'a family' and 'a conjugal union'" (Barrow, 1996, p. 458). Judged according to "Eurocentered ideals" Barrow explained that Caribbean families were described as deformed and malfunctioning and constituted a threat to the social order. According to European standards, families were stable units composed of a mother, a father, and their children, owned or officially adopted, living together in one household. Conjugal unions were defined as marriages – legally and religiously sanctioned, co-resident, permanent, and based on love and togetherness. The man was the head of the household and worked outside of the home and the woman worked within the home raising children, comforting her husband, and doing the housework. Caribbean households were described as incomplete and headed by women. Women were thought to have too many children who were left alone while they went out to work. Conjugal unions that did not involve co-habitation or marriage were thought to be temporary with little love, affection, or joint activity. Children were described as "illegitimate" and "outside" if they were born out of wedlock or to a parent who was in another committed relationship. Children were described as being shifted from one home to another. Parents migrated and aging grandmothers were saddled with the responsibility of training and disciplining the children. Boys allegedly grew up without their fathers as male role models. Barrow further explained that the task of colonial officials was to restructure Caribbean families and change the patterns of relationship, "what existed had to be removed, not understood. Social policy, therefore, along with the Church, the educational system and the law, set about constructing proper families in the Caribbean, in accordance with European ideals" (Barrow, 1996, p. 458). And, this reconstruction effort was merely an extension of similar efforts that began immediately after emancipation. Given Barrow's insights with respect to the colonial re-education effort as well as earlier post-emancipation efforts, it is not surprising that this colonial understanding of the traditional family seems to be the default backdrop of the Social Breakdown frame and the source of the participants' angst with respect thereto. In many ways, this default backdrop reflects the internalisation of colonial thinking and pathologises the realities of Caribbean family life.

Rebuttal argument 2: the traditional family and community were the site of crime

Feminists have long argued that because it is hidden and unregulated by its very nature, the private realm of domesticity is where women generally experience some of the more punitive aspects of gender relations that are grounded in domination and a denial of agency. This power dynamic coupled with the lack of governmental intervention and scrutiny allows discrimination, subordination, and violence against women to run rampant because such matters are simply dismissed as family matters or the actions of a private entity. Frances Olsen (1993) argued, that for the powerless, the private realm is frequently a sphere not of freedom but of uncertainty and insecurity. Participants in two of the peer group discussions drew on this kind of perspective to challenge the idea that crime stems from a breakdown of the traditional family and the traditional community. Indeed, for these participants, the traditional family and the traditional community were often the sites of crime and violence. For example, one participant said:

> I think that crime has changed because before there was whole lot of crime going on in the family that nobody talked about. You had a lot of incest, you had a tremendous amount of domestic violence and stuff like that that absolutely nobody talked about.

Similarly, in another discussion one participant emphatically rejected the view that life was so much better in the past and crime much less prevalent as he exclaimed:

> I don't believe in the good old days. The good old days to me were horrible when I was growing up here in Antigua. They were absolutely horrible . . . I think we as a society we were horrible. I saw a lot of exploitation.

Thus, both examples argue that crime is not more prevalent now than it was in the past; it is simply that the type of crime that occurs now is different.

Rebuttal argument 3: family and community breakdown does not cause crime

A minority of peer group participants argued that the frame accurately characterises the conditions of contemporary Antiguan society, but that those conditions do not cause crime, they merely provide more opportunity for it to flourish. For these participants, crime is caused by some other factor in spite of there being a breakdown in traditional family and community, and they did agree that neighbours banding together with the police may restore order to the communities.

Conclusion

The tepid performance of the Blocked Opportunities frame was in stark contrast to Social Breakdown's performance in the newspaper discourse where components of the Social Breakdown frame were invoked favourably and uncritically. The frame performed even better in the peer group discussions where nearly all participants agreed with the components of the frame. Although peer groups seemed more nuanced in their understanding, at times linking family breakdown to economic conditions, in the peer group discussions as in the newspaper discourse Blocked Opportunities had a weak showing.

The implications of this research are twofold. On a theoretical level, the remnants of post-emancipation and British colonial re-education efforts that can still be seen in Antigua's crime discourse support the contention that crime and crime policy in Antigua must be studied in light of the country's history. Analyzing crime from an ahistorical perspective is not likely to lead to effective policy. This finding underscores the call by post-colonial criminologists such as Biko Agozino (2004) to "decolonise" criminology by looking at crime through the prism of imperialism and colonialism to better understand criminal justice in post-colonial societies.

On a more practical level, the data suggest that criminal justice policy that is rooted in overtly structural conceptions of crime is not likely to succeed in Antigua. Both the news media and the public seem to have an aversion to explicit causal connections between crime and poverty, unemployment, poor education, bad housing, and class discrimination. This finding is hardly surprising given that Antigua is not a country with many social safety nets or the expectation thereof. While there are national social security and medical benefits schemes, there is no welfare, unemployment insurance, or universal health care scheme. Government subsidies are few and far between. Personal responsibility is a strong cultural meme. You pull yourself up by your bootstraps because there is no one else who will pull you up. Against the backdrop of Antigua's slave and colonial history, profound distrust of government as a source of support rather than oppression makes sense. Ever since emancipation, Antiguans have been devising ways to progress despite government rather than with the support of it (Lightfoot, 2015).

The participant quoted earlier in this study suggested that most Antiguans at some point would have had to overcome structural obstacles. Despite Lightfoot's (2015) work, that tells us that Antiguans used tactics that colonial authorities deemed unlawful to navigate a freedom that never fully delivered the promises of emancipation, in this participant's view structural obstacles are not excuses to turn to crime, they are the impetus to better oneself and get ahead. It is also important to note that rejecting this frame also insulates and protects politicians and public figures. Politicians and government agents are not held accountable in ways they might be if crime was seen more as a public failing.

Interestingly, however, attributing crime to a breakdown of the traditional family and traditional community resonates strongly with both the public and the news media. One could argue, that this is very much a structural argument especially given that some members of the public demonstrated a more nuanced understanding by locating the causes of this social breakdown in economic insecurity and inequality. As such, reframing the crime debate in terms of the Social Breakdown frame while incorporating subtle structural arguments will likely allow for more mature political discourse and as a result, a criminal justice policy differently oriented. It may be that Antiguans do not see this frame in such stark structural terms because the frame seems to contemplate a public private divide. That is, there is no reliance on or expectation of government. The unemployment, discrimination, poverty, and inadequate schools described by the Blocked Opportunities frame may well feel more like public problems falling squarely within the ambit of government while family, parenting, and neighbours looking out for each other may better comport with individual choice and personal responsibility. The government has no control over how and by whom children are disciplined and whether neighbours speak to each other. The components of Social Breakdown may initially be understood as private issues within the private domain. As such, although evaluations of the Chicago Area Project do not always support its crime preventive effects (e.g. Schlossman & Sedlak, 1983), criminal justice policy in Antigua should nevertheless exploit the resonance of the Social Breakdown frame by incorporating a bottom-up approach focused on social organisation and community stability.

Notes

1 CARICOM is an abbreviation for Caribbean Community and Common Market, which is a collection of 15 mostly English-speaking Caribbean countries and territories.

2 I chose to interview senior government officials – the Minister of National Security, the Police Commissioner, the Prison Superintendent, a criminologist, and a senior officer in the Criminal Investigation Department of the RPF, the Director of the Office of National Drug and Control Policy, the Director of Youth Affairs, and the Director of the Bureau of Gender Affairs – in order to get a better sense of existing criminal justice policy and to capture government reactions to the final catalogue of frames. I was interested to hear how these officials would describe the country's crime problem. I selected these government officials based on their position in the current government. From the Minister of National Security, the Police Commissioner, and the Prison Superintendent I was particularly interested in whether they were operating according to an articulated criminal

justice policy and how criminal justice policy was constructed. From the directors of Youth Affairs and the Bureau of Gender Affairs I was particularly interested obtaining any additional information they could provide with respect to youth and gender violence. I was interested in verifying newspaper reports of youth gangs and school violence and gang violence. I chose to interview the publisher of the newspaper not only to hear his views on crime and get his reaction to my catalogue of frames but also to have a sense of how the newspaper is produced.

3 The sample population is as geographically diverse as the population at large, according to the 2011 census. Based on a demographic questionnaire that participants completed at the end of each discussion, 58 per cent of the sample lives in the parish of St John as compared to 59 per cent of the larger population. The parishes of St Mary and St George are slightly over-represented as 12 per cent of participants reported living in St Mary (as compared to 9 per cent of the larger population) and 17 per cent in St George (as compared to 9 per cent of the larger population). The parishes of St Peter, St Phillip, and St Paul are slightly underrepresented with 2 per cent of the sample living in each of St Peter and St Phillip and 6 per cent living in St Paul (as compared to the larger population in which 7 per cent of the population lives in St Peter, 5 per cent in St Phillip and 6 per cent in St Paul). Ninety-two per cent of the sample is currently employed in the paid labour market while 6 per cent is retired and 2 per cent report being a student. Of those currently employed, 27 per cent work for the government in some capacity, which accurately reflects the 25 per cent of residents in Antigua who are employed by the government. Additionally, 33 per cent of the sample work in service-oriented jobs, 8 per cent work in clerical or administrative jobs, and 6 per cent worked in lower wage jobs such as domestic work or security. With respect to the major racial groups, the sample reflects the diversity of the larger population with 85 per cent of respondents identifying as Black (as compared to 91 per cent of the larger population) although White participants are over-represented (10 per cent as compared to 2 per cent) as well as those identifying as Syrian or Lebanese (4 per cent as compared to 0.6 per cent). The sample is more female than the larger population (71 per cent as compared to 53 per cent) and is comprised of more Antiguan nationals (85 per cent) than the larger population (70 per cent). With respect to age, the sample accurately reflects the proportion of those over 60 (17 per cent versus 16 per cent), although it significantly overrepresents those between the ages of 30 and 59 (63 per cent versus 38 per cent) and may slightly underrepresent younger residents between the ages of 18 and 29 (19 per cent as compared to 24 per cent). Additionally, the proportion of interviewees who reported being a victim of crime between 2009 and 2010 was in line with the UNDP crime survey (13 per cent compared with 11 per cent respectively).

4 Title and author of newspaper article unknown.

References

Agnew, R. (1992). Foundation for a generalism strain theory of crime and delinquency. *Criminology*, *30*(1), 47–88.

Agozino, B. (2004). Imperialism, crime and criminology: Towards the decolonisation of criminology. *Crime, Law and Social Change*, *41*(4), 343–358.

Atkinson, P., & Coffey, A. (2011). Analysing documentary realities. In D. Silverman (Ed.), *Qualitative research* (3rd ed., pp. 56–75). London: Sage Publications.

Barnes, A., Seepersad, R., Simpson, A., & Community, C. (2008). *Beyond boundaries: A comparative study on criminal deportation in Antigua and Barbuda, Guyana, Jamaica and Trinidad and Tobago*. Trinidad and Tobago: CARICOM Implementation Agency for Crime and Security (IMPACS).

Barrow, C. (1996). *Family in the Caribbean: Themes and perspectives*. Kingston: Ian Randle Publishers.

Bazeley, P. (2009). Analysing qualitative data: More than 'identifying themes'. *Malaysian Journal of Qualitative Research, 2*(2), 6–22.

Borah, P. (2011). Conceptual issues in framing theory: A systematic examination of a decade's literature. *Journal of Communication, 61*(2), 246–263.

Bowling, B. (2010). *Policing the Caribbean: Transnational security cooperation in practice*. Oxford and New York: Oxford University Press.

Braithwaite, J. (1979). *Inequality, crime, and public policy*. London and Boston: Routledge and K. Paul.

Braithwaite, J. (1989). *Crime, shame, and reintegration*. Cambridge and New York: Cambridge University Press.

Bryman, A. (2012). *Social research methods*. Oxford: Oxford University Press.

Caribbean Development Bank. (2007). *Living conditions in Antigua and Barbuda: Poverty in a services economy in transition*. Retrieved from www.caribank.org/uploads/2012/03/AntBarbCPAMainReport.pdf.

Commentary on Crimes of Violence. (1995, February 23). *The Daily Observer*, p. 7.

Creswell, J., & Clark, V.P. (2011). *Designing and conducting mixed methods research*. California: Sage Publications.

De Albuquerque, K., & McElroy, J.L. (1999). A longitudinal study of serious crime in the Caribbean. *Caribbean Journal of Criminology and Social Psychology, 4*(1/2), 32–70.

Downes, D.M., & Rock, P. (2011). *Understanding deviance: A guide to the sociology of crime and rule-breaking*. Oxford: Oxford University Press.

Gamson, W.A. (1992). *Talking politics*. New York: Cambridge University Press.

Garland, D. (1996). The limits of the sovereign state: Strategies of crime control in contemporary society. *The British Journal of Criminology, 36*(4), 445–471.

Garland, D. (2000). The culture of high crime societies: Some preconditions of recent 'Law and Order' policies. *British Journal of Criminology, 40*(3), 347–375.

Garland, D. (2001). *The culture of control: Crime and social order in late modernity*. Oxford: Clarendon.

Goffman, E. (1974). *Frame analysis: An essay on the organization of experience*. Boston: Northeastern University Press.

Government of Antigua and Barbuda (1995). Throne Speech 1995 delivered by His Excellency Sir James Carlisle GCMG, Governor General at Second Session of Parliament, March 1995.

Government of Antigua and Barbuda (1997). Government of Antigua and Barbuda Budget Speech Delivered by Hon. John E. St. Luce, Minister of Finance, March 1997.

Griffith, I.L. (2004). *Caribbean security in the age of terror: Challenge and change*. Kingston, Jamaica and Miami: Ian Randle Publishers.

Harriott, A. (2000). *Police and crime control in Jamaica: Problems of reforming ex-colonial constabularies*. Kingston, Jamaica: The University of the West Indies Press.

Hirschi, T. (1969). *Causes of delinquency*. Berkeley, CA: University of California.

Knight, F.W. (1989). *The modern Caribbean*. Chapel Hill, NC: The University of North Carolina Press.

Kvale, S. (2009). *Doing interviews, introduction to interview research*. Boston, MA: SAGE Publications.

Lightfoot, N. (2015). *Troubling freedom: Antigua and the aftermath of British emancipation*. Durham and London: Duke University Press.

Loseke, D.R. (2003). *Thinking about social problems: An introduction to constructionist perspectives* (2nd ed.). New York: Aldine de Gruyter.

Maertens, F., & Anstey, C. (2007). *Crime, violence, and development: Trends, costs, and policy options in the Caribbean.* Caribbean: United Nations office on drugs and crime Latin America and the Caribbean region of the World Bank; United Nations: UN Latin America and the Caribbean Regional Office.

Matthews, J. (2014). *Competing constructions: A mixed methods investigation of the popular and media framing of the Antigua crime story.* (Unpublished doctoral dissertation). The London School of Economics and Political Science (LSE). London.

Merton, R.K. (1938). Social structure and anomie. *American Sociological Review, 3*(5), 672–682.

Merton, R.K. (1957). *Social theory and social structure*. Glencoe, IL: Free Press.

Merton, R.K. (1968). *Social theory and social structure* (Revised ed.). New York, NY: Free Press.

Morgan, D.L. (1997). *Focus groups as qualitative research* (Vol. 16). London: Sage Publications.

Olsen, F. (1993). Constitutional law: Feminist critiques of the public/private distinction. *Constitutional Commentary, 10*(2), 319–328.

Oriola, T.B. (2006). Biko Agozino and the rise of post-colonial criminology. *African Journal of Criminology and Justice Studies: AJCJS, 2*(1), 104–131.

Osgood, D.W., & Chambers, J.M. (2000). Social disorganization outside the metropolis: An analysis of rural youth violence. *Criminology, 38*(1), 81–116.

Pearson, G. (1984). *Hooligan: A history of respectable fears* (1st American ed.). New York: Schocken Books.

Reiner, R. (2000). Crime and control in Britain. *Sociology, 34*(1), 71–94.

Reiner, R. (2012). *Casino capital's crimes: Political economy, crime, and criminal justice*. Oxford: Oxford University Press.

Reisig, M.D., & Cancino, J.M. (2004). Incivilities in nonmetropolitan communities: The effects of structural constraints, social conditions, and crime. *Journal of Criminal Justice, 32*(1), 15–29.

Richards, N. (2006a, February 8). Cops for Christ target the schools. *The Daily Observer*.

Richards, N. (2006b). Task force targets youth Violence, Drug Abuse in Barbuda. *The Daily Observer*.

Richards, N. (2007, February 23). Williams says the home, not gov't, key to child rearing. *The Daily Observer*.

Rock, P. (2012). Sociological Theories of Crime. In R. Morgan, M. Maguire, & R. Reiner (Eds.), *The Oxford handbook of criminology* (pp. 39–80). Oxford: Oxford University Press.

Sahay, R., Robinson, D.O., & Cashin, P. (2006). *The Caribbean: From vulnerability to sustained growth*. Washington: International Monetary Fund.

Sampson, R.J., Raudenbush, S.W., & Earls, F. (1997). Neighborhoods and violent crime: A multilevel study of collective efficacy. *Science, 277*(5328), 918–924.

Sandelowski, M., Voils, C.I., & Knafl, G. (2009). On quantitizing. *Journal of Mixed Methods Research, 3*(3), 208–222.

Sasson, T. (1995). *Crime talk: How citizens construct a social problem*. Hawthorne, NY: Aldine de Gruyter.

Schlossman, S., & Sedlak, M. (1983). The Chicago area project revisited. *NPPA Journal, 29*(3), 398–462.

Shaw, C.R., & McKay, H.D. (1942). *Juvenile delinquency and urban areas*. Chicago, IL: University of Chicago Press.

Shaw, C.R., & McKay, H.D. (1969). *Juvenile delinquency and urban areas.* (Revised ed.). Chicago, Ill. University of Chicago Press.

Siegel, L.J. (2011). *Criminology*. Belmont, CA: Wadsworth Cengage Learning.

Stemming the Rising Tide. (1998, February 10). Editorial. *The Daily Observer*, p. 2.

Surette, R. (2015). *Media, crime, and criminal justice*. Stamford: Cengage Learning.

Time to Take Our Country Back. (2005, February 16). Editorial. *The Daily Observer*, p. 2.

UNDP. (2012). *Caribbean human development report 2012: Human development and the shift to better citizen security*. New York: United Nations Development Programme.

Van Voorhis, P., Cullen, F.T., Mathers, R.A., & Garner, C.C. (1988). The impact of family structure and quality on delinquency: A comparative assessment of structural and functional factors. *Criminology*, *26*(2), 235–261.

When Mothers Cry. (2009, February 17). Editorial. *The Daily Observer*, p. 2.

Williams, K.S. (2012). *Textbook on criminology*. Oxford: Oxford University Press.

Wirth, L. (1931). Culture conflict and delinquency: Culture conflict and misconduct. *Social Forces*, *9*(4), 484–492.

Wirth, L. (1940). Ideological aspects of social disorganization. *American Sociological Review*, *5*(4), 472–482.

11 Psychosis and crime among Caribbean migrants

A social defeat perspective

David J. Vinkers

Post-colonial migration from the Caribbean and psychosis

Migration has been recognised as a risk factor for the development of psychosis since Ødegaard showed in 1932 that the incidence of psychosis in Norwegian immigrants to the United States was twofold increased (Ødegaard, 1932). This finding was replicated after World War II in Britain with the emergence of labour-related large-scale migration from Caribbean countries (Hemsi, 1967; Kiev, 1965; Sharpley, Hutchinson, McKenzie, & Murray, 2001). The increased prevalence of psychosis in Caribbean migrants was observed in the United Kingdom (Bhugra, Leff, Der Mallett, Corridan, Rudge, 1997; Harrison, Owens, Holton, Neilson, & Boot, 1988; Harrison et al., 1997; King, Coker, Leavey, Hoare, & Johnson-Sabine, 1994), as well as in the Netherlands (Schrier, Van de Wetering, Mulder, & Selten, 2001; Selten & Sijben, 1994; Selten, Slaets, & Kahn, 1997; Selten et al., 2001; Veling et al., 2006) and Canada (Anderson, Cheng, Susser, McKenzie, & Kurdyak, 2015). In general, the relative risk of psychosis in migrants is nearly three-fold increased as compared to natives (Cantor-Graae & Selten, 2005). However, Caribbean migrants have a nearly five-fold increased risk of psychotic disorders in the United Kingdom (Tortelli et al., 2015), which is comparable to the risk of developing psychosis found among black migrants (Cantor-Graae & Selten, 2005).

Overdiagnosis of psychosis?

It has been suggested that Caribbean migrants may be overdiagnosed with psychotic disorders, because Western psychiatrists are unfamiliar with Caribbean culture and misinterpret behaviour and language (Hickling, Gibson, & Hutchinson, 2013). For example, when compared with patients from European countries, Caribbean psychotic patients tend to be more likely to demonstrate an exuberant presentation of symptoms manifested by higher levels of impulsivity and hostile auditory hallucinations (Harvey, Williams, McGuffin, & Toone, 1990; Takei, Persaud, Woodruff, Brockington, & Murray, 1998). As the Caribbean cultural expression is more exuberant in behaviour and speech in general, this may be misconceived as psychotic (Harrison et al., 1988). Misdiagnosis of psychosis in Caribbean patients is especially likely when there is a negative interaction between these patients and

Western mental health services (Fernando, Ndegwa, & Wilson, 1998). The stereotyping of Caribbean migrants as "big, black and dangerous" may contribute to this negative interaction (SHSA, 1993). From the perspective of Caribbean migrants, a (compulsory) psychiatric assessment may be threatening, especially in light of colonial traumas from the past (Fernando, Ndegwa, & Wilson, 1998). As Fanon described in his seminal work (1967), white colonisation induced alienation and imposed feelings of inferiority on black people through oppression and slavery. The threat and oppression of compulsory psychiatric treatment may resemble this colonial trauma (Fernando et al., 1998), which may induce resistance in patients that could be misinterpreted as paranoia or psychotic symptoms.

However, it is unlikely that the increased rate of psychosis in Caribbean migrants can be explained solely by misdiagnosis of Western psychiatrists (Tortelli et al., 2015). A pertinent study, for example, evaluated the diagnosis of psychotic disorders by several British and one Jamaican psychiatrist working in the United Kingdom. The British psychiatrists classified 62 per cent of the 29 black Caribbean patients as having a psychotic disorder as compared to 55 per cent by the Jamaican psychiatrist (Hickling, McKenzie, Mullen, & Murray, 1999). Although agreement about the diagnosis in black Caribbean patients was less than in the Western white patients, the prevalence rate of psychotic disorders was similar across groups (Hickling, 2005). The increased rate of psychosis among Caribbean migrants has also been observed in studies using more rigorous semi-structured diagnostic interviews, which decrease the risk of cultural misdiagnosis. In general, misdiagnosis of psychosis is found across both white and black patients (Neighbors et al., 1999). Furthermore, there are no significant differences in structural brain abnormalities between Afro-Caribbean and European-British patients with a first psychotic episode (Morgan et al., 2010). When Afro-Caribbean migrants would be misdiagnosed with psychosis, they would lack the structural brain abnormalities found among psychotic patients. Although it is unlikely that the increased rate of psychosis in Caribbean migrants is fully explained by overdiagnosis, it may surely play a role in some cases. This is supported as well by the different course of psychosis in Caribbean migrants which will be discussed in the next paragraph.

Course of psychosis in Caribbean migrants

Caribbean migrants have a slightly more benign illness course of psychosis as compared with white European patients (McKenzie et al., 2001; Chorlton, McKenzie, Morgan, & Doody, 2012; Hickling et al., 2013). This more benign course in Caribbean migrants may also signal misdiagnosis, as most psychotic disorders actually have a chronic course of illness. Their beneficial prognosis of psychosis may also be related to cultural differences in social support and acceptance of aberrant behaviour (Jablensky & Sartorius, 2008). In Jamaica, for example, admission of psychotic patients to an open ward in the general hospital instead of a closed psychiatric hospital was related to better treatment outcomes and lower relapse rates (Hickling et al., 2013). The beneficial prognosis of psychosis in Caribbean countries may also be related to a lower level of stigmatisation of patients (Hickling et al., 2013), which may also be present among communities of migrated Caribbean nationals. Thus, although there are some indications that psychosis might be somewhat overdiagnosed among Caribbean migrants, the incidence rate of psychosis among Caribbean migrants living in Western countries is strongly increased when compared to native Europeans.

Possible explanations

As an explanation for the increased incidence of psychosis in Caribbean migrants it has been suggested that individuals with a predisposition to develop psychosis are more likely to migrate (Tortelli et al., 2015). However, if this was the case, a lower incidence of psychosis would in fact be expected among second-generation Caribbean immigrants, when in fact the opposite is true (Pinto, Ashworth, & Jones, 2008). Furthermore, in the 1970s, one-third of the population of Suriname migrated to the Netherlands when Suriname became independent. However, the prevalence of psychotic disorders in Suriname did not decrease, which would be expected when especially individuals with a predisposition to psychosis had migrated (Hanoeman, Selten, & Kahn, 2002). There is also no evidence of an increased genetic vulnerability to psychosis across the Caribbean, with incidence rates of psychotic disorders in Jamaica, Trinidad, and Barbados being equal to incidence rates of psychotic disorders among whites in Western countries (Hickling & Rodgers-Johnson, 1995; Bhugra, Hilwig, & Hossein, 1996; Mahy, Mallett, Leff, & Bhugra, 1999).

Another argument against a biological vulnerability for psychosis in migrants is that the incidence of psychosis in re-migrants from the United Kingdom to Jamaica is five-fold increased as compared to Jamaicans who never migrated (Hickling et al., 2013). In contrast, the incidence of psychosis in white immigrants to Jamaica is very low (Hickling, 1991). These findings may be related to the elevation in social class that white immigrants to Jamaica experience, in contrast to Jamaican re-migrants (Hickling et al., 2013). Most Jamaican re-migrants experience a decrease in social class in the country after remigration. For example, in a study of 126 Jamaican re-migrants, 37 per cent of the returned migrants were classified as a low social class I or II in Jamaica (from a total of five social classes) whereas they formed only seven per cent of the lower social classes in the countries from which they re-migrated (Hickling, 1991). These observations, in conclusion, show that social explanations rather than biological explanations are involved when explaining the increased incidence of psychosis among Caribbean immigrants (Selten & Cantor-Graae, 2005; Van Os & McGuffin, 2003).

Social defeat hypothesis

The *social defeat hypothesis* posits that the increased incidence of psychosis in migrants is explained by the negative experience of being excluded from the majority group (Selten, Van der Ven, Rutten, & Cantor-Graae, 2013). The social defeat hypothesis is supported by a high frequency of perceived discrimination, a weak or negative ethnic identity, and exposure to social disadvantages (e.g. low income, deprived neighbourhood) in psychotic immigrants (Hutchinson & Haasen, 2004; Hjern, Wicks, & Dalman, 2004; Veling, Hoek, Wiersma, & Mackenbach, 2010; Veling et al., 2007; Mallett, Leff, Bhugra, Pang, & Zhao, 2002). A recent review from the United Kingdom concluded that the increased rate of psychosis in Caribbean immigrants "will be most parsimoniously explained by increased exposure to social and economic disadvantage in the post-migratory environment" (Tortelli et al., 2015, p. 1053). Furthermore, psychotic disorders in immigrants have the highest incidence in neighbourhoods where they form a minority (Schofield, Ashworth & Jones, 2011; Veling et al., 2006; Veling et al., 2008) or where there is little support from ethnic peers (Kirkbride & Jones, 2011). Psychotic-like experiences in Caribbean immigrants to the United States are related to acculturative stress and younger age at immigration (Devylder et al., 2013). Already in the 1930s, Faris and Dunham (1939) stated that "the extended isolation of the person with the role of an outcast" and "lack of sufficient self-confidence" (p. 137) was related to psychosis in immigrants in Chicago. The study shows a differential rate of psychosis in neighbourhoods of Chicago, with highest rates in social disorganised areas. In conclusion, there is evidence from several sources supporting the hypothesis that the prolonged experience of social threats and defeat explains the increased rate of psychosis in Caribbean migrants in Western countries. Although all migrants may be subject to adverse social circumstances and social defeat, this may especially be the case in Caribbean migrants to former colonizing countries (Fernando et al., 1998). Social threats for Caribbean migrants in former colonizing countries involve experiences with institutionalised racism which has been related to feelings of hopelessness and hostility (Unnever & Gabbidon, 2011).

Institutionalised racism in treatment

Caribbean psychotic patients in the United Kingdom, the Netherlands, and Canada are five times more likely to be compulsorily detained in hospitals and secure forensic settings as compared with white patients (Audini & Lelliott, 2002; Bhui et al., 2003; Bhui, Ullrich, Kallis & Coid, 2015; Coid, Kahtan, Gault, & Jarman, 2000; McGovern & Cope, 1987; Vinkers, De Beurs, Barendregt, Rinne, & Hoek, 2011). Although the risk of psychosis in Caribbean migrants to Western countries may be increased up to five times (Cantor-Graae & Selten, 2005; Tortelli et al., 2015), only a fraction of psychotic patients is compulsorily detained. This means that the risk of compulsory treatment is also disproportionately increased among Caribbean migrants. Patient-related explanations for this phenomenon include a higher rate of challenging behaviour and violence, use of drugs, and less insight in their illness in Caribbean patients as compared with European patients (Bebbington et al., 1994; Goater et al., 1999; Thomas, Stone, Osborn, Thomas, & Fisher, 1993). Another patient-related explanation that has been suggested is the fact that Caribbean migrants with psychosis wait longer than other populations before they seek professional help (Harrison et al., 1989). Additionally, Caribbean migrants are also less likely to be referred to mental health services on a voluntary basis by general practitioners (Anderson et al., 2015).

Services-related explanations, on the other hand, state that mental health services do not understand black Caribbean patients, which seems related to poor engagement, misdiagnosis, and racism among mental health service providers (Commander, Sashidharan, Odell, & Surtees, 1997; Koffman, Fulop, Pashley, & Coleman, 1997; Odell, Surtees, Wainwright, Commander, & Sashidharan, 1997; Parkman, Davies, & Lesse, 1997). For example, referrals of black patients are more likely to present threatening behaviour (Fernando et al., 1998). Caribbean patients in the United Kingdom receive anti-psychotic medication at higher doses than white patients and more often through an intramuscular depot (Dunn & Fahy, 1990). This may be justified because Caribbean psychotic patients in Western countries more often show challenging behaviour (Price, Glazer, & Morgenstern, 1985). When adjusted for clinical and socio-demographic variables, medication differences between black and white psychotic patients are indeed reduced (Arnold et al., 2004).

Alternatively, high doses of anti-psychotic medication in intramuscular form may also be linked to prejudice or a lack of understanding of Caribbean culture and communication (Fernando et al., 1998). Afro-Caribbean patients are often perceived as "big, black and dangerous", which is also the title of a report about the death of three Caribbean patients in a UK forensic hospital (SHSA, 1993). This is underlined by the finding that referrals of black people to mental health services are more likely to present *perceptions* of threatening behaviour (Fernando et al., 1998). Institutional racism, which is the failure of an organisation to provide an appropriate service because of skin colour, culture, or ethnicity, is caused by prevailing negative racial stereotypes and perceptions (Fernando et al., 1998). Furthermore, as stated briefly in the previous paragraph, as a marker of social defeat, experiencing racism in and of itself is also associated with psychosis (Karlsen, Nazroo, McKenzie, Bhui & Weich, 2005). However, it should be noted that both patient-related and services-related explanations are largely unsupported by robust empirical evidence hitherto (Singh, Greenwood, White, & Churchill, 2007). Therefore, the strength of patient-related and services-related explanations for the high rate of compulsory detention and treatment of Caribbean psychotic patients remains largely unclear. However, the fact that equal treatment across race is still lacking in mental health services, causing an adverse effect on outcome, is undisputed (SHSA, 1993). Improvement of the relations between black and other ethnic minority patients and the mental health services should include more appropriate and responsive services, increased community engagement, and better information (Department of Health, 2005).

Offending rates among Caribbean migrants

Social defeat may also explain the elevated offending rates of migrants to former colonizing countries. This phenomenon is found in the Netherlands, the United Kingdom, and France (Jennissen, 2014; Smith, 1997). In contrast to popular myth, first-generation migrants typically have very low offending rates when compared to native populations, especially taking into account their high rates of unemployment and social and language barriers (Butcher & Piehl, 1998; Ousey & Kubrin, 2014). Second- and third-generation migrants tend to have crime rates comparable to native populations (Peterson & Krivo, 2005). This may be related to higher feelings of social exclusion in second- and third-generation migrants, who realise that they are discriminated against despite their (parents') efforts to integrate into society (Fernando et al., 1998).

Among Caribbean migrants to former colonizing countries, however, crime rates are especially increased among the first generation (Jennissen, 2014). The number of crimes committed per 1,000 persons by Caribbean nationals in the Netherlands is more than 100, compared to less than 20 by Dutch natives and to less than six in Caribbean nationals living in Curacao (Vinkers, De Beurs, Barendregt, Rinne, & Hoek, 2010). Furthermore, some studies have shown a distinctive age-crime curve for Caribbean migrants in the Netherlands. In general, the rate of offending decreases over time with age. However, for Caribbean migrants in the Netherlands this expected drop in the age crime-curve occurs significantly later when compared to other populations: not until age 45 years for Caribbean men and age 35 for Caribbean women (Jennissen, 2014). The number of drugs-related offences (i.e. drug trafficking) is especially increased; however, other offences are also involved in this prolonged age-crime curve (Jennissen, 2014). This finding has been related to adverse social circumstances in urbanised living areas, low educational levels, and poverty (Jennissen, 2014; Mares, 2010; Sampson & Wilson, 1995; Sampson & Groves, 1989; Smith, 1997). There may also be a link with single-parent and unstable family situations in Caribbean migrants (Bersani & DiPietro, 2014), although it remains unclear if the Caribbean matrifocal family structure *per se* is a risk factor for offending. The matrifocal single-parent family structure may be an adjustment to a poor or instable social situation instead of a risk factor for offending (Jennissen, 2014).

Racism and a lack of future perspective may also contribute to the increased crime rates in Caribbean migrants (Martinez, 2002; Hickling et al., 2013; Tonry, 1997). Unnever and Gabbidon have described in their theory of African American Offending (2011) that the involvement of African Americans in crime is related to racial stereotyping and a loss of bonds with institutions such as the school system and the labour market. This bidirectional interaction of racism and the experience of social defeat may also underlie the increased rate of offending in Caribbean migrants, especially of those migrating to former colonizing countries such as the United Kingdom and the Netherlands (Fernando et al., 1998). Caribbean and Surinamese people with a darker skin colour in the Netherlands indeed reported more experienced racism, which in turn was related to a higher rate of self-reported delinquency (Joosen, 2016). Institutionalised racism among police forces and the criminal justice system could also contribute to inflated (official) offending rates among black and ethnic minority populations (Smith, 1997). In the United Kingdom, Caribbean migrants were seen as a law-abiding community after World War II. From the 1978 Notting Hill Carnival onwards, however, several antipolice riots led to a negative interaction between Caribbean migrants and the police, which has resulted in an institutional bias against Caribbean migrants (Smith, 1997).

Like the toxic interaction between psychotic Caribbean patients and mental health, discrimination, racial prejudice, and hostility among police officers may have interacted with antagonism to white authority in Caribbean migrants (Smith, 1997). The perception that Caribbean migrants are involved in criminal activities may become a self-fulfilling prophecy through classification of Caribbean migrants as "big, black and dangerous" (SHSA, 1993). This conflict may have colonial roots, which could also explain why the increased rate of psychosis and crime in Caribbean migrants is especially found in former colonizing countries of the Caribbean. A history of conflict between Caribbean inhabitants and the former colonizing countries, originally stemming from a negative stereotyping of blacks in slavery, may continue through a toxic interaction between Caribbean migrants and psychiatric and judicial institutions of the host country, characterised by lack of understanding, racism, stereotyping, and antagonism (Unnever & Gabbidon, 2011).

While crime rates among first- and second-generation Caribbean migrants in former colonizing countries of the Caribbean (e.g. the United Kingdom and the Netherlands) are increased, the opposite is true for Caribbean migrants to Western countries which have not been involved in colonisation of Caribbean countries, such as Canada and Australia (Unnever & Gabbidon, 2011; Vinkers et al., 2010; Webster, 2007). This phenomenon may be related to the earlier described toxic interaction in former colonizing countries (Fernando et al., 1998). Among the Caribbean migrants who are sent back to their home countries as a consequence of criminal offending, very few commit crimes after their deportation (UNODC, 2007). For example, in criminal deportees to Jamaica, Barbados, and Trinidad and Tobago, recidivism was only 15 per cent, while in general recidivism rates are much higher (Webster, 2007). This finding suggests that indeed social factors such as racism and social exclusion in former colonizing Western countries could play a role in the increased rate of offending in Caribbean migrants (Fernando et al., 1998).

A similar toxic interaction plays a role in the high rate of offending among African Americans in the United States (Unnever & Gabbidon, 2011). Crime rates among Caribbean migrants in the United States are lower compared to the crime rate of African Americans (Peterson & Krivo, 2005). This may be related to a different cultural history, less unemployment, and less perceived discrimination in Caribbean migrants than African Americans living in the United States (Peterson & Krivo, 2005). Although Caribbean migration to the United States sometimes contributes to social disorganisation (Feldmeyer, 2009), it may also increase family cohesion, which decreases the likelihood of crime (Peterson & Krivo, 2005).

Psychosis and offending

In general, psychotic patients are more often convicted for crimes than the general population (Brennan, Mednick, & Hodgins, 2000; Fazel, Wolf, Palm & Lichtenstein, 2014; Wallace et al., 1998). Some studies show that psychosis is related to all types of crime (Modestin & Ammann, 1996; Mullen, Burgess, Wallace, Palmer, &

Ruschena, 2000; Taylor & Gunn, 1984; Wallace, Mullen, & Burgess, 2004), whereas other studies only find a relationship with violent offences (Lindqvist & Allebeck, 1990; Silver, Felson, & Vaneseltine, 2008; Tiihonen, Isohanni, Rasanen, Koiranen, & Moring, 1997; Wessely, 1997). Psychosis leads to social devaluation and psychotic patients often live in neighbourhoods where crime is highly prevalent (Logdberg, Nilsson, Levander, & Levander, 2004). It is not clear if psychotic disorders in themselves cause crime or if the relationship is mediated by other factors, such as substance abuse or poor impulse control, which are also frequently prevalent among psychotic patients (Fazel, Langstrom, Hjern, Grann, & Lichtenstein, 2009; Witt, Van Dorn, & Fazel, 2013). Caribbean migrants to former colonizing countries show higher incidences of psychosis and offending when compared to native white populations. What does this finding mean for the relation between psychosis and crime in Caribbean migrants?

In general, the prevalence of psychotic disorders among adult prisoners in the UK and the United States is *higher* than that of white adult prisoners (Baillargeon et al., 2009; Cope, 2001; Teplin, 1990), while the rate of psychotic disorders among black juvenile offenders is *lower* than in white juvenile offenders (Karnik, Jones, Campanaro, Haapanen, & Steiner, 2006; Teplin, Abram, McClelland, Dulcan, & Mericle, 2002; Vaughn, Wallace, Davis, Fernandes, & Howard, 2008). As psychotic disorders usually develop through adulthood, black experiences with social exclusion, for example through discrimination on the job market, adverse social circumstances, or being in prison, may explain the increased risk of psychosis in adults. In a similar vein, the lower rate of psychotic disorders in black juveniles may also be related to social circumstances (Unnever & Gabbidon, 2011). In the Netherlands, we found in a nationwide database of pre-trial reported defendants that psychotic disorders were more common in ethnic minority defendants than among native Dutch defendants (21.1 per cent versus 10.2 per cent). Caribbean defendants were 40 per cent more likely to be diagnosed with psychosis than native Dutch defendants after adjustment for age, gender, low IQ levels, and abuse of cannabis or hard drugs (Vinkers et al., 2010). In Caribbean and native Dutch juvenile defendants the prevalence of psychosis and other mental disorders was on a similar low level (Vinkers & Duits, 2011). We also compared the prevalence of psychosis in Caribbean defendants in the Netherlands to defendants in the Caribbean area itself (Vinkers et al., 2010). Defendants who are suspected to suffer from mental illness are pre-trial examined by a psychiatrist or psychologist. In absolute numbers, there were 140 Caribbean defendants with a psychotic disorder in the Netherlands versus 30 defendants with a psychotic disorder in the Dutch Caribbean area. The rate of psychotic disorders was, however, similar in the Netherlands and the Dutch Caribbean with 14.4 per cent versus 15.1 per cent. A recent study found a rate of psychosis of offenders in Jamaica similar to our study (Sewell et al., 2015). It should be noted that the relationship between mental illness and crime in Western countries is weaker, thus a lower rate of psychosis in Caribbean defendants in the Netherlands would have been expected (Large, Smith, Swinson, Shaw & Nielssen, 2008; Fazel & Seewald, 2012). These findings suggest that psychosis may be a small but important confounding factor explaining increased crime rates in Caribbean migrants. Furthermore, there is an overlap of causal factors of psychosis and crime in Caribbean migrants to former colonizing countries: a racial stereotyping of black people as dangerous and violent (SHSA, 1993).

Conclusion

This chapter describes the relation between adverse social circumstances and social defeat on the one hand and psychosis and crime on the other hand in Caribbean migrants residing in former colonizing countries. A toxic interaction between the psychiatric and judicial institutions of the host country seems to contribute to an increased rate of psychosis and crime in Caribbean migrants. Exposure to negative racial stereotypes stemming from colonial slavery (e.g. that Caribbean migrants are dangerous) may lead to loss of social bonds with the host country and its institutions for education and employment. It is important to understand this process in more depth in order to prevent such toxic interactions from continuing. Longitudinal studies among Caribbean migrants to former colonizing countries are therefore urgently needed.

References

Anderson, K.K., Cheng, J., Susser, E., McKenzie, K.J., & Kurdyak, P. (2015). Incidence of psychotic disorders among first-generation immigrants and refugees in Ontario. *Canadian Medical Association Journal, 187*(9), 279–286.

Anderson, K.K., Flora, N., Ferrari, M., Tuck, A., Archie, S., Kidd, S., . . . McKenzie, K. (2015). Pathways to first-episode care for psychosis in African-, Caribbean-, and European-origin groups in Ontario. *Canadian Journal of Psychiatry, 60*(5), 223–231.

Arnold, L.M., Strakowski, S.M., Schwiers, M.L., Amicone, J., Fleck, D.E., Corey, K.B., & Farrow, J.E. (2004). Sex, ethnicity, and antipsychotic medication use in patients with psychosis. *Schizophrenia Research, 66*(2–3), 169–175.

Audini, B., & Lelliott, P. (2002). Age, gender and ethnicity of those detained under Part II of the mental health act 1983. *British Journal of Psychiatry, 180*(3), 222–226.

Baillargeon, J., Penn, J.V., Thomas, C.R., Temple, J.R., Baillargeon, G., & Murray, O.J. (2009). Psychiatric disorders and suicide in the nation's largest state prison system. *Journal of the American Academy of Psychiatry and Law, 37*(2), 188–193.

Bebbington, P.E., Feeney, S.T., Flannigan, C.B., Glover, G.R., Lewis, S.W., & Wing, J.K. (1994). Inner London collaborative audit of admission in two health districts. II: Ethnicity and the use of the Mental Health Act. *British Journal of Psychology, 165*(6), 743–749.

Bersani, B.E., & DiPietro, S.M. (2014). Examining the salience of marriage to offending for black and Hispanic men. *Justice Quarterly, 33*(3), 510–537.

Bhugra, D., Hilwig, M., & Hossein, B. (1996). First-contact incidence rates of schizophrenia in Trinidad and one-year follow-up. *British Journal of Psychiatry, 169*(5), 587–592.

Bhugra, D., Leff, J., Der Mallett, R., G., Corridan, B., & Rudge, S. (1997). Incidence and outcome of schizophrenia in Whites, African-Caribbeans and Asians in London. *Psychological Medicine, 27*(4), 791–789.

Bhui, K., Stansfeld, S., Hull, S., Priebe, S., Mole, F., & Feder, G. (2003). Ethnic variations in pathways to and use of specialist mental health services in the UK: Systematic review. *British Journal of Psychiatry, 182*(2), 105–116.

Bhui, K., Ullrich, S., Kallis, C., & Coid, J.W. (2015). Criminal justice pathways to psychiatric care for psychosis. *British Journal of Psychiatry, 207*(6), 523–529.

Brennan, P.A., Mednick, S.A., & Hodgins, S. (2000). Major mental disorders and criminal violence in a Danish birth cohort. *Archives of General Psychiatry, 57*(5), 494–500.

Butcher, K.F., & Piehl, A.M. (1998). Cross-city evidence on the relationship between immigration and crime. *Journal of Policy Analysis and Management, 17*(3), 457–493.

Cantor-Graae, E., & Selten, J.P. (2005). Schizophrenia and migration: A meta-analysis and review. *American Journal of Psychiatry, 162*(1), 12–24.

Chorlton, E., McKenzie, K., Morgan, C., & Doody, G. (2012). Course and outcome of psychosis in black Caribbean populations and other ethnic groups living in the UK: A systematic review. *International Journal of Social Psychiatry, 58*(4), 400–408.

Coid, J., Kahtan, N., Gault, S., & Jarman, B. (2000). Ethnic differences in admissions to secure forensic psychiatry services. *British Journal of Psychiatry, 177*(3), 241–247.

Commander, M.J., Sashidharan, S.P., Odell, S.M., & Surtees, P.G. (1997). Access to mental health care in an inner-city health district. I: Pathways into and within specialist psychiatric services. II. Association with demographic factors. *British Journal of Psychology, 170*(4), 312–320.

Cope, R. (2001). Forensic psychiatry. In D. Bhugra, & R. Cochrane (Eds.), *Psychiatry in multicultural Britain* (pp. 264–283). London: Gaskell.

Department of Health. (2005). *Delivering race equality in mental health care: An action plan for reform inside and outside services and the Government's response to the Independent inquiry into the death of David Bennett.* London: DH publications.

Devylder, J.E., Oh, H.Y., Yang, L.H., Cabassa, L.J., Chen, F.P., & Lukens, E.P. (2013). Acculturative stress and psychotic-like experiences among Asian and Latino immigrants to the United States. *Schizophrenia Research, 150*(1), 223–228.

Dunn, J., & Fahy, T.A. (1990). Police admissions to a psychiatric hospital. Demographic and clinical differences between ethnic groups. *British Journal of Psychiatry, 156*(3), 373–378.

Fanon, F. (1967). *Black skin, white masks*. New York: Palgrave.

Faris, R.E.L., & Dunham, H.W. (1939). *Mental disorders in urban areas: Demography of urban psychotics with special reference to schizophrenia*. Chicago: University of Chicago Press.

Fazel, S., Langstrom, N., Hjern, A., Grann, A., & Lichtenstein, P. (2009). Schizophrenia, substance abuse, and violent crime. *Journal of the American Medical Association, 301*(19), 2016–2023.

Fazel, S., & Seewald, K. (2012). Severe mental illness in 33,588 prisoners worldwide: Systematic review and meta-regression analysis. *British Journal of Psychiatry, 200*(5), 364–373.

Fazel, S., Wolf, A., Palm, C., & Lichtenstein, P. (2014). Violent crime, suicide, and premature mortality in patients with schizophrenia and related disorders: A 38-year total population study in Sweden. *Lancet Psychiatry, 1*(1), 44–54.

Feldmeyer, B. (2009). Immigration and violence: The offsetting effects of immigration on Latino violence. *Social Science Research, 38*(3), 717–731.

Fernando, S., Ndegwa, D., & Wilson, M. (1998). *Forensic psychiatry, race, and culture*. London: Routledge.

Goater, N., King, M., Cole, E., Leavey, G., Johnson-Sabine, E., Blizard, R., & Hoar, A. (1999). Ethnicity and outcome of psychosis. *British Journal of Psychiatry, 175*(1), 34–42.

Hanoeman, M., Selten, J.P., & Kahn, R.S. (2002). Incidence of schizophrenia in Surinam. *Schizophrenia Research, 54*(3), 219–221.

Harrison, G., Glazebrook, C., Brewin, J., Cantwell, R., Dalkin, T., Fox, R., Jones, P., & Medley, I. (1997). Increased incidence of psychotic disorders in migrants from the Caribbean to the United Kingdom. *Psychological Medicine*, *27*(4), 799–806.

Harrison, G., Holton, A., Neilson, D., Owens, D., Boot, D., & Cooper, J. (1989). Severe mental disorder in Afro-Caribbean patients: Some social, demographic and service factors. *Psychological Medicine*, *19*(3), 683–696.

Harrison, G., Owens, D., Holton, A., Neilson, D., & Boot, A. (1988). A prospective study of severe mental disorder in Afro-Caribbean patients. *Psychological Medicine*, *18*(3), 643–657.

Harvey, I., Williams, M., McGuffin, P., & Toone, B.K. (1990). The functional psychosis in Afro-Caribbeans. *British Journal of Psychiatry*, *157*(4), 515–522.

Hemsi, L.K. (1967). Psychiatric morbidity of West Indian immigrants. *Social Psychiatry*, *2*(3), 95–100.

Hickling, F.W. (1991). Double jeopardy: Psychopathology of black mentally ill returned migrants to Jamaica. *International Journal of Social Psychiatry*, *37*(2), 80–89.

Hickling, F.W. (2005). The epidemiology of schizophrenia and other common mental health disorders in the English-speaking Caribbean. *Pan American Journal of Public Health*, *18*(4/5), 256–262.

Hickling, F.W., Gibson, R.C., & Hutchinson, G. (2013). Current research on transcultural psychiatry in the Anglophone Caribbean: Epistemological, public policy, and epidemiological challenges. *Transcultural Psychiatry*, *50*(6), 858–875.

Hickling, F.W., McKenzie, K., Mullen, R., & Murray, R. (1999). A Jamaican psychiatrist evaluates diagnoses at a London psychiatric hospital. *British Journal of Psychiatry*, *175*(3), 283–285.

Hickling, F.W., & Rodgers-Johnson, P. (1995). The incidence of first-contact schizophrenia in Jamaica. *British Journal of Psychiatry*, *167*(2), 193–196.

Hjern, A., Wicks, S., & Dalman, C. (2004). Social adversity contributes to high morbidity in psychoses in immigrants: A national cohort study in two generations of Swedish residents. *Psychological Medicine*, *34*(6), 1025–1033.

Hutchinson, G., & Haasen, C. (2004). Migration and schizophrenia: The challenges for European psychiatry and implications for the future. *Social Psychiatry Psychiatric Epidemiology*, *39*(5), 350–357.

Jablensky, A., & Sartorius, N. (2008). What did the WHO studies really find? *Schizophrenia Bulletin*, *34*(2), 253–255.

Jennissen, R. (2014). On the deviant age-crime curve of Afro-Caribbean populations: The case of Antilleans living in the Netherlands. *American Journal of Criminal Justice*, *39*(3), 571–594.

Joosen, K.J. (2016). De relatie tussen racisme en criminaliteit in Nederland: Een verkennende studie onder Surinaamse- en Caribische Nederlanders [The relationships between racism and crime in the Netherlands: An exploratory study among Surinamese- and Caribbean-Dutch]. *Proces*, *95*(6), 6–16.

Karlsen, S., Nazroo, J.Y., McKenzie, K., Bhui, K., & Weich, S. (2005). Racism, psychosis and common mental disorder among ethnic minority groups in England. *Psychological Medicine*, *35*(12), 1795–1803.

Karnik, N.S., Jones, P.A., Campanaro, A.E., Haapanen, R., & Steiner, H. (2006). Ethnic variation of self-reported psychopathology among incarcerated youth. *Community Mental Health Journal*, *42*(5), 477–486.

Kiev, A. (1965). Psychiatric morbidity of West Indian immigrants in an urban group practice. *British Journal of Psychiatry*, *111*(470), 51–56.

King, M., Coker, E., Leavey, G., Hoare, A., & Johnson-Sabine, E. (1994). Incidence of psychotic illness in London: Comparison of ethnic groups. *British Medical Journal, 309*(6962), 1115–1119.

Kirkbride, J.B., & Jones, P.B. (2011). The prevention of schizophrenia: What can we learn from eco-epidemiology? *Schizophrenia Bulletin, 37*(2), 262–271.

Koffman, J., Fulop, N.J., Pashley, D., & Coleman, K. (1997). Ethnicity and use of acute psychiatric beds: One-day survey in North and South Thames regions. *British Journal of Psychiatry, 171*(5), 238–241.

Large, M., Smith, G., Swinson, N., Shaw, J., & Nielssen, O. (2008). Homicide due to mental disorder in England and Wales over 50 years. *British Journal of Psychiatry, 193*(2), 130–133.

Lindqvist, P., & Allebeck, P. (1990). Schizophrenia and crime: A longitudinal follow-up of 644 schizophrenics in Stockholm. *British Journal of Psychiatry, 157*(3), 345–350.

Logdberg, B., Nilsson, L.L., Levander, M.T., & Levander, S. (2004). Schizophrenia, neighbourhood, and crime. *Acta Psychiatrica Scandinavica, 110*(2), 92–97.

Mahy, G.E., Mallett, R., Leff, J., & Bhugra, D. (1999). First-contact incidence rate of schizophrenia on Barbados. *British Journal of Psychiatry, 175*(1), 28–33.

Mallett, R., Leff, J., Bhugra, D., Pang, D., & Zhao, J.H. (2002). Social environment, ethnicity and schizophrenia: A case-control study. *Social Psychiatry and Psychiatric Epidemiology, 37*(8), 329–335.

Mares, D. (2010). Social disorganization and gang homicides in Chicago: A neighborhood level comparison of disaggregated homicides. *Youth Violence and Juvenile Justice, 8*(1), 38–57.

Martinez Jr., R. (2002). *Latino homicide: Immigration, violence, and community*. New York: Routledge.

McGovern, D., & Cope, R. (1987). The compulsory detention of males of different ethnic groups with special reference to offender patients. *British Journal of Psychiatry, 150*(4), 505–512.

McKenzie, K., Samele, C., Van Horn, E., Tattan, T., Van Os, J., & Murray, R. (2001). Comparison of the outcome and treatment of psychosis in people of Caribbean origin living in the UK and British Whites: Report from the UK700 trial. *British Journal of Psychiatry, 178*(2), 160–165.

Modestin, J., & Ammann, R. (1996). Mental disorder and criminality: Male schizophrenia. *Schizophrenia Bulletin, 22*(1), 69–82.

Morgan, K.D., Dazzan, P., Morgan, C., Lappin, J., Hutchinson, G., Chitnis, X., . . . Murray, R.M. (2010). Differing patterns of brain abnormalities between black and white patients with their first episode of psychosis. *Psychological Medicine, 40*(7), 1137–1147.

Mullen, P.E., Burgess, P., Wallace, C., Palmer, S., & Ruschena, D. (2000). Community care and criminal offending in schizophrenia. *Lancet, 355*(9204), 614–617.

Neighbors, H.W., Trierweiler, S.J., Munday, C., Thompson, E.E., Jackson, J.S., Binion, V.J., & Gomez, J. (1999). Psychiatric diagnosis of African Americans: Diagnostic divergence in clinician-structured and semi-structured interviewing conditions. *Journal of the National Medical Association, 91*(11), 601–612.

Ødegaard, Ø. (1932). Emigration and insanity. *Acta Psychiatrica Neurologica Scandinavia, Supplement, 4*(1), 1–206.

Odell, S.M., Surtees, P.G., Wainwright, N.W.J., Commander, M.J., & Sashidharan, S.P. (1997). Determinants of general practitioner recognition of psychological problems in a multi-ethnic inner-city health district. *British Journal of Psychiatry, 171*(6), 537–541.

Ousey, G., & Kubrin, C.E. (2014). Immigration and the changing nature of homicide in U.S. Cities, 1980–2010. *Journal of Quantitative Criminology, 30*(3), 453–483.

Parkman, S., Davies, S., & Lesse, M. (1997). Ethnic differences in satisfaction with mental health services among representative people with psychosis in South-London: Prism Study 4. *British Journal of Psychiatry*, *171*(3), 260–264.

Peterson, R.D., & Krivo, L.J. (2005). Macrostructural analyses of race, ethnicity, and violent crime: Recent lessons and new directions for Research. *Annual Review of Sociology*, *31*, 331–356.

Pinto, R., Ashworth, M., & Jones, R. (2008). Schizophrenia in black Caribbeans living in the UK an exploration of underlying causes of the high incidence. *British Journal of General Practice*, *58*(551), 429–434.

Price, N., Glazer, W., & Morgenstern, H. (1985). Demographic predictors of the use of injectable versus oral antipsychotic medications in outpatients. *American Journal of Psychiatry*, *142*(12), 1491–1492.

Sampson, R.J., & Groves, B. (1989). Community structure and crime: Testing social disorganization theory. *American Journal of Sociology*, *94*(4), 774–802.

Sampson, R.J., & Wilson, W.J. (1995). Toward a theory of race, crime and urban inequality. In J. Hagan, & R.D. Peterson (Eds.), *Crime and inequality* (pp. 37–54). Stanford, CA: Stanford University Press.

Schofield, P., Ashworth, M., & Jones, R. (2011). Ethnic isolation and psychosis: Re-examining the ethnic density effect. *Psychological Medicine*, *41*(6), 1263–1269.

Schrier, A.C., van de Wetering, B.J., Mulder, P.G., & Selten, J.P. (2001). Point prevalence of schizophrenia in immigrant groups in Rotterdam: Data from outpatient facilities. *European Psychiatry*, *16*(3), 162–166.

Selten, J.P., & Cantor-Graae, E. (2005). Social defeat: Risk factor for schizophrenia? *British Journal of Psychiatry*, *187*(2), 101–102.

Selten, J.P., & Sijben, N. (1994). First admission rates for schizophrenia in immigrants to The Netherlands. *Social Psychiatry Psychiatric Epidemiology*, *29*(2), 71–77.

Selten, J.P., Slaets, J.P., & Kahn, R.S. (1997). Schizophrenia in Surinamese and Dutch Antillean immigrants to The Netherlands: Evidence of an increased incidence. *Psychological Medicine*, *27*(4), 807–811.

Selten, J.P., Van der Ven, E., Rutten, B.P., & Cantor-Graae, E. (2013). The social defeat hypothesis of schizophrenia: An update. *Schizophrenia Bulletin*, *39*(6), 1180–1186.

Selten, J.P., Veen, N., Feller, W., Blom, J.D., Schols, D., Camoenie, W., . . . Kahn, R. (2001). Incidence of psychotic disorders in immigrant groups to The Netherlands. *British Journal of Psychiatry*, *178*(4), 367–372.

Sewell, C.A., Hickling, F.D., Abel, W.D., Smith, S., Paisley, V., Martin, J., & Shaw, J. (2015). Comparison of substance abuse and mental illness in male offenders in Jamaica and England and Wales. *West Indian Medical Journal*, *2*(1), 36–40.

Sharpley, M., Hutchinson, G., McKenzie, K., & Murray, R.M. (2001). Understanding the excess of psychosis among the African-Caribbean population in England. Review of current hypotheses. *British Journal of Psychiatry*, *40*, s60–s68.

Silver, E., Felson, R.B., & Vaneseltine, M. (2008). The relationship between mental health problems and violence among criminal offenders. *Criminal Justice and Behavior*, *35*(4), 405.

Singh, S.P., Greenwood, N., White, S., & Churchill, R. (2007). Ethnicity and the Mental Health Act 1983. *British Journal of Psychiatry*, *191*(2), 99–105.

Smith, D.J. (1997). Ethnic origins, crime, and criminal justice in England and Wales. *Crime and Justice*, *21*, 101–182.

Special Hospitals Service Authority. (1993). *Report of the committee of inquiry into the death in Broadmoor Hospital of Orville Blackwood and a review of the deaths of two other Afro-Caribbean patients: 'Big, black and dangerous?'* London: SHSA.

Takei, N., Persaud, R., Woodruff, P., Brockington, I., & Murray, R.M. (1998). First episodes of psychosis in Afro-Caribbean and White people: An 18-year follow-up population-based study. *British Journal of Psychiatry, 172*(2), 147–153.

Taylor, P.J., & Gunn, J. (1984). Violence and psychosis. I-Risk of violence among psychotic men. *British Medical Journal, 288*(6435), 1945–1949.

Teplin, L.A. (1990). The prevalence of severe mental disorder among male urban jail detainees: Comparison with the epidemiologic catchment area program. *American Journal of Public Health, 80*(6), 663–669.

Teplin, L.A., Abram, K.M., McClelland, G.M., Dulcan, M.K., & Mericle, A.A. (2002). Psychiatric disorders in youth in juvenile detention. *Archives of General Psychiatry, 59*(12), 1133–1143.

Thomas, C.S., Stone, K., Osborn, M., Thomas, P.F., & Fisher, M. (1993). Psychiatric morbidity and compulsory admission among UK-born Europeans, Afro-Caribbeans and Asians in central Manchester. *British Journal of Psychiatry, 163*(1), 91–99.

Tiihonen, J., Isohanni, M., Rasanen, P., Koiranen, M., & Moring, J. (1997). Specific major mental disorders and criminality: A 26-year prospective study of the 1966 northern Finland birth cohort. *American Journal of Psychiatry, 154*(6), 840–845.

Tonry, M. (1997). Race, ethnicity, crime, and immigration. In S. Bucerius, & M. Tonry (Eds.), *The Oxford handbook of ethnicity, crime, and immigration*, (pp. 1–29). New York: Oxford University Press.

Tortelli, A., Errazuriz, A., Croudace, T., Morgan, C., Murray, R.M., Jones, P.B., . . . Kirkbride, J.B. (2015). Schizophrenia and other psychotic disorders in Caribbean-born migrants and their descendants in England: Systematic review and meta-analysis of incidence rates, 1950–2013. *Social Psychiatry and Psychiatric Epidemiology, 50*(7), 1039–1055.

UNODC. (2007). *Crime, violence, and development: Trends, costs, and policy options in the Caribbean*. (Report no. 37820). Retrieved from www.unodc.org/pdf/research/Cr_and_Vio_Car_E.pdf.

Unnever, J.D., & Gabbidon, S.L. (2011). *A theory of African American offending: Race, racism, and crime*. London and New York: Taylor & Francis.

Van Os, J., & McGuffin, P. (2003). Can the social environment cause schizophrenia? *British Journal of Psychiatry, 182*(4), 291–292.

Vaughn, M.G., Wallace, J.M., Davis, L.E., Fernandes, G., & Howard, M.O. (2008). Variations in mental health problems, substance use, and delinquency between African American and Caucasian juvenile offenders: Implications for reentry services. *International Journal of Offender Therapy and Comparative Criminology, 52*(3), 311–329.

Veling, W., Hoek, H.W., Wiersma, D., & Mackenbach, J.P. (2010). Ethnic identity and the risk of schizophrenia in ethnic minorities: A case-control study. *Schizophrenia Bulletin, 36*(6), 1149–1156. doi: 10.1093/schbul/sbp032.

Veling, W., Selten, J.P., Susser, E., Laan, W., Mackenbach, & Hoek, H.W. (2007). Discrimination and the incidence of psychotic disorders among ethnic minorities in The Netherlands. *International Journal of Epidemiology, 36*(4), 761–768.

Veling, W., Selten, J.P., Veen, N., Laan, W., Blom, J.D., & Hoek, H.W. (2006). Incidence of schizophrenia among ethnic minorities in the Netherlands: A four-year first-contact study. *Schizophrenia Research, 86*(1–3), 189–193.

Veling, W., Susser, E., Van Os, J., Mackenbach, J.P., Selten, J.P., & Hoek, H.W. (2008). Ethnic density of neighborhoods and incidence of psychotic disorders among immigrants. *American Journal of Psychiatry, 165*(1), 66–73.

Vinkers, D.J., De Beurs, E., Barendregt, M., Rinne, T., & Hoek, H.W. (2010). Pre-trial psychiatric evaluations and ethnicity in the Netherlands. *International Journal of Law and Psychiatry, 33*(3), 192–196.

Vinkers, D.J., De Beurs, E., Barendregt, M., Rinne, T., & Hoek, H.W. (2011). The relationship between mental disorders and different types of crimes. *Criminal Behaviour and Mental Health, 21*(5), 307–320.

Vinkers, D.J., & Duits, N. (2011). Crime and mental disorders among native Dutch and ethnic minority juvenile defendants in the Netherlands. *International Journal of Law and Psychiatry, 34*(2), 131–134.

Wallace, C., Mullen, P.E., & Burgess, P. (2004). Criminal offending in schizophrenia over a 25-year period marked by deinstitutionalization and increasing prevalence of comorbid substance use disorders. *American Journal of Psychiatry, 161*(4), 716–727.

Wallace, C., Mullen, P., Burgess, P., Palmer, S., Ruschena, D., & Browne, C. (1998). Serious criminal offending and mental disorder: Case linkage study. *British Journal of Psychiatry, 172*(6), 477–484.

Webster, C. (2007). *Understanding race and crime*. Maidenhead: Open University Press.

Wessely, S. (1997). The epidemiology of crime, violence and schizophrenia. *British Journal of Psychiatry Supplement, 32*, 8–11.

Witt, K., Van Dorn, R., & Fazel, S. (2013). Risk factors for violence in psychosis: Systematic review and meta-regression analysis of 110 studies. *Plos One*, *8*(2), 55942.

12 Crime, identity and community

A post-colonial analysis on Kingston, Jamaica

Nicola D. Satchell

Introduction

Effectively problematizing identity and crime from an ecological perspective in the Caribbean requires an evaluation of the societal framework in which the self is negotiated as well as of the social representations from which collective and individual meanings are drawn. Post-colonial theorizing offers one such model, particularly because of its usefulness in facilitating a social psychological analysis, which interrogates notions of the identity, group formation, and larger processes of self-determination. Colonialism is instrumental to this process because of its role in informing essential reference points for identity formation such as the political system, culture, language, and the general way of life across the areas that have experienced it (Cesaire, 1972; Ghandi, 1998; McEwan, 2009; Nettleford, 1998). Social psychological theorizing also recognises that humans have a natural inclination to create meanings. These meanings, when internalised, inform: at the individual level, role identification and other person-specific processes; and, at the collective level, group formation and other social identity processes. The post-colonial moment, for the people of the Caribbean, is that pivotal period marked by an allegorical move from annexation (from France, the Netherlands, the United Kingdom, and the United States) towards self-determination. This move is characterised by significant challenges rooted in place, belonging, and social interaction (including interpersonal relationships and those with state actors).

The research postulates that shared meanings are imperative to the development of social identities and a predictor of behavioural outcomes. The interaction with those deemed significant others and environmental cues are crucial as they allow the individual to locate themselves in their everyday lived experiences. In an environment where there is: (a) collective trauma, (b) a subculture that facilitates self-help violence, and (c) social exclusion, there must be investments in understanding the exemplars and mental representations that generate conflict and inhibit the capacity of the community to develop internal social controls. The objective of this study is to highlight the importance of social identity processes, particularly *sensemaking*, in confronting the subculture of violence that has been a longstanding feature of the criminogenic communities in Kingston, Jamaica. First, I will provide a theoretical discussion of the link between post-colonial discourse, social identity, and crime; and how these concepts relate to the sensemaking process.

The Caribbean post-colonial community and the crime problem

Post-colonialism is a nuanced term, generally viewed as a deductive set of ideas produced outside of the West (Loomba, 1998; Young, 2003). It examines the *critical aftermath*, that is, the social influences that remained following the colonial experience (McEwan, 2009, p. 17). Post-colonial concerns include ecology, development, governance, self-hood, and identity (Fanon, 1963; Young, 2003) – all of which are concerns of this chapter/analysis. The people who were colonised, experienced dehumanisation – they were stripped of their language, religion, and all other existential reference points (Cesaire, 1972; Hall, 2001). This limited their capacity to make identity choices. The post-colonial moment was generally thought of as a period to reclaim that lost self-hood and identity. The challenge is that it could not be restored by the same processes that destroyed it, nor could it simply be reclaimed. This is especially true in Latin American and the Caribbean where large numbers of people were forcefully relocated and the autochthonous populations almost entirely annihilated (McEwan, 2009; Young, 2003).

The critical aftermath for these new peoples was a psychological space located between *thingification* (Cesaire, 1972) and *smaddification* (Nettleford, 1998), in other words they were moving from an inflicted categorisation of commodification towards self-determination and empowerment. Between these two existential realities (which Girvan, 2014, saw as *dialectic opposites*) lay major issues of efficacy, worth, and other intrapsychic interrogations of the self that were somehow inferior to the hegemonic culture. The negotiation within the psychological space created several outcomes, two of which have been heavily utilised in Caribbean sociological theorizing, namely: binarism and creolisation/hybridisation. Although the ontological contribution of binarism has been heavily criticised, it is being used here because of its value in expressing a separatist orientation among and within groups. This is evident in the social exclusion of particular groups of people, particularly those that were disenfranchised and displaced (Fanon, 1963).

This is not an attempt to rehash the discussions around reducing post-colonialism to two *antithetical groups in a third space* (Bhabha, 2004; Young, 1995) but rather, to show merit in the postulation that groups with strong links to the colonial power (cultural, ideological, political, or economic) are viewed as having the capacity to set the agenda for the majority, and those without those connections are regarded as powerless. Binarism is also expressed in the strong attachment to place and its influence on the processes involved in identity formation, and in particular that of *othering* (Ashcroft, Griffiths, & Tiffin, 2000, p. 161). This in-group/out-group categorisation creates social distance among the various social groups, making the development of social bonds, and the formulation and execution of collective goals difficult.

Although there is much in the post-colonial environment that creates fragmentation, creolisation – which facilitates some degree of syncretisation among the various racial groups – has also been experienced (Brathwaite, 1971). Creolisation or hybridisation acknowledges that there is relative acceptance of the new space and some amount of cultural fusion (Brathwaite, 1971). This idea is also linked to the notion of binarism as the assumptions are based on the dialectical theory which draws attention to "resistance that are inherent in the domination/subordination relationship between the metropole and the colony" (Bolland, 2002, p. 37). Fanon (1963) saw creolisation as a type of "perverted logic" which destroyed the colonised culture (p. 170). For this analysis it is accepted that creolisation has a strong link to the metropolis; however, the ideas are not limited to those emanating from the colonisers. The subalterns were given the opportunity to migrate and form a Caribbean diasporic community. This expanded the imaginations around the realities in the metropolis (Hall, 1990; Nurse, 2006; Patterson, 2003). A major assumption adopted in this chapter is that identity information is drawn from the supranational as much as from the local, because of the strength of the relationships to the metropole during and after the colonial experience. At the sub-national level, sociologists have described communities in the Caribbean: (a) as *plural* with a natural tension among the different groups (Premdas, 1996; Smith, 1965), (b) as *Creole*, implying an infusion of the various cultures and miscegenation creating a hybrid space (Bolland, 2002, Brathwaite, 1971), and (c) as reflective of the nuances of the plantation society where there is a natural ordering, that ascribes persons to different groups in society based on economic class and skin colour (Beckford, 1972).

The approach adopted for this chapter sees the community as a physical space with a set parameter (Brint, 2001); a space of social interaction (Kaufman, 1959), and an important point for understanding social problems and finding solutions (Levy, 2001, 2009). The importance of the community to self-hood and identity is irrefutable, as is the significance of identity and self-hood to the continued existence of community. Social identity is therefore seen as valuable to community research because it seeks to interrogate aspects of self, such as role identification, group formation, and collective behaviours (Either & Deaux, 1994; Hogg & Adams, 1998). It facilitates an analysis that "brings together both the structures of everyday lives and the socio-cultural and socio-political realities in which lives are lived" (Howard, 2000, p. 388). The discussion of identity negation (Lawrence, Duperly-Pinks, & Branche, 1999) highlights a people trying to organise themselves to transcend the negativity associated with slavery and the degradation which characterised the pre-emancipation, pre-independence era (Gopaul, Morgan, & Reddock, 1996; Hutton, 1996). Crime and violence are seen as adoptive strategies in the face of poverty and the political environment (Ellis, 1987; Fanon, 1963). There are some instances in which this is seen as expressive and others in which it is instrumental (Gray, 2004), or cathartic (Fanon, 1963).

The *garrison* is an example of how a salient identity, in this case political identity, can create fragmentation and in-group/out-group tensions that are violence producing (Charles, 2002, 2004; Espeut, 2005; Figueroa, 1994; Huddy, 2001; Jaffe, 2008) and which are transferred intergenerationally (Gayle, 2009). This typology is the most criminogenic community narrative in Jamaica. It is an expression of the link between criminal and political forces at the community level (Figueroa, 1994; Figueroa, Harriott, & Satchell, 2008; Figueroa & Sives, 2002, 2003; National Committee on Political Tribalism, 1997). The phrase was first used by Stone (1985) to describe constituencies in which seats of political power remain in the control of one of the two political parties. The development of this form of community signifies a turning point where the advent of high-intensity political violence in Jamaica leads to a polarised society (Eyre, 1984; Gray, 2004; Harriott, 2003b) and specifically what Jaffe (2008) referred to as a fragmented city.

The formation of these communities is accompanied by extreme violence and residents are kept loyal through the distribution of scarce benefits and other forms of *political patronage* (Chevannes, 1992; Gray, 2004; Harriott, 2003a, 2003b, 2009; Sives, 1998; Stone, 1980, 1985; Thomas, 2011). It is therefore in the interest of these residents to have their political party in power for as long as possible and to enforce the codes that ensure the loyalty of all the community members and the banishment of non-conformers. The political clientelism in an environment of uncertainty (especially in the absence of effective social safety nets) exacerbates this and strengthens community fragmentation. Political identity, therefore, becomes very salient and the narratives of *badness honour* (Gray, 2004, 2003), the *rude boy* (Hutton, 2010), and the *don* as defenders of that identity (Clarke, 2006a; Jaffe, 2013; Sives, 2002) become an enduring feature of these communities.

Sensemaking in high crime communities

"Sensemaking is what it says it is, making something sensible" (Weick, 1995, p. 17). It assumes that when an event takes place, there are social psychological processes, at the individual, as well as the collective level, which generate meanings that are cues for informing responses. After traumatic events (such as violence), there is a critical period during which individuals try to make sense of what occurred (Herman, 1997). This is done in order to do three things: first, to decide on next steps; second, to deal with the anxiety and fear that are associated with the event (Stein, 2004); and finally, to mitigate against reoccurrences (Gioia, Corley, & Fabbri, 2002). The social psychological tradition is rich with research focused on how people respond to the social situations in which they find themselves. Weick's postulations, though expressed in organisational psychology, are applied to this study because communities, like formal institutions, have an organisational structure (Weick, 1995; Weick, Sutcliffe & Obsfeld, 2005). Even within communities that are considered to be *disorganised* there is some semblance of organisation (Harriott, 2009; Sampson, Morenoff, & Gannon-Rowley, 2002). Three characteristics postulated in the Weickian notion are used to inform the current analysis namely: (a) the retrospective nature of sensemaking, (b) the thought that it is grounded in identity construction, and (c) is focused on and by identity cues (Weick, 1995; p. 17).

Sensemaking is retrospective in that individuals tend to rely on past experiences to make sense of current events. Even when sensemaking is future-oriented, that is, forward looking, there is still that retrospective element because the processes are established upon the events that have occurred (Gioia et al., 2002). For example, Harriott (2003b) showed that group identity could be infused with political identity in fragmented communities. This coupled with the history of political warfare generated the perceived need for group protection as all conflicts (even those that are domestic) were coded as a collective attack on in-group members. Sensemaking, in this case, is substantiated by group identity as well as retrospective events.

The issue of group identity is important to Weick's assumption that sensemaking is grounded in identity construction. It is embedded in the social psychological processes of the social categorisation. The interaction with those deemed the "generalised other" is imperative here as it allows the individual to locate him/herself in everyday lived experiences (Helm-Mills, Thurlow, & Mills, 2010). It can also be seen as constituting "subjective internalisations of collective representations of socially shared images of a group" (Van Knippenberg, 1978, p. 561). This is important in deconstructing and internalizing shared meanings, which inform attitudes and the general value orientation (Helm-Mills et al., 2010). For example, a critical question to be asked is, why partisan politics played such an important role in the interpretation of events in the era immediately after gaining universal adult suffrage and in post-independent Jamaica. The literature suggests that the sensemaker is not only able to extract the cues from his/her lived experiences but also reinforces and reproduces the supporting attitudes and behaviours that are deemed significant.

The current study

The study is conducted in Kingston, Jamaica – one of the largest cities in the Caribbean. Its history dates back to the early colonial era of the 1600s. Clarke (2006b) described Kingston during the colonial period (1692–1962) as a creole city highly stratified in accordance with the plantocracy; where the whites were at the top of the social and economic hierarchy and the blacks at the bottom. In between these two societal layers were confined the persons from other nationalities and the mixed population. Today the city remains fragmented (Jaffe, 2008) but more so in terms of class relations (Clarke, 2006b; Gray, 2004; Stone, 1985). There is an even greater concern about the city's criminogenic nature that dates back to the late colonial period after the granting of universal adult suffrage in 1944 (Sives, 1998).

Kingston is administratively linked to the parish of St Andrew and both have a combined population of 662,426 (Statistical Institute of Jamaica, 2013). The city has the reputation of being one of the most violent in the world. "Murder rates of 62 per 100,000 were recorded from 1994, placing the city second only to Bogotá among the 40 large cities for which such data was available for that year" (UNDP, 2000, p. 248 cited in Leslie, 2010). Leslie noted the murder rates for Kingston have been increasing exponentially, reaching 96.2 per 100,000 in 2008. In addition, he noted that an overall crime rate of as high as 1,000 per 100,000 has been noted in some of areas of the city. The problem of structural violence (from a criminal justice system that was state protected) and interpersonal violence (experienced as the communities tried to resolve its problems) is exacerbated by the existence of weak state apparatus, that could not effectively develop responsive institutions to generate and redistribute opportunities in an effective manner. This chapter unpacks the nexus between social identity processes and crime in two communities in Kingston, Jamaica. The study postulates an approach that is grounded at the meso level of analysis where identity is negotiated and relationships are concretised. The research question being explored here is formulated as follows: In the current identity moment, how are the urban poor making sense of the high violence around them?

Methods

Communities

For this study a two-community analysis was employed, which were both located in the established garrison constituencies of Kingston Central and St Andrew South.[1] The parameters used to establish a constituency or community as garrison are well developed in the literature and include: strong political identity and intolerance for supporters of competing political parties (Charles, 2004; Chevannes, 1992), evidence of homogeneous voting patterns (Figureroa & Sives, 2002; Sives, 2010), and political clientelism (Harriott, 2003a; Sives, 2010; Stone, 1980). The selected communities had high crime and violence rates. Haven Town[2] recorded a murder rate of 56 per 100,000 in 2012, which was above the national average of 44 per 100,000. Nature Town[3] recorded a lower than average rate of 39 per 100,000. Violence Related Injuries (VRIs) occurred at a rate of 1,103 per 100,000 for Haven Town and 913 per 100,000 for Nature Town.[4] The Police Division in which Haven Town is located had 51 gangs, while Nature Town had 21 (Ministry of National Security, 2015).

There was an attempt to keep all other socioeconomic variables equal across both communities.[5] The current design, however, did not assume a quasi-experimental methodology. Both communities consisted of four districts, had a comparable population size (Nature Town 10,144 and Haven Town 10,688), and youth population percentages were similar (19 per cent and 21 per cent respectively; Statistical Institute of Jamaica, 2013). Both communities had a household density of 3.7.[6] Furthermore, educational levels across both communities were comparable: Nature Town had 50 per cent of its adult population having at least a secondary school education, while this was the case for 45 per cent of residents in Haven Town.[7]

Procedure

The main data collection was through participant observation, interviews (life and event histories), and focus groups. For the participant observation – drawing on the use of ethnographic methodologies – an observer as participant model as developed by the seminal work of Gold (1958) was adopted. Attempts were made not to intervene significantly into the processes encountered in the social setting (Anderson, 1999; Atkinson & Hammersley, 1994). This was of particular concern for me as I traversed warring factions and interacted with the gangs/crews and the police. I had to be careful to present myself as a neutral party, this especially following the fatal shooting of two of my key informants in Haven Town.

The data collection was conducted between January 2013 and April 2014. It should also be noted that the fieldwork was more concentrated in the areas identified by the Peace Management Initiative, the Jamaica Constabulary Force, and data from the Mona Geoinformatics Institute as hotspots of crime and violence. A snowballing technique was used to select sites and participants from the observable groups within the community. Individual interviews were conducted with seven area leaders; 16 gang and crew members; eight persons from Non-Government Organisations and the Citizen Security and Justice Program; six persons from the Jamaica Constabulary Force and two gang experts. Four focus groups were also conducted.

Analyses

Thematic content analysis (Green & Thorogood, 2009; Hsieh & Shannon, 2005) was used to identify the common thoughts that emerged from the interview transcript, field notes, and secondary data utilised in the study. This method was preferred because it allows the researcher to analyse the messages being delivered in any modality, whether they be a manifested or latent content. NVIVO (qualitative data analysis software) was used to manage and organise the data as well as assist in identifying the major themes.

Results

Making sense of crime in a post-colonial environment

The primary data analysed in this study revealed that at the macro level, the political and economic forces were key to the sensemaking and organisational processes in the communities under study. While exploring the community dynamics, narrators cited: (a) the political violence of the 1970s and 1980s, (b) the limited access to meaningful employment, and (c) the lack of housing infrastructure as the main forces that negatively impacted the environment. The earliest identity stories of the communities, especially concerning the higher crime community which experienced more rapid homogenisation, reflected the narratives of the vulnerable urban poor and a society unable to adequately create opportunities for the masses (Gray, 2004; Sives, 1998; Stone, 1985; Thomas, 2011).

Political participation (largely through the labour movement) was seen as an avenue for a better life. But as discussed by Sives (2010) and Thomas (2011), the promised citizenship through political participation was fundamentally outside of the formal state structures and facilitated exclusion rather than empowerment. In other words, the community dynamics facilitated an insular orientation that created social exclusion as opposed to facilitating a national consensus, which by Anderson's (1991) account is at best imagined. Hence the groups who believed that the only way to traverse the post-independence environment was through self-help violence and building informal settlements saw these as viable options given the environmental cues at the international, national, and local levels. This encouraged the development of a subculture of violence that has been reinforced and transmitted trans-generationally. The country now finds it difficult to redevelop communities in the Kingston Metropolitan Area, and the second city of Montego Bay that has its geneses in this type of community formation.

Three overarching environmental cues guiding sensemaking in the current identity moment were identified in the current study. These are deemed to be important in the context of the high-violence environment in which communal identity is highly politicised such as the garrison in Kingston, Jamaica (Figueroa & Sives, 2002, 2003). They are not only important to an understanding of environmental cues but also point to possible policy imperatives. They were formulated as follows: (a) the orientation to peace building, (b) the economic environment created by the austerity measures and the new security agenda, and (c) everyday unfairness. Each of these environmental cues guiding sensemaking is discussed in the ensuing section.

Peace building

The peace-building efforts underway in both communities emerged as a central theme. The current wave of the peace process in Haven Town was facilitated by a dynamic leader of a Non-Governmental Organisation in the community in 2005. "Ms Sun",[8] explained that during the year, a peace dance was successfully staged, there was "relative peace following this but young men were not going to feel safe. This was however a year for change". In Nature Town, between 2006 and 2008 there was intense warfare among the gangs. The leaders expressed that they became tired of the fight and were desirous of a truce. This was supported by external actors such as the Citizen Security and Justice Program (CSJP), Peace Management Initiative (PMI), and the Police.

In spite of this orientation to peace, it was found that in a high-violence community, when a focusing event (i.e. one that shocks the collective conscience) occurs, community members may choose to do one of two things. They may rely on the scripts from the past that are associated predominately with violence and revenge-seeking behaviours, or tap into the current moment of peace for which there is fewer exemplars. This is seen as a dynamic continuous process as the sensemaker is not only drawing cues from the environment but also generating meaning that will inform behavioural responses. The observations made in two case studies were used to explore such peace processes. First, the killing of a four-year-old boy in Nature Town, which occurred following an interpersonal dispute between the boy's family and one of their tenants. Second, an internal gang feud in Haven Town where one man was shot several times, four persons were killed (thought to be related), and several families fled the community. Participant observation and interviews were conducted in both cases.

The first case involved the nuances surrounding the killing of the four-year-old. I spent the day on the corner (with one area leader, members of the defence crew,[9] and concerned community members) just outside the yard where the incident took place. The first observation was that the voice and posture of the area leaders were important in setting the tone for the reaction of the community. In this case both men were empathetic and sent a central message that reprisal was not an option, as that would negatively affect the peace process. Early intervention by the police reinforced that climate of peace. As the police commenced their formal investigations, the community activated their own informal operations. Before the day ended the community members had determined the identity of the killer. The suspect, according to the informal investigations, was not a gun owner, so the next step was to establish where he got the gun. There was an informal gun registry, and again, before the end of the day the source of the gun was also found, and the group was pleased to hear that the person identified as the loaner of the gun had fled the community. Although the family of the loaner of the gun was contacted, they were not forced to leave the community (which would have been demanded before this new era of peace). The way the community handled the matter showed a commitment to the peace process and signified that there was a system of internal social control in place to deal with conflict situations.

Immediately following the event, external agencies such as the PMI,[10] the CSJP,[11] the Police, and internal actors such as the area leaders, the political representatives, the church groups, and other community-based organisations were assisting with the sensemaking processes. They were a consistent voice reinforcing alternatives to the violence, which was important as the stories on the corner were all about what would have happened in the past. The mother of the child was taken in for grief counselling and the PMI team was on site with other family members. The Member of Parliament also visited the home and promised his support. The action of the state and non-state actors were important in helping the community to make sense of what had occurred and to determine the course of action.

In the second case in Haven Town, although members of the gangs and crews had an understanding that a peace process was underway, for some, there was dissonance concerning what that meant and how to operate within this new dispensation (even as the guns were still available and the gangs/crews remained active). One of the younger members of a criminal gang said "there can never be peace only a ceasefire". This sentiment reflected a strong revenge-seeking orientation in the community, which in the past fuelled the commission of heinous acts of violence against those deemed to be the enemy or anyone associated. Indeed, this mode of thought is difficult to transcend. It is interesting that this view was held even as their main rival gang in the community was working with the PMI to transform their identity from a criminal gang to a defence crew. They however saw this as the weakening of the other gang and an opportunity to concretise their own supremacy in the area.

Their major threat however was not external. I received a call early one morning from a key informant who told me that an associate of the gang had been shot several times but had survived and was in hospital. When the incident took place, there was quick intervention from the police but the gang members saw this as an internal attack. "Prof",[12] a high-ranking gang member, remarked: "they caught us napping but that nah happen again"[13]. I was given instruction not to return to that area of the community as a war (fighting) had begun and a gun battle was imminent. A reprisal was not an option, even as informal systems had pointed to a possible suspect. There was, however, great anticipation of another attack and so the group was in a defensive position. Prof was killed along with one of his sons and his entire family had to flee the community. The area leader[14] was also gunned down three weeks later just outside her business place. Though the police, and to a lesser extent the PMI, was present, the community was so tense that it was difficult for there to be any social intervention. The focus was law enforcement and order maintenance. This can be contrasted with Nature Town where the service arm of the police force functioned in conjunction with law enforcement and order maintenance producing a more favourable outcome.

The two cases highlight the challenges of peace building in an environment where there is persistent conflict that dates back to the late colonial period. Fragmented identities, the anti-essentialism, and the weak state structures have created an environment of hostility. The possibilities of success lie in the external support that challenges the dominant ideas at the community level.

The post-2010 environment

A major problem with small post-colonial states is their dependence on Foreign Direct Investment and other means of earning foreign exchange, as the economies are very open and vulnerable to internal and external shocks (Ffolkes-Goldson, 2016). Jaffe (2013) noted that the nature of the garrison system began to change in the 1980s with the structural adjustment program which drastically impacted government expenditure. This was occurring while the criminal dons were engaging in transnational organised networks and solidifying new sources of wealth and power (Blake, 2002; Harriott, 2008). The dons subsequently began providing services that would have been previously undertaken by the politicians.

Austerity measures were again undertaken in 2010 with noted reduction in discretionary government spending and stringent oversight mechanisms as the country worked assiduously to meet its International Monetary Fund (IMF) targets. Community leaders including gang/corner groups spoke of the fact that the Member of Parliament had not been able to implement all the programs they normally would. The reduction of discriminatory spending had also limited the issuance of state contracts. This became specifically acute during the Christmas season, where the road works and other employment would be generated around the festive season, and the "back to school season" when parents were preparing their children to return to school after the summer break. This had significantly affected the mode of operation of the observable groups, including the gangs, and the political activists as they now found it challenging to meet the expectations of the community and legitimise their importance in the space without the state support to which they were accustomed. Members of the two organised crime groups expressed that they had not been getting as many government contracts as before. Many of the groups now recognised that they had to find other sources of income.

A lesson learned from Nature Town is worthy to note. A group of residents took the decision to utilise the peace that was being experienced and the culture of street dances to generate income. The previously warring corners had been able to form an informal *round robin* which supported the staging of parties/street dances across the community almost every night. The round robin system required that each person or group paid into a revolving fund that was used by the party holder to procure liquor and other inputs necessary for the event to take place. Once the profit was made the seed funds were paid back into the pool and made available to the other person or group. Another feature, which took advantage of the new freedom of movement, was that all the groups supported the person who was staging the event. This meant that persons were moving across what was previously enemy territory to support the other group member.

The groups involved in this arrangement were very protective of the peace that supported it. The Police had been able to use the revoking of permissions[15] to hold the event as a system of reward and punishment to address burgeoning conflict situations. The parties also facilitated persons from the varying "corners" to cross borders and build relationships, thus reducing the community fragmentation. The CSJP and the PMI oversaw the group meetings as the members had little capacity to do so. This new group had also been able to identify community problems and with the help of internal and external stakeholders work on solutions.

A second feature of the post-2010 environment was that since the Tivoli joint military/constabulary operation,[16] the police had been given stronger legislation to deal effectively with gang reduction (Hall, 2010; Henry, 2013). Young men in Haven Town were reportedly dissuaded from assuming leadership roles in criminal gangs because this was seen as a new moment in the communities where the gangs were being vigorously attacked. This was exacerbated by the fact that there was a general feeling among the crews/gangs that their political representatives, especially the Member of Parliament, were now creating some distance. This undermined their legitimacy and some had expressed that they anxiously awaited the election season, which was fast approaching, to see if this trend would hold.

Everyday unfairness

A part of the negotiation process related to sensemaking is an understanding of what is deemed as the *everyday unfairness* within the social structure. A common theme expressed by those associated with the crews/gangs was that the society is fundamentally unfair. On a macro level, several indicators have shown the Jamaican economy to have high levels of corruption. A UNDP (2010) indicated that 47.9 per cent of Jamaicans thought that the society was fundamentally unjust and unfair. It is this belief about unfairness that supports differential associations to crime.

In both communities the story was told of politicians coming in during the late 1960s and early 1970s and giving selected groups the means to progress, changing the dynamics of the community. The development of this othering sparked gang violence. All this was developed without regard for innocent lives. The perceived dishonesty extended to those in leadership positions seen as indicative of a particular nature and ordering of the Jamaican society. This included the leaders of the church; in fact, in Haven Town one interviewee noted that the church leaders had enriched themselves at the expense of their congregants who remained poor. The urban poor therefore, have had to protect themselves and created innovation for their own advancement.

Dave, a young man in his late 30s, who was trained by an International Development Partner and later sent to the University of Technology said he no longer believed in volunteerism as he had given so much for the development of his community but felt as if his own development was being stymied. He said persons (including research students like myself) "come into the community and take". He noted that "outsiders" benefitted from the community as it was and they who were living in the community trying to develop found it difficult because of the social structural arrangements that prejudiced them but facilitated others (like myself). This for him was unfair.

Discussion

The current study investigated the ways in which the urban poor of two communities in Kingston, Jamaica, made sense of the high violence rates in their respective communities. Furthermore, it investigated how this sensemaking was related to the development and concretisation of social identities within a post-colonial environment. The research has shown that the post-colonial environment presents a unique space to explore crime, identity, and community because of the enduring socio-political structures that create exclusion and fragmentation.

The identity projects that an individual or group invest in may emerge abruptly in a crisis situation (or some other context that demands an immediate reaction), or through deliberate planning. The narratives from both communities suggest significant and long-term investment in the process of political polarisation. One of the outcomes of this is the garrison, a particular community prototype found in Jamaica (Figueroa et al., 2008). The findings from the research suggest that in the context of political garrisons, in spite of the changes in the governance structures since the late post-colonial period, the political processes have remained central in the development and concretisation of social identity. This makes it extremely difficult to build a strong notion of citizenship.

In the context of high community violence, when a traumatic event occurs within the community, storytellers either rely on the scripts from the past (which are associated with violence and revenge-seeking behaviours), or tap into the current moment of peace. The current data showed that gangs and crews are a rich source of community memory and they remain an important part of the sensemaking process. External partners such as the police, the CSJP, and the PMI are providing the much-needed support to help the community make sense of traumatic events and to reduce revenge-seeking behaviours. The communities, however, must build stronger mental representation and exemplars of conflict prevention and resolution. The identity project in criminogenic communities therefore needs to be recalibrated in a sustainable and feasible way. If the symbolic representations, including the badness honour, that facilitate the formation of observable groups with a criminal orientation are not removed, "there will never be peace, only a cease-fire".

Jamaica has to strive for the building of positive peace. This means systems that build mutuality and resilience (Barak, 2003) ought to be developed. The post-colonial environment requires a sociology that will create and promote a positive social movement at the community level and a criminology that is emancipatory, focusing not only on solutions from external international development partners but on the strengths and innovation of people at the grassroots level. This, with the goal of building a strong sense of belonging and citizenship that is empowering and encouraging of pro-social behaviours.

Notes

1 These are electoral boundaries
2 Pseudonym
3 Pseudonym
4 Calculated based on population data, major crime rates and VRIs complied by the Mona Geoinformatics Institute, University of the West Indies, Mona. The researcher at the Geoinformatics Institute noted that it was difficult to get a national average for VRIs because data is not collected from all Hospitals
5 Population, male population, youth population, and percentage of population with maximum secondary school education
6 Social Development Commission, 2009 and 2011
7 Data obtained from the Mona Geoinformatics Institute which uses Geographic Information Systems to map various social occurrences
8 Pseudonym
9 Defence crews, according to Levy, Ward, Hutchinson, and Weeks (2012), are conceptually distinct from a gang as their sole purpose is to defend the community against rival gangs. They are not motivated by economic gain.
10 The Peace Management Initiative is a civil society group brought together by the Minister of National Security in 2002 to help to defuse the upsurge of violence in Kingston and St Catherine. The mandate of the group has since spread to other sessions of the Island.
11 The Citizen Security and Justice Program is an initiative of the Ministry of National Security Jamaica focused on crime and violence prevention at the community level.
12 Pseudonym
13 That means, they caught us sleeping but that will not happen again as the necessary step have been taken to respond to such an attack.
14 An area leader is a community leader who has gained legitimacy usually through political affiliation and has acquired enough political, social, and economic capital to gain the respect of the community. They are able to navigate the legitimate as well as the criminal structures within the community.
15 Under the Law of Jamaica, a request must be made to the superintendent or the senior police officer in charge of the parish/division to host an event. Before the permit is granted the officer must be provided with accurate information about the type of event, the nature of the event, who your target group is, and the number of people that is expected to be in attendance.
16 In May of 2010 this joint operation resulted in more than seventy deaths in the Tivoli Gardens neighbourhood of Kingston, Jamaica. Tensions between the state and the community when in August, 2009 the US government requested the extradition of Christopher (Dudus) Coke. He was known as the country's most powerful "don", in Jamaica.

References

Anderson, B. (1991). *Imagined communities*. London, UK: Verso.

Anderson, E. (1999). *Code of the street: Decency, violence, and the moral life of the Inner-city*. New York: Norton.

Ashcroft, B., Griffiths, G., & Tiffin, H. (2000). *Key concepts in post-colonial studies*. London: Routledge.

Atkinson, P., & Hammersley, M. (1994). Ethnography and participant observation. In N. Denzin, & Y. Lincoln (Eds.), *Handbook of qualitative research* (pp. 248–261). Thousand Oaks: Sage Publications.

Barak, G. (2003). *Violence and non-violence: Pathways to understanding*. California: Sage Publications.

Beckford, G. (1972). *Persistent poverty: Underdevelopment in plantation economies of the third world*. Oxford, UK: Oxford University Press.

Bhabha, H. (2004). *The location of culture*. London: Routledge.

Blake, D. (2002). *Shower Posse: The most notorious Jamaican criminal organization*. New York: Diamond Publishing.

Bolland, O. (2002). Creolisation and creole societies: A cultural nationalist view of Caribbean society history. In K. Brathwaite, V. Shepard, & G. Richards (Eds.), *Questioning creole: Creolisation discourses in Caribbean culture* (pp. 15–46). Kingston: Ian Randle Publishers.

Brathwaite, K. (1971). *The development of Creole society in Jamaica, 1770–1820*. Oxford: Oxford University Press.

Brint, S. (2001). Gemeinschaft revisited: A critique and reconstruction of the community concept. *Sociological Theory*, *19*, 1–23. doi: 10.1111/0735–2751.00125.

Cesaire, A. (1972). *Discourse on colonialism*. New York: Monthly Review Press.

Charles, C.A.D. (2002). Garrison communities as counter societies: The case of the 1998 Zeeks Riot in Jamaica. *Ideaz*, *1*(1), 29–43.

Charles, C.A.D. (2004). Political identity and criminal violence in Jamaica: The garrison community of August Town and the 2002 election. *Social and Economic Studies*, *53*(2), 31–73.

Chevannes, B. (1992, November). *The Formation of garrison communities*. Paper presented at the Symposium — Grassroots development and the state of the nation in honour of Professor Carl Stone, University of the West Indies, Mona Campus, Jamaica.

Clarke, C. (2006a). Politics, violence and dugs in Kingston, Jamaica. *Bulletin of Latin American Research*, *25*(3), 420–440.

Clarke, C. (2006b). *Decolonising the colonial city: Urbanisation and stratification in Kingston, Jamaica*. Oxford: Oxford University Press.

Either, K., & Deaux, K. (1994). Negotiating social identity when context change: Maintaining identification and responding to threat. *Journal of Personality and Social Psychology*, *67*(2), 243–251.

Ellis, H. (1987). Crime and violence: The social and psychological dimensions. In P. Phillips, & J. Wedderburn. (1987, November). *Crime and violence: Causes and solutions*. Paper presented at the Symposium on Crime and Violence in Jamaica: Causes and Solutions, held at the Department of Government, University of the West Indies, Mona, Jamaica, in collaboration with the Friedrich Ebert Stiftung (FES).

Espeut, P. (2005, October 12). The mother of all garrisons. *The Jamaica Gleaner*. Retrieved from www.jamaica-gleaner.com/gleaner/20051012/cleisure/cleisure2.html.

Eyre, L.A. (1984). Political violence and urban geography in Kingston, Jamaica. *Geographical Review*, *74*(1), 24–37.

Fanon, F. (1963). *The wretched of the earth*. Middlesex: Penguin Books.

Figueroa, M. (1994, December). *Garrison communities in Jamaica 1962–1993: Their growth and impact on political culture*. Paper presented at the Democratization in Jamaica: Fifty Years of Adult Suffrage Lecture, Faculty of Social Sciences UWI, Mona, Kingston.

Figueroa, M., Harriott, A., & Satchell, N. (2008). *The political economy of Jamaica's inner-city violence: A special case?* Kingston: Ian Randall Publishers.

Figueroa, M., & Sives, A. (2002). Homogeneous voting, electoral manipulation and the garrison process in Post-Independence Jamaica. *Commonwealth & Comparative Politics*, *40*(1), 81–108.

Figueroa, M., & Sives, A. (2003). Garrison politics and criminality in Jamaica: Does the 1997 election represent a turning point? In A. Harriott (Ed.), *Understanding crime in Jamaica: New challenges for public policy* (pp. 63–88). Kingston: The University of the West Indies Press.

Ffolkes-Goldson, S. (2016). *Commonwealth Caribbean corporate governance*. New York: Routledge.

Gayle, H. (2009). Young boys learning to fear, hate and harm: A recipe for sustaining tribal political violence in Jamaica's garrisons. *IDS Bulletin*, *40*(1), 53–62.

Ghandi, L. (1998). *Postcolonial Theory: A critical introduction*. Sydney: Edinburgh University Press.

Gioia, D.A., Corley, K.G., & Fabbri, T. (2002). Revisiting the past (while thinking in the future perfect tense). *Journal of Organisational Change Management*, *15*(6), 622–634.

Girvan, N. (2014). Caribbean integration: Can cultural production succeed where politics and economics have failed? (Confessions of a way forward economist). In W.A. Knight, J. Castro-Rea, & H. Ghany (Eds.), *Re-mapping the Americas: Trends in region-making* (pp. 255–262). London: Routledge Taylor & Francis Group.

Gold, R. (1958). Roles in sociological field observation. *Social Forces*, *36*(3), 217–213.

Gopaul, R., Morgan, P., & Reddock, P. (1996). *Women, family and family violence in the Caribbean: The historical and contemporary experience with special reference to Trinidad and Tobago*. St Augustine: Centre for Gender and Development Studies. St Augustine.

Gray, O. (2003). Badness honour. In A. Harriott (Ed.). *Understanding crime in Jamaica: New challenges for public policy* (pp. 13–48). Kingston: The University of the West Indies Press.

Gray, O. (2004). *Demeaned but empowered: The social power of the urban poor in Jamaica*. Kingston: The University of the West Indies Press.

Green, J., & Thorogood, N. (2009). *Qualitative methods for health research* (2nd ed.). London: Sage Publications.

Hall, S. (1990). Cultural identity and diaspora. In J. Rutherford (Ed.), *Identity: Community, culture, difference* (pp. 222–237). London: Lawrence and Wishart.

Hall, S. (2001). Negotiating Caribbean identities. In B. Meeks, & F. Lindahl (Eds.), *New Caribbean thought: A reader* (pp. 24–39). Kingston: The University of the West.

Hall, A. (2010, January 23). Gang buster, security minister vows to disrupt criminal networks, *Jamaica Gleaner*. Retrieved from http://jamaica-gleaner.com/gleaner/20100123/lead/lead1.html.

Harriott, A. (Ed.). (2003a). *Understanding crime in Jamaica: New challenges for public policy*. Kingston: UWI Press.

Harriott, A. (2003b). Social identities and the escalation of homicidal violence in Jamaica. In A. Harriott (Ed.), *Understanding crime in Jamaica: New challenges for public policy* (pp. 89–112). Kingston: UWI Press.

Harriott, A. (2008). *Organized crime and politics in Jamaica: Breaking the nexus*. Kingston: Canoe Press.

Harriott, A. (2009, April). *Bending the trend line: The challenge of controlling violence in Jamaica and the high violence societies of the Caribbean*. Paper presented at the Professorial Inaugural Lecture, University of the West Indies, Kingston.

Helm-Mills, J., Thurlow, A., & Mills, A. (2010). Making sense of sensemaking: The critical sensemaking approach. *Qualitative Research in Organizations and Management, 5*(2), 182–195.

Henry, B. (2013, July 18) Anti-Gang Bill review starts September. *Jamaica Observer*. Retrieved from www.jamaicaobserver.com/news/Anti-Gang-Bill-review-to-start-September_14702584

Herman, J. (1997). *Trauma and recovery: The aftermath of violence – from domestic abuse to political terror*. New York: Basic Books.

Hogg, M., & Adams, D. (1998). *Social Identification: A social psychology of intergroup and group processes*. London: Routledge.

Howard, J. (2000). Social psychology of identities. *Annual Review of Sociology, 26*(1), 367–393.

Hsieh, H., & Shannon, S. (2005). Three approaches to qualitative content analysis. *Qualitative Health Research, 15*(9), 1277–1288.

Huddy, L. (2001). From social to political identity: A critical examination of social identity theory. *Political Psychology, 22*(1), 127–156.

Hutton, C. (1996). *Manufacturing violence shaping social psychology: Aspects of the Columbian holocaust in the Americas*. Unpublished essay. Department of Government, University of the West Indies, Mona, Kingston, Jamaica.

Hutton, C. (2010). Oh rudie: Jamaica popular music and the narrative of urban badness in the making of post-colonial society. *Caribbean Quarterly, 56*(4), 22–64.

Jaffe, R. (Ed.). (2008). *The Caribbean city*. Kingston and Miami: Ian Randle Publishers and Leiden: KITLV Press.

Jaffe, R. (2013). The hybrid state: Crime and citizenship in urban Jamaica. *American Ethnologist, 40*(4), 734–748.

Kaufman, H.F. (1959). Towards an interactional conception of community. *Social Forces, 38*(1), 8–17.

Lawrence, D., Duperly-Pinks, D., & Branche, C. (1999, February). *Narrative of attachment and identity: Alberto Melucci and the power of Black Power*. Paper presented at the 1st Annual Psychology Conference-Psychology and Caribbean Development. University of the West Indies, Mona, Kingston.

Leslie, G. (2010). *Confronting the Don: The political economy of gang violence in Jamaica*. Occasional Paper, Small Arms Survey, No. 26. Small Arms Survey, Graduate Institute of International and Development Studies, Geneva, Switzerland.

Levy, H. (2001). *They cry 'respect'! Urban violence and poverty in Jamaica*. Kingston: Centre for population, community and social change, department of sociology and social work, University of the West Indies, Mona, Kingston.

Levy, H. (2009). *Killing streets and community revival*. Kingston: Arawak Publications.

Levy, H. with Ward, E., Hutchinson, D., & Weeks, T. (2012). *Youth violence and organized crime in Jamaica: Causes and countermeasures: An examination of the linkages and disconnections*. Final Technical Report. (An unpublished monograph). Institute of Criminal Justice and Security, UWI/ International Development Research Centre (IDRC).

Loomba, A. (1998). *Colonialism/Postcolonialism: The new critical idiom*. London: Routledge.

McEwan, C. (2009). *Postcolonialism and development*. London: Routledge.

Ministry of National Security. (2015, November). *The Ministry of National Security Jamaica gang threat assessment: 2014*. Report prepared by The Organized Crime and Research and Evaluation Units of the Policy Directorate (Ministry of National Security) in conjunction with the National Intelligence Bureau.

National Committee on Political Tribalism. (1997). R*eport of the national committee on political tribalism*. Commissioned by Prime Minister P.J. Patterson. Kingston, Jamaica: Office of the Prime Minister.

Nettleford, R. (1998). *Mirror mirror: Identity, race and protest*. Kingston: LMNH Publishing.

Nurse, K. (2006). *Migration, diaspora and development in the Caribbean*. (Policy Paper, Focal FPP-04–6). Retrieved from www.focal.ca/pdf/migration_Nurse_diaspora%20migration%20development%20Caribbean_September%202004_FPP-04-6.pdf.

Patterson, P.J. (2003, October). *CARICOM beyond thirty: Connecting with the Diaspora*. Presentation made at the CARICOM 30th. Annual Lecture, Brooklyn, New York.

Premdas, R. (1996, December). *Ethnicity and identity in the Caribbean: Decentring a myth*. (Working paper #234). The Helen Kellogg Institute for International Studies. Retrieved from https://kellogg.nd.edu/publications/workingpapers/WPS/234.pdf.

Sampson, R., Morenoff, J., & Gannon-Rowley, T. (2002). Assessing "neighbourhood effects": Social processes and new direction in research. *Annual Review of Sociology*, *28*(1), 443–478.

Sives, A. (1998). *Violence and politics in Jamaica. An analysis of urban violence in Kingston, 1944–1996*. (Unpublished doctoral dissertation). University of Bradford, UK.

Sives, A. (2002). Changing patrons, from politician to drug don: Clientelism in Downtown Kingston, Jamaica. *Latin American Perspectives*, *29*(5), 66–89.

Sives, A. (2010). *Election, violence and the democratic process: 1944–2007*. Kingston: Ian Randle Publishers.

Smith, M.G. (1965). *The plural society in the British West Indies*. Berkeley and Los Angeles: University of California Press.

Social Development Commission. (2009). *Community profile: Greater Allman Town. (Kingston)*. Kingston: SDC.

Social Development Commission. (2011). *Community profile: Whitfield Town*. Kingston: SDC.

Statistical Institute of Jamaica. (2013). *Population and Housing Census, 2011: Jamaica Age and Sex, Volume 2*. Kingston: Statistical Institute of Jamaica.

Stein, M. (2004). The critical period of disaster: Insights from sense-making and psychoanalytic theory. *Human Relations*, *57*(10), 1243–1261.

Stone, C. (1980). *Democracy and clientelism in Jamaica*. Kingston: Blackett Publishers.

Stone, C. (1985). *Class, state and democracy in Jamaica*. New York: New Brunswick.

Thomas, D. (2011). *Exceptional violence: Embodied citizenship in transnational Jamaica*. Durham, DC: Duke University Press.

United Nations Development Programme [UNDP]. (2010). *United Nation Citizen Security Survey, Jamaica*. Unpublished raw data.

Van Knippenberg, A. (1978). Status differences, comparative relevance and intergroup differentiation. In H. Tajfel (Ed.), *Ingroup differences in social perception* (pp. 561–577). London: Academic Press.

Weick, K. (1995). *Sensemaking in organisations*. Thousand Oaks, CA: Sage Publications.

Weick, K., Sutcliffe, M., & Obstfeld, D. (2005). Organising and the process of sensemaking. *Organisation Science*, *16*(4), 409–421.

Young, R. (1995). *Colonial desire: Hybridity in theory, culture and race*. London: Routledge.

Young, R. (2003). *Postcolonialism: A very short introduction*. New York: Oxford University Press.

Section D

Criminal justice systems and policies

13 Perceptions of familial responsibility as a practical constraint in judicial decision-making

Focal concerns and gender bias in sentencing on the island of Barbados

Corin Bailey

Introduction

Offender gender and sentencing

Research on gender and sentencing has traditionally focused on two areas – gender relating to the victim and that of the offender. The present study is concerned exclusively with differential treatment that occurs in the courts, related to the sex of the offender. The notion that female offenders receive more lenient treatment in comparison to their male counterparts at sentencing, is one of the more consistent findings within criminological literature that focuses on court outcomes. Indeed, these findings have typically transcended both time and location. One of the earliest studies to explore the phenomenon was conducted by Martin (1934) and concluded that although females were no less likely to be sentenced to prison, they were more likely than men to receive suspended sentences. Similarly, Green (1961) demonstrated the increased likelihood among female offenders in the United States to receive non-custodial sentences such as probation, fines, and suspended sentences. Nagel and Weitzman (1971) too, concluded that among males and females charged with grand larceny, women were more likely to receive suspended sentences or probation. They framed these findings around the notion of *paternalistic protectiveness* that is based on the assumption that women need to be sheltered from "manly experiences" such as incarceration. Recent empirical work too, has generally supported early findings (Curry, Lee, & Rodriguez, 2004; Engen, Gainey, Critchfield, & Weis, 2003; Jeffries, Fletcher, & Newbold, 2003).

Not all studies however, have concluded that women enjoy favourable treatment before the courts. The theory of sex-role traditionalism argues that because criminality is seen by society as incompatible with traditional roles of women, they are subjected to even harsher treatment than men when they go before the courts. Proponents of the sex-role traditionalism theory maintain that as long as men continue to dominate the justice system, traditional attitudes about the role that women are supposed to play will influence decisions, and those women who behave "inappropriately" will be treated more harshly (Griffin & Woolridge, 2006).

These studies however have either pertained primarily to juveniles, or have been heavily based on historical data (Boritch, 1992; Chesney-Lind, 1977; Chesney-Lind & Shelden, 2004). Other studies have found family responsibilities to enjoy primary importance in sentencing decisions, indicating that only married women, or those with children receive milder sentences than men (Kautt & Spohn, 2002; Stacey & Spohn, 2006). This finding too suffers from a lack of consensus however, as research elsewhere has suggested that when compared to men, familied women are just as likely to receive milder sentences than those without families (Mustard, 2001; Spohn, 1999; Spohn & Beichner, 2000).

The implementation of sentencing guidelines and determinate sentencing in various jurisdictions was designed to reduce the propensity for bias and other personal factors to influence sentencing decisions. However, research suggests that even since the advent of these regulations, judges have still displayed a greater likelihood to demonstrate leniency towards female offenders through the consideration of various extra-legal factors (Koons-Witt, 2002). Williams (1999) for example, illustrated the manner in which judges in the state of Florida appeared to consider only legally relevant factors for male offenders, while punishments for females were based on other determinations.

Theoretical perspectives

Despite the absence of universal agreement, the relatively consistent determination among empirical research that women benefit from sentencing leniency when compared to men has precipitated a large body of work seeking to explain how and why this operates within the context of judicial decision making. Among the range of theoretical perspectives aimed at explaining this phenomenon, two theories have emerged as particularly influential. The *chivalry thesis* emerged in the 1950s and is based on societal assumptions and cultural stereotypes concerning gender. Second, the *focal concerns theory* examines the nature and dynamics specific to judicial decision-making. It is important to note here that neither of these theories have been examined specifically within the Caribbean context.

Chivalry and the justice system

Though chivalry as an institution, originating in tenth-century medieval Europe has long since disappeared, it has been argued that in many parts of the world, practices of chivalry continue to be a large part of accepted social codes (Moulds, 1980). When applied to the justice system, the chivalry thesis argues that gendered stereotypes surrounding men and women operate to influence the nature of sentencing decisions. It has often been used in conjunction with the term *paternalism*, a concept the roots of which can be traced to a type of behaviour that is associated with the treatment of a daughter by her father. Three basic premises of paternalism exist, namely (1) a child is ignorant, such that he/she can be deceived and manipulated to serve the needs of his parent, (2) a child is not fully aware of his/her role and so is in need of guidance, and (3) a child is defenceless and in need of protection (Sills, 1968). Moulds (1980) suggested that the inevitable effect of a society which has been allowed to absorb these beliefs is that the actions of those who affect the law either directly or indirectly become inconsistent with the operation of a democratic state. This is what she referred to as "A basic denial of self-determination" (Moulds, 1980, p. 419).

One of the most influential writers on the subject of chivalry in the justice system was Otto Pollack. He explained:

> One of the outstanding concomitants of the existing inequality between the sexes is chivalry and the general protective attitude of the man toward woman. This attitude exists on the part of the male victim of crime as well as on the part of the officers of the law, who are still largely male in our society. Men hate to accuse women . . . Police officers dislike to arrest them, district attorneys to prosecute them, Judges and Juries to find them guilty.
>
> (Pollack, 1950, p. 151)

The views of Pollack greatly influenced the direction of research undertaken from the 1970s as the belief persisted among some that society did not see female offenders as criminals but in terms of their relation to men as daughters, mothers, sisters, and wives. In this way, citizens and criminal justice officials acting chivalrously conceal the criminality of the female offender. In short, society's preoccupation with the protection of women leads to increased leniency towards them (Rodriguez, Curry, & Lee, 2006).

Focal concerns theory

The more recent development of the focal concerns theory (Steffensmeier, 1980; Steffensmeier, Kramer, & Streifel, 1993; Steffensmeier, Kramer, & Ulmer, 1995) was precipitated by a need for a more nuanced perspective that explained sentencing disparities. Central to the theory is the notion that judges take three focal issues into account when making sentencing decisions: blameworthiness, dangerousness (community protection), and practical constraints. As it relates to blameworthiness, judges consider the type and severity of offence. Dangerousness relates to the nature of prior convictions or whether or not a weapon was used, while practical constraints take social costs such as the offender's ability to serve time, as well as organisational factors such as the offender's familial responsibilities into consideration. It is suggested that time constraints on the part of the judiciary cause judges to receive incomplete information on offenders and cases. As a result, these decisions are affected by generalisations and personal bias (Rodriguez et al., 2006). Judges may make assumptions for example, based on the sex of the defendant. Female offenders may be viewed as less dangerous to the community, males may be assumed to be better equipped to handle the rigours of incarceration, or women may be assumed to be the ones primarily responsible for child rearing (Albonetti, 1991; Steffensmeier, Kramer, & Ulmer, 1998). Indeed, it is the assumed social costs associated with the incarceration of women as it relates to caring for dependent children that was identified by Steffensmeier (1980) as contributing greatly to gender disparities in sentencing.

There have been several attempts to explain how ties to families, and in particular children, can influence sentencing decisions. Kruttschnitt's (1982) theory of informal social control argued that the level of social control an individual is subjected to increases the more tied they are to others. Since social controls reduce the likelihood of future offending, the assumption in the eyes of the court, that these informal social controls are greater in the lives of women, leads to more lenient treatment for them. Kruttschnitt believed that informal social control was greater in the lives of women, as a result of their greater propensity to be economically dependent on others. While the work of Kruttschnitt was informative, Daly (1987) challenged its conclusions on the basis that (1) there was a lack of specification as to the locus of informal control, and more importantly, (2) the gender differences observed in court decisions could not be adequately explained by it: while women may be more dependent on others, they are also more likely than men to have others dependent on them. As an alternative, Daly combined the notion of practical considerations with Kruttschnitt's informal social control, to suggest that there was an important distinction between the courts desire to protect women (female paternalism) and the desire to protect children (familial paternalism). Familied offenders were seen as more anchored in the normative social order because their day-to-day lives are restricted by having family responsibilities (Daly, 1987). Daly posited that the courts are reluctant to punish children, by incarcerating the person on whom they depend.

While the view that familied women are treated more leniently than familied men has received considerable support within the literature (Albonetti, 1997; Engen et al., 2003; Rodriguez et al., 2006), others have argued that of critical importance is familial role. It is suggested that judges privilege the importance of emotional support for children over purely financial responsibilities. As a result, the effect of gender on sentencing decisions is reduced, if the defendant is integral to the emotional development of his/her children (Bickle & Peterson, 1991; Freiburger, 2010).

The present study

As stated earlier, the focal concerns theory suggests that due to the possession of incomplete information on offenders and cases, judges are forced to make assumptions that are based on generalisations and biases as they relate to criminality. Few studies have sought to explore the nature of perceptions that may fuel generalisations held by the judiciary, particularly as they relate to male and female offending. Indeed, this form of inquiry remains absent from the research agenda of Caribbean criminologists. The large proportion of males in Caribbean prisons when compared to their female counterparts necessitates an investigation into the factors that may contribute to differential treatment when they come before the court. The present study seeks to fill this need by examining the impact of perceptions among magistrates, relating to familial responsibilities, as a practical constraints concern, on sentencing decisions for male and female offenders.

Methods

Participants

In order to achieve the desired aims of the study, and to generate rich insights into judicial perspectives that may influence sentencing decisions, a qualitative methodology was utilised. The island of Barbados is separated into two judicial levels: the Magistrate's Courts, and the Supreme Court (further divided into the High Court, and the Court of Appeal). The Magistrate Courts have jurisdiction over civil, family, and criminal matters and operate within eight judicial districts. At the time of data collection, there were eleven magistrates employed on the island. Although attempts were made to include all eleven magistrates in the interview process, the eventual participation rate was 60 per cent. That is, nine out of the 11 judges sitting in 2014 participated in the study. Only two of the magistrates interviewed were women.

Procedure

Semi-structured interviews have long been used as a means of capturing data in sentencing research and thus were employed in the present study to explore the origin and current nature of magistrates' perceptions on gender roles, and the manner in which these may affect decisions as they relate to possible leniency. The interview schedule was guided by the following research question:

> How do perceptions of gendered family roles affect judicial decision-making regarding the sentencing of male and female offenders?

Interviews were conducted in August and September 2015. After receiving initial permission from the Barbados Chief Justice to approach individual magistrates, letters of request were mailed to each magistrate to determine whether or not they would be willing to take part in the study. Those that consented were later visited in their chambers at which time the interviews were conducted. Each interview lasted an average of 90 minutes and was conducted by a trained moderator and note taker.

Data analysis

Quality assurance checks were employed to ensure accurate reading of the data collected. A standardised protocol was developed by way of a written list of issues to be covered in each interview. In addition, a manual for data collection was developed and consulted before each research day to ensure that the moderator followed the same pattern and research techniques for each interview. Along with the use of a tape recorder, the note taker was asked to capture verbatim accounts of the discussion and to record non-verbal activity. Communication cues were developed between the moderator and note taker such that the moderator would know when to employ techniques in order to slow down the interview, or ask the participant to repeat or rephrase what was said. Notes were reviewed immediately following each interview and any gaps in the discussion filled in. Finally, full transcripts were produced by the note taker as soon as possible with the assistance of the interview recordings. Before analysis the data was examined and new themes were added to the existing themes that were decided upon before commencing the study. Coding took place during the analysis and sections of the data were labelled. Extensive discussions with the note taker followed, to ensure a consensus on the findings, interpretation, and conclusions.

Caribbean patriarchy and gender role expectations

Central to debates surrounding notions of familial roles, and the impact these may have on perceptions of childcare, are the predominantly male-centred ideologies that continue to pervade Caribbean cultures. The roots of these ideologies can be traced to the post-emancipation period, during which Caribbean women benefitted from few opportunities for political, civil, or educational involvement and as such, were severely limited in their occupational choices (Blank, 2013). Among women, and importantly, in the eyes of men, domestic responsibilities therefore took precedence, with child rearing in particular assuming considerable importance. So much so that Caribbean women often assumed the role of primary care for children that were not their own, in order to assist families suffering from economic hardship (Safa, 1995; Sobo, 1993). Today, the matrifocal family is commonplace throughout the Caribbean region with as many as 70 per cent of children in the Eastern Caribbean being born into non-nuclear families (Blank, 2013). This is however, a unit that operates in conjunction with a deeply entrenched system of patriarchy, enforced by cultural norms (Momsen, 2002).

Contemporary Caribbean society continues to maintain an inexorable link between women and their domestic responsibilities. Evidence suggests for example, that Barbadian society still views women primarily as nurturers and caregivers, despite their higher participation and performance in education, and despite the expectation that they must provide a meaningful economic contribution to the home as well (Barrow, 1986; Dann, 1987). Indeed, despite societal preoccupation with women's domestic responsibilities, in a country in which a large percentage of households are headed by women, their role in ensuring both the emotional and economic well-being of their children is now seen as critical. The close relationship between mothers and children is seen by men as the manifestation of the fact that women are biologically predisposed to the task of raising children, rather than a function of societally cultivated neglect on the part of fathers. In an earlier study examining gender role perceptions among Barbadian shop owners confronted with male and female shoplifters, it is instructive to note that male participants not only viewed the role of the mother in child rearing as critical, but also as considerably more important to the long-term development of children than that of the father (Bailey, 2012). Chevannes (2001) felt that at the heart of this issue was an image problem. The role of caregiver was almost incompatible with the perceived status of the Caribbean man, who had appropriated the view that providing was the most important role of the father. One of the participants in his study said that: "Most men think that 'gentle' is not macho, and that loving your children is strictly for female" (Chevannes, 2001, p. 137).

It was against this background that the majority of the magistrates interviewed were raised. Participants were asked to expand on the nature of familial roles within their households as children. The majority described the existence of clearly defined, and strictly adhered to, gender roles between both parents. Despite evidence suggesting the contemporary dominance of single-parent families throughout Caribbean society (Blank, 2013; UNICEF, 2002), participants were typically raised by both parents, with fathers generally assuming the role of principal breadwinner. Mr Joseph, a 42-year-old male magistrate explained:

> I lived with both parents. I am from a traditional family. A country home. My father was no doubt the leader of the house. He substantially did the work (public service). My mother worked from time to time doing some subbing in government. Mainly outside of that she was a seamstress. Roles between my parents were specified. My father was the breadwinner, my mother the homemaker. She did the cooking and cleaning. Mother was the nurturing one as far as the children were concerned but both were involved in decision making.

This situation was common to the majority of those interviewed. Mr Jennings, a 49-year-old magistrate described similar circumstances:

> I lived with both parents. As a child of the 60s and 70s we had the more traditional family unit where the father was the breadwinner. My mother was the stay at home type. My father saw himself as the breadwinner and joint disciplinarian. My mother was the foundation of everything – nurture, discipline. In the initial stages my mother went out to work and so at that point breadwinning was joint but that didn't last long. After a while she stopped and concentrated on domestic things. She did all the cooking and cleaning and other things around the house.

Caribbean children are socialised into these gender norms and roles from an early age. While boys for example, are typically given toys such as trucks and water guns, girls tend to be given dolls and kitchen utensils and are encouraged to assume domestic responsibilities in servitude of both their male siblings and their father (Senior, 1991). When boys are given domestic responsibilities, these tend to be outdoors, where they also primarily spend their leisure time playing sports and socializing with friends, while girls are often left to assist mothers inside the home. The outdoor activities of girls tend to occur at school, and end before it gets dark (Blank, 2013). This too was a common feature of the socialisation of the majority of magistrates interviewed. The experience of Mr Edmond, a 60-year-old magistrate, was instructive:

> I had to do chores like maintaining the animals we kept. My sister would mostly do the housework. My sister had to learn to cook because my mother

> thought it was a priority for her to learn to cook. It was not a priority for me to cook, although she would casually tell me I should learn, she never really enforced that.

It was apparent from the testimonies, that as children, with few exceptions, participants were heavily socialised into the belief that child rearing and other domestic responsibilities were almost exclusively the domain of women. Although 53-year-old magistrate, Ms Anderson, was the only female participant involved in the study, she described a situation in keeping with that majority of those interviewed:

> My parents' roles were different. Although both worked, my father was clearly the breadwinner of the family. At home he did stuff outside. He wouldn't even iron his clothes. My mother did all the cooking and domestic responsibilities. As girls we would help with washing and cleaning. My father was very good at barking orders, but my mother was very nurturing. She was very lovey-lovey with us.

Indeed, young children internalise these patriarchal ideologies such that before long, they too grow to prioritise the maternal functions of Caribbean women at the expense of other responsibilities. Relatively few Caribbean women now refer to themselves as housewives, yet one study demonstrated that among young children in Barbados, Dominica, and Jamaica, there was an expectation that in male and female cohabiting relationships, the primary responsibility for the economic upkeep of the family rested with the male, while women were to place domestic and family responsibilities first, although in many cases, still working outside of the home (Bailey, Branche, McGarritty, & Stuart, 1998).

Practical constraints

Familial responsibility as a practical constraint

Focal concerns theory posits that judges make their sentencing decisions based in part on a set of critical assessments of which practical constraints are a part. One important aspect of practical constraints, and the effects of these on court outcomes, relates to the manner in which the criminal justice system as a whole, is impacted by sentencing decisions. As stated earlier, judges take into consideration a range of organisational factors. These may include ensuring a regular flow of cases, being cognisant of issues of overcrowding and resources in state penal facilities, as well as ensuring the maintenance of productive relationships among prosecutors and defence attorneys (Daly, 1987; Dixon, 1995; Hartley, Maddan, & Spohn, 2007; Steffensmeier, 1980). However, also of critical importance are the consequences of these sentencing decisions at the micro level, with respect not only to the individual offenders, but also to their immediate and extended families, as well as to the wider community in which they exist. These are the possible social costs that result from the incarceration of offenders including special needs, health concerns, and disruption to the family unit, with children of particular concern.

Due to time constraints, judges develop what has been referred to as a *perceptual shorthand*, based on assumptions and stereotypes that they themselves apply to offenders (Hawkins, 1981). Such assumptions and stereotypes are linked to a variety of characteristics that may include race, age, economic status, and particularly relevant to the present study – that of gender. Steffensmeier (1980) argued that the responsibilities associated with being the primary caretaker of dependent children were of great importance to members of the judiciary. Participants in the present study were particularly vocal about the role that they believed they played in the protection of children. Mr Harris, a 42-year-old magistrate expanded:

> I feel that as an officer of the court, I have an obligation to protect children. Because there is a myth that we just lock up people, but there is wider responsibility. The child is really important. All the persons around the child that may have an impact, we have to address it. The consequences of hastily removing the parent from the home is that we will repeat the cycle of dysfunctional families. So if a chance can be given to the parent, we can ultimately impact the child in a positive way.

Daly's (1987) contention that among the judiciary, there is a reluctance to remove from the home, the person upon whom children most depend is of notable relevance here. Considering the large proportion of single-parent families in the Caribbean, judges consider the range of detrimental effects of parental incarceration. If no other parent is available, children may be placed under the care of neighbours, relatives, or in some cases, foster care (Raeder, 1993). The negative effects of this on the long- and short-term development of children are well established. Data has supported the link between parental incarceration and a host of behavioural and developmental consequences for children including depression, sleep disorders, as well as an increased likelihood of future criminal involvement and incarceration (Parke & Clarke-Stewart, 2001). While one magistrate believed that State mechanisms were such that there were enough safeguards to protect children if their primary provider was incarcerated, the possible detrimental effects were almost unanimously of concern to the magistrates interviewed.

Gendered assumptions of familial responsibility

There is little doubt that for the judiciary, the measurement of these utilitarian practical concerns, against those of the need for punishment and deterrence represents an arduous task. Such decisions are influenced heavily by personal biases, assumptions, and political beliefs. If it is generally accepted among magistrates however, that they have a responsibility for the protection of children, then it follows that gendered assumptions have the propensity to influence sentencing outcomes as they assign a particular level of perceived familial involvement to those that come before the court.

It was evident from the testimony of the participants that there were indeed gendered assumptions made relating to the nature of familial involvement of offenders. Following on from the socializing effects of the childhood experiences of the majority of the magistrates interviewed, there was the common belief that it was women who played the dominant role in the critical developmental stages of the lives of their children. Mr Richards, a 39-year-old magistrate described the prevailing assumption:

> women obviously are the ones that do most of the nurturing. So the mothers principally who appear before me, are really the ones running the households. In the case of the men, they are not the ones in the household a lot. Maybe they are the main source of finance, but that's about it.

In keeping with the findings of previous research (Barrow, 1986; Dann, 1987), it was the belief of the participants that within the typical Barbadian family, women cared for children, while men were either absent, or played a minimal role in their development. As a result, the presence of the mother was considered more important. Mr Edmond opined:

> I believe that children really need their mothers because in Barbados, to my mind, and maybe this is my own socialisation, the children gravitate towards the mother more so than men in our society.

Closely linked to the assumptions made regarding the differing roles played by men and women in the lives of their children therefore, were the beliefs about their respective motivations when they offend. Work in the area of shoplifting is instructive in demonstrating the contrasting manner in which the motivations of male and female perpetrators have been handled within the literature. Men are portrayed as being likely to steal items that are of no particular use to them since stealing is a manifestation of a desire to display masculinity (Steffensmeier & Allan, 1996). In an environment in which displays of machoism are glorified, crimes such as these have the effect of increasing critical masculine capital and garnering much coveted respect (Alder & Polk, 1996; Hochstetler & Copes, 2003; Katz, 1988; Messerschmidt, 1993; Mullins, 2006; Oliver, 1994). Crime, and in particular, street crime, is used by men in order to enhance their manhood on the streets.

By contrast, female shoplifters are depicted as passive actors who engage in crime due to psychiatric issues, or as a result of financial hardships faced by them and their families (Allen, 1987; Heidensohn, 1994). Bailey (2012) too, found this to be the dominant view among his sample of Barbadian shop owners. The narratives of the magistrates in the present study suggested the existence of similar assumptions. Magistrates were generally unsympathetic to the possible motives for male offending, while assuming a close association between female crime and their familial responsibilities. Mr Leacock, a 53-year-old magistrate explained:

> In Barbados, quite often, what I find disturbing is that for the most part when it comes to child rearing, you see females in the street . . . school time, shopping

> for children, in the church you see the mother, christening you see the mother. But you never ever see the father. And so it follows that most mules for example, from my experience are females. Swallowers who are promised a sum of money by a male who disappears after they are caught. So most of the time it is money. Trying to get them and their children out of their economic rut. Saying they are going to do it once, and then they get sucked in and do it more than once. Most of the time for the women it is out of need. For men it is more greed and ego. Who can manage the largest Cartel? Who can use brute force? Who can manipulate women to do their bidding?

The view was not unique among the participants. Mr Jennings too argued:

> The male offender is driven by a mixture of ego, driven by his desire not to be seen as weak by his peers, materialistic attainment. They are not generally driven by the more spiritual side of things. There are a lot of bravado and masculinity issues. Economic crimes are to keep up with what is seen in the movies and media. A heavy impact from America and a lesser impact from Jamaica. For female offenders they often don't know where the next meal is coming from and their children have needs.

The magistrates, based on their personal experiences and assumptions relating to the role of women in the typical Barbadian home, were assigning the responsibility of principal caregiver to female offenders, thus, making them indispensable to the family unit, and more importantly, to the lives of their children. Although recognizing that for them, the protection of children was of critical importance, and although admitting that the possibility existed that a male offender could be the main source of care, as Mr Edmond explained, magistrates found it difficult to believe this likely to be the case:

> It could move me if a man says he is sole provider, but not in the same way. And regardless he would have a lot to do to convince me. Just because of how society is today I am less likely to believe that a man is committing crime to take care of his family as sole provider. I have had instances in which they come saying that they are supporting children and when I ask them to bring the mother, the mother says that she is receiving no support.

Effect on court outcomes

In 1987, Federal Sentencing Guidelines were enacted in the United States, the aim of which was to ensure that all offenders that came before the court were afforded uniform punishment through the removal of avenues for disparate sentencing (USSC, 1987). The Sentencing Commission determined that characteristics such as race, nationality, religion, class, and gender should be irrelevant to the potential severity of punishment. As such, it was mandated that judges follow a prescribed model, by which offenders were sentenced using a baseline that corresponded with a particular crime (Berberian, 1999). Judges were allowed to use their discretion only to a limited degree.

By contrast, the Barbados Penal System Reform (Amendment) Act, passed in 2014, while recognizing the need for consistency in sentencing, encouraged a greater consideration of the mitigating factors that may have caused offenders to engage in criminality. The Act applies specifically to those offences for which sentencing by judges is discretionary in nature (Penal System Reform Act, 2014). The Act was designed to persuade judges to utilise where applicable, the range of alternatives to imprisonment that are available to them. By encouraging a greater consideration of mitigating factors however, rather than enforcing a uniform set of guidelines for punishment with limited room for discretion as with the US Federal Sentencing Guidelines, the Act has increased the scope for individual biases and assumptions to affect sentencing outcomes.

It is apparent, that with little exception, such individual biases and assumptions have a significant gendered effect. If the protection of children is a priority for decision makers, then one would expect that both men and women without children would be afforded limited leniency. Indeed, there was the common assertion among participants, that this was in fact the case. Ms Anderson for example argued that non-familied women were treated in the same way as non-familied men in her courtroom:

> If my issue is with who is taking care of children, then I have to treat men and women who do not have children the same. How in that situation could I justify giving a woman a slap on the wrist, if I treat a man in the same situation differently?

More importantly, one would assume that if judges view it as detrimental to remove familied women from the home, the same would be true for familied men. Generally, magistrates articulated the propensity for favourable treatment, where possible to be afforded to those with sole responsibility for childcare. If evidence could be supplied that showed this to be the case for a male offender, most participants claimed a willingness to take this into consideration. Mr Leacock's stance for example was typical:

> If they can prove sole care, maybe through the pre-sentencing report, that would give me the information necessary. If you find that the report is pointing in that direction, then you would factor in all of those factors. Depending on what the offence is, what can be done. For example, a community based sentence, or a bond. One last chance to pull their life around. You could afford that to him.

The gendered nature of familial paternalism in this context however, as a result of pre-existing beliefs about familial responsibilities, meant that the burden of proof for male offenders to show sole responsibility was much greater than that of their female counterparts. Consequently, favourable treatment appeared to be primarily applied to mothers as opposed to fathers. Daly (1987) found that in reality, the equal treatment of familied men and women is rarely demonstrated in court outcomes. She concluded therefore, that gender differentiation was the result of the assumption that the social costs of removing mothers from the home were greater than those of removing fathers. Magistrates in the present study were almost unanimously aware of the manner in which their individual perceptions affected sentencing decisions. Mr Edmond explained:

> It would be dishonest for me to say that my personal opinions don't affect my decisions. Sometimes you have an offender who is pleading guilty. I dig down to find out whether or not they have children, knowing that in single parent families, if you put away the mother it will be very, very difficult for the children . . . So you have two people charged for the same crime – a woman with children and a man with children. The mother tends to get a little lighter sentence. It's a sort of a little bias that comes out.

Similarly, 40-year-old magistrate, Mr Brathwaite echoed similar sentiments:

> There's a high price for incarcerating mothers. I know that. A higher cost than incarcerating men. You would hardly find the type of caring gentleman involved with a female that goes to prison. Hence he is not the person to step up to the plate when she goes to prison. You would find it the other way around though. Where a woman would take care of children when the man is in prison. But when she is gone, children are left in the man's charge, and most time he is irresponsible. Many times they are left with a grandmother or aunt. The man doesn't assist in the real child rearing and instilling values. That plays a part in my decisions.

Discussion

The results of this study cannot be interpreted to be representative of the views of all judicial decision makers in Barbados – nor was this the aim. The research was limited to a sample of magistrates that typically adjudicate on matters that include the crimes of shoplifting and various drug offences. The purpose of the study was to build on the dearth of literature on the intersection between offender gender and sentencing outcomes in the Caribbean through an exploration into a subset of magistrate perceptions. It is important to note here too, that although not the foci of the current paper, a number of other variables were identified by participants as being integral to the decision-making process. Indeed, factors such as remorse, repeat offending, and the seriousness of the crime were all identified by magistrates as playing critical roles in determining the nature of punishment. These factors too, can be analysed against the theoretical background of the focal concerns theory (i.e. remorse, repeat offending; blameworthiness; seriousness of crime; dangerousness). The preceding testimonies however, represent a valuable contribution specifically to the role of familial responsibilities as a practical constraint. This represents an important area of scholarship that has been relatively ignored within the West Indian context.

The findings are consistent with the theoretical perspectives supporting focal concerns that suggest that as a practical concern, magistrates consider the social costs associated with the incarceration of offenders. Of primary importance among these social costs appears to be the protection of children. Thus, the evidence suggests that against the background of pre-existing notions of male and female familial roles, women benefit disproportionately from perceptions held by magistrates, relating to the role that they play in their children's lives. As stated earlier, the magistrates interviewed were products of traditionally patriarchal Caribbean societies, in which women's presumed primary role was that of caregiver, while men were responsible for the financial upkeep of the home.

Lewis (2007) argued however, that the notion of the male as the sole breadwinner today exists to a large extent only in the form of ideology. In reality, the concept of the male breadwinner has been under threat for some time as global forces have rendered the Caribbean male in crisis, leading to the dislocation of traditional gender roles. While fathers continue to be absent from the day to day running of many Caribbean households, mothers have been left to be the main sources of all aspects of support for children (Blank, 2013). Despite cultural norms enforcing patriarchy and male authority, Safa (2002) argued that even when present, Caribbean male household authority was limited to an earning capacity that is increasingly threatened by female financial participation. Momsen (1993) saw this conflation of female domestic responsibilities with an increased economic burden in the Caribbean as evidence of an ideological unity of patriarchy existing side by side with a growing tradition of female economic autonomy. Ironically therefore, although the father's primary role is still believed to be that of provider, in privileging the presence of mothers, magistrates were demonstrating the perception that Caribbean women today play the critical role in both the emotional and financial aspects of their children's lives.

Overall, the evidence demonstrates an intrinsic link in the Barbadian context between practical constraints relating to the protection of children, and the concept of familial paternalism. Although paternalism has often been identified as being responsible for the lenient treatment of women, it is important to make the distinction between familial paternalism and the concept of chivalry, which assumes that women need to be protected as they occupy a position of social, physical, and legal weakness when compared to men. The application of chivalry here would indeed erroneously place the focus on the protection of women. Similarly, it is important to note also that although marriage is a part of the concept of familial paternalism, which views the institution as part of one's family responsibility, the fact that no magistrate made mention of marriage suggests that it was not a practical constraint that had any substantial effect on leniency within this context.

In reality, the testimony of the magistrates indicates that of paramount concern is the protection of children. The fact that mothers appear to benefit disproportionately from the associated leniency does not negate this conclusion, but rather illustrates the shared assumption among magistrates, that to this end, mothers are the ones whose presence is most critical.

Implications

The findings raise important questions as to the responsibility of the courts for the consideration of social costs such as the protection of children, and the manner in which these are balanced against fairness, and the need for uniformity in sentencing. While many criminologists find the consideration of the effects of sentencing on children a necessity, there are those that argue that these extra-legal concerns cannot outweigh the need for punishment and deterrence. Nagel and Johnson (1994) for example, in defence of the US Sentencing Guidelines, suggested that culpability and crime control must be the foremost considerations where sentencing is concerned, rather than exogenous factors such as the effect on children. It should be noted here as well that such considerations are based on the possibly erroneous assumption that in some instances, children may, in reality, not be better off without a parent that is in conflict with the law.

There is no doubt that in Caribbean societies in which spiralling levels of crime are cause for increasing concern, the need for deterrence must not be understated. There is however enough evidence that points to the deleterious effects of parental incarceration, and particularly that of the mother, on children, to necessitate its serious consideration. The aim here is not to advocate for the disproportionately lenient treatment of all mothers when they come before the courts. However, the attempt to achieve uniformity in sentencing when children are involved, either suggests that such considerations are unimportant, or presupposes a Caribbean reality in which men and women generally play equal roles in their children's lives. The participants in the present study generally appear to reject the need for uniformity, and instead are choosing to apply the discretion allowed for by the Penal System Reform Act to balance the need for punishment with that of the protection of future generations.

References

Albonetti, C. (1991). An integration of theories to explain judicial discretion. *Social Problems, 38*(2), 247–266.

Albonetti, C. (1997). Sentencing under the federal sentencing guidelines: Effects of defendant characteristics, guilty pleas, and departures on sentence outcomes for drug offenders, 1991–1992. *Law and Society Review, 31*(4), 789–822.

Alder, C., & Polk, K. (1996). Masculinity and child homicide. *British Journal of Criminology, 36*(3), 396–411.

Allen, H. (1987). *Justice unbalanced gender, psychiatry and judicial decisions*. Milton Keynes: Open University.

Bailey, C. (2012). Familial paternalism examined: The case of shoplifting in Barbados. *Social and Economic Studies, 61*(2), 73–98.

Bailey, W., Branche, C., McGarritty, S., & Stuart, S. (1998). *Family and the quality of gender relations in the Caribbean*. Jamaica: Institute of Social and Economic Studies.

Barrow, C. (1986). Male images of women in Barbados. *Social and Economic Studies, 35*(3), 51–64.

Berberian, S. (1999). Protecting children: Explaining disparities in the female offender's pretrial process, and policy issues surrounding lenient treatment of mothers. *Hastings Women's Law Journal, 10*(2), 369–407.

Bickle, G., & Peterson, R. (1991). The impact of gender-based family roles on criminal sentencing. *Social Problems, 38*(3), 372–394.

Blank, S. (2013). An historical and contemporary overview of gendered Caribbean relations. *Journal of Arts and Humanities, 2*(4), 1–10.

Boritch, H. (1992). Gender and criminal court outcomes: An historical analysis. *Criminology, 30*(3), 293–325.

Chesney-Lind, M. (1977). Judicial paternalism and the female status offender. *Crime and Delinquency, 23*(2), 121–131.

Chesney-Lind, M., & Shelden, R. (2004). *Girls, delinquecy, and juvenile justice*. Pacific Grove, CA: Brooks/Cole.

Chevannes, B. (2001). *Learning to be a man: Culture, socialisation and gender identity in five Caribbean communities*. Jamaica: The University of the West Indies Press.

Curry, T., Lee, G., & Rodriguez, S. (2004). Does victim gender increase sentence severity? Further explorations of gender dynamics and sentencing outcomes. *Crime and Delinquency, 50*(3), 319–343.

Daly, K. (1987). Structure and practice of familial-based justice in a criminal court. *Law and Society Review, 21*(2), 267–290.

Dann, G. (1987). *The Barbadian male: Sexual attitudes and practices*. London: Macmillan.

Dixon, J. (1995). The organisation context of criminal sentencing. *American Journal of Sociology, 100*(5), 1157–1198.

Engen, R., Gainey, R., Critchfield, R., & Weis, J. (2003). Discretion and disparity under sentencing guidelines: The role of departures and structured sentencing alternatives. *Criminology, 41*(1), 99–130.

Freiburger, T. (2010). The effects of gender, family status, and race on sentencing decisions. *Behaviour Sciences and Law, 28*(3), 378–395.

Green, E. (1961). Judicial Attitudes in Sentencing. London: Macmillan

Griffin, T., & Woolridge, J. (2006). Sex-based disparities in felony dispositions before versus after sentencing reform in Ohio. *Criminology, 44*(4), 893–923.

Hartley, R., Maddan, S., & Spohn, C. (2007). Concerning conceptualisation and operationalisation: Sentencing data and the focal concerns perspective: A research note. *Southwest Journal of Criminal Justice, 4*(1), 58–78.

Hawkins, D. (1981). Causal attribution and punishment for crime. *Deviant Behaviour, 2*(3), 207–230.

Heidensohn, F. (1994). Gender and crime. In R. Maguire, R. Morgan, & R. Reiner (Eds.), *The Oxford handbook of criminology* (pp. 336–369). Oxford: Clarendon Press.

Hochstetler, A., & Copes, H. (2003). Situational construction of masculinity among male street thieves. *Journal of Contemporary Ethnography, 32*(3), 279–304.

Jeffries, S., Fletcher, G., & Newbold, G. (2003). Pathways to sex-based differentiation in criminal court sentencing. *Criminology, 41*(2), 329–353.

Katz, J. (1988). *Seductions of crime: Moral and sensual attractions of doing evil*. New York: Basic Books.

Kautt, O., & Spohn, C. (2002). Cracking down on black drug offenders? Testing for interactions between offender race, drug type, and sentencing strategy in federal drug sentences. *Justice Quarterly, 19*, 1–35

Koons-Witt, B. (2002). The effect of gender on the decision to incarcerate before and after the introduction of sentencing guidelines. *Criminology*, *40*(2), 297–328.

Kruttschnitt, C. (1982). Women, crime, and delinquency: An application of the theory of law. *Criminology*, *19*(4), 495–513.

Lewis, L. (2007). Man talk, masculinity, and a changing social environment. *Caribbean Review of Gender Studies*, *1*, 1–20.

Martin, R. (1934). The defendant and criminal justice. Study 9, Bulletin 3437. Austin, Texas: University of Texas Bureau of Research in the Social Sceinces.

Messerschmidt, J.W. (1993). *Maculinities and crime: Critique and reconceptualisation of theory*. Lanham: Rowan and Little Field.

Momsen, J. (Ed.). (1993). *Women and change in the Caribbean: A pan-Caribbean perspective*. Bloomington, IN: Indiana University Press.

Momsen, J. (2002). The double paradox. In P. Mohammed (Ed.), *Gendered realities: Essays in Caribbean feminist thought* (pp. 44–55). Centre for Gender and Development: The University of the West Indies Press.

Moulds, E. (1980). Chivalry and paternalism: Disparities of treatment in the criminal justice system. In S. Datesman, & F. Scarpitti (Eds.), *Women, crime, and justice* (pp. 277–299). New York: Oxford University.

Mullins, C. (2006). *Holding your square: Masculinities, streetlife and violence*. Cullompton, England: Willan.

Mustard, D. (2001). Racial, ethnic and gender disparities in sentencing: Evidence from the U.S. Federal Courts. *Journal of Law and Economics*, *44*(1), 285–314.

Nagel, L., & Johnson, B. (1994). The role of gender in a structured sentencing system: Equal treatment, policy choices, and the sentencing of female offenders under the United States sentencing guidelines. *Journal of Criminal Law and Criminology*, *85*(1), 181–221.

Nagel, L., & Weitzman. L. (1971). Women as Litigants. Hastings Law Journal, 23, 171–198

Oliver, M. (1994). *The violent social world of the black male*. New York: Lexington Books.

Parke, R., & Clarke-Stewart, K. (2001). *Effects of parental incarceration on young children*. Presented at the National Policy Conference. Washington DC.

Pollack, O. (1950). *The criminality of women*. Philadelphia: University of Pennsylvania Press.

Raeder, M. (1993). Gender and sentencing: Single moms, battered women, and other sex-based anomalies in the gender-free world of the federal sentencing guidelines. *Pepperdine Law Review*, *20*(3), 905–990.

Rodriguez, S., Curry, T., & Lee, G. (2006). Gender differences in criminal sentencing: Do effects vary across violent, property, and drug offenses? *Social Science Quarterly*, *87*(2), 318–339.

Safa, H. (1995). *The myth of the male breadwinner: Women and industrialization in the Caribbean*. Colorado: Westview Press.

Safa, H. (2002). Questioning globalisation: Gender and export processing in the dominican republic. *Journal of Developing Studies*, *18*(2–3), 11–31.

Senior, O. (1991). *Working miracles: Women's lives in the English-speaking Caribbean*. London, England: James Currey and Bloomington/Indiana University Press.

Sills, D. (1968). International Encyclopedia of the Social Sciences. New York: Macmillan

Sobo, E. (1993). *One blood: The Jamaican body*. Albany, New York: State University of New York Press.

Spohn, C. (1999). Gender and sentencing of drug offenders: Is chivalry dead? *Criminal Justice Policy Review*, *9*(3–4), 365–399.

Spohn, C., & Beichner, D. (2000). Is preferential treatment of female offenders a thing of the past? A multisite study of gender, race and imprisonment. *Criminal Justice Policy Review*, *11*(2), 149–184.

Stacy, A., & Spohn, C. (2006) Gender and the social costs of sentencing: an analysis of sentences imposed on male and female offenders in three U.S. District Courts. *Berkeley Journal of Criminal Law*, *11*, 43–75.

Steffensmeier, D. (1980). Assessing the impact of the women's movement on sex-basd differences in the handling of adult criminal defendants. *Crime and Delinquency*, *26*(3), 344–356.

Steffensmeier, D., & Allan, E. (1996). Gender and crime: Towards a gendered theory of female offending. *Annual Review of Sociology*, *22*(1), 459–487.

Steffensmeier, D., Kramer, J., & Streifel, C. (1993). Gender and imprisonment decisions. *Criminology*, *31*(3), 411–446.

Steffensmeier, D., Kramer, J., & Ulmer, J. (1995). Age differences in sentencing. *Criminal Justice Quarterly*, *12*(3), 701–719.

Steffensmeier, D., Kramer, J., & Ulmer, J. (1998). The interaction of race, gender, and age in criminal sentencing: The punishment cost of being young, black and male. *Criminology*, *36*(4), 763–797.

UNICEF. (2002). *THe OECS family law and domestic violence legal and judicial reform project. Children in focus 15 (2)*. Bridgetown, Barbados: UNICEF Office for Barbados and the Eastern Caribbean.

USSC. (1987). *United States sentencing commission guidelines manual*. Washington, DC: United States Sentencing Commission.

Williams, M. (1999). Gender and sentencing: An analysis of indicators. *Criminal Justice Policy Review*, *10*(4), 471–490.

14 Intellectual disability among male prisoners in Bonaire

Translating and validating psychological and intellectual diagnostic tools in the local Creole language

Micha van de Vorst

Introduction

Intellectual impairment is very prevalent among criminal offenders; approximately 7 to 10 per cent of the prison population worldwide suffer from intellectual disabilities (Hellenbach, Karatzias, & Brown, 2017). People with an intellectual disability are more likely to violently and sexually offend than those without intellectual disabilities (Fogden, Stuart, & Daffern, 2016). The prevalence of intellectual disabilities is especially high in Dutch Caribbean Papiamento-speaking suspects (Vinkers, Heijtel, Matroos, Hermans, & Hoek, 2010b; Vinkers, 2011). The prevalence of intellectual impairment among this population is 22.4 per cent of the psychiatrically assessed suspects in the Netherlands and 15.1 per cent in Curacao (Vinkers, Barendregt, Beurs, Hoek, & Rinne, 2010a), although reasons why remain unclear. However, the lack of the ability to adapt, which is necessary to diagnose intellectual disabilities, does not seem to be the reason (Koster van Groos, 2001). A common problem on the Dutch Caribbean islands is undereducation, related to truancy and leaving school (Boonmann, Vinkers, & Doreleijers, 2012; Van Hulst & Bos, 1993). For example, the dropout rate in 2011 of students 10 to 14 years old was 25.3 per cent (Centraal Bureau voor de Statistiek, 2014). Also, Dutch – the language used to assess Dutch Caribbean suspects in the Netherlands – is in many cases not the native language of Dutch Caribbean suspects, which may influence the result of their IQ test (Stuurman et al., 2008; Luteijn & Barelds, 2004; Bochhah, Kort, Seddik, & Vijver, 2001; Hofstee, 1990). Cultural differences, the degree of acculturation, and the amount of time spent in the Netherlands (Bleichrodt & Vijver, 2001) should also be considered when interpreting test results of Dutch Caribbean nationals in the Netherlands. In fact, the prevalence of intellectual disabilities among Dutch Caribbean suspects in the Netherlands varied between 19.6 and 47.7 per cent, depending on the intellectual diagnostic tool used (Vinkers, 2011). The prevalence of intellectual disabilities among Dutch Caribbean Papiamento-speaking suspects both across the Dutch Caribbean as in the Netherlands, and the fact that they are over-represented as crime suspects compared to other ethnic groups living in the Netherlands (see Table 14.1) (Blom, Oudhof, Bijl, & Bakker, 2005), stresses the need for translated

Table 14.1 Number of suspects and origin in the Netherlands

Origin	*Dutch native*			*Morocco*			*Former Dutch Antilles and Aruba*			*Suriname*			*Turkey*		
Year	2013	2014	2015	2013	2014	2015	2013	2014	2015	2013	2014	2015	2013	2014	2015
N	110	101	92	591	560	499	677	638	565	450	421	383	350	319	286

Note: Source Centraal Bureau voor de Statistiek, 2015b; *N* = Number of registered suspects per 10,000 inhabitants

and validated psychological and intellectual diagnostic tools for this specific group of offenders and suspects.

At the time of writing this chapter, only one effort has been made to study the possibility of translating and validating psychological and intellectual tools for the Papiamento language (Vorst, Vinkers, Matroos, Hoek, & Heijtel, 2015). The study was conducted in the local prison on the island of Bonaire. Currently, there are no other psychological or intellectual diagnostic tools translated and validated for the Papiamento-speaking to be found. Clinicians working on Aruba, Bonaire, and Curacao tend to use psychological and diagnostic tools which are widely used in countries like the United States or the Netherlands. The diagnostic tools available in Papiamento are often translated by a Papiamento-speaking clinician, who wants to use the tool in his practice. For some assessments, multiple translations made by separate clinicians of the same diagnostic tool circulate, resulting in different, non-validated translations. Due to the lack of local norm tables, it is common work practice to calculate scores based on Dutch or American norm tables. Although there is consensus among local clinicians about, for example, illiteracy, truancy, or neglect being the cause for low scores on diagnostic tools assessing intelligence, the actual incidence and prevalence of intellectual disabilities among the Papiamento-speaking general population across the Dutch Caribbean and the Netherlands has never been reported.

This lack of measures for the Papiamento-speaking population might negatively impact diagnostic reliability. There are two risks: (a) deciding a male suspect is not intellectually disabled when he is, or in contrast, (b) misdiagnosing a male suspect with an intellectual disorder when he does not in fact have one (Chafetz, 2011). Both diagnostic failures can be relevant for the level of accountability determined in psychological pre-trial assessments. Also, suspects with intellectual disability are prone to have comorbid mental health issues like personality and conduct disorders and anxiety (Hellenbach et al., 2017; Kendall & Owen, 2015).

Translating and validating psychological and intellectual diagnostic tools for the Papiamento language, which is mainly spoken as opposed to written, is challenging, especially when the aim is to use these tools in the local prisons. The current chapter aims to discuss this challenge as pertaining to the Dutch Caribbean specifically. However, this challenge is not endemic to the Dutch part of the Caribbean as many creole languages are spoken in the Caribbean, such as Haitian Creole and Jamaican Patois. Even outside the Caribbean, comparable challenges concerning languages occur, including Warlpiri and Tiwi spoken by Aboriginals in Australia (Dingwall, Pinkerton, & Lindeman, 2013), for example. Recommendations are made in this paper concerning spelling, choosing an adequate diagnostic tool for translation based on requirements in the forensic field, and common local psychological patterns to consider. The recommendations are based on research in the prison of Bonaire, a review of literature concerning cultural translations, and the historical development of the Papiamento language. Three descriptions of real cases are added to the chapter to give the reader insight into challenges court reporters working with Papiamento-speaking suspects are confronted with (see Box 14.1).

Box 14.1 Case examples

Case A – High functioning and illiterate

Mr K was a 30-year-old male, suspected of stabbing a man with a knife multiple times. The victim had to be hospitalised. Mr K was a first-time offender and had never been in contact with the justice system. He never had treatment for mental health problems. Due to the seriousness of the accusations, a psychiatric and psychologic evaluation was ordered by the prosecutor. Mr K explained to the psychologist that the victim, known as a troublemaker in the community, had been harassing him for a long time. The victim sabotaged his car by pouring sugar in his fuel tank and stabbing the tires, threatened Mr K and his girlfriend, and would follow him to his job. Mr K had filed a complaint at the police station twice, but without any result. He took precautions against a possible confrontation. He bought a fuel cap with a lock, took alternate routes to work and would leave work through the backdoor. Mr K works as a chef in a hotel and is known by his co-workers as a friendly and hardworking man.

Before he was administered, he explained that he finished elementary school, finished various courses successfully, and started working as a cook at the age of eighteen. Mr K warned the psychologist he does not like personality tests and would prefer not to take one. He gave a nervous impression during the assessment of his intelligence and was not capable to follow simple instructions. The test had to be stopped before completion. Mr K was asked to read an article of the newspaper and then admitted he could not read or write. He explained that he had been hiding his illiteracy and became a chef by learning to recognise the written orders so he would know what to cook. He learned cooking by memorizing recipes from looking at other cooks. He explained that hiding his illiteracy had been stressful. When the victim started harassing him, the tension became too much. The day the victim confronted Mr K with a knife after he left his job through the backdoor of the hotel, Mr K felt desperate. He managed to take over the knife and stabbed the victim until he backed off. Both the psychiatrist and the psychologist found Mr K less accountable for his act and assessed the risk of recidivism low. They stated that Mr K did as much as he could within his limits to avoid a confrontation. When a confrontation occurred, he panicked and lost self-control. No cognitive impairment was determined, due to the fact that there were no signs of functional impairment.

Case B – Social system concealing pathology

Mr L was a 20-year-old, accused of stabbing a near 30-year-old man, while being under the influence of alcohol. He had never been in prison before. Although several witnesses testified against him, Mr L denied the accusations and told the police that the victim fell on broken glass. Mr L was sent to the Department of Young Adults where he was observed. Mr L was impressed by the whole situation, but not in an emotional way. He was rather captivated, like a child can be when seeing an airplane for the first time. He was cooperative and polite, but did not connect well with the other prisoners at the department. His behaviour at the department was described as somewhat childish. An early intervention report from a probation officer stated that Mr L, after attending regular primary school, was sent to a special education school because he could not keep up with the pace at school. After primary school, he showed interest in becoming an electrician. At the time of his detention, he had been working as an assistant electrician; his employer was satisfied with his work. His employer was willing to pay school for Mr L so he could earn a degree. Mr L. had a girlfriend for a year and played on a soccer team in his free time.

He had never received treatment from a psychologist or a psychiatrist. Due to the seriousness of the accusations, a psychiatric and psychologic evaluation had been ordered by the prosecutor. When a personality test was administered, problems with reading were observed. When reading words with more than two syllables, he created non-existent words and did not seem to comprehend what he was reading. Surprisingly, Mr. L scored 93 on the IQ test, which is an average score and higher than expected based on his reading skills. The results on the IQ subtests, however, were inconsistent. He scored above average at the performance tasks and below average at the verbal tasks. When his mother was interviewed, she explained that there were complications at birth. Mr L had to stay in an incubator for several months. According to his mother, Mr L was slower in his development than his brother. Getting insight into his emotions and thoughts had always been difficult. He never had friends, not even on the soccer team. His brother helped him to get his first few jobs. His current employer happened to be his uncle, the brother of his mother. His social system seemed to be very supportive and made it possible for Mr L to participate in the community. He was diagnosed with an autism spectrum disorder, which also explained the inconsistencies in the IQ test results.

Case C – Personality traits related to low IQ

Mr M was a 40-year-old male, who had repeatedly been arrested for different felonies. Throughout his criminal history, he had never been a prime suspect, yet he would always end up getting long imprisonments. He had a history of substance abuse, but quit using hard drugs almost three years ago. The last time he had been discharged from prison was three years ago. Mr M was a short, but athletic man. In prison, he was known to have aggressive outbursts, followed by him crying and hugging the prison workers he had been aggressive toward. His mood highly depended on the ambiance in the department. He was easily influenced and copied behaviour from other prisoners. He was vulnerable to psychopathic prisoners looking for "soldiers". This time, Mr M. was accused of mistreating the mother of his children and threatening her with a knife. A psychological and psychiatric evaluation was ordered by the prosecutor. He had never been evaluated before. During the evaluation, he frequently numerated everything he had done for the victim and blamed the victim for being in prison. He explained, proudly, how he managed to have a stable family life by raising his children, working every day, and being drug-free for almost three years. He also explained that, a couple of months before he was arrested, the victim suggested to separate. The victim explained that Mr M. tended to get bossy at home. Mr M became homeless and slept elsewhere every day. He kept working and would give the victim the money he earned to support his children. He did not relapse into substance abuse. An intelligence test was administered and he scored an IQ of 76. Hypervigilant narcissistic traits (compensatory narcissistic traits) were found in his personality, meaning he had the tendency to mask his shortcomings by using a rather positive self-presentation. If experiencing pressure, he only had anger and aggressiveness as coping strategies. Mr M stayed for a couple of weeks in a special care department, where he developed himself as a model-prisoner. Both the psychiatrist and the psychologist found Mr M less accountable for his actions, due to his low IQ and the amount of stress he had been experiencing. The reports stated that his low IQ, in combination with poor coping skills, increased the risk of recidivism if Mr M would not receive any guidance.

Why diagnostic tools for the Papiamento language do not exist

Development of the Papiamento language and post-colonial influences

Reviewing the different theories about its origin and post-colonial influences might answer the question. The origin of Papiamento and its development was comprehensively studied and described by Jacobs in his dissertation (2012a). Aruba, Bonaire, and Curacao were discovered in 1499 by the Spanish (Dalhuisen, 2009). It was not until 1634, when The Dutch West Indian Company claimed Curacao, that Curacao became a centre for slave trade. It is believed that during this period, when slaves of differing ethnicity met, the Papiamento language emerged on the island (Jacobs, 2009b). There is an ongoing discussion about whether Papiamento is a Spanish-based creole language or a Portuguese-based language, influenced by Spanish. The fact that Papiamento is spoken in a Spanish-speaking region, contributes to the theory that the origin of Papiamento is to be found in the Spanish language. However, through Dutch colonisation, Peter Stuyvesant brought many Portuguese-speaking slaves from the ex-Dutch Brazilian colonies (Jacobs, 2009a). Therefore, the development of Papiamento might have been highly influenced by the Portuguese language. The most recent point of view on the development of Papiamento is built on an earlier study by Quint (2000). Papiamento seems to be "genetically" related to the Portuguese-based creole varieties of upper Guinea, spoken on the Cape Verde Islands, in Guinea-Bissau, and Casamance. Between 1650 and 1680, slave trade between Curacao and those regions was at its peak (Jacobs, 2012a). Nowadays, Papiamento is developing increasingly in the direction of the socially dominant European languages such as Spanish and, to a lesser extent, Dutch. Thus, Papiamento is losing much of its original Portuguese influence (Jacobs, 2016).

Papiamento seems to differ between generations. This is probably related to the different roles Papiamento has played in politics and the education system. Until the mid-1980s, Papiamento was not supposed to be spoken in schools and it was not acceptable to speak Papiamento in the local parliament (Fouse, 2002). A riot on May 30, 1969, when the Papiamento-speaking "Children of the Island" protested the influence of the Netherlands and the influence of the white European working class on local politics, resulted in an increased use of Papiamento (Eckkrammer, 2007). In the past, the Curacaoan education system was more influenced by the Dutch language compared to nowadays. In the early nineteenth century for example, the teachers of the Catholic schools on Curacao were Dutch-speaking friars from Tilburg (Robben, 2006). Since 2004, Papiamento has become an accepted language in primary schools (Eckkrammer, 2007). On October 10, 2010, Bonaire, Saba, and St Eustatius became special municipalities of the Netherlands, which for these islands meant an increased Dutch influence, also regarding local schools and educational policies. From this moment onwards, schools had to meet the Dutch educational standards, which meant some schools were forced to close after inspection, while other schools had to reorganise.

The status of Papiamento in the post-colonial era

Compared to other creole languages, Papiamento does not have an "endangered" status. This is even more remarkable considering the fact that inhabitants of Aruba, Bonaire, and Curacao speak four languages (Papiamento, Dutch, Spanish, and English). A reason for its vitality might be that in the eighteenth century, the elite on Curacao were not only comprised of the Dutch, but also of a group of Spanish- and Portuguese-speaking Sephardic Jews. Papiamento made communication possible among the elite, consequently spreading the language among the white elite as well (Jacobs & Van der Wal, 2015). Another reason is that a relatively big group of slaves, who had Papiamento as its first language, was freed and formed an important socioeconomic group in the early eighteenth century (Jacobs, 2012b). Furthermore, Jacobs (2016) has stated that the strength of Papiamento seems to correlate with the socio-historical fact that the language served as a marker of group identity of the original slave population – with predominantly African, but also Amerindian roots – opposing the Dutch colonial masters (Jacobs, 2016).

In case of the southern Dutch Caribbean islands, Papiamento is still the most spoken language (Centraal Bureau voor de Statistiek, 2014; Coomans-Eustatia, 2015). However, it should not be forgotten that Curacao's official language, until 2007, was Dutch (Koninkrijksdeel Curaçao, 2007), before it was agreed to also include Papiamento and English as official languages. Furthermore, it was not until 2008 that the government of Curacao agreed to a law concerning spelling guidelines for Papiamento (Nederlandse Antillen, 2015). Although the guidelines exist, in practice it is not uncommon that newspapers continue to use different spelling. The fact that (a) Papiamento only recently became fully accepted as a language, (b) variations in spelling used in daily life continue to exist, and (c) Papiamento only recently became compulsory at local schools, might answer the question why an effort to use the language in psychological and intellectual diagnostic tools has never been made.

Challenges and suggestions for translation and validation of psychological and intellectual diagnostic tools for small forensic populations

As mentioned earlier, translating and validating psychological and intellectual tools in small communities and adapting them to forensic requirements can be challenging. Knowledge on how to start, and what to consider when doing research in small (Caribbean) communities is required. The following paragraphs aim to contribute to this knowledge.

Guidelines for cross-cultural translation and validation

Several guidelines for conducting a cross-cultural translation and validation have been published. In 1993, Guillemin, Bombardier, and Beaton (1993) proposed guidelines for cross-cultural adaptation in order to adapt health-related, quality-of-life, which included the following five steps: (1) translations and (2) back translations by qualified people, (3) committee review of the translations, (4) pre-testing for equivalence, and (5) re-examination of the score weighting. While the authors advised the back translators to, preferably, not be aware of the intent or concepts of the material to prevent bias, no requirements for the translators of the first translation were mentioned. The committee reviewing the translation should be multidisciplinary: experts in the disease, in intent and in concepts to be explored, and bilingual members. For pre-testing two techniques were proposed: a probe technique and appraisal by bilingual individuals. Using the probe technique, participants are asked to explain their answers to the translated questions. Administering the translated measure to a group of bilingual individuals to detect possible discrepancies, after which asking them to rate the equivalence of each item was proposed as an alternative. In addition, the authors made a remark on assessing bilingual immigrants; they advised letting the participant express his preference for the assessment language. As an alternative, a dual-format measure in two languages was suggested. For the re-examination of the weighting scores, consideration for adapting the weights of scores to the cultural context was also advised.

Beaton, Bombardier, Guillemin, and Ferraz (2000) published an adaptation of these guidelines, including a description of more specific requirements concerning the translators. During the first translation into the target language, the use of one *informed* and one *uninformed* translator was advised. An informed translator is described as being aware of the concepts being translated, whereas an uninformed translator is not aware of the underlying concepts. During the second stage, a merge of the two translations occurs. The back-translation process remained unchanged; however, two separate translations were advised. Methodologists, developers, language professionals, and translators were added to the expert committee in step four. This committee was in charge of evaluating the written reports drafted after completion of each stage and creating the pre-final version of the translation. In step five, a population of 30 to 40 was to test the translated questionnaire. In this step, the probe technique, to check for comprehension of the questions, was recommended. During step six, authors proposed for the translation process and the written report to be reviewed, in order to make sure all the steps were followed.

In 2013, Ziegler and Bensch (2013) wanted to raise awareness of problems regarding validation efforts. They stated that as new traits and constructs are suggested, the demand of questionnaires increases. According to the authors, a fair amount of studies relies on factorial validity, neglecting construct validity-related evidence. Three aspects to be followed were recommended: (a) the trait being measured should be clearly defined and embedded within a nomological network, (b) besides convergent validity, discriminant validity is important, in order to gain a complete picture of the validity of an instrument, and (c) effects of method variance should be modelled.

In 2015, Epstein, Santo, and Guillemin (2015) aimed to review the best cross-cultural adaptation methods. They found no evidence for a best method. The majority of the methods used back translations, a variety of expert committees, and focus groups. Clues were found indicating that back translation might not be necessary. The use of a certain method seemed to be a matter of preference or logistics. Although guidelines for cross-cultural translations are not set in stone, the method proposed by Beaton and colleagues (2000) seems to be standing the test of time. Small changes might be necessary to fit local needs. For example, removing back translation from the process will save translation fees. Reviewing the guidelines for cross-cultural translation, no study was found concerning languages which are mainly spoken.

Spelling

The official orthography of Papiamento is a phonemic orthography, meaning that Papiamento is written the way it is spoken. In practice, it means that a lot of accents are used, making it hard to read. Frequent observations made while administering intellectual diagnostic tools in Papiamento included participants (i.e. prisoners with and without intellectual disabilities) reading the questions out loud themselves to understand them better. A recommended way to overcome this challenge is to value the aim of the diagnostic tool above the use of correct orthography. The final translation of the Groninger Intelligence Test 2 (Luteijn & Barelds, 2004) and the Barkley Functional Impairment Scale (Barkley, 2011) into Papiamento, for example, were largely based on the official orthography but changes to the spelling were made to make the questions easier to read (Vorst et al., 2015). It is important that participants understand what they read. If written language is not possible, an alternative would be letting a computer voice, using text-to-speech (TTS), read the written material. Promising efforts have been made to make speech synthesis more natural (Trilla, 2009). In some studies, the use of TTS is studied for treatment or training (Cassidy et al., 2016). The influence of timbre of different TTS voices, and emotion recognition are increasingly studied (Nayak & Pradhan, 2015). School personnel are encouraged to provide TTS for students with disabilities and suggestions are made to keep the costs within the school budget (Bone & Bouck, 2016). A possible alternative is applying Audio Computer Assisted Self-Interview (ACASI) (O'Reilly & Lessler, 1997). Research suggests that ACASI can remove the literacy barriers for self-administration (Mierzwa, Souidi, Friedland, & Littlefield, 2013) and it may enhance the validity of self-report data in research and clinical settings by reducing measurement bias (Brown, Swartzendruber, & DiClimente, 2013).

Selecting psychological and intellectual diagnostic tools regarding forensic requirements

If there is no scientific research available on which instrument would fit the characteristics of the local population, it is recommended to evaluate instruments which are already in use. As mentioned in the introduction, on the islands of Aruba, Bonaire, and Curacao, several unofficially translated assessment tools circulate among psychologists. Although not validated, talking to the psychologists using them can give information on how the instrument suits the needs of the clinician.

To maintain the scientific standard, it is recommended to determine if the instrument in use is translated in a scientifically approved way. Otherwise, a correct valid translation should be undertaken. It is also recommended to study the requirements of the publisher before selecting an assessment tool. The Minnesota Multiphasic Personality Inventory-2-RF (MMPI-2RF), for example, is a personality questionnaire adequate for forensic psychological use (Ben-Porath & Tellegen, 2008). However, one of the requirements to translate and validate the MMPI-2-RF is that the translation be administered to 50 native English speakers, who are also native speakers of the target language. Those might be difficult criteria to meet in a small community, let alone in a local prison. For the first translation, it is recommended to select assessment tools with a structure that is not too complicated. Especially when, like Papiamento, the language is mainly spoken and there is no certainty that the written language can be used for psychologic assessment.

Translators and inclusion criteria for a forensic setting

The process of translating can be expensive and time-consuming. Also, the Beaton criteria, although very useful, can be hard to meet in a small community or a forensic setting. Specialists, like official translators and methodologists with knowledge of the local (forensic) situation, can be hard to find. Working on a translation with schoolteachers and experienced psychologists using diagnostic tools on a regular basis is a good way to determine if a language that is mainly spoken is adequate for use in assessment tools. A benefit of small communities like the ones in the Dutch Caribbean is that it is often easier to get colleagues involved than would be the case in big communities.

In a small island community, inclusion criteria of origin should be defined carefully. In the case of the pilot study conducted in the prison of Bonaire (Vorst et al., 2015), the criteria of origin were too strict. Suspects born on the island of Bonaire, with both parents born on the island, were included. This resulted in 23 inclusions after a year-and-a-half. It is advised to select native speakers, born in the studied region, with at least one parent born in the same region. Depending of the development of the language and its origin, comments can be made on the participants' origin and the influence on the outcomes.

When including participants from a forensic setting into a study, knowledge on the organisation of the imprisonment before trial is required to prevent participants dropping out, because they are released from custody. For example, in Curacao suspects are taken into custody for 48 hours before being presented to an Investigative Judge. The remand in custody can be prolonged three times with eight days. After each of these eight days, the custody needs to be evaluated. If the investigation needs the suspects to be kept in custody, it can be prolonged 60 days and another 30 days after these first 60 days (Openbaar Ministerie, 2017). After the first 20 days, it is safe to include the suspect from the forensic setting into the study, because the suspect will probably stay another 30 or 60 days. However, to prevent bias, suspects subject to court-ordered psychological evaluation should not be included. Offenders subjected to court-ordered psychological evaluation might try to influence the outcome of their assessment. For example, if they are simulating a low IQ as part of a defence strategy, they will probably simulate a low IQ during the assessment related to the study, too.

Consensus among clinicians concerning psychopathological patterns

When translation and validation for a certain population has never been done before, clues from the local field can give information about whether the score on the translated intellectual diagnostic tool makes sense. The first recommendation of Ziegler and colleagues – clear definition of measured trait embedded in the nomological network – (Ziegler & Bensch, 2013) should be considered in the pre-testing stage or during reunions with the expert committee. Also, the level of acceptance, in the community or a local prison, of certain forms of psychopathology should be mapped. Case B (see Box 14.1), describing a man with an intellectual disability, apparently well-functioning in the community, is not an exceptional case on the islands of Bonaire and Curacao. In this case, his reading skills and his mother were key to revealing the dysfunctional behaviour. People with, for example, an intellectual impairment without major behavioural problems seem to be able to participate in a small community, often because of family being supportive and offering them jobs in the family business. This also means that they might not be known by the mental health department, which means that sometimes, like for cases A and B, psychopathology is not evident. When translating tools into new languages, individuals with intellectual impairment, severe mental illness, or without the capacity to consent should be excluded as study participants; this is also the case with illiteracy. The percentages in Table 14.2 explain why it is important to check for illiteracy.

Although it has never been studied, psychologists on the island of Curacao agree to the fact that there are remarkable differences between intelligence assessments of persons in their twenties and persons older than fifty, when Dutch versions of assessment tools are used. It seems that persons older than fifty (which

Table 14.2 Information on school dropout percentages in Curacao, Census 2011 of Curacao

Age ranges	*School dropout rates*		
	Male (%)	*Female (%)*	*Total (%)*
10–14	29.2	20.5	25.3
15–24	37.2	26.8	32.3
25–34	25.9	20.9	23.1
35–44	28.0	27.5	27.7
45–54	28.5	31.5	30.2
55–64	32.8	40.3	37.0
65+	48.2	65.2	58.1
Total	33.1	37.3	35.5

Note: Adaption of "E-12 Dropouts by age"; Source Centraal Bureau voor de Statistiek, 2015a

is a rough estimate), born and raised on the island, score higher on the Dutch assessment tools than persons in their twenties who were also born and raised on the island. A possible explanation would be the differences in education systems. Because Papiamento-speaking participants can either have a Dutch or Papiamento-dominated education, language preference should be asked for before assessment. Furthermore, it is recommended to score correct answers, given in Dutch on assessment tools translated to Papiamento, as right answers (and vice versa).

Conclusion

Despite the number of guidelines to conduct a cross-cultural translation being proposed in the last two decades, little is known about translating and validating assessment tools for languages which are mainly spoken. Translated tools are in particular needed in the forensic work field. The Papiamento language, alive, developing, and still dominant on the islands of Curacao, Bonaire, and Aruba, deserves more attention from the psychological, scientific field. The post-colonial influence must be taken into account when using the language for written assessment tasks, for the Papiamento language is a quickly changing language, in the middle of a complicated, cultural transition. Also, historical political changes in language policies, the impacts over time on the different roles of the Papiamento language within the Dutch Caribbean educational systems and, consequently, the differences between generations in language fluency might be of influence on study outcomes. More research on psychological assessments using mainly spoken languages as well as the possibilities of the use of audio in psychological assessments is greatly needed, especially within multi-lingual Caribbean societies and populations.

References

Barkley, R. (2011). *Barkley functional impairment scale (BFIS for Adults)*. New York: Guilford Press.

Beaton, D.E., Bombardier, C., Guillemin, F., & Ferraz, M.B. (2000). Guidelines for the process of cross-cultural adaption of self-report measure. *Spine*, *25*(24), 3186–91.

Ben-Porath, Y., & Tellegen, A. (2008). *Minnesota Multiphasic Personality Inventory-2-RF*. Minnesota: University of Minnesota Press.

Bleichrodt, N., & Van Vijver, F. (2001). *Diagnostiek bij allochtonen: Mogelijkheden en beperkingen van psychologische tests [Diagnosis in immigrants: Possibilities and limitations of psychological tests]*. Lisse: Swets en Zeitlinger.

Blom, M., Oudhof, J., Bijl, R., & Bakker, B. (2005). *Verdacht van criminaliteit: Allochtonen en autochtonen nader bekeken [Suspected of criminality: A closer look on immigrants and natives]*. Den Haag: WODC/CBS.

Bochhah, N., Kort, W., Seddik, H., & Van Vijver, F. (2001). *Deskundigen over het testen van etnische minderheden [Experts on testing ethnic minorities]*. Rotterdam: Landelijk Bureau ter bestrijding van Rassendiscriminatie (LBR); Nederlands Instituut van Psychologen.

Bone, E., & Bouck, E. (2016). Accessible text-to-speech options for students who struggle with reading. *Preventing School Failure: Alternative Education for Children and Youth*, *61*(1), 1–6.

Boonmann, C., Vinkers, D., & Doreleijers, T. (2012). Pro justitia reported Antillian adolescents. A study on psychiatrich disorders, intellectual disabilities, accountability and treatment advice. *Maandblad Geestelijke Volkgezondheid, 67*(1/2), 46–57.

Brown, J., Swartzendruber, A., & DiClimente, R. (2013). The application of Audio Computer-Assisted Self-Interviews (ACASI) to collect self-reported health data: An overview. *Caries Research, 47*, 40–45. doi:10.1159/000351827.

Cassidy, S., Stenger, B., Van Dongen, L., Yanagisawa, K., Anderson, R., Wan, V. . . . Cipolla, R. (2016). Expressive visual text-to-speech as an assistive technology for individuals with autism spectrum conditions. *Computer Vision and Image Understanding, 148*, 193–200. doi: 10.1016/j.cviu.2015.08.011.

Centraal Bureau voor de Statistiek. (2014). *Papiaments de meest gesproken taal op Bonaire, en Engels op Saba en Sint Eustatius [Papiamentu is mainly spoken in Bonaire and in Saba and St. Eutatius it is English]*. Den Haag: CBS. Retrieved from Wikipedia.

Centraal Bureau voor de Statistiek. (2015a, December 26). *Education Characteristics*. Retrieved from website Central Bureau of Statistics Curaçao. Retrieved from www.cbs.cw/document.php?m=1&fileid=673&f=de68599ef0a4406d9088b89f48d22fc5&attachment=1&c=121.

Centraal Bureau voor de Statistiek. (2015b, December 26). *Verdachten; delictgroep, geslacht, leeftijd en herkomstgroepering [Suspects; crime group, gender, age and ethnic background]*. Retrieved from website Centraal Bureau voor de Statistiek http://statline.cbs.nl/Statweb/publication/?DM=SLNL&PA=81947NED&D1=0-1,12,18,22,25-28,39,45,49,52-53&D2=0&D3=0&D4=a&D5=13-15&HDR=G2,G1,G3,G4&STB=T&VW=T.

Chafetz, M. (2011). The psychological consultative examination for Social Security disability. *Psychological Injury and Law, 4*(3–4), 235–244.

Coomans-Eustatia, M. (2015). *Bibliography of the Papiaments language*. Bloemendaal/Willemstad: Stichting Libri Antilliani/Fundashon pa Planifikashon di Idioma.

Dalhuisen, L.D. (2009). *Geschiedenis van de Antillen [The History of the Antilles]*. Zutphen: Walburg Pers.

Dingwall, K., Pinkerton, J., & Lindeman, M. (2013). "People like numbers": A descriptive study of cognitive assessment methods in clinical practice for Aboriginal Australians in the Northern Territory. *BMC Psychiatry, 13*(42), 1–13.

Eckkrammer, E. (2007). Papiamentu, cultural resistance, and socio-cultural challenges: The ABC islands in a nutshell. *Journal of Caribbean Literatures, 5*(1), 73–93.

Epstein, J., Santo, R., & Guillemin, F. (2015). A review of guidelines for cross-cultural adaptation of questionnaires could not bring out a consensus. *Journal of Clinical Epidemiology, 68*(4), 435–441.

Fogden, B., Stuart, D., & Daffern, M. (2016). Crime and victimisation in people with intellectual disability: A case linkage study. *BMC Psychiatry, 16*(1), 1–9.

Fouse, G. (2002). *The story of Papiament: A study in slavery and language*. Lanham: University Press of America.

Guillemin, F., Bombardier, C., & Beaton, D. (1993). Cross-cultural adaptation of health-related quality of life measures: Literature review and proposed guidelines. *Journal of Clinical Epidemiology, 46*(12), 1417–1432.

Hellenbach, M., Karatzias, T., & Brown, M. (2017). Intellectual disabilities among prisoners: Prevalence and mental and physical health comorbidities. *Journal of Applied Research in Intellectual Disabilities, 30*(2), 230–41.

Hofstee, W. (1990). Toepasbaarheid van psychologische tests bij allochtonen [The applicability of psychologic test on immigrants]. *De Psycholoog, 25*(6), 291–294.

Jacobs, B. (2009a). The origins of Old Portuguese features in Papiamento. In N. Faraclas, R. Severing, C. Weijer, & L. Echteld (Eds.), *Leeward voices: Fresh perspectives on Papiamento and the literatures and cultures of the ABC Islands* (pp. 11–38). Curacao: FPI/UNA.

Jacobs, B. (2009b). The Upper Guinea origins of Papiamentu. *Diachronica, 26*(3), 319–379.

Jacobs, B. (2012a). *Origins of a creole: The history of Papiamento and its African ties.* Berlijn: De Gruyter Mouton.

Jacobs, B. (2012b). On the Dutch presence in 17th-century Senegambia and the emergence of Papiamento. In T. Green, & J.L. Nafafe (Eds.), *Brokers of change: Atlantic commerce and cultures in pre-colonial "Guinea of Cape Verde"* (pp. 191–214). Oxford: Oxford University Press.

Jacobs, B. (2016, August 12). *Papiamentu, healthy Creole.* Retrieved from website Sorosoro http://blog.sorosoro.org/en/papiamento-healthy-creole.

Jacobs, B., & Van der Wal, M. (2015). The discovery, nature, and implications of a Papiamento text fragment from 1783. *Journal of Pidgin and Creole Languages, 30*(1), 44–62.

Kendall, K., & Owen, M. (2015, May 26). Intellectual disability and psychiatric comorbidity: Challenges and clinical issues. Retrieved from www.google.com/url?sa=t&rct=j&q=&esrc=s&source=web&cd=2&ved=0ahUKEahU3OPL–LSAhVHPiYKHSRzBjYQFggnMAE&url=http%3A%2F%2Fwww.psychiatrictimes.com%2Fprintpdf%2F211426&usg=AFQjCNGpfzBCjnnhOVyrJ2BovlOa2r2DHg&cad=rja.

Koninkrijksdeel Curaçao. (2007). *Landsverordening officiële talen [Land ordinance official languages].* Willemstad: Koninkrijksdeel Curaçao.

Koster van Groos, G. (2001). *Handleiding diagnostische criteria DSM-IVTR.* Amsterdam: Swets & Zeitlinger.

Luteijn, F., & Barelds, D. (2004). *Groningen intelligence test 2 (GIT-2): Manual.* Amsterdam: Harcourt Test Publishers.

Mierzwa, S., Souidi, S., Friedland, I., & Littlefield, S. (2013). Effective approaches to user-interface design with ACASI in the developing world. *Interactions, 20*(3), 58–61.

Nayak, B., & Pradhan, M. (2015). Text-dependent versus text-independent speech emotion recognition. In S. Satapthy, K. Raju, J. Mandal, & V. Bhatej (Eds.), *Proceedings of the second international conference on computer and communication technologies* (pp. 153–161). New Delhi: Springer India.

Nederlandse Antillen. (2015, 12 26). *Landsbesluit schrijfwijze Papiamentu en Nederlands [Governmental decision on writing Papiamento and Dutch].* Retrieved from website Dutch Government http://decentrale.regelgeving.overheid.nl/cvdr/xhtmloutput/historie/Nederlandse%20AntilAnt/14666/14666_1.html.

Openbaar Ministerie. (2017, February 12). *Custodial coercive measure.* Retrieved from website Openbaar Minsterie www.openbaarministerie.org/en/faq-en#custodial-coercive-measures.

O'Reilly, J., & Lessler, J. (1997). Mode of interview and reporting of sensitive issues: Design and implementation of audio computer-assisted self-interviewing. *NIDA Research Monograph, 167*, 366–382.

Quint, N. (2000). *Grammaire de la langue cap-verdienne. Étude descriptive et compréhensive du créole afro-portugais des Îles du Cap-Vert [Grammar of the Cape Verdean language. Descriptive and comprehensive study of the Cape-Verdean Afro-Portuguese Creole].* Paris: L'Harmattan.

Robben, P. (2006). *Het geheugen van Tilburg [The memory of Tilburg].* Retrieved from http://geheugenvantilburg.nl/verhalen/lees/11740/fraters-van-tilburg-naar-de-antillen.

Stuurman, S., Mulder, A., Van Straaten, B., Kruijt, P., De Baan, M., & Mulder, N. (2008). *Intelligentieonderzoek bij patiënten van assertive community treatment (ACT)-teams [Intelligence assessment in patient of ACT-teams].* Rotterdam: Bavo Europoort.

Trilla, A. (2009). *Natural language processing techniques in text-to-speech synthesis and automatich speech recognition.* Department de Tecnologies Media Enginyera la Salle. Barcelona: Universitat Ramon Llull.

Van Hulst, H., & Bos, J. (1993). *Pan i Rèspèt: Criminaliteit van geïmmigreerde Curaçaose jongeren [Bread and respect: Criminality of immigrated Curacao youth].* Utrecht: Onderzoeksbureau OKU.

Vinkers, D. (2011). Borderline intellectual functioning in Antillean suspected offenders. *Tijdschrift voor Psychiatrie*, *53*(1), 9–14.

Vinkers, D., Barendregt, M., Beurs, E.D., Hoek, H., & Rinne, T. (2010a). Etnische verschillen tussen pro Justitia gerapporteerde verdachten. *International Journal of Law Psychiatry*, *53*(11), 801–811.

Vinkers, D., Heijtel, F., Matroos, G., Hermans, K., & Hoek, H. (2010b). Pre-trial psychiatric reports on suspected Antillean Offenders in the Netherlands and on the Dutch Antilles. *Tijdschrift voor Psychiatrie*, *52*(11), 745.

Vorst, M.V., Vinkers, D., Matroos, G., Hoek, H., & Heijtel, F. (2015). Validation of tools for assessing the intelligence and the functional impairment of Papiamento speaking suspects. *Tijdschrift voor Psychiatrie*, *58*(11), 785–93.

Ziegler, M., & Bensch, D. (2013). Lost in translation: Thoughts regarding the translation of existing psychological measures into other languages. *European Journal of Psychological Assessment*, *29*(3), 157–61.

15 Crime control and punishment in Dominica

Perspectives of community leaders and offenders

Kyra Paul

Introduction

Crime in the Caribbean emerged as a serious issue on the research agenda of criminologists when rates began to show sharp increases in the 1980s (UNODC & World Bank, 2007). In particular, law enforcement and the prison exert social control through arrests, convictions, and punishment for those who violate acceptable social norms and the law. Yet, after decades, the increasing crime surge continues to pose a challenge to the justice system. The crime rate in Dominica is relatively minimal in comparison to its counterparts such as Jamaica and Trinidad and Tobago where violent crimes are most prevalent. For example, according to the Jamaica Crime and Safety Reports, in 2013, there were 1,193 murders, 1,227 shootings, 580 aggravated assaults, 792 rapes, 2,631 robberies, and 2,443 break-ins recorded, and available data for Trinidad and Tobago reveal that there were 379 murders, 579 wounding and shootings, 933 rapes, incest, and other sexual offences, and 4,436 robberies. For that same calendar year, there were 12 murders, four shootings, 54 grievous bodily harm, 150 sexual offences, 62 robberies, and 899 burglaries recorded in Dominica. According to St Jean (2005, 2006), however, since the 1980s the structure of crime in Dominica has been dominated by property crimes, especially theft and burglary, that are associated to economic disenfranchisement.

According to the crime statistics, for every year between 2011 and 2015 during the year over 500 convicted or pre-trial detainees are committed in a prison which was built for an official capacity of 300.[1] The data also show that more than 56 per cent of the annual prison population fall within the ages of 20 to 39 year olds, and of that approximate figure over 95 per cent is male (Central Statistics Office, 2016). The compilations of statistics from the Dominica State Prison indicate that the rate of return to prison was high for the years of 2013 to 2016. According to the statistics more than 45 per cent of individuals committed to the prison annually are recidivists who return to prison within one year of incarceration. Additionally, there was an 18 per cent increase in the number of recidivists between 2013 and 2016. A recent study by the Organization of American States (OAS) conducted in 2012 produced similar results. The researchers found that more than 60 per cent of prisoners in Dominica are repeat offenders, primarily for stealing and physical assaults. Furthermore, up to 75 per cent of the inmates had been to prison at least four times or more.

According to the formulated aims, "the Dominica Prison Service leads in the professional advancement on corrections, promoting integrity, ethics, good practices through rehabilitation and reform to change for the better with dignity for our nation's future" (Dominica Prison Service, n.d.). However, the rate of return, the size, and the characteristics of the offences and offenders suggest that the prison's goal of integrating offenders back into society is not being realised. The criminal justice systems across the Caribbean, including Dominica, are preoccupied with law and order, which often translates to a focus on incarceration instead of the rehabilitation of offenders (Platzer, Mirella, & Nestares, 2004). Although fines and community service are handed down for less serious offences, this punitive approach to crime control is premised on ensuring the protection of the general public by excluding the offender from society through measures such as incarceration.

This seems to contradict the fact that scholars have recognised that the approach to crime control – as an agent of social control – must balance the needs of the victim, the offender, and the general public. In response to public demands for more safety provided by the justice system, many Caribbean states are attempting to reform and modernise their criminal justice organisations by focusing on increased and effective deployment, strengthening staff capacities, upgrading of facilities, introducing new technologies and information systems, and revising regulations and legislations (Ellison & Pino, 2012; Harriott, 2000b; Singh, 2004). However, there have been little regional efforts to reform the strategies of the prison as an institution of crime *prevention.*

The criminal justice system as a social institution, including the police and correction officers, plays a critical role in controlling the behaviour of citizens, and hence, the successful outcome of the criminal justice system's social control function is hinged on the engagement of all key stakeholders including offenders. The direct experience of individuals and the accounts of families and friends with law enforcement officers and correction officers influence their perception of the legitimacy of the system which also stimulates their behaviours. It stands to reason that citizens who view the criminal justice system as fair and legitimate are more likely to comply with the law or to assist criminal justice agents in carrying out their work. Likewise, offenders who view the system positively are more likely to avert crime because they may be more accepting of the sanctions imposed on them (Sunshine & Tyler, 2003).

This suggests that deterring crime and rehabilitating offenders necessitates a movement away from a punitive approach (Deosaran & Ramdhanie, 2003) towards the adoption of tactics built on understanding the perceptions of offenders and the general public about the efficacy of current strategies and procedures, and the needs and concerns of offenders, particularly during and after incarceration. Still, few regional studies have explored the views of the general public towards the criminal justice system, even though they are the direct beneficiaries. The current study seeks to add to the literature on crime and criminology in the Caribbean by providing insights into present-day crime control and punishment in the Commonwealth of Dominica from the views of community leaders and prisoners.

The crime control theory

The punitive approach to crime management in the Caribbean region has its roots in the history of colonialism which has been perpetuated by the continuous use of the *Crime Control Theory* that views offenders as a threat to society and deserving of punishment (Harriott, 2000a; Johnson, 1991; King, 2009). The focus of this model is based on reducing the risk posed by a delinquent individual, through a watch-man style of policing in order to decrease the occurrence of crime in society. Harriott (2000a) posited that this top-down style of policing is reinforced by the rigid class structure still found in Caribbean police forces. According to this model, law enforcement and the prison are central in limiting behaviours through arrests and detainments as a means of removing them from society. This *law and order* approach, therefore, entrusts crime control agents with high levels of trust and leeway to determine the expected behaviour of released prisoners beyond serving their time in prison.

According to King (2009), these policing tactics are problematic. The traditional style of policing in the region makes it difficult for the police to balance reactive protection with active interventionist approaches such as community policing (Harriott, 2000a) or to support the rehabilitation of offenders (King, 2009; Skeem & Manchak, 2008). The rehabilitation process is also compounded by limited resources to support its programming which often leads to undesirable prison conditions (Deosaran & Ramdhanie, 2003). At present, the prison in Dominica also serves as remand centres, and there is no differential treatment for female, male, or youth offenders. Individuals who come in direct contact with the jail are either in detention, pending court hearings, are serving short-term or long-term sentencing, or are juvenile delinquents (OAS, 2012). This non-separate facility approach implies that offenders committed for petty crimes share spaces with hard-core criminals and juveniles are housed with adult detainees – together providing opportunities for a natural progression from petty to more serious crimes or habitual offending (Fagan, Kupchik, & Liberman, 2007). Correctional systems without a focused purpose of transforming the lives of offenders do very little to solve the crime problem (Deosaran & Ramdhanie, 2003). Rather, it helps to perpetuate a situation whereby first-time, petty crime, and youth offenders resort to serious crime after their correctional experience in adult facilities (Fagan et al., 2007).

Post-colonial impacts on Caribbean crime control policies

Crime control remains a key development priority if the region as a whole is to advance towards sustainable development. Yet, the complexities of post-colonialism pose a great contest to the pursuit of an appropriate Caribbean development model (Grenade, 2007). The high volumes of homicides, assaults, and property crimes – characteristic of the region – question the impact and efficacy of the law and order approach in an age of intense mobility, trade liberalisation, and globalisation. There are limited studies of the legitimacy of the criminal justice system from the vantage point of different stakeholders. However, in cases where research has been conducted, most studies of police organisations in the Caribbean have found that militaristic police practices are ineffective, often linked to incompetence, corruption, and/or misuse of political power, and lead to poor police-citizen relations (e.g. Harriott, 2000a; King, 2009; Pino & Johnson, 2011; St. Jean, 2006).

It is best to understand crime control within the context of the post-colonial period which has left many islands in the Caribbean characterised by highly indebted open, undiversified market economies with multiple vulnerabilities, high unemployment rates, political fragility, and high crime levels (Girvin, 2012). Colonisation introduced the process of supremacy versus inferiority, and transplanted economic policies that heavily relied on constant movement of people, and a trading system of cash crop agriculture and commodities to the interest of Europe and the disadvantage of the indigenous colonised countries and their cultures. The colonial legacy left behind a socially unjust society where social exclusion thrives. Following emancipation, crime control strategies necessitated the maintenance of existing structures or discipline subordinate groups who were often marginalised from the labour markets (Harriott, 2000a; Johnson, 1991). In consequence, dissatisfaction with the outcomes of engaging with the criminal justice system continues to lead to self-regulation of social problems in ways that may be deemed unpopular or illegitimate (Meares & Fagan, 2008).

Criminal justice system agencies are therefore tasked with balancing state security and crime control in an era when human rights and gender equality are high on the development agenda (Grenade, 2007; Harriott, 2000a). Attaining this goal within the context of the Caribbean is compounded by several factors that make crime management problematic, particularly in the areas of public reporting, lasting solutions, and adaptive strategies (Harriott, 2000a; St. Jean, 2006). These complicating factors include high levels of crime, the emergence of *garrison* communities and the underground economy, the social embeddedness of criminals in society, growing mistrust of the judicial system, a reluctance to provide police with information, the irreconcilable differences between perception and legal definitions of crime categories, and the concurrent handling of public disorder and criminal offences. Instead of merely focusing on community policing or law enforcement, exploring new ways to deal with the crime problem and focusing resources in rehabilitative programs are in the interest of achieving the development goals of the Caribbean.

Local crime control programs

Like many other Caribbean islands, crime control in Dominica is based on three divisions which have their origin in the British Westminster legal system: the Commonwealth of Dominica Police Force, the Judiciary, and the Dominica State Prison. The focus of this paper is on the police force and the prison, but it is important to note that all three bureaucratic models were designed to maintain an established social order within the context of law enforcement, justice, and punishment. The Commonwealth of Dominica Police Force (CDPF) is the principal agency engaged in the reproduction and maintenance of social order and crime control and is based on a military structure. This crime control function is achieved through surveillance and patrols, criminal investigation and intelligence-gathering, detailing of government officials, prosecution, border control, securing of state property, transportation of prisoners to courts, and search and rescue operations (Dominica Government, 2002). From observations, in their guardianship functions, the police also engage in softer informal duties such as community and family mediation, collection of vending fees, and apprehension of psychiatric patients, among others, so as to guard against laxative residents or to prevent any disorder from escalating (personal communication, August 18, 2011).

The CDPF is profoundly structural with eight ranks starting with constables who assist with routine tasks. At the higher end of the hierarchy is the Chief Commissioner who provides directive and instructions to the organisation. Several intelligence units and investigative squads within the force are charged with specific mandates and work collectively to attain the surveillance, protection, and responsive goals of the police (Police Act of, 1940, 1991). Over the years, the CDPF initiated a few action-oriented programs such as the gun control scheme that targeted the drug trade and armed robberies. They have also initiated several outreach programs such as community-oriented policing in selected communities and the "On the Beat" radio talk show to provide the public with information on protecting themselves and their property. These programs, however, are mainly focused on police activity and have not been effectively incorporated or evaluated to assess whether they are addressing the direct needs and issues of different communities, forms of crime, and age groups. The police also collaborate with "Crime Stoppers Dominica" to enhance communication between the police force and the public in the determination to solve crimes. However, little effort has been made to evaluate the crime control programs to determine whether programs should continue, modify, or stop; or to determine which program is most effective against which type of crime. Measures of effectiveness of crime control programs remain practically non-existent, particularly in the case of how those socially and economically disadvantaged respond to these programs. Therefore, the dominant measure of police effectiveness continues to rely on official crime data (Paul, 2016).

The only existing correctional facility in Dominica is the Dominica State Prison which operates under the leadership of a Superintendent, a Deputy Superintendent, and a Chief Prison Officer. At the time of writing, the State Prison had roughly 68 prison officers of which 53 were males. As stated previously, the Dominica Prison envisions rehabilitating offenders. However, no structured or systematic rehabilitation program links offenders to skills training, work opportunities, and social assistance beyond imprisonment. Some literacy, social skills, formal training, and vocational skills programs are offered on an ad-hoc basis by a few government departments, religious groups, or local organisations (Dominica Prison Service, n.d.). The Prison also established a Visiting Committee that provides a link between the prison and society. The Committee visits on a weekly basis to assess the efficiency of the jail, and to advise prison superintendence on matters relating to social welfare, economic well-being, and social development of prisoners (Dominica Prison Service, n.d.). The members of the Visiting Committee include staff from the Social Welfare Division, civil society organisations, Court system, and police (personal communication, April 06, 2017).

Current study

As stated elsewhere, there has been little effort in the Caribbean region to explore the perspectives on the criminal justice system of those who had direct experience with its agents, particularly for this study in Dominica. The salience of recidivism suggests that current practices are not working, and therefore, necessitates an inquiry into the public's attitude toward the criminal justice system; and how their experiences with law enforcement officers and correction officers impact offender rehabilitation and reintegration into society. This study uses ethnographic methods to respond to these concerns by exploring the views of both offenders who have direct experience with the criminal justice system and community leaders who act on behalf of the community. Both these insider views are important, as these participants have different interactions and expectations from the criminal justice system. The data from these informant interviews was supported with information from field notes, government reports, magazine articles, and academic material.

Methods

Participants

As part of a larger study that specifically sought to examine the impact of social capital on crime among three poor communities in Dominica, focus group discussions with offenders[2] and community leaders from a middle-crime and high-crime community were held to understand their views of the justice system. Two rounds of discussions, lasting approximately 1 hour and 20 minutes were conducted between September 2012 and February 2013. By way of convenience sampling, 12 prisoners were selected with the help of prison management and 25 community leaders were mobilised with the assistance of the local government authorities. The selected prisoners were a mix of recidivists and hard-core offenders. Community leaders were chosen because of their varying involvement as school personnel, religious leaders, village council members, community health workers, and leaders of civil society organisations, to ensure that their views were grounded in differential experiential knowledge of the criminal justice system in Dominica.

Procedure and data analysis

The focus group discussions with prisoners were conducted after receiving permission to access the prison and obtaining signed consent forms from the prisoners who agreed to participate in the research. The discussions with inmates took place within the confines of the prison and the presence of an authorised prison officer facilitated a controlled environment. Prisoners were assured that their participation would be confidential and verbatim use would be anonymous. The group meetings with the community leaders, on the other hand, were located at venues within their home communities. A separate protocol was developed to guide the interviews with each group of participants based on theoretical concepts discovered in the literature review.

A note taker also assisted with documenting observations and important verbatim quotes, while the discussions were audiotaped to maintain data integrity and to complement the note taker's transcripts. The data from these interviews were transcribed within two weeks of completion in order to prevent misinterpretation of the data. Microsoft Word was used to analyse the data according to the themes outlined in the protocol to make the information easier to manage and to understand the patterns of similarities of differences that emerged. This format also allowed for cleaning and verification after repeated analysis.

Results

Offender attitudes towards law enforcement and punishment

Offenders and former prisoners need to feel supported by the criminal justice system, but this entails a change in attitudes towards them. After years of imprisonment, feelings of alienation, compounded by unemployment and having no profession increase the odds of recidivism. Chappell (2002) argued that professional training behind bars increases the chances of becoming productive citizens as such trainings can provide ex-prisoners with livelihoods. Offenders are not necessarily unskilled or uneducated individuals. Efforts should be made to channel their skills and talents into productive assets that can benefit the individual, their families, their communities, the state, and the region. Re-schooling offenders to meet labour market demands can assist with turning around their lives and reintegrate them into society. However, the possession of skills does not necessarily translate into occupations or reintegration. Several factors impede successful integration, including (a) the characteristics and behaviours of ex-prisoners, (b) the negative stereotypes and mistrust towards former prisoners by potential employers, and (c) a lack of a supportive framework and enabling environment with legitimate opportunities for released prisoners. With regards to the needs of offenders, Goldthief proposed:

> What I think is lacking is some more constructive programs in the prisons and they need to set up a system with halfway houses for us. Inmates making big time prison, especially for those five years and upwards, so that they can prepare that inmate for his release with certain skills and prepare him for certain jobs. We are stigmatised by the people out there. They consider us to be vole' and thief and whatever. Now when we go out there, we should

> have halfway houses and they will put you straight. You will go out there and have a paper that says yes you can do this. You see people like us that keep coming back to prison, we should have some kind of tough rehabilitation and human activities right. You spend three to five years in prison but when you go out there you supposed to have a potential to show. There is supposed to be a system within the prison that is supposed to work with outside there to provide jobs for us. Unless we get that sort of program in Dominica prison you will not see change.

The prisoner articulated the opportunities that are critical in society to meet their needs during the process of returning to society, particularly a halfway house that would act as a transition agency and would link offenders to employment, accommodation, and information. The interviews with offenders revealed that practitioners did not fully comprehend the needs of prisoners, and neither did they appreciate their starring function in crime prevention. Deosaran & Ramdhanie (2003) opined that preventing recidivism necessitates the investment of adequate resources to support prison release planning. The critique of release policies by offenders suggested that key components of release planning such as transportation, food financial resources, housing, support systems, and cooperation with potential employers were often overlooked. Matt had this to say about prison release planning:

> Sometimes you leave the prison and don't have a ten cent to pay your bus much less to drink a coke.
>
> Inside here, ask for a phone call you don't get so you have no contact with family so we could discuss problems to them. Letters don't post here.
>
> They putting you out there and don't even know if you have homes or if you have somewhere to sleep.

Effective release planning provides opportunities to connect ex-prisoners with society after discharge, but the activities require the engagement of the released prisoner, supervised releases, and collaboration with agency partners (Deosaran & Ramdhanie, 2003). There was agreement among inmates that communication, coordination, and follow-up were critical to their re-entry into communities. In the words of Skell:

> It should have some other function out there for us to get us occupied and look out for us.
>
> We need some observers to know our whereabouts, what is our plans and what is our intention for the future.
>
> They need to ask us questions so that they can help you. Now your debt finish they just calling you and tell you going home today. They don't know if you know how outside looking because after all, things can change. So they have to investigate if you have people, if you know where you going, if you know what your where about.

Skell's explanation is typical of recommendations in the literature of the importance of identifying the needs of released prisoners, including the designing of programs to meet their individual circumstances, thus reducing the risk of recidivism (Deosaran & Ramdhanie, 2003; Maguire & Raynor, 2003; Shoham & Timor, 2014; Visher & Travis, 2003). All of the interviewed prisoners shared the sentiment that their successful reintegration into the wider society was stifled by the stigma attached to their identity that extended beyond their imprisonment and release. Society was generally of the view that prison was a self-verifying environment which resulted in little sympathy for offenders among the general public of Dominica, including law enforcement officers. The fixation of crime control agents on law and order often resulted in the unfair treatment of former prisoners, which robbed them of opportunities. It was in this setting that Horses[3] said:

> I'm interested in doing mechanics but what happen is every time I come out of prison, and I want to work . . . the police run me out . . . and I didn't even do anything . . . But I mean because I'm a bad dog and bad habits, the sergeant there tell me is best I go back when I come out, and I missed the opportunity to work. So I see no hope for me in Dominica.

Ex-prisoners often have limited or severed social support systems in their home communities, and the stigma associated with imprisonment reduces their ability to access social services and labour market opportunities. Horses's articulation is one of low confidence in the system because of the limited focus on individual restoration to society post-sentencing, including a lack of appreciation by criminal justice agents of their roles in the rehabilitative process. This difficulty manifested most in ex-prisoners attempts to secure employment after release, despite overwhelming existing empirical evidence that there is an inverse relationship between employment and recidivism (e.g. Healy, 2010).

The idea of constant harassment of the released prisoner reinforces the social label of ex-prisoners as chronic criminals who are prone to continuous criminal activity, and who should be monitored after release in the interest of protecting the public (Graham & Lowery, 2004). In this particular case, the police believed that the prison would serve to suppress opportunities for committing crimes, resulting in a more peaceful community. However, this approach does not help to reduce the problem of recidivism (Deosaran & Ramdhanie, 2003). Offenders are often times made to feel like criminals and are not taken seriously even in cases where they or family members are victims of crime. The following quote suggests of a cover-up or the lack of prosecution of people who do wrong depending on their status in society, or their connections with the police. The words of Casper, a notorious burglar were instructive:

> I will never stop crime. I have to come back here. It have a fella that chook his hand in my first daughter vagina at nine years. The whole community know about it but through who he is in society . . . I make a report to police and up till today that doh go nowhere. There are some people who are willing

> to speak but the fella does be assisting the police. Welfare come, everybody come, doctor say yes and up till now. They tell me leave it in their hands and they prevent me from doing what I had to do when the heat was on and I leave it in their hands and you see how it die out? But it doh finish yet. Don't be surprise, I have to come back here. I have to come back here.

The offender's conviction of returning to prison points to frustration with achieving fair access to justice and the potential consequence of retaliation against the suspect in an effort to find his own form of justice. As previously discussed, the status of the offender, and that of the victim have implications for how crime reports are addressed.

Community leaders' attitudes concerning the police

In both communities, leaders claimed to have low levels of trust and confidence in the police servicing their communities. The low view of the police was associated with problem-solving inabilities especially when reports were made. This is consistent with literature showing that police-citizen relations are relevant for crime control and the engagement of the general public in the production of social order (Jackson & Bradford, 2010; Renauer, 2007). Focus group discussions with community leaders revealed that the police are always under public scrutiny and the reluctance of the public to report originated from the lack of confidence in the professional handling of crimes. When questioned on how deviant behaviours were addressed in communities and whether these actions were effective in controlling behaviours, leaders held a deep belief that the police often did not take certain crimes seriously, shelved reports, or mismanaged information communicated to them. Three leaders from Castle Bruce[4] explained:

> It have some situations where you would report certain things to the police, and they might not handle it immediately, or sometimes they just don't respond the way that they should. I think that this is a problem.
>
> So everywhere you go, and you supposed to get some level of encouragement about accountability, it is just not there.
>
> But then again when you do report . . . you are asked so many questions, and you are turned left, right and centre. Then they want your name to report that you were the person who reported the crime . . . there is the fear of being exposed as the one who reported the crime.

These comments indicated a lack of trust in the police's ability to uphold a certain standard of confidentiality. Globally, researchers have long argued that many crimes go unreported and several factors account for this pattern, including fear of mishandling of reports by the police (Felson & Pare, 2005; Singer, 1988; Skogan, 1990). Leaders opined that this was most realised if the reports involve those within their networks or if the defendant is from the upper echelons of society which affected how authority was applied. Mr John, sports officer explained:

> Yes, there is a police station but there is no policing in the community. There are certain incidents that happen and because of one policeman loving somebody in the community they will pass certain people straight and pretend like they did not see.

Ms Dear from St Joseph also echoed sentiments regarding failure of the general public to make reports to the police as a result of the social standing of offenders:

> Image is everything eh. That is why people don't report or expose things. . . . We have compromised too much. We have given into too much. So what used to be wrong then is now acceptable and so there is an acceptance on our part. If we don't talk and we treat it silent and the persons who we choose or who ought to be good role models honouring that, then those things become a revolving one.

To Ms Dear, failure to disclose offences committed by persons from the upper echelons of society is a reflection of the socialisation and normalisation processes of victimisation by those who are seen to have the power. This has some serious consequences to society, particularly crime occurrence.

Harriott (2000a) put forward that class differential policing in Jamaica is softened by the recognition of the value of community norms, which often results in a reluctance to enforce some of the more unpopular laws around, for example, illegal occupation of land, or street vending. Paul (2016) argues that in the context of Dominica, sexual abuse of young girls and praedial larceny are matters that are usually dealt with internally by families which have implications for enforcement of laws. In other words, the patterns of crime and society's response shape the behaviour of the police (Harriott, 2000a). The personal experiences of individuals or those recounted by friends and family members shape the public's perceptions of the police. Citizens usually judge the efficacy of police work based on how the police treats them. There was general consensus among the leaders of St Joseph that citizens were likely to comply with police authority if they perceived the police as legitimate, trustworthy, and free of prejudice. Mr John's opinion summarised the general consensus on this matter:

> I believe that the police has to give a proper response to the community so that the community will say I will be there when you call on me and not the other way around. The police have to be somewhat integrated and build a relationship, with the community. If you don't do that, then it's going to be difficult to get the response of the community. . . . If there is a relationship that exists where the police is integrated, and people see the presence of the police, you are more likely to get a response from the people if something happens.

Police-community engagement can lead to improved police work since the citizens will feel more comfortable communicating and making reports to the police on matters of security. However, leaders purported a failure of the police to respond to calls for assistance due to lack of vehicles, and unwillingness to engage in foot patrols in the absence of transportation. Mrs Belle, a school teacher claimed: "There have been instances where you have an incident in the community and you call the police and they say they have no transport. Right in the village and they say they have no transport". On the other hand, this negative perceived attitude may be a function of limited resources since local research has shown that lack of resources to assist with surveillance and investigations pose a challenge for the Dominica Police Force (St Jean, 2006).

Focus group participants also shared the sentiment that the police were always under public scrutiny particularly with regards to the application of authority. With respect to police-community relations, Mr John lamented:

> I feel there is a lack of police and villager's communication . . . It is so much like they not involved in the community at all. . . . On various occasions, I have called them and they never show up. Too many things happening and there is no presence of the police at all. They are not living up to what they are expected to be doing!

Negative attitudes towards the police in executing their duties and low investments in capacity have implications for crime control (St Jean, 2006). The results may be detrimental to victims and their families, offenders, and the general public. Victims may not get the justice that they deserve, reports filed may not be followed through, or feelings of insecurity may emerge. Another factor that contributes to the public's confidence in the police is also based on judgments of police deportment as a tool to command respect. Tasia gave an example of dissatisfaction with police behaviour:

> It have some policemen working there in the community and I have never ever ever seen them in their uniform. They always dressed up like they going town. They in the station; they dress up. Come on, what's your job? Not even patrol they doing. How can I have confidence in them? You go to the station; a whole set of bottles lined up. It have a particular police when I see him I used to be afraid, but they send him St Joe, he is a fashion police now.

It is evident that police officer's demeanour impacts the public's perception of police legitimacy. The unprofessional demeanour of a police officer creates negative impression of the department or police station where the officer is assigned. Other officers are therefore perceived to be behaving the same way manner. On that matter, Moise shared his experience:

> I had an incident which I though was so grave. I wrote a letter to the commissioner of police but I also copied it to the officer in charge here and hand delivered him the copy and spoke to him about it. But the police here did not seem happy I had taken it to the commissioner. They felt that maybe it was something I should have come to them. There may be the element of fear that

people are afraid to speak out and say what is affecting them in the presence of the police.

Moise's experience raises fundamental questions about the process of lodging complaints with the police which starts at the level of the police serving the complainant's community. He argued that this process can impede reporting behaviours, creating a situation where concerns regarding criminal victimisation are replaced with failure to disclose offences to the police.

Discussion and implications

As this paper suggests, the current rate of recidivism appears to be the outcome of larger structural and social causes of crime that have shaped the island's crime policies. Until recently, Caribbean criminology focused on establishing the relationship between high rates of crime and traditional Western economic and social theories, and failing to take into account the social reality of prisoners and ex-prisoners experiences with the criminal justice system agents. Consequently, most crime policies recommend simplistic and penal enforcement responses (namely arrests, convictions, and incarceration) to complex social issues, employing assumptions about offenders in relation to law-biding citizens, with limited empirical support.

This study offers great insights into criminology within a Dominican setting. The evidence presented makes two chief contributions to the literature. First, it provides substantive insight into the views of members of the public on of the legitimacy of law enforcement and correction in Dominica. The analysis presented highlights that some practices in the criminal justice system ignore the needs of offenders, allowing for limited response options in terms of offender needs, and as such correctional programming tends to model a public safety-oriented focus. The analysis, therefore, raises questions about the effective functioning of current crime control and punishment strategies in an era where the observance of human rights is recognised as a pillar of development. Second, from the vantage point of offenders, it makes recommendations for an improved focus on the rehabilitation and reintegration of offenders into their communities. The predominant and traditional approach to crime management in Dominica disavows the voices of offenders, who can in fact offer insights into existential needs that must be addressed as part of the efforts to reintegrate these prisoners into the community. The process of giving more credence to offenders' rights and local community laws and knowledge require significant institutional change in order to transform the police and the prison system into institutions that embrace greater social inclusion of all. This has broader implications for public policy on crime prevention in Dominica and the broader Caribbean region.

From the accounts of community activists and offenders, the perceived attitudes of law enforcement agents have the potential to undermine the goal of crime control. The research participants highlighted several factors that affected their perception of the criminal justice system. Specifically, lack of systematic rehabilitation, improper release planning, negative interactions with the police, police misconduct, and the military-like approach were identified as issues that tainted their views of police and correction officers' legitimacy. These factors are typical of the Crime Control Theory and law and order practices – lingering effects of the colonial experience which determine how law enforcement agents interface with the general public. The findings suggested that offenders' perceptions of the state and its agents are failing to provide for their social and economic well-being within and outside of prison, which have implications for their re-involvement in crime after serving prison sentences. The punitiveness towards offenders is hinged on fear of uncertainty about the characteristics and behaviours of criminals and their potential damage to social order.

As previously stated in the review of the literature, the attitude of criminal justice agents is significant to the successful reintegration of released prisoners in society. Nonetheless, the labelling of offenders facilitates the disassociation of the public from them (Graham & Lowery, 2004) and social exclusion makes it difficult to secure employment, socialise, or re-connect with family (Travis, 2002). The stigmatisation of prisoners as unfixable no doubt often hurts their self-image and forces them to re-associate with other offenders and to commit offences again, creating a self-fulfilling prophecy (Maguire & Raynor, 2006). There is no doubt that close support from family members and positive and stable relationships with the community aids in the successful reintegration of ex-offenders into society (Clark, 2007; Roman & Travis, 2006).

This research was conducted with a small group of participants and, therefore, the findings cannot be generalised. Nevertheless, the accounts provide valuable insights into what the public thinks about crime control in Dominica, and the information can be used to inform a wider debate on the issue across the Caribbean. The results suggest that more research on the extent to which practitioners' behaviours and attitudes affect crime control outcomes is essential. Addressing the internal issues that affect police attitudes is imperative so that citizens enjoy the benefits of good police character. Police attitudes impact public perceptions and relationships with victims, offenders, and communities – good or bad. The current findings also advocate for the revision of prison programs to ensure that rehabilitation is actionable and more than a vision. Focusing on a rehabilitative approach is even more attainable given that each Caribbean island has either one or two prisons that can make release planning more manageable and a beacon in the crime control landscape. Prisoners should be afforded opportunities to become employable and adequate resources to reconstruct their lives. So too, the Commonwealth of Dominica Police Force must renew its relationship with citizens and review its crime control programs to ensure that these are designed to meet both victims and offender needs. Additionally, reporting protocols with redress mechanisms for breaches of confidentiality need to be formulated or strengthened.

The signal for the shift in approach to dealing with crime in Dominica was documented in the Policy on Crime Prevention and Control prepared by Dr. Peter K. B. St Jean[5] and approved in 2006. This policy appealed for a greater emphasis on crime prevention as a tool for crime reduction by proposing 12 main goals that included restructuring institutional arrangements to address national security, crime prevention and control, a public education program, and modernisation of the criminal and juvenile justice systems. Nonetheless, such implementation of policy requires substantive funding and political support. Moreover, public buy-in and a philosophical shift are critical so that policy makers and criminal justice agents can be held accountable for their commitments.

The results presented show that current policies have not yet contributed to attaining the crime prevention goals and that the call for a new paradigm that moves the world from an industry of violence, to an industry of peace[6] must be adhered to. St Jean's recommended courses of actions through a multi-agency approach promised to lower crime rates and to promote Dominica as a safe haven to both visitors and nationals. Given Dominica's regionally acclaimed *Nature Island* brand and *smallness* character, the country is in a prime position to first test the peace concept as a sustainable development tool that can be replicated in other parts of the world, once proven successful (St Jean, 2011). This can be a great alternative for the colonial based approach of response to the problems of crime and violence in society, which is not sufficiently problematised as a left-over effect of colonisation for the most part. This aspiration is even more prudent when the reputation of the Caribbean as a violent place where everyone, including locals, is at risk of serious criminal victimisation, is reflected upon. As discussed in the literature review, the laws are created to protect the interests of a few, and penalise many of the actions of those who use innovate means to move themselves from systems of economic and other oppression, with disproportionate enforcement. A few of the quotes by the respondents indicate that those in control do not sufficiently get punished, and those with less power, the vulnerable most especially, do not find justice deserved. Consequently, at times they predict their recidivism in an attempt to find justice on their own.

If the Caribbean is to move away from post-colonial law enforcement practices, countries like Dominica must embrace the prospect of becoming pioneers of justice designed for citizens who seek to promote their care for each other, including offenders, rather than reliance on a failing crime model developed by the colonials, and practiced in modern day (St Jean, 2011). In other words, the re-creation and localisation of our criminal justice institutions presents opportunities to ensure that criminal justice practices are more in sync with Caribbean people's interest, needs, and values (Harriott, 2000b). Unless this paradigm changes sufficiently to replace the current system which makes crime and violence profitable with a peace industry development model, the doors of recidivism will continue to swing and revolve.

Notes

1 Up until 2010, the prison had a capacity of 270 and was operating beyond its capacity.
2 Offenders refer to individuals who have been found guilty of a crime.
3 Note that the names of participants were changed to maintain anonymity.
4 In the methods section I indicated that two communities were represented in the sample. Castle Bruce is the poor middle-crime community.
5 Dr St Jean is a Dominican-born criminologist residing in the United States, but has remained closely tied to his land of birth.

6 In 2011, Dr St Jean submitted a 'Proposal for Maintaining and Improving Peaceful Dominica' to the Government of Dominica that recommends moving away from the reactive approach of crime control to the instead adoption of a proactive approach of building an economy of peace which was not officially adopted.

References

Central Statistics Office. (2016). *Crime Statistics*. Central Statistics Office, Ministry of Finance, Dominica Government.

Chappell, C.A. (2002). Post-secondary correctional education and recidivism: A meta-analysis of research conducted 1990–1999. *The Journal of Correctional Education, 55*(2), 139–144.

Clark, A. (2007). *Understanding community: A review of networks, ties and contacts*. National Center for Research Methods Working Paper Series, University of Leeds; Economic and Social Research Research Council, London. Retrieved from http://eprints.ncrm.ac.uk/469/1/0907_understanding_community.pdf?origin=publication_detail.

Deosaran, R., & Ramdhanie, I. (2003). *Prison recidivism: Towards reduction, rehabilitation and reform*. Paper submitted to the Office of the Prime Minister, Government of the Republic of Trinidad and Tobago. Retrieved from www.inspectorofprisonstt.com/wp-content/uploads/2013/11/Policy-Research-Report-2003-pt1.pdf.

Dominica Government. (2002). *Strategic plan of action 2002–2007*. Roseau, Dominica: Police Force.

Dominica Prison Service (n.d.). *About Us*. Retrieved from http://prisons.gov.dm/about-us.

Ellison, G., & Pino, P. (2012). *Globalization, police reform and development: Doing it the Western Way?* New York: Palgrave Macmillan.

Fagan, J., Kupchik, A., & Liberman, A. (2007). *Be careful what you wish for: Legal sanctions and public safety among adolescent felony offenders in juvenile and criminal court*. (Columbia Law School Public Law Research Paper No. 03–61). Retrieved from https://papers.ssrn.com/sol3/papers.cfm?abstract_id=491202.

Felson, R.B., & Pare, P.P. (2005). The reporting of domestic violence and sexual assault by nonstrangers to the Police. *Journal of Marriage and Family, 67*(3), 597–610.

Girvin, N. (2012). *Colonialism and Neo-colonialism in the Caribbean: An Overview*. Paper presented at the IV International Seminar Africa, The Caribbean and Latin America, St. Vincent and The Grenadines. Retrieved from http://normangirvan.info/wp-content/uploads/2013/01/Girvan-St-Vincent-paper.pdf. Accessed April 28, 2017.

Graham, S., & Lowery, B.S. (2004). Priming unconscious racial stereotypes about adolescent offenders. *Law & Human Behavior, 28*(5), 483–504.

Grenade, W. (2007). *Balancing economic development and security: The case of tourism and HIV/AIDS in Grenada*. Paper presented at the SALISES 8th Annual Conference, Trinidad & Tobaga. Retrieved from http://sta.uwi.edu/conferences/salises/documents/Grenade%20W.pdf. Accessed April 28, 2017.

Harriott, A. (2000a). *Police and crime control in Jamaica: Problems of reforming ex-colonial constabularies*. Kingston, Jamaica: The University of the West Indies Press.

Harriott, A. (2000b). Police reform in the Commonwealth Caribbean. *Open Journal Systems, 6*(1/2), 107–119.

Healy, D. (2010). *The dynamics of desistance: Charting pathways through change*. Cullompton: Willan.

Jackson, J., & Bradford, B. (2010). What is trust and confidence in the police? *Policing: A Journal of Policy and Practice, 4*(3), 241–248.

Johnson, H. (1991). Patterns of policing in the post-emancipation British Caribbean, 1835–95. In D. Killingray, & D. Anderson (Eds.), *Policing the empire: Government, authority and colonial control, 1830–1940* (pp. 71–91). Manchester: Manchester University Press.

King, K. (2009). *Policing your brother as the other: An analysis of policing in Trinidad and Tobago "measuring paramilitarism"*. Paper presented at the SALISES Tenth Annual Conference, Cavehill, Barbados.

Maguire, M., & Raynor, P. (2006). How the resettlement of prisoners promotes desistance from crime: Or does it? *Criminology & Criminal Justice*, *6*(1), 19–38.

Meares, T.L., & Fagan, J. (2008). Punishment, deterrence and social control: The paradox of punishment in minority communities. *Ohio State Journal of Criminal Law*, *6*(1), 173–229.

Organization of American States. (2012). *Exploring the relationship between drugs and crime: A comparative analysis of survey data from prisoners in four Caribbean Countries, Dominica, Saint Kitts and Nevis, Saint Lucia, Saint Vincent and the Grenadines*. Washington, DC: OAS, Inter-American Drug Abuse Control Commission. Retrieved from www.cicad.oas.org/oid/pubs/CaribbeanPrisons2012.pdf.

Paul, K. (2016). Variation in levels of crime among three poor communities in Dominica: Is social capital an agent? (Unpublished doctoral dissertation). University of the West Indies, Cavehill Campus, Barbados.

Pino, N.W., & Johnson, L.M. (2011). Police deviance and community relations in Trinidad and Tobago. *Policing*: *An International Journal of Police Strategies and Management*, *34*(3), 454–478.

Platzer, M., Mirella, F., & Nestares, C.R. (2004). Illicit drug markets in the Caribbean: Analysis of information on drug flows through the region. In A. Klein, M. Day, & A. Harriot (Eds.), *Caribbean drugs: From criminalisation to harm reduction* (pp. 189–223). New York: Zed Books.

Police Act of 1940, Act 25 of Laws of Dominica, Chapter 14:01 (1991).

Renauer, B.C. (2007). Neighborhood policing related to informal social control? *Policing: An International Journal of Police Strategies and Management*, *30*(1), 61–81.

Roman, D., & Travis, J. (2006). Where will I sleep tomorrow? Housing, homelessness, and the returning prisoner. *Housing Policy Debate*, *17*(2), 389–418.

Shoham, E., & Timor, U. (2014). Once a criminal, always a criminal? Attitudes towards reintegration of released prisoners among Israeli public. *Canadian Social Science*, *10*(6), 104–116.

Singer, S.I. (1988). The fear of reprisal and the failure of victims to report a personal crime. *Journal of Quantitative Criminology*, *4*(3), 289–302.

Singh, W. (2004). Drugs and the prison system: Impact of legislative changes on the prison crises in the commonwealth Caribbean region. A. Klein, M.D., & A. Harriott (Eds.), *Caribbean drugs: From criminalization to harm reduction* (pp. 101–119). New York: Zed Books.

Skeem, J.L., & Manchak, S. (2008). Back to the future: From Klockars' Model of effective supervision to evidence-based practice in probation. *Journal of Offender Rehabilitation*, *47*(3), 220–247.

Skogan, W.G. (1990). A review: The national crime survey redesign. *Public Opinion Quarterly*, *54*(2), 256–272.

St. Jean, P.K.B. (2005). *More money more crime: Trends in Dominica over the last 21 years*. Unpublished paper. Retrieved from www.da-cademy.org/randdmoremoney.html.

St. Jean, P.K.B. (2006). *Lessons from Grand Bay*. Brampton, ON: Pond Casse Press.

St. Jean, P.K.B. (2011). *Proposal for maintaining and improving peaceful Dominica*. Chicago, Illinois: Quality of Life Solutions Inc. Retrieved from http://da-academy.org/Peaceful_Dominica_Proposal.pdf.

Sunshine, J., & Tyler, T.R. (2003). The role of procedural justice and legitimacy in shaping public support for Policing. *Law & Society Review*, *37*(3), 513–548.

Travis, J. (2002). Invisible punishment: An instrument of social exclusion. In M. Mauer, & M. Chesney-Lind (Eds.), *Invisible punishment: The collateral consequences of mass imprisonment*. Retrieved from http://webarchive.urban.org/UploadedPDF/1000557_invisible_punishment.pdf.

United Nations Office on Drugs and Crime. (2007). *Crime, violence, and development: Trends, costs, and policy options in the Caribbean*. A Joint Report by the United Nations Office on Drugs and Crime and the Latin America and the Caribbean Region of the World Bank. Washington, DC: UNODC. Retrieved from www.unodc.org/pdf/research/Cr_and_Vio_Car_E.pdf.

Visher, C.A., & Travis, J. (2003). Transitions from prison to community: Understanding individual pathways. *Annual Review of Sociology*, *29*(1), 89–113.

16 Migrant sex work or sex trafficking? Reflections on "trafficking in women"

A Caribbean post-colonial perspective

Joan Phillips

> What is certain is that beyond those who suffer as victims, crime is in danger of becoming embedded in Caribbean society, changing the quality of Caribbean life and engendering a fear, albeit suppressed into a kind of silent complicity, that if allowed, will over time enable those involved to challenge legitimate economic growth and development. . . . Regrettably for a still peaceful region, the last two and a half decades have seen murder, armed robbery, kidnapping, organized crime, narcotics trafficking, the sale and smuggling of arms, piracy, money laundering, people trafficking, extortion and corruption, in almost every nation in the Caribbean.
>
> (Jessop, 2013)

Introduction

Criminology has become a popular field for academics, politicians, and policy makers to wax lyrically about the effects of crime on the region's development. The excerpt from the article "Caribbean Development", speaks to a kind of neo-colonial angst endemic to Caribbean criminology. Commentators, like Jessop (2013) present a trope of the idyllic Caribbean slowly being destroyed by this criminal scourge, and Caribbean governments helpless in the face of this menace. However, albeit though there may be some validity to these panicked cries, there is also the awareness of "facts as truth" that circulate in this type of neo-colonial discourse and the nature of this "truth", since it is often the truth reflective of the neo-colonialist (Spivak, 1988). Such is the case of epistemology[1] writing, which continues to support the historical "situatedness" of the Caribbean and its people, viewed as helpless without a (neo) colonial direction, along with the tacit compliance of the neo-colonial.

This chapter aims to provide an analysis of the hegemonic discourse which speaks for and on behalf of the countries of the global South, and in doing so, has silenced many other voices in relation to understanding, analyzing, and determining what is crime. For, in presenting a picture of the Caribbean in which politicians, academics, and policy makers faithfully follow the common law and judiciary dictates set out by their former colonial masters, the criminological literature demonstrates a particular silencing of alternative voices in relation to the concept of crime (Bhabha, 1983; Spivak, 1988)

In exploring questions relating to the ways of seeing and interpreting what is crime and determining criminality, I propose that the use of post-colonial perspectives provides us with an opportunity to explore how Western neo-colonialism hegemony has shaped our understanding of crime in the region (Spivak, 1988). I suggest like other commentators writing from the post-colonial perspective, that such a reproduction, such "faithful following" only serves to perpetuate the perceived inferiority of the Caribbean voice and the superiority of a Western standard (Cunneen & Rowe, 2014). I argue that if we take the stance that racialised discourses that produce knowledge and practice about crime and race are embedded in Caribbean criminology (Cunneen & Rowe, 2014), we acknowledge that there has been little scope for the development of an indigenous criminology.

Using newspaper articles, other secondary available data, and drawing on the work of other post-colonial feminists (De Shalit, Heynen, & Van der Meulen, 2014, p. 387; Kempadoo, 2007, 2016; De Sousa Santos, Gomes, & Duarte, 2010), I will argue that the application of the criminological approach used by many Caribbean governments to the issue of sexual trafficking speaks to a tacit compliance with a neo-colonial Western dictate that negates Caribbean sovereignty and undermines political self-reliance. Further, by condemning all foreign sex workers as "trafficked", Caribbean governments obscure the multiple realities in which sex work takes place.

Sexual trafficking of women: silencing the "Other" in sex work

The publication of the United Nations Against Transnational Crime signed by 140 countries and ratified in 2003, along with the "Protocol to Prevent Suppress and Punish Trafficking in Persons" (US Department of State, 2004) has made sexual trafficking part of the political agenda of many states (Sharma, 2015) The Caribbean is by no means an exception. However, a review of the literature offers an understanding of how sex trafficking can be framed within a post-colonial feminist discourse. For example, De Shalit et al. (2014, p. 387) suggest that the discourses of trafficking, sex work, and prostitution are often intertwined and present powerful narratives of good and evil, exploiter and exploited. Yet these discourses are rarely interrogated and support suppressive political agendas around labour and migration. It is through this particularly post-colonial lens of national and international security agendas that Sharma (2015, p. 89) demonstrates the ways in which women and children are controlled through anti-trafficking laws. She frames this discussion within the conceptualisation of "global apartheid", a UN policy used to regulate and criminalise the mobility of the Other. She further maintains this is facilitated by a moral panic that "simultaneously obscures the vulnerability of the migrant women in the nexus of state and capitalist practices while representing them as victims solely of traffickers" (Sharma, 2015, p. 90).

Kempadoo's (2007, 2016) approach is similar to Sharma's (2015) with regards to her analysis of sexual trafficking. Kempadoo (2016) argues that the hegemonic discourses on human trafficking seek to mask the real issue at hand: that of the strengthening of a neo-liberal capitalism which has made the divide greater between the rich and poor. She opines the problem of sex trafficking is never about the inequalities within global capitalism but rather on individual components of the system: the individual, the corporation, or the agency. This epistemology inherently supports claims of the everyday occurrence of sexual trafficking, as something commonplace.

She identifies three dominant, hegemonic movements which explain the intervention programs for sexual trafficking in women: (a) abolitionist feminism, (b) modern day slavery, and (c) celebrity humanism. According to Kempadoo (2016) abolition feminism is based on the premise that prostitution is viewed as exploitation and a function of patriarchy. She notes that the abolition feminist coined the term "sex trafficking", and supported the criminalisation of the demand side of sex work. She examines modern day slavery as another hegemonic campaign in which sexual trafficking is likened to an indentureship rather than slavery of the Atlantic trade. The term "slavery" in this campaign has a more expanded focus than sexual trafficking, and includes a focus on debt bondage, serfdom, arranged marriages, and child servitude. Kempadoo identifies a third hegemonic trend in relation to sexual trafficking in women, namely that of "celebrity humanitarianism". In this case celebrities use their status as a platform to combat sexual trafficking through a number of (media) outlets: through the foundation of NGOS, motion pictures, and as UN ambassadors.

The author concludes that these three campaigns demonstrate a white knight neo-colonial discourse: "neo-liberal white chivalrous crusade born of a moral sense of goodness that shores up the power of subjectivity of the North, with the 'developing' Global South and East as dumping grounds for helping imperatives involving rescue and charity" (Kempadoo, 2016, p. 17). I further argue that this *white knightism* is born out of a post-colonial mentality which speaks for and on behalf of the Other. Furthermore, implicit in this knowledge construction is the superiority of a Western standard of "getting the job done".

De Sousa Santos et al. (2010, p. 169) also present an analysis of sex trafficking in women worthy of note. The authors argue along similar lines as Kempadoo (2007, 2016), stating that sex trafficking must be understood in the context of the stark disparities between North and the developing South. They propose that the emergence of sex trafficking can be viewed through a conceptualisation of Marx's *primitive accumulation of capital*. Sexual trafficking can be viewed as part of an exploitation and commodification of labour which is part and parcel of a neo-liberal globalisation. The authors point to such factors such as the desocialisation of capital, the rise in privatisation of a global economy, and the development of a global sex industry, which have fostered the growth of sexual trafficking in women. With regards to the desocialisation of capital, the authors maintain that the rise of neo-liberal capitalism has precipitated an erosion of social rights and an increased vulnerability of the most powerless.

Taking these factors into consideration presents us with the necessary conditions in which the over-exploitation of labour comes into play, where migrants are the most vulnerable to exploitation. Sexual trafficking must be understood in the context where usually (migrant) women sell their sexual labour with or without consent. De Sousa Santos et al. (2010) suggest that the issue of sexual trafficking comes with a myriad of challenges for governments and policy makers. Perhaps the basis of such challenges is the fact that there is very little consensus on the definition of trafficking for sexual purposes. Consequently, evidence is vague with regards to solid reliable data. The authors further agree with commentators that government policy around trafficking is more about border control and monitoring migration flows, and legislation often results in the criminalisation of those "trafficked". Governments in the Caribbean face a similar dilemma where the legislative response appears to condemn rather than support those who are "trafficked" into the region.

There is also criticism offered by post-colonial writers who argue against an essentialist, universal approach to trafficking which is dictated from the North. This presents little space for the voices of the South to be heard in relation to the development of legislative and other alternatives to deal with the issue.

> Police have smashed what they believe is a human trafficking ring here, and for the first time have charged individuals with this crime. As a result, a man and a woman will appear in court today jointly charged with human trafficking. Police public relations officer Inspector David Welch yesterday confirmed that the two were charged following a police raid of a bar in Nelson Street, The City, last Thursday. Reliable sources told the "Daily Nation" that the 22-year-old man and the bar's 36-year-old proprietress were arrested after police found five female Guyanese nationals, dressed only in bathing suits, working in the bar.
>
> (Price, 2013)

The above excerpt is typical of the Caribbean's governments' response to migrant sex work in the region. A response that clearly demonstrates that for many policy makers and commentators sex work falls under a purview of sexual trafficking. For example, websites like End Human trafficking in the Caribbean use the slogan "most acts of prostitution amount to sex trafficking" (CurbCrime, n.d.). The website uses the statement from former UN rapporteur who maintains with prostitution must come exploitation. This anti-trafficking ideological framework makes no allowances for the experiences of migrants to be heard, or explanations behind their migrations given. Rather, under the anti-trafficking framework migrants are criminalised and often sent "home" as quickly as possible under national and international security agendas (Sharma, 2015), as the Barbados government like many other Caribbean islands treat these "cases" as immigration cases.

Governments like Barbados – like many others – appear to use deportation to solve the issue of migrant sex work (Kempadoo, 2007, 2016). This is a reflection of a neo-colonial viewpoint where the "troublesome" Other in this context must be got rid of; like many of the recalcitrant slaves on the plantation who did not quite fit the stereotype of the "happy slave" were sold off. One is left unsure about the status of these "foreign nationals" detained in sex work clubs. We know little about their stories, working conditions, and their final outcomes. However, at the same time we are very aware that anecdotal evidence about migrant sex workers presents a much more complicated narrative than policy makers, and governments would have us believe. The *prostitute as victim* is a narrative that we know well. However, other evidence suggested by informal interviews shows us a different narrative, where migrant women from Trinidad, Dominican Republic, and Guyana come to Barbados to use their exoticism as currency to successfully compete against local sex workers. Yes, they may be deported but they will return in a few weeks to ply their trade again.

It is in this particular context that Spivak (1988) questions whether the subaltern can speak from such a "powerless" space. Sharma (2015) too opines that the ideology of sex trafficking and by extension sex work makes migrants completely invisible. I challenge this view and say we see mobile sex workers on every street corner, they are certainly not invisible, and their voices can be heard clearly: "I come here to make money". I concur on the one hand that sexualised spaces are therefore invisible and not regarded as worthy of social protection and support (Cabezas, 2016, pp. 46–47), but if we accept this stance, we ignore the agency and entrepreneurship embedded in all kinds of sex work.

The use of a post-colonial approach in criminology as it applies to sex trafficking in the Caribbean opens the doors to an interrogation about the US political and economic neo-colonial maneuvering in the region (Kempadoo, 2016). The anti-trafficking discourse, which is intertwined with sex work narratives, according to Kempadoo "allows women's sexual purity to be rescued in the national imagination. . . . Caribbean women are restored to respectability and moral rectitude" (2016, p. 81). In this discourse, as argued by both Cabezas and Kempadoo, migrant sex workers are stereotypically represented as the sexual Other who challenges the respectability of the Caribbean woman, thus she does not deserve any social help, she does not deserve saving. Rather, as pointed out by Kempadoo, she becomes a target of "racial discrimination, harassment, detention, and deportation" (2016, p. 81).

In a climate where state borders have become sites for policing migrant bodies, this anti-trafficking discourse is urgent for criminologists to challenge in the region (Pickering & Ham, 2013). Moreover, as Kempadoo argues, the Caribbean cannot simply buy into US international discourses regarding the state. It is time that Caribbean nations develop our own frames of analysis regarding post-coloniality, sex work, and trafficking. Research needs to be undertaken in order to present a counter discourse to voice racial and ethnic differences, and thereby, empower the silenced sex worker whose history and life begins in the sex club.

Discussion

The use of a post-colonial theoretical framework in criminology, according to Cunneen and Rowe (2014), means an articulation of the ways in which the discourse criminalises and silences the voices of the disadvantaged, and marginalises – in this case – migrant sex workers. In "Doing criminology from the periphery: Crime and punishment in Asia", Lee and Laidler (2013) raise the epistemological question about the situatedness of criminology. A discipline backed by a discourse, which has remained centred in the North to the detriment of the South. According to Lee and Laidler (2013), this construction of knowledge in the North has led to the neglect and distortion of many problems in the South not covered by any Anglo-American criminology text (Keim, 2010, p. 16). The authors put out a similar call to those writing from the post-colonial South, with their proposal to develop more frameworks of knowledge, thus breaking away from the ethnocentric discourses that have framed discourses in the South.

The purpose of the chapter was to provide a new understandings of the way in which Caribbean criminology is linked with post-coloniality by exploring governments and policy makers' response to the complexities involved in sex trafficking and migrant sex work. The chapter also focused on the ways in which such neo-colonial discourses continue to undermine indigenous knowledge and experiences in criminology, and the need to develop indigenous frameworks. Throughout this chapter, I have argued that Caribbean governments' adherence to neo-colonial criminological laws and practices does not offer any challenges to the inherent ontological weaknesses inherent in a discipline whose theories and paradigms do not speak to the Caribbean experience. I have used the example of how regional governments have jumped on the bandwagon of "sex trafficking" with very little empirical evidence to justify this "jump". Further, in adopting this neo-colonial framework for understanding sex trafficking, governments and agencies also limit understandings of the multiplicities of the way in which indigenous migrant sex work is played out, along with the resilience of Caribbean women to survive.

Note

1 I use epistemology here to refer to 'knowledge as truth' construction.

References

Bhabha, H. (1983). The Other question. . .Homi K Bhabha reconsiders the stereotype and colonial discourse. *Screen*, *24*, 18–36. Retrieved from http://courses.washington.edu/com597j/pdfs/bhabha_the%20other%20question.pdf.

Cabezas, A. (2016). Invisible Dominican women: Discourses of trafficking into Puerto Rico. *Cadernos Pagu*, 1–30. doi: 10.1590/18094449201600470007.

Cunneen, C., & Rowe, S. (2014). Changing narratives: Colonised peoples, criminology and social work. *International Journal for Crime, Justice and Social Democracy*, *9*(16), 49–67.

CurbCrime (nd). *Prostitution and sex trafficking*. Retrieved from https://endhumantrafficking.wordpress.com.

De Shalit, A., Heynen, R., & Van der Meulen, E. (2014). Human trafficking and media myths: Federal funding, communication strategies, and Canadian anti trafficking programs. *Canadian Journal of Communication*, *39*(3), 385–412.

De Sousa De Sousa Santos, B., Gomes, C., & Duarte, M. (2010). The sexual trafficking of women: Representations of illegality and victimization. *RCCS, Annual Review*, *2*,

167–191. Retrieved from https://estudogeral.sib.uc.pt/bitstream/10316/36619/1/The%20 Sexual%20Trafficking%20of%20Women_Representations%20of%20Illegality%20 and%20Victimisation.pdf.

Jessop, D. (2013, January 25). *Crime is damaging the Caribbean development*. Retrieved from Caribbean Council website www.caribbean-council.org/wp-content/uploads/ 2014/09/coljan25-Crime-and-development.pdf.

Keim, W. (2010). The internationalization of social sciences: Distortions, dominations and prospects. In International Social Science Council (Hg.) (Ed.), *World social science report: Knowledge divides* (pp. 169–170). Paris: UNESCO Publishing.

Kempadoo, K. (2007). The war on human trafficking in the Caribbean. *Race and Class*, *49*(2), 79–84.

Kempadoo, K. (2016). Revitalizing imperialism: Contemporary campaigns against sex trafficking and modern slavery. *Cadernos Pagu*, *47*, 1–18. doi: doi.org/10.1590/ 18094449201600470008.

Lee, M., & Laidler, K. (2013). Doing criminology from the periphery: Crime and punishment in Asia. *Theoretical Criminology*, *17*(2), 141–157.

Pickering, S., & Ham, J. (2013). Hot pants at the border: Sorting sex work from trafficking. *British Journal of Criminology*, *54*(1), 2–19.

Price, S. (2013, April 22). Ring busted. *Nationnews*. Retrieved from www.nationnews.com/ nationnews/news/52362/story-ring-busted.

Sharma, N. (2015). Anti-trafficking: Whitewash for anti-immigration programmes. *Open Democracy Blog*. Retrieved from www.opendemocracy. net/beyondslavery/nandita-sharma/antitrafficking-whitewash-for- antiimmigration-programmes.

Spivak, G. (1988). Can the subaltern speak? In C. Nelson, & L. Grossbert (Eds.), *Marxism and the interpretation of culture* (pp. 280–316). Urbana: University of Illoinis Press.

U.S. Department of State. (2004). *Victims of trafficking and violence protection act of 2000: Trafficking in persons report* (U.S. Department of State Publication 11150). Retrieved from www.state.gov/documents/organization/34158.pdf.

Discussion

Katharina J. Joosen

This edited volume was designed to add to the existing body of scientific, empirical, and theoretical work on crime (victimisation), and criminal justice in the Caribbean. First, we believed that the impact of post-colonialism on crime needed to form a significant part of such a volume. This is especially so, as ties to the former colonial powers are still manifested throughout the various Caribbean societies either directly through semi-independence or indirectly through language, lingering cultural identities, and migration movements to the former "mother country". Second, we wanted to shed light on the impact that gender, by way of an examination of gender roles, perceptions of femininity, and motherhood have on victimisation, offending, and sentencing within what are predominantly, matrifocal Caribbean societies. To investigate these impacts on a developing Caribbean criminology, the chapters in this volume have focused on how impacts of post-colonialism and/or gender throughout the Caribbean impacted on (a) types of offending, (b) victimisation, and (c) criminal justice system responses and policies.

Impacts of post-colonialism

An analysis of the various chapters covering criminological topics across the former Dutch, French, and English Caribbean reveals a number of critical points of note. In describing the importance of a post-colonial or counter colonial criminology, Agozino (2003, 2004) called for a decolonisation of the *Establishment Criminology* (see Oriola, 2006). To this end, he highlighted a number of areas concerning crime and criminal justice in the Caribbean that had been neglected within the academic literature. First, he emphasised the need to focus on the crimes committed during the transatlantic slavery, colonialism, and subsequent neo-colonialism. In keeping with this call, Chapter 1 has demonstrated the manner in which the resistance strategies of female slaves in the Dutch Caribbean and Suriname should be reframed and decriminalised in order to do justice to the "right to rebel as fundamental human right" (Oriola, 2006, p. 105). Furthermore, Bijnaar, Lurvink, and Joosen have argued that this criminalisation of such a basic human right, added to the dehumanisation of the enslaved by interpreting potential behavioural responses to trauma and loss as proof for the hypersexualised stereotype of the *Jezebel*, or for the unruly and savage character of blacks – or as so perceived and recorded in history by the coloniser. Last, Chapter 1 has shown how this unjust criminalisation by former colonisers still can contribute to the over-representation of black women in official crime rates and prison populations of former "mother countries". This study highlighted the link between the criminalised resistance strategies of female slaves, and the continued unjust representations of the behaviour of black females as dominant, angry/violent, and hypersexual (e.g. Brennan, 2006), and black female offenders as "beyond reformation" (Brennan, Chesney-Lind, Vandenberg, & Wulf-Ludden, 2015). In doing so, Chapter 1 has shown that – indeed as suggested by Cunneen (2011) – the potential of a post-colonial perspective on criminology includes an understanding of the relationships between colonisation and the ongoing over-representation in "crime" of the formerly enslaved.

Second, Agozino (2003, 2004) emphasised the role of institutionalised racism and its importance for criminological studies both in former colonies as well as former colonizing nations (see also Cunneen, 2011). Within the current volume, two chapters in particular have focused attention on the impact of institutionalised racism and racist stereotypes on criminological relevant topics, such as victimisation rates and the treatment and diagnoses given by (forensic) mental health organisations. Quantitative analyses in Chapter 4 presented an intriguing discrepancy between official registered and self-reported data concerning victimisation rates among various ethnic groups in Trinidad and Tobago: official data showed a stark over-representation across offence types of victims of African descent which in fact is not found in self-reported data. Explanations provided by the authors included the expectation that over-policing among people from African descent, and in neighbourhoods where persons of African descent reside, could contribute to such inflated official victimisation rates, as compared to official victimisation rates among other ethnic groups. This study is particularly interesting as former empirical criminological studies have "been overly concerned with minorities, particularly black minorities, as offenders" (Phillips & Bowling, 2003, p. 282). Furthermore, Chapter 11 discussed the high prevalence of psychosis among Caribbean migrants in Western countries as a potential risk factor for offending. In this discussion, racism was discussed as a risk factor for psychosis, a risk factor for offending, as well as a potential explanation for misinterpretation of behaviour as violent, psychotic, and in need of compulsory treatment. In addressing these so-called "toxic interactions" institutionalised racism takes centre stage within these complex relationships between migration, social defeat, psychosis, and offending among Caribbean nationals abroad.

Third, Agozino's work (2003, 2004) highlighted the imbalance between the large numbers of criminological studies focusing on offences committed by the poor, and the lack of attention for those white-collar crimes committed by the rich: such as public fraud, corruption, and embezzlement. Chapter 3 of this volume examined the prevalence of public fraud and corruption in the Dutch Caribbean and discussed what the impact of post-colonialism might be on this prevalence. According to Schotborg-van de Ven, there are several possible impacts of post-colonialism on the current-day perpetration of fraud and corruption: (a) societies based on gain as opposed to common good, implying that colonial actions based on self-enrichment have been copied by politicians and high-ranking public officials in former colonies, (b) *political patronage*, which entails relationships based on loyalty and the exchange of goods and services, (c) the forced upon Dutch political structures which are ineffective for small-scale island nations, and vulnerable for bad governance, and (d) a culture of fear/silence that implies a translation of the colonial fear of the slave master into a fear of authority in general, causing a lack of mutual trust, and a fear to take responsibility or to contradict authorities. However, it is also discussed by the author of Chapter 3 that the current prevalence of fraud and corruption across Dutch Caribbean islands should also be interpreted beyond post-colonial impacts, taking into account the current-day media attention and coverage of high-profile cases and the impact this has on political and diplomatic relations, the islands' reputation, stigmatisation, public scrutiny, and subsequent fears of reporting on and prosecuting of so-called "big fish" in organised crime circuits.

A fourth point emphasised by Agozino (2003, as cited in Oriola, 2006) was the need for ethnographic methods to balance out the focus on quantitative methods in Establishment Criminology. This is necessary foremost to voice the lived experiences, realities, and perspectives of Caribbean nationals, and also to enable a critical examination of the existing quantitative "facts as truth" concerning offending rates among (Afro-) Caribbean nationals (Phillips & Bowling, 2003). Or as formulated by Oriola (2006, p. 113) "people must be studied not as some subdued or captive subjects with western eyes, but in the context of their cultural milieu". For example, Chapter 12 on Kingston's garrison communities focused on sense-making and identity formation processes in high-violence environments in which community-identity is politicised. With her ethnographic study Satchell showed that a great level of "everyday unfairness" was experienced in these communities. Furthermore, corruption among politicians and church leaders seems to have led to the conviction among almost half of Jamaicans that their society is fundamentally unjust and unfair. Her findings are in line with a recent study by Thame (2011) that discussed the relationship between decolonisation and the experience of violence in post-colonial Jamaica. She stated that identities based on race and class spawned the acceptance and tolerance of violence against the poor. As the failure to live up to colonial patriarchy's notions regarding man's role in the family (i.e. as breadwinner) and society (i.e. in contributing to the economy) demeaned poor blacks in particular, black men in garrison communities armed themselves in response to the (post-)colonial violence inflicted upon them. This is also in line with the impacts on their environment as cited by narrators in Satchell's study such as political violence, the limited access to meaningful employment, and the insufficient available housing infrastructure. According to Satchell, these environmental impacts led to the emergence of self-help violence and informal settlements in the post-independence society of Jamaica, which fostered the development of a subculture of violence. Or as formulated by Thame (2011, p. 79) communities in which there is constantly a "suspended atmosphere of violence".

In addition, Chapter 10 presented a frame analysis on the perceptions of the public on causes of crime in Antigua. With data from newspaper articles and focus groups, Matthews highlighted a strong public support of family and community disintegration as the main cause of Antigua's crime rates, while explicit connections between crime, poverty, marginalisation, and discrimination were refuted. These findings are interesting as they show that family disintegration is perceived in conflicting ways. On the one hand, data seems to show a certain internalisation of the European two-parent family ideal, which was forced upon Caribbean societies during post-colonialism: as Caribbean matrifocality has long been pathologised by the West as the main cause of crime rates among black populations (Phillips & Bowling, 2003). On the other hand, some focus groups explicitly emphasised that family disintegration in Antigua's society should be interpreted as the disintegration of *extended* family networks. Moreover, as discussed by Matthews, the fact that the *blocked opportunities* frame received little support as a cause of crime, underlines the fact that unreliable governments have created a public perception that is more willing to focus on family- and community-related causes of crime – which are outside of direct governmental influence – than causes related to economic and social marginalisation which should be dealt with by these governments.

A last point that has been stated as important for the development of a post-colonial criminology is a critical reflection on the Eurocentric colonial and post-colonial structures that still continue to form the base of many Caribbean justice systems and crime policies. This is particularly worrisome as the justice systems of such former colonizing nations are widely known to suffer from institutionalised racism contributing to inflated, arrest rates, prosecutions, convictions, and imprisonment of (black) ethnic minorities (Cunneen, 2011). In Chapter 15 Paul discussed the emphasis placed upon law-and-order approaches in which imprisonment of offenders is approached merely as a way to protect the public from criminals, while little investment is made towards successful reintegration and the prevention of recidivism. These programs have had little success in Europe and the United States (see American Society of Criminology, 2017); therefore, it should come as no surprise that these policies do little to help Caribbean nations attain crime prevention goals. Furthermore, the neo-colonial military-like approach of Dominican police was one of the factors contributing to limited perceptions by offenders and the public of the legitimacy of police and correction officers' conduct. In a post-colonial light, especially, an emphasis on incarceration of those marginalised by society should also be considered as "an extension of dispossession and the abuse of human rights" (Cunneen, 2011, p. 5).

In addition, Chapter 16 presented a discussion regarding such Eurocentric crime policies, in particular, relating to sex trafficking and sex work. Phillips presented a strong case for the importance of voicing the perspective of the sex worker, against the assumption that all sex work involves sex trafficking. This assumption denies female migrant sex workers any agency while some of them in fact might make more deliberate choices – as opposed to being mere victims of exploitation – regarding their strategies for economic survival. Furthermore, she critically addressed the adaptation by Caribbean governments of the American and European movement towards *crimmigration* policies (Stumpf, 2006), in which legislative responses concerning sex trafficking end up mainly focused on the control of borders and migration flows, labelling migrant sex workers as violators of migration laws as opposed to groups vulnerable for exploitation.

Last, in Chapter 14 van de Vorst added to this perspective that Dutch Caribbean judicial systems are in dire need of valid translations of psychological and intellectual measures in the local Creole *Papiamento* to improve diagnoses of (male) prisoners in light of their pre-trial forensic psychiatric evaluations. In this chapter the author discussed the impact the enforcement of Dutch as a first language up until recently might have had on the language development of the local Creole. Papiamento only recently became an official language; schools have only recently begun teaching in Papiamento; and measures for psychological and intellectual ability have only recently started to become validated in Papiamento. This control over language might, one the one hand, have caused a lack in literacy and school attainments of economically marginalised people in the Dutch Caribbean. On the other hand, it might have contributed to inflated rates of (migrated) Dutch Caribbean nationals diagnosed with intellectual disabilities impairments; creating and enforcing racist stereotypes of (black) Dutch Caribbean nationals as dumb and dangerous. Through these chapters, authors from the Caribbean, Europe, and the United States together have aimed to contribute to break the silence that Agozino (2004) described concerning the development of a post-colonial criminology. Therefore, we hope this volume provided a timely perspective to oppose imperialist reason, and to create a greater international platform for Caribbean relevant criminological empirical studies.

Impacts of gender on victimisation and crime

Throughout the current volume several chapters have addressed the impact of gender on: (a) victimisation (Chapters 4, 5, 6, and 7), (b) offending (Chapters 2, 8, and 9), and (c) sentencing (Chapter 13) of Caribbean nationals in the Caribbean and abroad. Concerning gendered victimisation in the Caribbean, several chapters in this volume have highlighted the higher rates of certain types of victimisation among women as compared to men. Chapter 4 showed that – across ethnic groups – almost 100 per cent of victims of sexual offences in Trinidad and Tobago were female. According to the study of Hayes, DeJong, Dathorne, and Lawrence, in St Lucia, this was especially the case for forced sexual contact and rape. However, Chapter 7 also highlighted the fact that self-reported victimisation rates for sexual offences might be higher among men, than is shown by official data. In the St Lucia study, one in eight male participants reported sexual victimisation during their lifetime, and although not significantly different, more men than women reported victimisation through attempted oral or anal sex. Indeed, in Trinidad and Tobago a previous study has shown similar percentages across gender regarding self-reported sexual victimisation (Le Franc, Samm-Vaughan, Hambleton, Fox, & Brown, 2008). This potential underreporting of male sexual victimisation could be related to the cultural taboo and stigma that remains attached to male sexual victimisation across the Caribbean.

Nevertheless, Seepersad and Wortley also showed that again for domestic violence, women across ethnic groups were more prevalent as victims in the official data. In Chapter 6, DeShong presented gendered narratives of intimate partner violence (IPV) on the island of St Vincent and discussed how these narratives are constructed in order to justify, rationalise, and support the perpetration of IPV by men towards women. Applying theoretical notions of decolonial feminism (e.g. Lugones, 2010, 2016), DeShong demonstrated how gender norms – as dictated by colonialism and imbedded in Caribbean societies still – cause men to inflict their "rational" and "effective" physical violence upon women to control female sexuality and recalcitrance: to tame her. These qualitative gendered narratives regarding IPV perpetration were also supported by the quantitative finding of Hayes et al. in St Lucia regarding the greater support of rape myths among men as compared to women. According to Thame (2011, p. 78), in the post-colonial Caribbean "working class men were not able to exercise patriarchy in relation to the society as a whole since they were to be dominated by middle class men, but they could use violence against their women". These colonial legacies seem to be enforced by the fact that more recently, the position of Caribbean women has improved due to higher educational levels and the ability to earn an independent income, which according to some scholars has led men to repair this erosion of their power – in part – by domestic violence (Blank, 2013; Momsen, 2012; Kibbelaar, 2010).

Regarding the victimisation of girls in the Caribbean, Faedi Duramy presented findings on Haiti concerning the phenomenon of *restavèk*, or child domestic slavery (Chapter 5). These children – mainly girls – suffer extreme physical and emotional neglect, and are at increased risk for physical and sexual abuse. Such systematic victimisation and exploitation of ethnically and economically marginalised girls bears resemblance to the violence perpetrated by the white coloniser during the era of transatlantic slavery. Therefore, within a Caribbean context it is difficult to see impacts of gendered victimisation completely separate from impacts of post-colonialism as gender intersects with (or perhaps shapes) societal structures, expectations, and attributions which seem to stem from the colonial era, post-colonial socioeconomic policies, and patriarchy. In slavery enslaved women and children were deemed of less worth, and it seems that – although improving in many ways – the position of (Afro)-Caribbean women (especially in lower socioeconomic strata) is still one of a certain degree of submissiveness to (colonial) patriarchal notions of Man and Woman. In this position girls and women are vulnerable to sexual and physical abuse at the hands of those either strange or related to them.

These gendered notions seem to also impact on gendered risk factors for (violent) youth offending and the buffering role of social capital in this relationship. As Matthew showed, adolescent girls in her sample particularly benefitted from the protective effect of positive family attachment on the risk for violent offending. Boys on the other hand were at decreased risk for violent offending if they reported more neighbourhood cohesion, and when they grew up in two-parent families. In general, these findings concerning Trinidad and Tobago are in line with the perception of Antiguan people regarding the disintegration of families and the community as the cause of crime (Chapter 10). Moreover, a recent study on Dominica also showed that across three poor neighbourhoods experienced social capital decreased crime at the community level (Paul, 2015). From a more gendered perspective, it remains interesting in the light of Caribbean patriarchal gender norms that girls did not seem to benefit from a protective effect of neighbourhood cohesion or school-related social capital. It could be that female gender norms keep women in the house out of the need to protect them from the described victimisation of sexual and physical assaults. Following that line of thinking, girls that lack family attachment or parental involvement are not kept at home, and therefore, at increased risk for delinquent friends and (violent) offending. However, if girls are kept at home, they also have fewer opportunities to form positive relationships within their communities, and thus miss out on the protective effects of such social capital. If from a young age, girls are also stimulated to form positive neighbourhood social ties, they might have a safety net – as is the case for boys concerning delinquency – in case family attachments and involvement are falling short in protecting them from adolescent delinquent behaviour.

In this light, the role of matrifocality also deserves attention. As stated, Matthew showed that only for boys growing up in a two-parent family decreased the risk for violent offending. As most Caribbean single-parent families are headed by women, this finding implies that absent fathers might contribute to boys' violent offending, but that this is not the case concerning girls violent offending. This is not to state that (Dutch) Caribbean girls are not affected by father absence (Girigori, 2015), however, perhaps less when predicting offending risk. In fact, a recent study among Dutch Caribbean women showed that more self-reported delinquency was related to growing up with an uninvolved biological mother, while having an uninvolved biological father did not have such an impact on offending (Joosen, Slotboom, & Bijleveld, 2017). This could be due to the fact that boys in particular miss out on male role models to prevent the development of violent antisocial behaviour, while women are particularly affected when – within the norm of matrifocal Caribbean societies – they have to grow up without their mothers. Or as phrased by Blank (2013, p. 2): "Slave mothers were the sole recognised parent; paternity was not considered to matter unless the father of the child was the slave master".

What about the link between matrifocality and the offending of single mothers themselves? As discussed in Chapter 9 among criminally active Caribbean women incarcerated in the Netherlands, being single was in fact more strongly related to periods of incarceration then was the case for single motherhood. Moreover, having a substance-(ab)using partner or even a violent partner was inversely related to periods of incarceration. Thus, while gendered intimate partner violence might have many negative impacts and consequences – as addressed in Chapter 6 – it did not seem to be related to the exact moments that criminally active Caribbean women ended up incarcerated across their life course. Rather, having any relationship seemed to be better than having no relationship at all. As having debts was also related to periods of incarceration, the idea of a feminisation of poverty (e.g. Sudbury, 2013) seems to fit with these findings: when these high-risk Caribbean women were single and in debt they were more likely to experience periods of incarceration. However, while taking care of children (regardless of the effects of relationship status and debts) was a factor that kept these women out of prison, single motherhood was in fact not related to the timing of incarceration for these women. Momsen's (2012) double paradox between matrifocality and patriarchy seems a fitting frame to understand these intricate relationships between both the positive and negative impacts intimate relationships can have on (criminally active) Caribbean women. On the one hand, strong, financially independent women form the centre of most Caribbean households. However, as there is no matriarchy, men remain the official head of the home when he is in fact present (Blank, 2013; Brown & Chevannes, 1998); moreover, even in matrifocal families, girls remain socialised to conform to patriarchal gender norms and roles.

Last, Chapter 13 showed that these patriarchal gender roles are also of influence regarding sentencing decisions of magistrates on Barbados. Bailey showed in his qualitative study that female offenders are more likely to receive milder sentences when they have children to take care of. Again the double paradox between matrifocality and patriarchal gender roles seems at play here. First of all, magistrates indicated that offending fathers were – despite their fatherhood – less likely to receive a more lenient treatment by the court as was the case when mothers appeared in court as defendants. From a patriarchal perspective, women are perceived to assume most of the caregiving responsibilities. However, in matrifocal families, fathers do not always fulfil their patriarchal financial responsibilities, which could have an additional impact on sentencing decisions regarding mothers who stand trial. These gendered policies are further illustrated in Chapter 16 through a discussion of gendered sexual norms regarding female sex work and in Chapter 1 by reframing the criminalisation of survival sex of victimised female slaves. In patriarchal Caribbean societies "boys have sexual freedom and are generally encouraged to experiment sexually, whereas girls may be beaten if they are suspected of pursuing sex" (Blank, 2013, p. 5).

"What got you here won't get you there": future directions for criminological research in the Caribbean

This discussion aims to highlight the rich body of studies on Caribbean crime and criminal justice as presented in the current volume. At the same time we need to discuss where the road of a post-colonial criminology will need to lead next. Bennett and Lynch (1996) formulated four major impediments for the future of criminological studies in the Caribbean: (a) governments and funding agency needed to be persuaded of the importance of a scientific approach in understanding crime and criminality, (b) there should be readily gained access to available crime data, (c) and accessibility to social and economic data (neighbourhood and community level), which should be combined with individual level data enabling multi-level analyses of crime problems, (d) the need to use different mediums for collecting data, beyond the use of registered police data. As we have learned from the various chapters in the current volume, great strides have been made since then. Several of the larger Caribbean islands have developed and implemented policies and systems to structurally collect crime data on both the individual as well as the community and neighbourhood level. Furthermore, both quantitative as well as qualitative measures and analyses are being conducted in Caribbean criminological studies. So what is next?

First, despite the development of systems to develop registered crime data, there are few large-scale Caribbean studies to date, that combine both official data on offending with self-reported questionnaires on delinquency and offending. Second, there are few if any population-based longitudinal studies investigating the development of antisocial behaviour and delinquency from infancy to adulthood, in which factors from genetic, psychological, as well as sociological perspectives are combined. This seems particularly pertinent in light of the increasing rates of violent (youth) offending across Caribbean nations, which cannot – and should not – be simply and uncritically explained and acted upon based on empirical evidence-based policies developed in the West. There is also much to discover beyond the realm of prevalence rates of various types of victimisation towards the identification of underlying explanatory mechanisms of the differential impact of such experiences within the specific context of Caribbean societies.

However, such studies require great amounts of funding and time: in short, a long-term vision that needs to be supported by local (sometimes fleeting) governments. Nevertheless, there is much to be gained from policies that are empirically driven, as efficient policies to prevent crime, lower risks of recidivism, and increased legitimacy of Caribbean law enforcement agents can only be more cost-effective as well. Thus, the message should perhaps be that empirical criminological studies generate – as opposed to – cost more governmental spending. Moreover, as crime in the Caribbean and in other nations continues to become interlinked across country boundaries due to organised international crime networks, empirical and theoretical work on crime and criminal justice in the Caribbean will continue to be of interest to many scholars and policy makers worldwide. However, even though decolonial criminology in our opinion should remain an inclusive field of study, interested international scholars will need to look critically at their own imperialist upbringing in order to be open to a decolonial collaboration with Caribbean scholars. In doing so, great things might be expected for the future landscape of decolonial criminology.

References

Agozino, B. (2003). *Counter-colonial criminology: A critique of imperialist reason.* London: Pluto Press.

Agozino, B. (2004). Imperialism, crime and criminology: Towards the decolonisation of criminology. *Crime, Law, & Social Change*, *41*(4), 343–358.

American Society of Criminology (2017). *Statement of the American Society of Criminology Executive Board concerning the Trump administration's policies relevant to crime and justice.* Retrieved from www.asc41.com/policies/ASC_Executive_Board_Statement_on_Trump_Administration_Crime_and_Justice_Policies.pdf.

Bennett, R.R., & Lynch, J.P. (1996). Towards a Caribbean criminology: Prospects and problems. *Caribbean Journal of Criminology and Social Psychology*, *1*(1), 8–37.

Blank, S. (2013). An historical and contemporary overview of gendered Caribbean relations. *Journal of Arts and Humanities*, *2*(4), 1–10.

Brennan, P.K. (2006). Sentencing female misdemeanants: An examination of the direct and indirect effects of race/ethnicity. *Justice Quarterly*, *23*(1), 60–95.

Brennan, P.K., Chesney-Lind, M., Vandenberg, A.L., & Wulf-Ludden, T. (2015). The saved and the damned: Racial/ethnic differences in media construction of female drug offenders. *Radical Criminology*, *5*, 47–98.

Brown, J., & Chevannes, B. (1998). *"Why man stay so": An examination of gender socialization in the Caribbean*. Kingston: University of the West Indies/UNICEF.

Cunneen, C. (2011). Postcolonial perspectives for criminology. In M. Bosworth, & C. Hoyte (Eds.), *What is criminology*, (pp. 1–15). Oxford, UK: Oxford University Press.

Girigori, O. (2015). *Father Absence: The consequences for reproductive behavior and mating strategies among females*. (Unpublished doctoral thesis). University of Groningen, Groningen.

Joosen, K.J., Slotboom, A.-M., & Bijleveld, C. (2017). The relationship between experienced racism and delinquency among Dutch Caribbean women. Paper presented at the meeting of SALISES, Trinidad.

Kibbelaar, P. (2010). *Vrouwen van de Nederlandse Antillen en Aruba [Women from the Dutch Antilles and Aruba]*. Retrieved from Rijksoverheid website: www.rijksoverheid.nl/documenten/rapporten/2010/04/20/onderzoek-vrouwen-van-de-nederlandse-antillen-en-aruba.

Le Franc, E., Samm-Vaughan, M., Hambleton, I., Fox, K., & Brown, D. (2008). Interpersonal violence in three Caribbean countries: Barbados, Jamaica, and Trinidad and Tobago. *Revista Panamericana de Salud Pública*, *24*(6), 409–421.

Lugones, M. (2010). Toward a decolonial feminism. *Hypatia*, *25*(4), 742–759.

Lugones, M. (2016). The coloniality of gender. In W. Harcourt (Ed.), *The Palgrave handbook of gender and development* (pp. 13–33). Houndsmill: Palgrave Macmillan.

Momsen, J.H. (2012). Patriarchy in absentia: Women and development in the Caribbean. In A. Buang, & J.H. Momsen (Eds.), *Women and empowerment in the NAM world: Different contexts, different facets* (pp. 71–86). Kuala Lumpur: NAM Institute for the Empowerment of Women.

Oriola, T. (2006). Biko Agozino and the rise of post-colonial criminology. *African Journal of Criminology and Justice Studies*, *2*(1), 104–131.

Paul, K.S. (2015). *Variations in levels of crime among three poor communities in Dominica: Is social capital an agent?* (Unpublished doctoral dissertation). University of the West Indies, Cave Hill, Barbados.

Phillips, C. & Bowling, B. (2003). Racism, ethnicity, and criminology. *British Journal of Criminology*, *43*(2), 269–290.

Stumpf, J. (2006). The crimmigration crisis: Immigrants, crime, and sovereign power. *American University Law Review*, *56*(2), 367–419.

Sudbury, J. (2013). Mules, "yardies", and other folk devils: Mapping cross-border imprisonment in Britain. In J. Sudbury (Ed.), *Global Lockdown: Race, gender, and the prison-industrial complex* (pp. 167–184). London/New York: Routledge.

Thame, M. (2011). Reading violence and postcolonial decolonization through Fanon: The case of Jamaica. *The Journal of Pan African Studies*, *4*(7), 75–93.

Index

abolitionist feminism 320
Aboriginal youth victimisation 74
absent fathers 180
accountability and bribery 63
acculturation process 75
Act on the Prohibition and Elimination of All Forms of Abuse, Violence, Ill treatment or Inhumane Treatment against Children 109, 119
action-oriented programs 304
acts against children 90
African American crime 37
African American women 25–26, 125, 153
African cultural tradition 211
Afro-Caribbean women 125, 189–190, 203
Afro-Guyanese women 125
age-crime curve 237
age-graded informal control 165
Agozino, Biko 226
agricultural economy 36
American Barometers Survey 97
analysis of variance (ANOVA) 78–79, 96
antebellum Southern slavery 11
anthropological resistance framework 11
anti-psychotic medication 236
anti-trafficking activism 321–322
anti-trafficking laws 319
Antigua *see* crime in Antigua
antisocial groups 182
antithetical groups in a third space 248
arrest rates in Trinidad and Tobago 77–78
autonomous positional identity 2
autonomy/agency of slaves 19–21

badness honour 250
Barbados *see* gender bias in sentencing
Barbados Penal System Reform (Amendment) Act 278
bidirectional interaction of racism 237
bilingualism 292
binarism 248–249
biological vulnerability for psychosis 234
bivariate results 175–177, **176**
blame in intimate partner violence 133–137
blameworthiness 269
Blocked Opportunities frame 216–219, 226, 227, 328
Bonaire *see* intellectual disability among male prisoners
Braithwaite, John 222
break-ins in Trinidad/Tobago *85,* 85–88, *86,* **87,** 92
breaking rules, as criminalised resistance 17–19, **18**
bribery 58
bribes/bribery 55, 58, 63–64
Brigade for the Protection of Minors 119
British colonial re-education efforts 226
buggery in Trinidad/Tobago 84
Bureau Rijbewijzen (Bureau of Drivers' Licensing) 60
burglary in Trinidad/Tobago *85,* 85–88, *86,* **87,** 92

cannabis use 239
Caribbean crime: changing nature of 1–2; economically depressed areas and 219; embezzlement crime 54, 58, 60–61, 326; forgery crime 58, 60–61, 63; future directions 332–333; gender considerations 2; organised crime 2, 67–68; overview 3–4; post-colonialism 3; social capital 165–167; *see also* fraud and corruption; intimate partner violence; post-colonial theorizing on crime

Caribbean Development Bank (CDB) 211–212
Caribbean Netherlands (BES) 36
Catholic Church 114
celebrity humanism 320
Central Statistical Office 76, 102
chi-square tests 197
Chicago Area Project 220, 223, 227
child domestic slavery in Haiti: domestic legislations 108–109; findings and discussion 110–118; international law 106–108; introduction to 105; methods of study 109–110; responses to 119; summary of 119–120, 330
Child Protective Services 196
child sexual abuse 22
childcare impact on incarceration 201–202
chivalry thesis 268–269
choking violence 132
Christian churches 211
Christianity/Christianisation 16–17, 21, 211
Citizen Security and Justice Program (CSJP) 253, 254–255, 257–258
civil servants law 53
Coalition Haïtienne pour la Defense des Droits de l'Enfant (COHADDE) 118
cohesion scale 170
collective efficacy 210
colonial/modern gender system/logic 123–125, 132, 136
colonialism 124, 247
colonisation 153, 233
Committee on the Rights of the Child 109
Commonwealth of Dominica Police Force (CDPF) 303–304
community breakdown 226
community crime prevention 210
community interest groups 182
community leaders' attitudes toward police 309–312
community-oriented policing 304
community solution needs 223–224
Computer Assisted Personal Interview (CAPI) 195, 196–197
conformity 180, 209, 215
conspiracy of rebellious slaves 14
Convention on the Elimination of all Forms of Discrimination against Women 107
Coomaraswamy, Radhika 112
Cops for Christ 221
Council of Europe Convention 38
Court of Appeal 59, 64
court-ordered psychological evaluations 294–295
court outcome effects 277–279
creole language 287, 290–291, 329
creolisation 248–249
crib death *see* Sudden Infant Death Syndrome
Crime and Problem Analysis (CAPA) 74, 76, 90
crime control and punishment: community leaders' attitudes toward police 309–312; crime control theory 302, 313; current study 305; discussion and implication 312–314; introduction to 300–302; local programs 303–305; methods of study 305–306; offender attitudes toward law enforcement 306–309; post-colonial impact 302–303; results of study 306–312
crime control theory 302, 313
crime in Antigua: Blocked Opportunities frame 216–219, 226, 227, 328; informal economies 211–213; introduction to 208; methods of study 214–216; results of study 216–226; Social Breakdown frame 220–226; social control theory 210–211; social disorganization theory 209–210; socioeconomic causes of 213–214; summary of 226–227; theoretical background 208–211
crime of necessity 217
crime-proneness 99
criminal justice organisations 301
criminogenic risk factors 194, 199–200, **200**
crimmigration policies 328–329
critical aftermath 248
cuckolding festival 133
cultural values shift 222–223
cultural victimology 155
culture of fear 56
culture of silence 56
culture of victimisation 56
Curacao, domestic violence 39
"Curinta-affair" case 64

dangerousness 269, 279
de Vries, Hendrika Reims 14–15, *15*
deception crime 58
decision-making processes 105, 279
decolonial feminist approach of IPV 124–125, 126

decolonisation 34–36, 325, 327
definite pressure 209
dehumanisation 153, 248, 325
delinquent acts analyses 177
Dementricia, Virginia 17–18
depersonalisation of slaves 21
deprived families 33
descriptive results 175–177, **176**
diagnostic tools, Papiamento-speaking population 287, 290–291, 329
disorganisation, as social change 210
diversification 1, 212
domestic responsibilities, gender roles 274
domestic servitude in Haiti *see* child domestic slavery in Haiti
domestic violence: Curacao 39; female victimisation 330; Haiti 117; Trinidad/Tobago 89–94, *90, 91,* **92, 93**
Dominica Police Force 311
Dominican sex work industry 62
double counting 90
drug-connected men 190–191
drug-connected women 190–191, 202
drug culture 40, 62, 191, 239
drug running 213
Dutch Bureau of Statistics (Centraal Bureau voor de Statistiek) 36
Dutch Caribbean female offenders *see* female prison population in Netherlands
Dutch Caribbean female slaves *see* female slaves
Dutch Centre of Expertise on HBV 42
Dutch Prison Project 196
Dutch West Indian Company 290

economic marginalisation of Afro-Caribbean women 203
economically depressed areas and crime 219
embezzlement crime 54, 58, 60–61, 326
employment impact on incarceration 201–202
ends justify means 218
escaped slaves 17–19, **18**
Ethics Committee of the Faculty of Law (CERCO) 195
ethnicity and crime victimisation, Trinidad/Tobago: burglary and break-ins *85,* 85–88, *86,* **87**; concept of race and 75–76; discussion of 98–101; domestic violence 89–94, *90, 91,* **92, 93**; introduction to 73; larceny *88,* 88–89, *89*; murder statistics 77–79, **78,** *78, 79*; overview 73–75; results of study 77–98; robbery *81,* 81–82, *82*; sexual offenses 82–85, *83,* **84,** *84,* 140; study data and method 77; summary of 102–103; survey data 94–98, **95, 97, 98**; woundings and shootings 79–81, *80*
ethnographic methodologies 252
European bourgeois 137
everyday unfairness 257–258, 327

factor loadings of sexual violence 157–158
familial responsibility 274–275
family attachment 170, 179
family breakdown 226
family realm criminality 225–226
family violence 38–39, 39–41
favouritism 58, 63, 66
Federal Sentencing Guidelines (US) 277, 281
female domestic responsibilities 280
female-headed households 167, 192–194
female offenders: dangerousness of 269; drug smugglers 191; as struggling mothers 193; youth problem behavior 167, 179–181
female prison population in Netherlands: analyses 197–199, **198, 199**; criminogenic risk factors 194, 199–200, **200**; current study on 194; discussion 202–204; drug-connected women 190–191; gendered pathways to offending 191–192; incarceration period variables 200–201; introduction 189; matrifocality impact on 192–194; measures 195–197; methods of study 194–199, **198, 199**; procedure 195; results of study 199–202, **200**; summary of 204
female slaves, criminalised resistance: autonomy/agency of slaves 19–21; breaking rules 17–19, **18**; current studies on 12–13; current viewpoints 25–26; discussion of 24–26; gendered types 11–12; historical views on 10; introduction to 9–13; methodology of study 13; murder by 14–16, *15*; non-violent resistance 12–13, 16–21, **18,** *19, 20*; protests by 13–14; results of study 13–24; rules and bureaucracy 16–17; summary of 26–27; trauma and loss by 21–24; violent resistance of 13–16, *15*
feminisation of poverty 192–193
financial dependency of women 40

fiscal imbalance 212
focal concerns theory 268, 269–270
Fondasyon Limyè Lavi 119
Foreign Direct Investment (FDI) 256
forgery crime 58, 60–61, 63
formal economies 212
Foyer Maurice Sixto (Maurice Sixto Home) 119
fraud and corruption: bribes/bribery 55, 58, 63–64; current study 57; data on 57; defined 53–54; existing literature on 54–55; favouritism 58, 63, 66; grand corruption 62; grand fraud 58, **60,** 61; introduction to 53–57; limitations to 58–59; methods 57–59; perpetrators, organisation/positions 65; petty corruption 58, 62; petty fraud 58, 59, 60, **60**; political corruption 58, 63–64; political fraud 58, **60,** 61–62; procedure 58; results of study on **59,** 59–65, **60**; summary of 65–68; verdicts on 64
French colonisation 112

gang culture: among youth 40; female involvement 180; Haven Town gangs 257; post-colonial theorizing 255–256
gangster girlfriend 193
garrison and identity 249
gender 2, 124, 329–332; *see also* honour-based violence
gender bias in sentencing: chivalry thesis 268–269; court outcome effects 277–279; discussion 279–281; familial responsibility 274–275; focal concerns theory 268, 269–270; focus of 267–268; gender role expectations 271, 272–274, 332; gendered assumptions 275–277; introduction to 267–270; methods of study 271–272; practical constraints 274–279; present study 270; theoretical perspectives 268
gender in youth problem behaviour: analyses 171–175, **172, 173, 174, 175**; control variables 171; descriptive and bivariate results 175–177, **176**; discussion 178–183; implications 182; introduction 163–164; limitations 183; methods of study 168–175, **172, 173, 174, 175**; results of study 175–178, **176**; sample/data collection 168–169; self-reported measures 169–170; social capital measures 170–171; social capital overview 164–168; summary of 183
gender-neutral policy 41
gender non-conformity 153
gender norms 123, 153
gender role expectations 271, 272–274
gendered assumptions 275–277
gendered pathways to offending 191–192
gendered portrayals of IPV 126–130
general strain theory 165
global apartheid 319
global organisations 58
grand corruption 62
grand fraud 58, **60,** 61
green insularity 35
Groninger Intelligence Test 2 translation 293
guilt 142
gun-toting youths 43

habitual offending 302
Haiti *see* child domestic slavery in Haiti
Haitian Institute for Childhood 116–117
Haitian Ministry of Social Affairs and Labour 119
hard-core offenders 305
Haven Town gangs 257
heterosexist posturing 123
high class 146
high-intensity political violence 250
Hindustani community 42, 44
homicidal behaviours of female slaves 14–16, *15,* 24
homosexuality 42, 153
honour-based violence (HBV): causes/prevalence of family violence 38–41; decolonisation in Dutch Caribbean 34–36; family structures 36–37; introduction to 33–34; matrifocality 37–38; as motive for violence 41–42; *rèspèt* (respect) and honour 42–44; summary of 44–45
Hooligan (Pearson) 222
human trafficking 60, 212; *see also* migrant sex work/trafficking
hybridisation 248
hypersexual behaviour by slaves 22

ILO Convention No 29 on Forced Labour 107
ILO Convention No 138 on Minimum Age 108
ILO Convention No 182 on the Worst Forms of Child Labour 107–108
ILO International Program on the Elimination of Child Labour (IPEC) 117

Immigration Grace Period 61
in-groups 248, 251
incarceration/incarcerated offenders: African American women in US 25; arrest rates in Trinidad and Tobago 77–78; black *vs.* white women, in US 25; court-ordered psychological evaluations 294–295; emphasis on 328; harassment of 308; male Caribbean inmates 170; period variables 200–201; recidivism 238, 305; stigmatisation of prisoners 313; *see also* intellectual disability among male prisoners
incest, in Trinidad/Tobago 84
indecent exposure, in Trinidad/Tobago 84
indentured labourers 36, 42, 75
indirect taxation 212
individualism 167, 222
Indo-Guyanese women 125
informal economies 193, 211–213, 218
informal friendship networks 168
informal social control theory 270
inhumane work conditions of slaves 25
innovation 209
Institut Psycho-Social de la Famille (IPSOFA) 114
Institutional Review Boards 146
institutionalised racism 235–236, 326
intellectual diagnostic tools 287
intellectual disability among male prisoners: case examples 288–289; cross-cultural translation/validation 291–293; forensic requirements 293–294; high functioning 288; introduction to 285–287, **286**; Papiamento-speaking population 287, 290–291, 329; personality traits 289; psychopathological patterns **295,** 295–296; social system and pathology 288–289; spelling barriers 293; summary of 296; translation/validation diagnostic tools 291–296, **295**; translators/inclusion criteria 294–295
interculturation process 75
International Covenant on Civil and Political Rights 106
International Covenant on Economic, Social and Cultural Rights 106
International Development Partner 258
international law on child domestic slavery 106–108
International Monetary Fund (IMF) 256
International Youth Survey 170
intimate partner violence: colonial/modern gender system/logic 123–125, 132, 136; decolonial feminist approach of 124–125, 126; gendered portrayals of 126–130; introduction to 123; methods of study 125–126; provocation and blame 133–137; rates of 1; summary of 137
Istanbul convention 38

Jamaica Constabulary Force 253
Jamaica Crime and Safety Reports 300

Kingston Metropolitan Area 254

Labour Code *(Code du Travail)* 108–109
lagged variables 201
land ownership patterns 101
larceny, in Trinidad/Tobago *88,* 88–89, *89*
Latina women 125
law-abiding 57
law and order approach 302, 328
Lesire, Johanna 14
Life History Calendars (LHC) 195–196
light manufacturing 1
local crime control programs 303–305
long-lasting intimate relations 38
long-term sentencing 302
loss of female slaves 21–24
low-income concerns 40, 218
lower-class crime 3
Lugones, Maria 123

Ma Cato (slave) 18–19
machismo (macho culture) 37, 41
male Caribbean inmates 170
male dominance 37
male offenders and masculinity 277
male youth problem behavior 167, 179–181
malicious woundings 90
Man as The Human 137
Maroons 18–19
marronage communities 18, *20*
masculinity 153, 276
matrifocality 37–38, 178, 192–194, 211, 332
men's linguistic strategies 130
mental health outcomes 166
Michigan University's Institutional Review Board 146
middle class 146

migrant sex work/trafficking: discussion 322–323; intervention programs 319–322; introduction to 318–319
migration and psychosis 232
militaristic police practices 303
Ministry for the Status of Women 111
Ministry of Education 168
Ministry of Social Development and Family Services 102
Minnesota Multiphasic Personality Inventory-2-RF (MMPI-2RF) 294
modern day slavery 320
modes of adjustment 209
Mona Geoinformatics Institute 253
Moravian missionaries 17
mother-centeredness 37
Moya, Antonio de 133
multi-problem families 33
multivariate outcomes 197
murders (homicides): by female slaves 14–16, *15*, 24; high-volume 302–303; rates of 1; Trinidad and Tobago 77–79, **78,** *78, 79*

National Coalition for Haitian Rights 114
National Dutch Institute on Slavery 12
National Longitudinal Study of Adolescent Health 165–166
National Violence Sexual Resource Center 152
native-language concerns 285, 287
Nature Town killing 254, 257
negative binomial regressions 172
neo-liberal capitalism 320
(neo)colonialism 43
new economic realities 212
non-Aboriginal youth victimisation 74
non-conformity 153
non-governmental organisations (NGOs) 253, 254
non-nuclear families 272
non-violent resistance of female slaves 12–13, 16–21, **18,** *19, 20*
NVivo software 215

offenders 277, 305–309; *see also* female offenders; incarceration/incarcerated offenders
offending rates of Caribbean migrants 236–240
OLS analysis 172
Olsen, Frances 225
open-*versus*-hidden classification 11, 12
opportunity bias 218–219
Optional Protocol to the Convention on the Rights of the Child on the Sale of Children 107
organised crime 2, 67–68
Organization of American States (OAS) 300
out-group 248
over-exploitation of labour 320
Overseas Countries & Territories (OCT's) 61

Papiamento-speaking population 287, 290–291, 329
Papiamentu language 55
Parent Teachers' Association 182
parental lack of responsibility 223
parental monitoring on risky behaviour 166, 170, 177–181
partner deviancy 201
paternalism 267, 268, 278–279
patriarchy *vs.* matrifocality 330, 332
peace building 254–256
Peace Management Initiative (PMI) 253, 254–258
peer delinquency 177, 180
Penal Code 54
perceptions of threatening behaviour 236
perceptual shorthand 275
perpetrators of fraud and corruption 65
personality traits 289
petty corruption 58, 62
petty fraud 58, 59, 60, **60**
phonemic orthography 293
plural society 75
poison, as murder weapon 15–16
Police Service 102
policing practices 102
political corruption 58, 63–64
political dependency relationships 42
political fraud 58, **60,** 61–62
political patronage 55, 250, 327
political polarisation 258
Pollack, Otto 269
polygamous family structures 38
poor families 33
Portuguese-based creole 290
post-colonial theorizing on crime: analyses 253; current study on 251–252; discussion 258–259; everyday unfairness 257–258, 327; impact of 55, 325–329; introduction to 3, 247; methods of study 252–253; overview of 248–50;

patriarchy and 330; peace building 254–256; results of study 253–258; sensemaking 247, 250–251, 327
primitive accumulation of capital 320
privatisation of global economy 320
property crimes 166
PROSAF-Surviving Sexual Abuse in the Caribbean 145
prostitute/prostitution: defilement of inmate/mental person 141; economy built around 212; by slaves 22; street women 192; underground economy 213; victims of 118, 319–322
protests by female slaves 13–14
provocation in intimate partner violence 133–137
psychological abuse 90, 91, 197
psychological consequences of rape 143
psychological diagnostic tools 287
psychopathological patterns of intellectual disability **295,** 295–6
psychosis of Caribbean migrants: course of 233–234; institutionalised racism 235–236; offending rates 236–240; overdiagnosis of 232–233; possible explanations for 234; post-colonial migration 232; social defeat hypothesis 234–235; summary of 240

quality-of-life concerns 292
quasi-adoption 111–112

racial bias/disparities (racism): bidirectional interaction of racism 237; enforcing stereotypes 329; increased rates of crime 237; institutionalised racism 235–236, 326; in police practices 73; segregation 101; in victimisation 76, 100
rape 142, 143
rape myth: acceptance of 154–155; belief in **150**; culture of 143–145; defined 152; rating scale 148
rebellion 11, 209
recidivism 238, 305
reciprocity in corruption 54
regression coefficients 172
relapse rates with psychosis 233
rereatism 209
rèspèt (respect) and honour 42–44
restavèk see child domestic slavery
ritualism 209
robbery in Trinidad/Tobago *81,* 81–82, *82*
rules and bureaucracy as criminalised resistance 16–17
runaway slaves 17–19, **18**

schemata of interpretation 214
school connectedness 178
self-blame 142
self-determination 247, 248, 269
self-esteem 41
self-fulfilling prophecy 238
self-governance 36
self-harming behaviour of slaves 21
self-help violence 327
self-hood and identity 248
self-reported violence 166, 169–170, 329
self-rewarding behaviours 180
sensemaking 247, 250–251, 327
Sephardic Jews 291
service industries 1
7-point Likert-scale 148
sex-role traditionalism 267–268
sex work industry 62
sexual abuse/assault: childhood victimisation 191–192; of female slaves 10, 14, 22, 26; Haiti 111; rape 142, 143; self-reporting of 329–331; Trinidad/Tobago 82–85, *83,* 84, **84,** *84,* 94, 140; of working class 146, 154
sexual coercion by strangers 152
Sexual Experiences Survey (SES) 146
sexual objectification of black women 153
sexual violence in St Lucia: current study on 145; defining/reporting/handling 141–143; discussion about 152–156; factor loadings 157–158; introduction to 139–140; limitation of study 155–156; methods of study 145–148; prevalence of 140–141, 146–147; rape myth culture 143–145; resource items 148; results on survey 145–148; summary of 156; support provider reactions 147; victimisation history 148–152, **150, 151**
sexualised behaviour problems 22
shared biological children 130
shootings in Trinidad/Tobago 79–81, *80*
short-term sentencing 302
single-parent households 192, 224–225, 331
slaves/slavery: autonomy/agency of 19–21; conspiracy of rebellious slaves 14; depersonalisation of 21; escaped slaves 17–19, **18**; homicidal behaviours of 24; honour and 42–43; inhumane work

conditions 25; loss of female slaves 21–24; modern day slavery 320; self-harming behaviour 21; sex trafficking and 320; suicide behavior 24; trauma of female slaves 21–24; *see also* child domestic slavery in Haiti; female slaves
slavesome society 224
smaddification 248
Social Breakdown frame 220–226
social capital: crime and 155–157; defined 164–165; gender and 167–168; measures of 170–171; resources 181
social control theory 210–211
social defeat hypothesis 234–235
social devaluation and psychosis 239
social disorganization theory 209–210, 222
social identity 249, 251–252
social psychological analysis 247
Social Welfare Division 306
socialisation practices 179
socioeconomic status 164, 208
spatial stability 75
Special Rapporteur on Contemporary Forms of Slavery 117
St Jean, Peter K.B. 313–314
St Lucia *see* sexual violence in St Lucia
St Lucian criminal code 142
St Lucian Gender Relations 145
St Lucia's Institutional Review Board 146
St Maarten's Point Blanche prison 60
stereotypes of female slaves 10
stigmatisation of prisoners 313
stigmatisation of psychosis 233–234
strain theory 208–209
street women 192
stressful life events 217–218
strict (gender) rules 41
structural violence 251
subcultural theories of crime 76
substance-abusing partners 202–203
substance use in adolescents 166
Sudden Infant Death Syndrome (SIDS) 25
sugar cane plantations 35
Sugar Duties Act (1846) 211
suicide behavior of slaves 24
support provider reactions 147
supremacy *vs.* inferiority process 303
Suriname 35–36, 39, 234
Suriname female slaves *see* female slaves

t-tests 151
task-oriented behaviour 57
teenage pregnancies 36
text-to-speech (TTS) 293
theft crime 58
theft of their own body 17–18
thingification 248
Thomas, Amand 13–14
time-invariant dichotomous variables 196, 197
time-variant variables 196
Tobago *see* ethnicity and crime victimisation; gender in youth problem behaviour
trafficked funds 60
translation diagnostic tools 291–296
Transparency International 58
trauma of female slaves 21–24
Treaty of Breda 35
Trinidad *see* ethnicity and crime victimisation; gender in youth problem behaviour
Trinidad and Tobago Police Service (TTPS) 74, 76, 77, 89
two-parent households 177, 179–181

UN Convention on the Rights of the Child 106–107
UN Supplementary Convention on the Abolition of Slavery 107
undereducation concerns 285
UNDP crime survey 208
United Nations Against Transnational Crime 319
United Nations Development Programme (UNDP) 77, 96, 101
Universal Declaration of Human Rights 106
University of Manchester Ethics Committee 125
University of Technology 258
urbanisation 1
US Air Force Assessment of Sexual Violence 146
US National Crime Victimization Survey 73–74
US Sentencing Guidelines 277, 281

validation diagnostic tools 291–296
van der Biest, Jan 17–18
verdicts on fraud and corruption 64
victimisation: Aboriginal youth victimisation 74; failure to report 100; of female slaves 10, 21–24; gender impact on 329–332; introduction to 2; psychological abuse 90, 91, 197; racial disparities in 76; rape history in St Lucia

148–152, **150, 151**; *see also* ethnicity and crime victimisation; migrant sex work/trafficking; sexual abuse/assault
violence: degrees of seriousness 132; family violence 38–9, 39–41; gender accounts of 133; honour, as motive for 41–42; legitimisation of 43; peer influence on 177; rates against females 1; self-help violence 327; *see also* honour-based violence; intimate partner violence; murders; sexual violence in St Lucia
violent resistance of female slaves 12, 13–16, *15*
VIP project 194
VU University Amsterdam 195

white-collar crimes 326
white knightism 320
Williams, Winston 220
Willoughby, Francis Lord 35
working class and sexual assault 146, 154
World Bank 58, 110
World Trade Organization (WTO) 212
woundings in Trinidad/Tobago 79–81, *80*
Wynter, Sylvia 137

zero import-duty regulation 61